TIME FLIES

THE HISTORY OF PACWEST RACING

JOHN OREOVICZ

DOCUMENTARY MEDIA | SEATTLE, WASHINGTON

TIME FLIES: THE HISTORY OF PACWEST RACING

Publisher:
Documentary Media LLC
books@docbooks.com
www.documentarymedia.com
(206) 935-9292

First Edition
Printed in Canada

Author: John Oreovicz
Editor: Tori Smith
Book Designer: Ryan Long
Featured Photographer: Dan R. Boyd
Cover concept: John Creak
Editorial Director: Petyr Beck, Documentary Media LLC

ISBN: 978-1-933245-62-1
Library of Congress Control Number: 2020908536

DEDICATED TO JOHN "ANDO" ANDERSON, 1945–2010

hollywood
PacWest

VISA
PacWest

TO THE TEAM, OUR FRIENDS, AND SUPPORTERS

BRUCE R. McCAW | BELLEVUE, WASHINGTON

THIS BOOK BEGAN as a well-intended project to help celebrate the 15th anniversary of PacWest's creation. The anniversary occurred in 2009, so however well-intentioned it might have been, we only missed that deadline by a decade. I believe that, for a long time, Oreo [John Oreovicz] secretly hoped I would forget about it. However, that did not happen, and he has now survived many more years of my input, comments, and editing. I admire his stamina and patience with me and, most of all, his talent for bringing these stories to life.

John Anderson was the catalyst of the entire organization. When we lost him in 2010, it left a permanent void in all of our lives. He was one of a kind and loved by everyone. This is really his story and I was determined to finish it to say thank you to Ando and all of you who were part of PacWest. I was very proud to lead this team—or at times, to try not to impede its progress. The old adage "Lead, Follow, or Get Out of the Way!" has never been so appropriate. I am very thankful to have been a part of it.

After years of reflection, I am more deeply than ever moved by the quality of the people who made PacWest what it became. From the beginning, the plan was for the team to be all about the people. That is why it never carried the name of an individual(s), and we were almost unique in that manner.

Jolene and I cherished our relationship with the team, and we always looked forward to seeing everyone. When our daughter Skye was born during the parade lap of the 1998 season opener at Homestead, Russ Cameron dutifully raised a Pink Flag in the pits to welcome her arrival. She would become a frequent attendee at the races until the birth of her brother, Wynn, and the challenge of having two kids on a race weekend began to keep Jolene home. Even then, Jolene would be watching and often calling me so that she could keep up.

PacWest became an extended family, and those bonds today seem stronger than ever. Clearly, the deep commitment made by so many was the reason for the team's success. Indeed, the entire CART community was very much like a family comprised of an extraordinary group of dedicated people who loved what they were doing. It was a wonderful time during the pinnacle era of open-wheel racing, perhaps never to be repeated.

Our first race as a two-car team was in Australia to start the 1994 season. Since we were new and did not have a franchise, we had to pay to ship everything there. Following a rain delay, both cars got collected in the first-lap crash and received considerable damage. We did not have running spare cars nor many spare parts, so getting things running again was quite a challenge and a tribute to the guys. As the race finished in darkness, I recall thinking, "What am I getting into?"

The roller coaster ride of highs and lows that followed in the next eight years provided some of the most rewarding times of my life. This was never to be a hobby and I knew it must run as a business. It was a difficult moment when I finally had to step aside. I had hoped the pieces were there for the team to survive and prosper, but sadly some setbacks would preclude that.

Living and working in Seattle was always a challenge, mainly due to the extra travel. I missed being in the race shop so much and we needed to communicate with faxes and conference calls. Getting a dedicated video link helped, but it was never the same. So, except for race weekends, I always felt a bit disconnected.

I am often asked if I miss it, and if I would ever get back in. My response is that I very much miss the people, but I am not sure we could ever recreate what we once had. I was surrounded by a very fine group of people and took immense pride in knowing and working with each of them. When I visit the races today, it is gratifying to see so many familiar faces. I am very proud of the success that many have achieved and the fact that they got their start at PacWest.

It is our honor to know each of you. We salute you and thank you from the bottom of our hearts.

FOREWORD

ANDREW CRAIG | CEO, CHAMPIONSHIP AUTO RACING TEAMS, 1994-2000 | TROY, MICHIGAN

THE FIRST TIME I met Bruce McCaw was at the PPG IndyCar World Series race at Phoenix International Raceway in 1994. I had recently started as CEO of Championship Auto Racing Teams, and there was a lot of uncertainty surrounding CART at the time.

Carl Hogan, one of the veteran team owners, came up to me and said, "There's a new team owner that I think we should bring into the franchise meeting." Those meetings are normally closed, but Carl wanted Bruce to get a sense of what the sport is all about.

So we had the meeting, which was very informal, and sitting at the back of the room was Bruce McCaw. I was struck immediately by his modesty and his understated approach. But from his comments to me after the meeting, it was clear that this was somebody who had a clear vision and a high degree of determination.

Bruce eventually served on CART's Franchise Board and, following the company's initial public offering, on its Board of Directors. He brought a level of thoughtfulness to the Franchise Board meetings which, quite frankly, wasn't always the case with some of the team owners. I believe his views were respected because when he spoke, it was because he had something to say—something that he had thought through carefully, normally after having taken counsel or advice from experts in that particular field. He was also a very thoughtful and thorough director of the public company—always well prepared, always well organized, and ready to offer advice and guidance.

Bruce always put what was in the best interests of IndyCar ahead of personal benefit. Sometimes in motor racing you could make decisions that would benefit one individual but not the series, but Bruce always put the series first. If he believed in what you were doing, or what you were saying, he could be relied upon to support you.

He came into Indy car racing at a time when the sport was in crisis. The day after I had joined CART, Tony George announced the formation of the Indy Racing League. Bruce, therefore, came to us at a time when he easily could have taken a different direction. And he was absolutely committed to CART. There was never any question that he would be with anyone but us, and I know the organization appreciated his loyalty. You could always rely on him throughout that crisis—shoulder to shoulder, being part of the series and helping us through a very difficult time.

In business, you can really separate the true leaders from the rest by those who remain calm and cool and analytical when times were bad. Bruce's quiet, unflustered character served him well in the world of motor racing, where sometimes things go well, and sometimes they don't. I never saw him panic—ever. Even under the most difficult circumstances—like in the 1997 Detroit Grand Prix when Bruce gambled and didn't bring in his two cars for the final fuel stop. They were running 1-2 when they both ran out of fuel on the last lap, handing the victory to the late Greg Moore. I happened to be standing in the PacWest pit when it happened, and if ever there was an example of super-cool, that was it. Most people would be rolling on the ground in anguish, but Bruce was cool as could be. They rolled the dice, it didn't work out, and life moves on. I remember that very well and it left a strong impression.

In the 1990s, the CART series really was the best of all worlds. Having a multiplicity of chassis and engine manufacturers was a very important ingredient, along with having a large field of interesting and talented international and American drivers, and some very compelling sponsors. All those components were in the right place at the right time; the planets were aligned.

Of course, the team owners in the series also played an essential role, and Bruce McCaw represented a new breed of team owner. Bruce brought a focused, business-first approach to racing that stood in stark contrast to the generally casual attitude of the wealthy sportsmen who had fielded cars in prior decades.

Bruce's leadership built PacWest Racing into a winning team in an incredibly difficult arena, during an era when Indy car racing was arguably at its peak. That meant going up against the sport's legendary teams including Penske Racing, Newman/Haas Racing, and Ganassi Racing, along with other formidable contenders like Patrick Racing, Forsythe Racing, and Bobby Rahal's organization. PacWest also launched the career of Scott Dixon, who has developed into one of the greatest Indy car drivers of all time.

Anyone who followed Indy car racing in the 1990s will enjoy this book as it captures the back-story of the life and times of PacWest Racing. For readers new to the sport, it is an opportunity to delve into the past of a great American race series and one of its most significant race teams.

TABLE OF CONTENTS

The start of the 1997 U.S. 500 at Michigan Speedway, with Mauricio Gugelmin leading Scott Pruett and Raul Boesel.

Paul Webb

INTRODUCTION

ORGANIZED AUTOMOBILE RACING in America dates to the start of the twentieth century. The American Automobile Association (AAA) formed in 1902. The organization created a Contest Board to govern and officiate events, beginning with the inaugural William K. Vanderbilt Cup Race on Long Island in 1904. The AAA was also selected to sanction the first racing events at the newly built Indianapolis Motor Speedway (IMS) in 1909, establishing a relationship with IMS that would span five decades.

The first Indianapolis 500 was staged in 1911 and the race was soon renowned as the most important auto race in the United States, if not the world. By staging just one event a year, with a full month of build-up, the original owners of IMS created a mystique to the "500" that has never eroded. Tony Hulman, a businessman from Terre Haute, Indiana, purchased the Speedway from World War I hero 'Captain' Eddie Rickenbacker in 1945, and Hulman's enthusiasm and leadership fueled the post-war growth of the Indy 500 into an American institution.

The year 1955 unfolded into the deadliest in the history of auto racing with a series of tragic events and the AAA decided to withdraw from its racing activities. Tony Hulman responded quickly. He put up five thousand dollars in seed money and recruited the necessary staff to create a new sanctioning body known as the United States Auto Club (USAC). The move strongly enhanced the Speedway's position of influence and power. Starting in 1956, USAC took over sanction of both midget and sprint car racing, the traditional path to Indianapolis, as well as the "Championship Cars" that competed at the Indy 500 and a few other paved ovals. USAC added a few road races starting in the mid-1960s. A handful of dirt ovals remained an important part of the equation until 1970 as the sport struggled for direction.

Little apparent effort went into marketing or growing the sport outside of the Indianapolis 500, but 'The Greatest Spectacle in Racing' continued to thrive. The "500" was invigorated by an influx of international stars in the 1960s, including Jim Clark, Graham Hill, and Jackie Stewart, and by rapid-fire technological advances that produced record speeds. But the USAC Championship Trail as a whole went into decline in the 1970s,

Dan Gurney and Roger Penske were instrumental in the formation of Championship Auto Racing Teams.

consisting of Indianapolis' once-a-year phenomenon and a handful of other paved oval tracks hosting poorly promoted and attended events. Ironically, this is the period when people started using the term "Indy cars" to generically describe the increasingly specialized machines comprising the field for the '500' and the other races in the USAC series.

With Indy car racing stumbling under USAC's leadership—exacerbated by the death of Tony Hulman in 1977—racing legend Dan Gurney composed a "White Paper" in early 1978. He encouraged his fellow team owners to band together to help build the sport to insure their survival as business entities. Gurney cited the example of Bernie Ecclestone, who had formed a group called the Formula One Constructors Association (FOCA) to take control of the marketing and promotional aspects of F1; he believed the USAC car owners could replicate FOCA's success and suggested naming the USAC car owner group Championship Auto Racing Teams, or CART.

As the 1978 season rolled on, Gurney's proposal gained momentum and a series of meetings resulted in the formation of CART. With Roger Penske and fellow team owner U.E. "Pat" Patrick as point men, CART proposed a revised government structure giving the new organization primary responsibility for the marketing and promotion of the sport, including television, while clearly stating it wanted USAC to retain control of actually running the races.

Spurned by USAC, CART acted quickly, announcing that it would break away and stage its own series of Indy car races in 1979. USAC continued to resist and tried to unsuccessfully prevent several CART teams from participating in the Indianapolis 500. From 1979 to 1981, USAC and CART both staged Indy car championships, with CART's PPG IndyCar World Series emerging as the sole survivor. However, and of critical importance, USAC maintained sanction and control of the Indianapolis 500, a points-paying round of the CART championship. This fight for leadership between the car owners and IMS management would impact Indy car racing for nearly 30 years.

In the 1980s and into the 1990s, Indy car racing enjoyed a period of impressive growth attracting worldwide attention to the sport. CART successfully combined the best elements of F1's Grand Prix style road racing with American oval racing, into a series of races anchored by the classic Indianapolis 500. That diverse challenge attracted international stars like Emerson Fittipaldi to challenge the established Americans, including Mario and Michael Andretti, Rick Mears, Al Unser Jr., Danny Sullivan and Bobby Rahal.

In 1994, Indianapolis Motor Speedway president Tony George (the 34-year-old grandson of Tony Hulman) announced plans for IMS and USAC to establish a new Indy car championship featuring the Indy 500. The Indy Racing League came into existence in 1996, sparking a twelve-year battle for control of the sport, ultimately resulting in the demise of CART and dramatically reducing the sport's popularity and economic base.

When George announced the IRL in March 1994, CART had considerable momentum. The field featured a strong entry of teams and drivers, including Nigel Mansell, the 1992 Formula 1 World Champion. Mansell had switched to the CART series in 1993, promptly claiming a second consecutive major international championship as a 40-year-old "rookie."

Even after the IRL started staging races in 1996, CART continued gaining strength. It maintained solidarity and appeared to hold the upper hand over the IRL through the end of the 1990s. CART completed a successful initial public offering in 1998 and its series, as a whole, was considerably stronger than the IRL in almost every measure through the turn of the century. But the Indianapolis 500 remained far more popular and influential than any other Indy car race sanctioned by CART or the IRL—as CART quickly learned when it attempted to stage competing events on Memorial Day weekend from 1996 to 1998.

Confusing matters, the Indianapolis Motor Speedway revoked its agreement allowing CART to use the trademarked term "IndyCar." The rebranded FedEx Championship Series attempted to revive the "Champ Car" nomenclature from the 1950s and 1960s without success and CART's fortunes began to fade. One by one, the CART teams chose to enter cars in the IRL-sanctioned Indianapolis 500, beginning with Chip Ganassi Racing in 2000 and Penske Racing in 2001. By the end of 2003, most of the top CART teams had switched their full-time participation to the IRL.

CART went through a series of management changes as it continued to battle the IRL, spending more than $100 million from the 1998 IPO, prior to descending into bankruptcy by late 2003. A trio of team owners acquired CART's key assets and continued to operate as the Champ Car World Series until Champ Car was finally merged into the IRL in early 2008. With title sponsorship from the IZOD apparel company (2010–2013), Verizon Wireless (2014–2018), and Japanese communications giant NTT, the IRL-sanctioned IndyCar Series demonstrated slow growth in a generally tough market for motorsports. On November 4, 2019, Roger Penske announced he had concluded a deal to acquire Hulman & Co., including the IndyCar Series and the Indianapolis Motor Speedway.

Late in the 1993 season, when Nigel Mansell reigned as king and Indy car racing was attracting a historical level of international attention, a start-up team joined the highly competitive arena of the PPG IndyCar World Series for a handful of races.

The two years Nigel Mansell spent racing Indy cars gave the CART series a massive international boost.

PacWest Racing, led by Seattle businessman Bruce McCaw, in partnership with Tom Armstrong, Wes Lematta, and Dominic Dobson, made its debut in the Molson Indy Vancouver. Dobson drove a year-old Galmer G92-Chevrolet to a 14th place finish.

From those humble roots, PacWest grew into one of the most professional and respected organizations in Indy car racing, developing into a regular race winner and championship contender within four years. Yet the second half of PacWest's eight-year run in the CART series turned into a cautionary tale about how quickly a competitive racing team's fortunes can change through an unpredictable combination of economic conditions, misplaced loyalty, and industry politics. CART's rapid decline, and the effect it had on PacWest and many other competitors in the series, is an important underlying theme in this book.

While PacWest's time in operation was relatively short, many of the individuals who drove or worked for the team went on to accomplish great things in Indy car racing and other forms of motorsport around the world. While they played "behind-the-scenes" management and engineering roles, John Anderson, Paul "Ziggy" Harcus, Allen McDonald, and Guillame "Rocky" Rocquelin all became familiar personalities to television viewers. Perhaps the most notable PacWest alumnus is Scott Dixon, who emerged as the most successful Indy car driver of the 21st century and one of the sport's all-time greats.

In his many business endeavors, Bruce McCaw always believed in creating a family atmosphere. And while PacWest eventually grew to include more than 100 team members, the organization always remained close-knit. Here, often in their own words, is the story of the PacWest Racing family—the people who made the memories.

Bruce McCaw captured this image of Jim Hall at Pacific Raceways. He proudly sold Hall prints and never cashed the check.

Bruce McCaw

1

THE ROOTS OF PACWEST

CARS WERE ALWAYS a major part of Bruce McCaw's life; family memories include his semi-successful attempt as a toddler to move his father's 1948 Buick from the driveway into the garage. Long before he obtained a driver's license, Bruce sometimes drove family vehicles on the lightly traveled (and lightly patrolled) roads of The Highlands, the community where the McCaws resided near Seattle, Washington. Even as a teenager, Bruce treated driving seriously and took any opportunity to hone his skills. He subscribed to *Road & Track* magazine and read and re-read a pair of influential books: *The Racing Driver,* by Denis Jenkinson, and Paul Frere's *The Theory and Practice of Fast Driving.*

At the same time, McCaw was developing a fascination for airplanes and flying. As home to The Boeing Company, greater Seattle played an important role in the history of aviation, and Bruce was drawn to highly advanced aircraft and the charismatic figures who created and flew them. McCaw began flying as a pilot at the age of 21, sparking a lifetime involvement in the aviation industry.

Once he obtained his driver's license, McCaw started attending car races at nearby tracks. He frequented a temporary road course at the Shelton Airport, but spent more time at Pacific Raceways, a 2.25-mile road course in Kent that hosted a renowned sports car race called the Grand Prix Northwest from 1962 to 1968. That event attracted an international field of stars, including Dan Gurney, Innes Ireland, Jim Hall, Joachim Bonnier, Pedro Rodriguez, Mark Donohue, Peter Revson, George Follmer, and even a young Roger Penske prior to his retirement from driving.

Although he could drive his car around the track for a dollar, Bruce's interest in attending those races was often fueled by photography. One of his fondest memories is selling a set of black-and-white images he captured of Jim Hall at Pacific Raceways in his iconic Chaparral 2A sports car. "In the mid '60s, I was pretty keen on international racing—sports cars and Formula 1, and all of the cool cars," McCaw recalled. "I started a photography business and whenever I could, I'd go to the track and take some pictures. I was so proud of the first check that I got from Hall that I never cashed it."

Bruce McCaw is seen with his 1959 Mercedes 220SE and a friend's Porsche 356 Speedster.

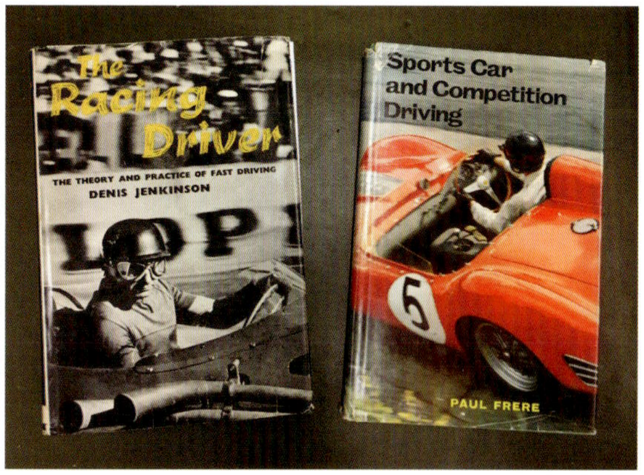

McCaw credits these classic racing books with sparking his love of driving.

In 1967, Bruce drove a single-seat racer for the first time (a Formula 4 car powered by a 700-cc BMW Isetta engine) owned by renowned local racer Warren Gibbons. McCaw acquired Sports Car Club of America (SCCA) and International Conference of Sports Car Clubs (ISCCC) licenses in the Spring of 1968, and his first racing car later that year: an SCCA H-Production class Austin-Healey Sprite McCaw and his friend, John Black, campaigned first in primer gray, before converting it to a very bright orange with a handful of spray cans.

As he got more serious about racing in 1968, McCaw bought a C-Sports Racing Elva-Climax, a purpose-built sports car. Bruce, then 23, was at Pacific Raceways running the Elva on August 17, 1969, when he learned of his father Elroy McCaw's unexpected passing at the age of 57. He continued to race on a limited basis after his father's death (including competing in the 1970 SCCA National Runoffs at Road Atlanta), but entered the new decade devoting the bulk of his time and energy to his family's businesses and laying the groundwork for his own business career in the aviation industry.

McCaw's aviation business interests in the Los Angeles area brought him into frequent contact with Sam Hanks. Prior to World War II, Hanks was revered as one of America's finest Midget car racers. After serving in the Army Air Corps based out of Wright Field near Dayton, Ohio, he claimed the 1953 AAA Champ Car title in addition to his career-capping 1957 Indianapolis 500 triumph where, in Victory Circle, he famously announced his retirement as a driver following the race. Hanks remained closely involved with the Indianapolis Motor Speedway after his retirement, driving the pace car a record six times and serving as Director of Competition from 1958 to 1979.

Hanks, along with his wife, Alice, introduced McCaw to a social circle that included aviation legends Herman 'Fish' Salmon, Tony LeVier, and Chuck Yeager. Hanks was also instrumental in stoking McCaw's interest in the Indianapolis 500 and Indy car racing, and as such, the retired champion played an important indirect role in the conception of PacWest Racing.

"Sam loved aviation as much as he loved racing cars and that's how he and I really got to know each other," McCaw related. "We used to see each other at the air races at Reno and Mojave and in those days our relationship was all about airplanes and had nothing to do with automobile racing. He flew his airplane, a Piper Comanche, tail number N500V (Victor) to and from Indianapolis every May and really loved it. And he stayed an active pilot until he was just too old to fly. Sam also flew supersonic with Yeager and Jerry Gentry and hung out with many of the best pilots.

"When Sam was the Director of Competition at Indy, he started to get me more interested," Bruce added. "Until I met Sam, I really only followed road racing and I really didn't understand oval racing. He was pretty passionate, and he was a good road racer too, though he had spent most of his time on ovals. I knew some other drivers from the northwest like Jerry Grant, but I didn't pay much attention to the 500."

McCaw attended the Indianapolis 500 for the first time in 1973 when a scheduled visit to Indianapolis on Air Travel Club Association business coincided with the rain-delayed conclusion of the Memorial Day classic. It was a difficult year for an Indianapolis baptism, marred by a pair of fatalities that McCaw did not witness. But as his friendship with Hanks blossomed, McCaw regularly began to return to the Speedway—though he still wasn't particularly enamored with oval track USAC Champ Car racing.

"In the early '80s, I started going to Indianapolis more often, just to be with Sam. He was like a king around there and he and I would just take off on a golf cart and have fun all day. We'd watch the race from the Hulman Suite and we had free run of the place. I didn't follow the racing too much, but I enjoyed being there, period." Later in the 1980s, they were joined by McCaw's friend Howard Leendertsen. Leendertsen owned the US license for the Wolff Tanning System and sponsored Michael Andretti, and several other drivers, billed as 'The World's Fastest Tanning Team.'

As the 1980s unfolded, the McCaw Communications Company, for which Bruce acted as Vice President and Director, experienced tremendous growth. McCaw Cablevision had grown from a tiny, fledgling operator into the 20th largest cable system in the United States, with 250,000 subscribers from Alaska to Missouri. When cell phones came along, Bruce and his brothers were quick to embrace what was still an expensive niche technology. In a manner similar to their cable company, McCaw Cellular expanded under Craig McCaw's leadership into a major national provider that was ultimately acquired by AT&T.

In the latter part of the 1980s, Bruce pulled his Elva out of storage and began entering vintage racing events. In that period, McCaw met Dominic Dobson, who was an aspiring driver working a 'day job' as an instructor at the Bob Bondurant High Performance Driving School to support his racing endeavors. Born in Stuttgart, Germany, in 1957, Dobson was raised in Seattle and started racing go-karts at age nine. He made his Indy car debut in 1985, driving a March entered by legendary mechanic A.J. Watson. Splitting his schedule between open-wheel and IMSA sports car events, Dobson qualified for the Indianapolis 500 for the first time three years later.

Bruce McCaw is seen working on his Sprite at Westwood Motorsport Park in the late 1960s.

1973 Indianapolis 500 winner Gordon Johncock (No. 20) is flanked by Bobby Allison (left) and the late Peter Revson (right).

AVIATION AND RACING

Like cars, airplanes have been a passion for Bruce McCaw throughout his life. Much of his business career was centered around almost every aspect of the aviation industry. Bruce's father, J. Elroy McCaw, was a friend of Bill Lear and director of Lear Jet Corporation. Elroy acquired Jetair Corporation, which operated just north of Seattle at Paine Field, as a Lear Jet dealer. It later transformed into a fixed-base operations flight service (FBO) with aircraft maintenance and sales.

After attending Colorado College and the University of Washington, Bruce joined Jetair as the office manager in 1968. He quickly formed strong friendships with the company's co-founders, Joe Clark and Chuck Lyford. Jetair included a flight school as well as a fuel and turnaround facility for cargo aircraft and weather-related diversions from Seattle-Tacoma International Airport. Lyford taught McCaw how to fly jets, and in 1970, Bruce was named president of the company.

By then, McCaw had already formed Argosy Travel Club, operating a pair of Douglas DC7s. His next move was to co-found Delta Aviation Insurance Brokers Inc., later to become Westar Insurance Co. and Forbes-Westar. Bruce also served as the executive director of the Air Travel Club Association, a group of clubs that flew Boeing 707 and Douglas DC7 and DC8 aircraft on trips for members.

McCaw co-founded Horizon Air in 1981, later serving as both a board member and vice president of operations. The carrier started with just two aircraft and 12 pilots, but quickly grew to employ more than 400 pilots with 35 aircraft. It was the fourth largest regional airline in the US prior to its 1987 acquisition by Alaska Airlines.

Along with his longtime friends Clark and Clay Lacy, McCaw conceived and organized "Friendship One Around the World for Kids." The globe-circumnavigating flight in January 1988, in a Boeing 747 donated by United Airlines and captained by Lacy, raised more than $530,000 for children's charities. It also set a still-unbroken record for large aircraft of 36 hours, 54 minutes and 15 seconds. Passengers aboard the historic flight included Neil Armstrong (the first man to walk on the moon), along with Lyford, Bill Lear's widow Moya, and legendary pilot R. A. "Bob" Hoover.

Many of Bruce's closest friendships developed through a mutual love of aviation, most notably with Clark, Lacy, and Lyford. Clark's company, Aviation Partners, Inc., developed the performance enhancing and fuel-saving 'Blended Winglets' now common on many aircraft. Lacy, McCaw's senior by 14 years, is a renowned pilot who participated in the development of the original Lear Jet 23 and operated the first jet charter company on the west coast. Lacy was United Airlines' most senior Captain when he retired in 1992 after more than 42 years of incident-free flying. He also revolutionized air-to-air cinematography by developing the Astrovision camera system, used most notably in the 1986 blockbuster *Top Gun.*

Cable television pioneer Bill Daniels was another key figure with similar interests to McCaw's. Daniels was an accomplished Navy fighter pilot during World War II and the Korean War, retiring with the rank of full Commander. In 1970 and 1971, Daniels' Cablevision firm sponsored the Indy car driven by Lloyd Ruby in the Indianapolis 500 and the USAC National Championship. Introduced to Daniels by Elroy McCaw, the relationship helped Bruce meet Apollo 12 astronaut Charles "Pete" Conrad for what turned into a long friendship. Daniels would play a very key role with McCaw and his brothers Craig, Keith, and John, as they grew Twin City Cablevision from roughly 3,000 subscribers to nearly half a million, making it the 20th largest cable provider in the United States.

"I've had the opportunity to spend time with so many incredible people from the world of aviation or aerospace, including Clay Lacy, Bob Hoover, Bill Lear, Bill Boeing Jr., Kelly Johnson (the Lockheed engineer who contributed key design input on many notable aircraft), Allen Paulson (who built Gulfstream into the executive jet class leader), and I think ten of the twelve men who walked on the moon," McCaw reflected. "It's been a real privilege."

But McCaw has also done plenty to give back to the industry. His growing interest in aviation as a teenager coincided with the founding of the Pacific Northwest Aviation Historical Foundation in 1965. Over the years, Bruce became deeply involved with what was eventually renamed the Museum of Flight, functioning as a Trustee since 1985 and serving as board chair from 2003 to 2005. Highlights during McCaw's chairmanship include the Museum's acquisition of many notable aircraft, including the first Boeing 737, a British Airways Concorde, and the Champlin Collection of World War I and II fighters, along with a priceless collection of papers documenting the Wright Brothers successful early endeavors. McCaw was presented with the Museum of Flight's Pathfinder Award in 2013 as well as the Red Barn Heritage Award; the latter was presented previously only to William E. Boeing Jr. and The Boeing Company. Bruce is also an emeritus board member of the Smithsonian National Air and Space Museum in Washington, DC, and a recipient of the Living Legends of Aviation Award.

McCaw's experience in aviation-related businesses convinced him there is a significant amount of transfer between aviation and top-level motorsports—in particular, the attitudes and disciplines necessary for proper development of technology and maintenance of equipment. Those views were cemented a few years before the creation of PacWest Racing, during his short-lived involvement in unlimited hydroplane competition when Leendertsen sponsored Jim Harvey and Miss T-Plus. Though the team won two races with driver Steve David, who went on to win multiple national championships as one of the most successful drivers of all time, McCaw noticed serious shortcomings in the documentation of the team's discipline with setup, operating, and maintenance procedures.

"I've used an analogy about racing with people over the years: It's about the same as running an airline," McCaw noted. "You have to build consistency, you have to develop expectations, you have to be clear on things like appearance and procedures. Pilots and race drivers are very much of the same mold: mechanics are mechanics. The mindsets are very much identical. The engineering team focuses on the strength and lifting of components, whereas mechanics take them and change them. Then you get into the hospitality people, not unlike flight attendants, along with sales and marketing, and accounting. Reliability was crucial and being reliable as a company was crucial.

"By the time I got involved in auto racing, CART featured such a blend of technology that it required a lot of aerospace skill sets and aviation disciplines," he added. "Having run an FAA 121-certified airline, including both flight operations and maintenance, with a particular focus on maintenance and record-keeping, component life, and reliability of things, I felt that those were some of the disciplines that I really helped instill into the mechanical side of PacWest. PacWest's mechanical reliability was among the highest in the business."

McCaw Collection

Clay Lacy and Joe Clark became great friends with Bruce McCaw through their aviation interests.

Bruce McCaw, Joe Clark, and Clay Lacy with the record-setting Friendship One.

Dominic Dobson made his Indy car debut in this Leader Card March at Laguna Seca Raceway in 1985.

Indianapolis Motor Speedway

Dobson leased a spare car from Raynor Racing to qualify for his first Indianapolis 500 in 1988. After the race, Tom Armstrong purchased the car and Dobson Racing ran four additional CART races with this Lola.

Through aviation channels, McCaw was also acquainted with one of Dobson's backers—Dominic's uncle Wes Lematta, who established Columbia Helicopters in 1957, initially to give rides at the Washington State Fair. The company developed into one of the world's largest heavy-lift helicopter operators, specializing in forestry, construction and firefighting.

Immediately after his rookie race at Indianapolis in 1988, Dobson attracted the support of another successful businessman from the Pacific Northwest—Tom Armstrong. Armstrong had recently retired after selling his company, Ridgway Packaging, to James River Corporation.

"Tom's daughter worked with a relative of mine; he came by the garage on the Monday morning after the Indy 500, when we were kind of cleaning up the shop and fixing to give the car back to the team we had leased it from [Raynor Racing]," Dobson related. "He introduced himself and we had a nice little visit. I told him I didn't know what was next, but that we hoped to do some more races. He went outside to talk to his son Brad for five minutes, and when he came back in, he stuck his hand out and said, 'Congratulations, I'm your new car owner! Who do I pay?' He went and bought the car from Raynor, and we took that car and our team that I had assembled—the foundation of Dobson Motorsports—and we ran a couple additional CART races later that year."

Dobson's performances with his shoestring operation helped land him a paid ride in the CART series in 1989 and 1990 with Bayside Racing. He also co-drove Bayside's Porsche 962 with team owner Bruce Leven in IMSA endurance races. But Leven sold the team after the 1990 season and Bayside's chief sponsor, Texaco/Havoline, was keen to field Mario Andretti's youngest son Jeff in the Indy car in 1991. That put Dobson on the sidelines.

For the Indianapolis 500, Dominic teamed up with Thom Burns, an Indianapolis-based contractor whose previous auto racing experience involved co-owning a successful team fielding USAC Midgets for veteran Mel Kenyon. Dobson destroyed Burns Racing's two-year old Lola in a big practice crash at the exit of Turn 4 before the remains came to a rest at the IMS pit road entrance. The wreck left him mystified, saying he wasn't even fully up to speed when the car snapped loose.

Bruce McCaw was watching from Jeff Stoops' suite above the pit entry and actually witnessed the accident. "He ended up right below us with car parts everywhere," McCaw remembered. "It was the first time I had seen one of those things come pretty well apart—at least with somebody I knew in it—and it left an impression."

After the May 12 crash, Dobson recalled that McCaw assisted the Burns team by helping them acquire a pair of Judd engines. Dominic hyperextended his left knee in the accident, and he was still walking with the aid of a cane when he drove to a 13th-place finish 12 days later.

McCaw's exploratory venture with Dobson's 1991 Indianapolis 500 effort coincided with a desire to pursue other forms of professional sports as a business. He was encouraged by his friend Bob Walsh, a Seattle entrepreneur responsible for bringing more than 90 major sporting and cultural events to the city, including the Goodwill Games and the NCAA Basketball Final Four for women and men. McCaw incorporated RaceSport Management in September 1991, as a holding company for his long-term investments in professional sporting endeavors.

"Bob came to Seattle with Bill Russell to work for the Seattle SuperSonics in the '70s and he was one of those creative people who make things happen," McCaw said. "I liked him a lot and he later helped us build relationships when we were trying to develop sponsorships."

In 1992, McCaw was approached by Jim Hayhoe and America's Cup skipper Dennis Conner to sponsor Jimmy Vasser's rookie season in the CART series. The plan was to field a "Stars and Stripes" car with General Motors/Cadillac support in tandem with Conner's entry in the 1992 America's Cup competition. But McCaw wasn't comfortable with the proposal and instead returned to Indianapolis with Dobson and Burns Racing, and increased his involvement for the coming year.

"I thought if I could buy a car and then lease it, I could make some sense from a business standpoint," he recalled. "We ended up negotiating for a '91 Lola from Galles Racing for I think $95,000, which looked like a pretty good deal because it came with some spares. We had a hard time getting an engine from Ilmor Engineering (manufacturer of the Chevrolet-badged engine that dominated the CART series in the early '90s), but we finally got the thing put together, got on track Thursday before the second weekend, and just qualified."

Dobson went on to claim 12th place in a race won by Al Unser Jr. in his Galmer/Chevrolet. It was the closest finish in Indianapolis 500 history—0.043 seconds over Scott Goodyear in a Lola. The finish paid Burns Racing $179,983. "It was a reasonable amount of money," McCaw said. "I had the car paid down after that race to about $15,000. I thought that wasn't too bad and figured we could try it again or bring it back next year—which we did, as a spare car."

On race day, the Burns entry ran a "Tobacco Free America" livery—which was ironic because the engine that Dobson used to qualify was acquired from Marlboro Team Penske.

Dobson first teamed with Burns Racing in 1991 when he drove this Lola-Judd to a 13th-place finish at Indianapolis.

Dobson's 1992 Indy engine was sourced from Marlboro Team Penske. "Mr. Penske was very respectful of our sponsors and that was a Marlboro motor!" laughed Thom Burns.

Dominic Dobson at speed in the 1993 Indianapolis 500.

"A group of Indianapolis physicians helped us put it together," said McCaw. "With all the tobacco sponsorship in CART at the time, we weren't terribly popular."

For the 1993 Indianapolis 500, Thom Burns purchased a 1992 Galmer chassis similar to the one that Unser drove to victory at Indy the year before. The Galmer project was commissioned by Rick Galles, whose Indy car team campaigned customer March, Eagle, and Lola chassis from 1983 to 1991, winning the CART championship with Unser in 1990. Drawing inspiration from Penske Racing (which started designing and constructing its own Indy car chassis in 1977) and Newman/Haas Racing (the works Lola team that enjoyed a direct pipeline to the factory for rapid development on its cars), Galles teamed up with designer Alan Mertens to form Galmer Engineering in 1988 with the goal of eventually producing his own chassis. The resulting Galmer G92 claimed pole position for its first race, but the Galmer chassis didn't attract outside customers despite Unser's victory at Indy and an additional win by Danny Sullivan at the Long Beach Grand Prix. Galles shelved the project at the end of the 1992 season, much to Mertens' disappointment.

Crucially, when Burns ran the Galmer at Indianapolis in 1993, he and Dobson obtained the support of Mertens and engineer/aerodynamicist Andy Brown, the men responsible for the car's creation and development. Mertens and Brown first worked together alongside Adrian Newey during a star-studded era at March Engineering. March had produced a series of successful Indy cars in the 1980s prior to the marque's return to Formula 1.

Brown and Mertens formed an effective partnership at Galmer. "In '93, Andy was asked to support Dominic's efforts at Indy in the year-old car," Mertens said. "He agreed, somewhat reluctantly at first, but he enjoyed the experience and, as he and I discussed, recognized it could lead to bigger and better things for Galmer."

The year-old chassis benefitted from a USAC rule change to the underbody making its aerodynamics more effective in 1993 superspeedway trim. Dobson's qualifying speed of 218.776 mph was only 3 mph slower than Unser ran in the same car the year before, compared to a 10-mph average reduction for the entire field. But if the Galmer G92 was comparatively fast in 1993 specification, it was also a handful to drive. During practice, Dobson managed to escape a high-speed spin without hitting anything, sliding sideways down the "Short Chute" between Turns 1 and 2.

"I've had people tell me that my qualifying run was the scariest four laps they have ever witnessed, and I'd have to say those were probably the scariest four laps I've ever driven!" he said after earning the 27th position on the 33-car grid.

"I've had people tell me that my qualifying run was the scariest four laps they have ever witnessed, and I'd have to say those were probably the scariest four laps I've ever driven!"

Dominic Dobson

THE 1993 EUROPEAN GRAND PRIX

A few weeks prior to participating in the 1993 Indianapolis 500 as the co-entrant of the Burns Racing car, Bruce McCaw attended the Formula 1 European Grand Prix at Donington Park. He was the personal guest of McLaren Technology Group CEO Ron Dennis. That was the landmark weekend when Ayrton Senna claimed perhaps the most famous of his 41 Grand Prix victories, and McCaw called the entire trip "a transforming moment."

"Ron Dennis invited me to the Donington race and was looking to see if he could get me involved somehow in what he was doing, financially," McCaw explained. "He knew I was collecting some cars and I think he had visions that I might be a customer for his spare fleet of old McLaren Formula 1 cars. It was an impressive collection of cars and I think they ultimately went to Dubai or Bahrain for a large sum of money.

"Howard Leendertsen came with me, and of course Michael Andretti was driving for McLaren," McCaw continued. "I knew Michael and Mario well and we ended up staying in this wonderful manor house out in the country. We flew to the track in a helicopter. It became a really extraordinary experience because we all stayed together for five or six days. It was a small group of people—Ron and Lisa Dennis, Mansour Ojjeh, and his wife Kathy, Mansour's brother Aziz, Udo Zucker from TAG Electronics, Bill Smith from McLaren engines in the US, and of course Senna, Michael, and Mario. During the week, there was a lot of entertaining. There were several dinners. We never left the estate. I think on two different nights we had these murder mystery dinners that everybody was into. It was a perfect setting for something like that."

Dennis had visions of grandeur to grow McLaren from a constructor of Formula 1 cars into a full-fledged manufacturer of ultra-high-performance road cars to compete with the likes of Ferrari, Lamborghini, and Bugatti. He viewed McCaw as a potential customer for the McLaren F1 road car that was being designed and developed by Gordon Murray prior to its 1995 introduction.

"They had a prototype shipped up there so I could look at it," McCaw said. "I remember sitting in the car with Mario in this old horse stable or empty ballroom. It was a big empty space with this car stuck in the middle. But I also remember making a decision that I didn't see any real need to buy a McLaren F1. I guess I just thought it was just too much car to put on the street, certainly in the United States."

At the time, Michael Andretti was having a difficult baptism to Formula 1, having crashed in his first two races. He was uncomfortable driving the highly complex McLaren, which featured a computer controlled "active suspension" and other complex electronic systems, and McCaw could understand why.

"Michael was really struggling just to understand the car and was quite frustrated, though he was actually going fairly well," McCaw recalled. "He was studying this manual on how to run the car, and I borrowed it from him one afternoon and read it for an hour or two. It was the most complicated thing. I've flown some pretty sophisticated airplanes and read a lot of stuff about electronics and I was lost in this thing. It was pretty extreme. I told Dr. Zucker, 'If you want to be more successful with Michael, put this into a language he can understand.' I spent some time talking to him and it was ridiculous to give him a technical manual. Tell him what he needs to do when he's driving the car, not how to build the system."

Donington would result in another opening-lap crash, with Andretti's misfortune magnified by Senna's brilliance on a rain-soaked track. It was a contract year for Senna, and the legendary Brazilian was motivated to perform at his peak throughout 1993 while engaging in an extraordinary game of brinksmanship with Dennis over his salary. By the time they reached Donington in April, the tension between Dennis and Senna over the Brazilian's unresolved contract reached its peak.

"It was actually quite an interesting time because Senna was on a race-to-race deal with Ron, and as of race morning they still hadn't agreed on his compensation," McCaw said. "On Sunday morning, he and Dennis finally had to go finalize the contract terms. The Andrettis and Senna had a priest come in to do Sunday mass, and then Ron and Ayrton went into the library and closed the door for about an hour. Ayrton walked out with what I later found out was a million dollars in cash for the weekend. I think that is actually when they agreed that he would do the rest of the

"Ayrton walked out with what I later found out was a million dollars in cash for the weekend."

Bruce McCaw

season for a million dollars a race. I really got to know Senna well at that time and I was right in the McLaren garage during the race."

The Donington race is famous because Senna was in a class by himself in the pouring rain, lapping every competitor other than second-place finisher Damon Hill. Ayrton's bitter rival Alain Prost finished a distant third. McCaw felt privileged to have a front row seat for one of Senna's most memorable performances, but more importantly, the Donington experience opened his eyes to the technological possibilities in auto racing and undoubtedly contributed to his decision to form PacWest Racing later in 1993.

"Of course, seeing that race and being that close to Senna at probably one of the most brilliant drives ever was just a phenomenal experience for me," McCaw said. "But the biggest thing was getting a chance to see how that team functioned and the details and the discipline and the computer systems. I was just amazed at the level that I saw there. It was really a different perspective from what I had seen at Indy, which was still really a grassroots thing. It gave me a different picture. A few sports car teams were probably more professionally run than a lot of the teams at Indy and even in CART. It brought a whole new perspective about racing to me."

McCaw Collection

Howard Leendertsen and Bruce McCaw attended a private viewing for prospective customers of the upcoming McLaren F1 road car.

Burns Racing enjoys the traditional Indianapolis post-qualifying photo. Bruce McCaw is toward the left in a red shirt.

Unusually light attrition meant that Dobson finished only 23rd despite completing the same number of laps as he did in finishing 12th the year before (193 of 200). The effort netted $146,703. “We had no horsepower with the old Chevy ‘A’ engine, but that car was so fast in the turns,” observed Burns. “Dominic ran with Mario Andretti for about 20 laps and Mario was very quick, so we wondered what would have happened if we had the latest Chevy ‘C’ motor. Everybody was so pleased with the car, so the finish position wasn’t important.”

Most significantly, Bruce McCaw began to think about a full-time involvement in the CART series. “Bruce started getting excited in ’93,” Dobson confirmed. “The McCaws were in the process of selling their cellular company (McCaw Cellular Communications), and I think he saw on the horizon his ability to participate from a time standpoint, and certainly to fund a team. I remember getting together with Tom, Wes, and Bruce after Indy, having a couple of late-night meetings at the hotels there, just putting together the structure of how a team would work and how it would be funded. We had a name and didn’t even have a logo developed, but it was the basis of seeing if this group of guys could work together.”

Things moved forward quickly, but without Burns, who withdrew when he balked at matching the other partners’ long-term financial commitment. “I smiled and said, ‘I’m flattered you asked me, but stunned you think I could make my first payment, much less my second payment,’” Burns recounted. “But I had a great time with those guys, and I would hope they would say the same about me. Everyone was honorable and credible, and I look back now and think that’s how it should be.”

During the summer of 1993, Pat Wall, a Michigan-based motorsports consultant with whom Dobson and Armstrong had worked since 1991, assisted in drafting a basic business plan for a team. The decision was made to initially lease the Galmer, along with pit equipment from Burns, and enter a handful of road races later in the 1993 season as PacWest Racing. McCaw initially contributed $200,000 to the effort, Lematta $175,00, and Armstrong $50,000. McCaw also entered negotiations to acquire Rick Galles’ share of Galmer Engineering.

Mertens and Brown played a key role in convincing McCaw to forge a deeper involvement with Indy car racing. “Galles Racing was starting to fall apart, and I think Alan and Andy felt their car deserved some vindication,” McCaw related. “As I got to know Mertens, I took a look at what Rick Galles had done and hadn’t done with his team and with Galmer. Rick put together some great stuff, but he clearly didn’t run it well as a business, though he had some great people and some great success. We got to know Mertens and Brown over a two- or three-week period during the month of May and that's when they started talking about trying to keep the Galmer going."

"It was at Indy in '93 that we met Bruce and pitched the idea to him that we form a team together," Brown confirmed. "As they say, timing is everything, and with Bruce looking to expand his racing activities, our aims were mutually beneficial. The idea was that I would move to Indy and help establish the team, using a customer chassis. Once the team was established, I'd return to the UK and we'd restart the Galmer chassis build program."

PacWest Racing was chosen as the name to symbolize the ownership group's ties to the Pacific Northwest, while purposely not highlighting McCaw or any of the other owners.

"We were certainly one of the first teams to be created without putting the owner's name in it, and that was very intentional," he explained. "I didn't want it to become 'McCaw Racing' for two reasons. One, I felt if you did that you weren't building as much of a team identity. It was just all centered around the individual. We consciously early on went through the formalities of running as a corporate business with officers, and not succumbing to the old 'car owner' mentality, which I thought was sort of a dinosaur. I really wanted the focus on what we could build and accomplish as a team instead of somebody trying to figure out who I was or what I stood for. That was always very important to me. Most people that know me well know that I don't tend to seek the limelight. I think it becomes a distraction for a lot of people.

"I can certainly understand the value of some people using their name because of their long association with racing, whether it's Penske or Bettenhausen; at Newman/Haas, Carl Haas certainly had a tradition, and Paul Newman had thirty-some years in the sport," he added. "But with what we were trying to set out to do, it really didn't make much sense to try to associate it with my name. We did see some value in trying to associate it with this region. We felt there was a chance to perhaps build a fan base for the team here and have some Northwest identity."

The team's first appearance as PacWest came the last weekend in August 1993 at the Molson Indy Vancouver. Dobson qualified 23rd out of 26 entries, and although many laps behind, he was running at the finish in 14th place. Two weeks later at Mid-Ohio, the Galmer failed to make the start, sidelined by a gearbox problem. "With the Galmer being such a bespoke chassis, we didn't have the required spare parts," explained Andy Brown. However, the season finale at Laguna Seca produced another finish, and McCaw warmed

Ready for travel, summer 1993: (left to right) Tim Love, Mike Huppert, Tom Bloom, Andy Brown, Gary North, Buddy Bivens, Matt Huth. "It was a bloomin' hot day in Indy," Brown recalled. "The photographer's insistence to hose down the parking lot only added to the humidity."

With a Columbia Helicopters logo now adorning the Galmer's rear wing, Dobson runs in a pack at Laguna Seca led by Mario Andretti. Following the PacWest car are Scott Goodyear, who finished fourth in the race, and Bobby Rahal.

up to the notion of taking majority ownership in a full-time Indy car team, comfortable with CART's increasingly international flavor centered around road and street races, but still anchored by the Indianapolis 500.

"By then I was starting to think there was an opportunity to put a team together and move forward," he said. "After the last race of the 1993 season at Laguna Seca, I stayed over for a day or two with Mertens and Brown at Monterey, and they were prepared to leave what they were doing. They were very supportive and they really wanted to see the car run. They obviously had some pretty strong reputations, and it appeared Rick Galles was losing interest and was thinking about getting out, so we put some ideas together and left there with a framework of what we would do for a team. The defining moment came in those meetings after Laguna when we sat down with Alan and Andy and really talked about getting Galmer on board. The opportunity to acquire some top-level engineering talent for a start-up team was critical to the organization."

For Mertens, the partnership with McCaw and PacWest gave his company a new lease on life, even though the Galmer chassis project was never revived ("Big shame, it would have been mega!" asserted Brown). Meanwhile, the association with Galmer, along with the presence of Mertens and Brown, gave the new PacWest team the kind of credibility it needed to attract quality personnel in an extremely competitive industry. Mertens would remain based in England to manage Galmer, while commuting to CART races to contribute to the engineering effort. Brown relocated to Indianapolis and fully committed to PacWest.

"Bruce, towards the end of '93, saw that the Galmer/Galles era was coming to an end and negotiated with Rick Galles to buy out Rick's shares," recalled Mertens. "For all intents and purposes, he became a partner in Galmer and created PacWest at the same time. Initially Bruce drew on my experience to build the team from scratch around Dominic, with support from Tom Armstrong."

Armstrong described Mertens and Galmer as a sort of secret weapon to accelerate PacWest's progress. "We had a strategy of building the team around a star person, and we chose Alan as that person," Armstrong said. "He not only brought engineering experience and the knowledge of how to win, but he brought Galmer Engineering. If you have an Emerson Fittipaldi kind of driver, that's maybe your competitive edge. But if you don't have a Fittipaldi kind of driver, maybe a Galmer Engineering is your competitive edge, or an Alan Mertens. I really think you have to have every one of the elements—the cars, the development program, the drivers, the money, the strategy."

With McCaw involved in the sale of McCaw Cellular Communications to AT&T (a transaction finally completed in 1994) and other business activities, Dobson generally functioned as the lead man in terms of guiding PacWest's transformation from a part-time entity into a professional organization that strove to compete with the top teams in American open-wheel racing. But Dominic disputed the notion that he was responsible for the creation of the team.

"I don't know that I want to take credit for that," he said. "I wanted to start a team to go Indy car racing and I was able to find a group of people who shared my vision. I kind of pulled the group together, I guess. I planted the seed and Bruce and Tom provided the water and the fertilizer. But from the very beginning, it was Bruce's vision to do a two-car team. No one had ever really started from scratch with a two-driver team and at that time, there were only a few two-driver teams, period. Most teams had one driver and certainly for a new team it was unheard of."

McCaw was no stranger to the process of building successful enterprises from the ground up, and he approached founding PacWest with the same philosophy that applied to all of the start-ups he had been involved in.

"It was very purposeful," he added. "Before we started, we wrote an extensive business plan. From the start, PacWest Racing was built as a business intended to be profitable and sustainable. A lot of racing teams are not necessarily created for that purpose, but PacWest was not an ego trip for any of us. We saw CART's growth and recognized that there was a shake-out of the lesser teams, as part of the process of the sport moving to a higher level. It somewhat mirrored the development of the NBA and NHL, and we saw a window of opportunity to enter the business of Indy car racing."

McCaw and early PacWest partners Tom Armstrong and Wes Lematta had a sense of humor about the team's humble beginnings.

The PacWest team poses for a group photo on the grid at Phoenix, April 10, 1994.

2

GROWING PAINS

ALTHOUGH BRUCE McCAW was the principal figure behind PacWest Racing, he remained mostly in the background as the organization began its expansion into a full-time business entity. The team's entry into the 1994 PPG IndyCar World Series was announced via press release on October 31, 1993.

"Our strategy is to attract the very top people available and then provide them with the most advanced equipment, testing, and development support from Galmer Engineering," said McCaw. "We expect to start the '94 season with the capabilities of an established team and an association of people with the highest business ethics and integrity."

During that gestation period in late 1993 into 1994, Dominic Dobson and Tom Armstrong were tasked with planning and building the basic infrastructure for the team. Tom and Susan Armstrong's son Brad experienced a sudden medical issue and died in January 1993. McCaw thought the race team would be a good outlet for the grieving father.

"Brad Armstrong had been a regular participant in vintage racing and his passing was a major shock, especially to his family," McCaw said. "Having recently sold his company, Tom was having a hard time finding something to do with himself. When we really started moving ahead, that's when I thought to get Tom immersed in it because they were having a really tough time. I thought it would be good therapy for Tom and I still had a pretty busy year in front of me. So, Tom got put in charge as General Manager and I figured he could dive in there and really help bring Dominic up to speed and get the budgets put together."

The perception was that Bruce couldn't devote time to PacWest because his family was in the process of selling McCaw Cellular Communications to AT&T Inc. But RaceSport Management was also deeply involved in putting together the Vancouver Grizzlies NBA expansion franchise. It was also building the new GM Place arena that would be the home for the Grizzlies and the Vancouver Canucks NHL team. "I think I had also just gone on the board of Alaska Airlines at that time and I had two or three other projects going," McCaw said. "I really needed somebody on site who could focus on the team in

Mike Huppert confers with Scott Sharp at one of PacWest's earliest 1994 test sessions at Phoenix International Raceway.

Among the first hires, office manager Colleen Howerton was indispensable to PacWest.

detail because I just didn't have the time to spend in Indy." McCaw still had his finger firmly on the pulse of how the team was developing despite his lack of physical presence.

While PacWest's racing operations functioned with relative autonomy in Indianapolis, the team's accounting and other key functions were controlled by RaceSport from Washington. "RaceSport held the driver's contracts so that we could retain confidentiality, and the senior management was employed by RaceSport," McCaw said. "As the PacWest brand grew, each of the individual race team entities were owned by RaceSport—so PacWest, PacWest Lights, and Touring Car were entities owned by RaceSport and not subsidiaries of PacWest. RaceSport provided the senior management of the team, including me. That's something that I think even people in the team didn't fully understand. But that was intentional—the reason we managed all the accounting out of Seattle was to try and keep us in control of the money, which I knew could wreck us faster than anything else."

Tom Bloom, the chief mechanic for Burns Racing who'd performed the same role for PacWest's debut races, and Galmer Engineering's Alan Mertens were tasked with making the initial hires. By early 1994, PacWest had 15 employees. At the end of 1994, its first season as a full-time entrant in the CART series, PacWest still employed just 25 people. Four of those 'original' team members—office manager Colleen Howerton, gearbox specialist Tim "Doc" Love, lead mechanic Mark Moore, and purchasing manager Nigel Bloom—remained with PacWest from start to finish.

The most important early hire was a manager to run the team's racing operations. John "Ando" Anderson was the man chosen for the job. By the end of his seven seasons with the team, Ando would be synonymous with PacWest. The Australian native worked for Frank Matich's Formula 5000 team before moving to America in 1981 to wrench for VDS Racing in the second-generation SCCA Can-Am series. Anderson then landed in Vermont working for Bill Alsup's Indy car team in 1983. He remained in the CART series for the next decade, working for Rick Galles, Truesports, and A.J. Foyt.

"I got a call from Alan Mertens, so I came up and had a chat with him and I interviewed with Tom Armstrong," Anderson recalled. "At the time, Tom Bloom had run Dominic in a couple of races in '93. Colleen was working there as the secretary, and they had Tim Love. That was about it. They decided to give me a shot, and away we went, down on Gasoline Alley. We started pulling some key people in. I'd been around the scene for a few years and had seen different guys in action as mechanics. We got Nigel Bloom. We got Ziggy (Paul "Ziggy" Harcus). It was bloody asses and elbows for some time. We had nothing but a workshop, a will, and a bloody good core of people."

Nigel Bloom was hired as a truck driver, a job that also entailed organizing and preparing tires at the track. He was later promoted to purchasing and parts manager. He remembers that eighteen-hour days were the norm as the small but growing crew prepared the team for the opening race of the 1994 season.

"Ando and I, the first few months, we'd work until midnight every night," Bloom said. "When we were done doing our jobs, we'd go back in the fabrication area to help make bottle guards and the pit equipment. We had nothing. The trucks were from the Nissan sports car program and they hadn't rolled in a year. You had to get all that equipment together and get a group of guys and learn how to do pit stops together and all that. We were scrambling to get enough wheel guns at first. Sue Armstrong was like the mother hen, the first year at the track, sewing patches on our uniforms with Colleen. Some of the mechanics were sewing patches onto their own fire suits. It was a very family-oriented team.

"It was really intense, but fun. I really enjoyed working alongside Ando. Our day jobs probably didn't reflect our true passion; tinkering, welding, and fabricating stuff is probably more up our alley. But we had to do our assigned jobs first."

The workshop was, in modern terms, tiny. But 150 Gasoline Alley was just a mile from the Indianapolis Motor Speedway and an easy five-minute ride from Interstate 465. Led by Anderson, the team began to customize the shop to its specifications. Despite its small size and lack of amenities, Gasoline Alley would serve PacWest for two full seasons of CART competition and remains in use as a functioning race shop more than 20 years later.

"We put a little extension on the shop, to house some machinery—a lathe and a mill and a few bits and pieces of fabricating stuff," Anderson said. "Then it was a matter of getting things like pit equipment together. That took a couple of months. But you could walk in that place in the morning, have a pee, collect the mail, make a phone call, and build up the car without moving your feet."

While Anderson recruited mechanics and fabricators, Dobson and Mertens worked to secure a supply of engines and chassis during a period of burgeoning manufacturer involvement in the PPG IndyCar World Series. The Lola chassis had dominated CART racing since the late 1980s, but a competing British manufacturer, Reynard Racing Cars, was entering American racing for the first time. Reynard had the unique distinction of winning first time out in every formula it competed in. Indy cars would prove to be no exception as Michael Andretti won for Ganassi Racing on Reynard's CART debut at Surfers

The rental property at 150 Gasoline Alley served PacWest for nearly three years.

Nigel Bloom was hired as a truckie, but he soon took over responsibility for purchasing and parts inventory.

John Anderson recruited Paul "Ziggy" Harcus from Galles Racing to serve as crew chief. Harcus eventually created and managed PacWest's championship-winning Indy Lights team.

Paradise, Australia. In addition, Penske Racing had year-old chassis available for sale, cars that had won nine races in 1993 in the hands of Emerson Fittipaldi and Paul Tracy.

Engines from Ford-Cosworth and Ilmor Engineering (badged as Chevrolet from 1985 to 1993) had proven almost equal since Cosworth rejoined the series in 1991. Meanwhile, Honda was entering CART competition in 1994 with Bobby Rahal's team, and Toyota was starting the due diligence process that would culminate in the Japanese giant joining the CART series in 1996. In the end, PacWest opted for the proven combination of Lola and Ford-Cosworth.

Unfortunately, Lola had an off year. Penske Racing's expanded three-driver lineup featuring Al Unser Jr., Fittipaldi, and Tracy won 12 of 16 races, with Unser easily locking up the CART championship. Reynard took three wins and Lola just one.

"We probably selected the wrong car, but we needed to make the decision earlier than we did and that was the deciding factor why we ended up with the Lola," Dobson noted. "I think the Reynard was a better car that year, but Lola was the proven choice. Those Lolas were aerodynamically pretty good on the ovals, but I think they lacked traction on the road courses and weren't very consistent. But we got a late start, and you can't just snap your fingers and expect everything to show up on your doorstep. You take what you can get, and in this case, what we could get was Lola."

Championed by Armstrong, the plan to run two full-time cars was not embraced by all. Armstrong was enamored by Scott Sharp, the 1993 SCCA Trans-Am champion and 26-year-old son of noted sports car racer Bob Sharp. Scott Sharp made his single-seat debut driving for Tony Bettenhausen's team in September 1993 in the CART finale at Laguna Seca Raceway.

"We were looking to race just Dominic, and somehow Tom Armstrong fell in love with the idea that we would run Scott Sharp," said Pat Wall, the consultant hired by Dobson to assist with sponsorship sales and the initial business plan for PacWest. "Chevy paid Derrick Walker to test Scott at Mid-Ohio in 1993 and I had a view of that. My opinion was that Scott needed to go race Indy Lights. It was a bridge too far. But Armstrong convinced Bruce to put up the money to run the second car. I don't think there was anybody involved with the team that thought that was a good idea, other than Armstrong."

McCaw knew of Bob Sharp's reputation as a racer and a developer of other drivers, most notably Paul Newman. The actor caught the racing bug filming *Winning* at the

One of PacWest's 1994 Lola chassis is seen at Galmer Engineering's UK base.

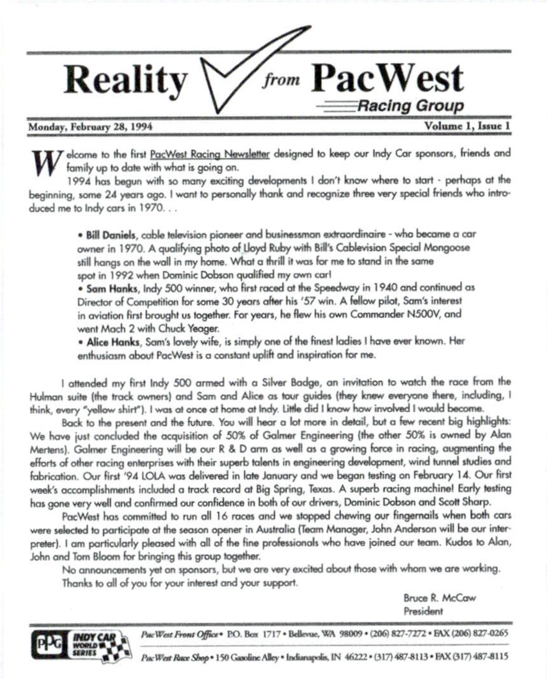

Reality *from* **PacWest** Racing Group

Monday, February 28, 1994 — **Volume 1, Issue 1**

Welcome to the first PacWest Racing Newsletter designed to keep our Indy Car sponsors, friends and family up to date with what is going on.

1994 has begun with so many exciting developments I don't know where to start - perhaps at the beginning, some 24 years ago. I want to personally thank and recognize three very special friends who introduced me to Indy cars in 1970. . .

- **Bill Daniels**, cable television pioneer and businessman extraordinaire - who became a car owner in 1970. A qualifying photo of Lloyd Ruby with Bill's Cablevision Special Mongoose still hangs on the wall in my home. What a thrill it was for me to stand in the same spot in 1992 when Dominic Dobson qualified my own car!
- **Sam Hanks**, Indy 500 winner, who first raced at the Speedway in 1940 and continued as Director of Competition for some 30 years after his '57 win. A fellow pilot, Sam's interest in aviation first brought us together. For years, he flew his own Commander N500V, and went Mach 2 with Chuck Yeager.
- **Alice Hanks**, Sam's lovely wife, is simply one of the finest ladies I have ever known. Her enthusiasm about PacWest is a constant uplift and inspiration for me.

I attended my first Indy 500 armed with a Silver Badge, an invitation to watch the race from the Hulman suite (the track owners) and Sam and Alice as tour guides (they knew everyone there, including, I think, every "yellow shirt"). I was at once at home at Indy. Little did I know how involved I would become.

Back to the present and the future. You will hear a lot more in detail, but a few recent big highlights: We have just concluded the acquisition of 50% of Galmer Engineering (the other 50% is owned by Alan Mertens). Galmer Engineering will be our R & D arm as well as a growing force in racing, augmenting the efforts of other racing enterprises with their superb talents in engineering development, wind tunnel studies and fabrication. Our first '94 LOLA was delivered in late January and we began testing on February 14. Our first week's accomplishments included a track record at Big Spring, Texas. A superb racing machine! Early testing has gone very well and confirmed our confidence in both of our drivers, Dominic Dobson and Scott Sharp.

PacWest has committed to run all 16 races and we stopped chewing our fingernails when both cars were selected to participate at the season opener in Australia (Team Manager, John Anderson will be our interpreter). I am particularly pleased with all of the fine professionals who have joined our team. Kudos to Alan, John and Tom Bloom for bringing this group together.

No announcements yet on sponsors, but we are very excited about those with whom we are working.

Thanks to all of you for your interest and your support.

Bruce R. McCaw
President

PPG INDY CAR WORLD SERIES

PacWest Front Office • P.O. Box 1717 • Bellevue, WA 98009 • (206) 827-7272 • FAX (206) 827-0265

PacWest Race Shop • 150 Gasoline Alley • Indianapolis, IN 46222 • (317) 487-8113 • FAX (317) 487-8115

PacWest created a newsletter called "Reality Check" that was faxed or mailed to team sponsors and supporters.

Scott Sharp followed in his father's footsteps as a champion sports car driver, but had a difficult time transitioning to winged open-wheel cars as a PacWest Indy car rookie.

Sharp chats on the grid at Phoenix with his godfather, the famous actor and Newman/Haas Racing co-owner Paul Newman.

Indianapolis Motor Speedway in the late 1960s. With Sharp as a tutor and mentor, "P.L. Newman" developed into a respected racer who earned four SCCA National Championships and claimed a pair of class wins at the Daytona 24 Hours. Newman also finished second overall in the 1979 24 Hours of Le Mans, sharing a Porsche 935 with Rolf Stommelen and Dick Barbour. Newman also branched into team ownership, at first as Haas' main competitor in the SCCA Can-Am Series (see Chapter 17).

"Paul was not only Carl Haas' partner at Newman/Haas Racing, but he was Scott's godfather," McCaw said. "Paul called me and encouraged me to give Scott a chance, noting that the seats at Newman/Haas were obviously spoken for by Mario Andretti and Nigel Mansell. Gregg Pickett, the father of Scott's fiancée, was likewise highly successful in the Trans Am championship. Everyone was committed to support Scott and to help bring in some of his current sponsors as well as future prospects."

Clean-cut, American, and from a successful racing family, Sharp looked like a can't-miss prospect. But in retrospect, his limited open-wheel experience proved difficult to overcome and his lack of improvement over the course of the 1994 season clearly caused some dissention within the PacWest team.

"PacWest is still the only team that has gone into its first full year as a two-car team, which was a very ambitious program," said engineer Andy Brown. "I think the plan to run two cars was because they felt it would help Dominic in his driver development and give him a yardstick. Speaking honestly, I thought Scott Sharp was a strange choice if that was the case because he was another unknown quantity, and what we probably needed to help Dominic was a driver with more experience. But I think they wanted an all-American lineup. If there was anything about Bruce, and especially Tom, it came across that they were extremely patriotic. You could tell by the color scheme of the cars—basically un-sponsored, but red, white, and blue."

With that all-American flavor, PacWest Racing made its official debut as a full-time entity on March 20, 1994, more than 7,000 miles away on Australia's Gold Coast. Carrying the logos of local sponsors Red Back Bitter beer and FAI Insurances, the cars lined up 18th (Sharp) and 27th (Dobson) on the grid for the FAI Indy 300 at Surfers Paradise. They represented thousands of hours of work and four months of effort. But when the green flag flew, the weary PacWest crew didn't catch a break. A first-lap multi-car accident swept in Dobson within seconds.

"At Australia, there were two red flags at the start of the race, and Dominic was in both of them," recounted John Anderson. "So, the boys all jump in. The guys off the other car jumped in and helped as well. You couldn't even see Ziggy because he was buried in the cockpit. His head was down around the pedals as he was putting the wishbone in from the inside. At one stage, I looked up and I couldn't see the car because there were bodies all over it. It was like a swarm of bees. We got it back in the race, but it started raining, and there was a bit of a spin, and Dominic happened to get collected. There's another red flag. He came in and we repaired the damage and finished the race. Afterwards, the feeling was that we had won as a team and started to gel. The team spirit generated was just fantastic."

"I'd love to have a picture of that car in Australia with Ziggy," added McCaw. "Ando and I walked over, and all the corners and wheels were gone. All we could see was Ziggy's feet poking out of the tub, and we laughed so hard. It was quite a sight."

With Sharp leading the way in 11th place, both PacWest cars finished in the points on the team's official debut as a full-time entrant.

At Phoenix International Raceway, Sharp improved to a ninth-place finish in his first-ever oval race, while Dobson was eliminated in a multi-car accident triggered by Hiro Matsushita. "There was a yellow for Matsushita's spin and rookie Jacques Villeneuve cut him in half," said Anderson. "Villeneuve slides around the rest of the track, hits Dominic, who had backed off. Villeneuve ends up in the pit lane and we're looking at this thing laying there with two eyeballs poking out of a helmet and no wheels on it. He stopped in our pit! And poor old Dom was taken out."

Sharp then had a rough weekend at Long Beach. During the Saturday practice, his car suffered a front wing failure and he crashed heavily in qualifying near the hairpin with a 57 G impact. "I was watching from there and when I went over there to get him, he didn't know me from Adam," recalled Pat Wall. "I turned him into the medical staff because he had a concussion. It was a big hit, and in those days, there wasn't any concussion protocol."

When the month of May rolled around, the PacWest drivers slowly worked up to speed before ultimately topping 225 mph in practice. Both were first-day qualifiers for the Indianapolis 500. Dobson averaged 222.970 mph to qualify 12th, while Sharp's 222.091 mph run was good for 17th on the 33-car grid.

In additional to the usual photo ops and media interviews drivers submit to after an Indianapolis qualifying run, Sharp was greeted in pit lane by PacWest's owners who

John Anderson (standing, right) supervises the repair of Dominic Dobson's car in Australia.

Dominic Dobson was involved in several accidents in PacWest's debut race. He awaits assistance from the CART Safety Team after landing atop Hiro Matsushita's car.

INTERNATIONAL BAPTISM

Not only did PacWest Racing start the 1994 season as a newly expanded two-car operation, the team's first event took place thousands of miles away in Surfers Paradise, Australia. In addition to the usual preparation necessary for a new team or a new season of racing, PacWest had to acquire the equipment and knowledge necessary for shipping its operations overseas. Nigel Bloom was in charge of preparing and packing for international events.

"One week prior to the race we had two primary cars ready for our two drivers, and the day prior to taking everything to the airport, we received our third Lola rolling chassis in its birthday suit—black carbon," Bloom said. "We had very few car spares at that time and no time to do anything to the new car. So, we loaded it in the transporter as-is and took it to the airport with the rest of our equipment for Australia. That car sat in the garage behind the pit boxes, ready in case we needed to rob parts off it.

"The race started in the rain and on the first lap there was a big shunt and a red flag. Dominic damaged his car, so the crew goes to work robbing parts from the new car to repair his. On the first lap after the restart, there was another shunt, another red flag, and Dominic's car required more repairs—the other end this time, and more parts robbed. Finally, the race gets under way, still under rainy conditions, and due to all the delays, the race finished so late that it was almost dark, and the street lights were on."

For Bloom, the long day was not nearly yet completed. "In the past, the teams had flown out on the Monday after the event, but for some reason the organizers thought they would fly the crews out on the Sunday night instead," he said. "As soon as the race was over the teams were frantically trying to prep the cars for their return trip, pickling the engines, removing and disassembling the wings so the cars could be loaded on the car racks."

Shortly after the race, John Anderson approached Bloom with some bad news. "Ando says, 'Nugget Head, I'm sorry to do this to you, mate, but we're running out of time for the team to get back to the hotel to pack and get the bus back to the airport. Who would you like me to leave with you to finish the packing and loading?' Mark Moore was my roommate and I knew he would be a great help, so when everyone left, Mark and I started the task of packing all the equipment up, loading it on to the aluminum cargo flats, and loading the cars on the shipping racks. That poor donor car—when Mark and I loaded it that night, we literally loaded an underwing with a tub. There were no wheels on it or anything—the suspension was all gone, and it was no longer a roller.

"Mr. Moore! You have to get up—we've found you a flight home!"

"Finally, Mark and I finished the load and got back to the hotel after one in the morning. We headed straight to the bar, dropping our crew bags on the dance floor, and drank till they kicked us out. That's when we remembered that we had not eaten since midday and were famished. We decided to get cleaned up, then headed into downtown Surfers to a 24-hour bakery; we stocked up on meat pies and pastries then headed for the beach to eat our breakfast while the sun came up. Mark had missed his flight and had no clue how or when he would be able to fly home. Mark stuffed the phone under his bed so we would not be disturbed, and we went to sleep. A few hours later there was a loud pounding on our door with someone shouting, 'Mr. Moore! You have to get up—we've found you a flight home!' He hurried to pack while I went back to sleep because I wasn't flying home until the next day on the cargo plane."

Tom Armstrong (left) and Bruce McCaw enjoy PacWest's first event as a full-time two-car team.

Indianapolis Motor Speedway

Mike Groff (Car No. 10) pinched Dominic Dobson into the Turn 1 grass, sending both cars spinning out of the Indianapolis 500.

Dobson smacks the wall hard after the initial contact with Groff.

were brandishing a three-year contract extension for the American rookie. "We thought it would be the most positive statement we could make of our confidence and pride in Scott," Armstrong told the gathered media. "This contract gives our prospective sponsors, the team, and Scott the benefits of long-term stability. We can now go forward according to our business plan."

"I think this speaks well of our relationship," Sharp added. "I think I am being taught by a great bunch of guys and I am looking forward to being with PacWest for three more years."

Sharp's Indy 500 debut was compromised by a gearbox malfunction that locked his Lola's transmission in neutral, requiring a 16-minute pit stop to repair. Although he finished 16th, 14 laps behind winner Al Unser Jr., he showed his potential by setting the seventh fastest lap of the race. Dobson, meanwhile, suffered bruised legs when he was taken out in a crash triggered by Mike Groff on the 30th lap.

A quarter of the way into the season, Armstrong remained bullish about Sharp and the overall performance of the PacWest team. "I think it's unprecedented that we've come into the sport like a mature team instead of like a team that just shows up," he said. "Last October, we decided we would do at least a partial season with new equipment and top people. But a few weeks later we talked ourselves into two teams and a full season because we had a chance to hire Scott Sharp. We're trying to come into the sport not at 30th place and three years later be at 15th. We're trying to come in at P10 or P12 and work our way up into the top 10. Our goal is to qualify in the top 10, finish in the top 10, and finish both cars."

During that first season, there were occasional flashes of brilliance tempered by moments of anguish as the new organization struggled to find consistency. The Milwaukee weekend brought more highs and lows when Dominic qualified a CART-career-best sixth, only to crash the car in Turn 3 just two minutes into the warm-up session. He finished 13th, just behind Sharp in the race.

"The first year, I think we went six months before we loaded both cars in on all four wheels," Bloom said. "It seemed every weekend the primary car was crunched so the backup came out, and there was a wreck in most races. Every weekend we were loading cars up on dollies. Finally, we got to a point where we were rolling them in on wheels and that lifted the whole team. You know, with a brand-new team and such a small group of people, that was a lot of work for everybody."

In June, PacWest added a key new team member. At age 28, Russell Cameron already boasted five years of Indy car experience with Galles Racing, Granatelli Racing, and Patrick Racing. He joined PacWest as crew chief for Dobson's No. 17 car just in time for the team's "home" race at Portland International Raceway. Although Dobson and Sharp finished only 17th and 18th at Portland, it was the first time that year both PacWest cars made it through a race without incident.

The highlight of the season came in the Marlboro 500 at Michigan International Speedway. Sharp crashed in practice, but Dobson had a strong weekend from start to finish. He qualified ninth and claimed third place, PacWest's first-ever podium finish. Dominic suffered some bad luck during his final scheduled pit stop when he was already committed to pit lane when the yellow flag flew for a blown engine by leader Al Unser Jr. That cost Dobson second place to Arie Luyendyk.

"We could have won that race!" Brown said. "Dominic passed the pace car, and we told him to get back behind the pace car, but instead of slowing down and letting the pace car by him, he accelerated and completed a full lap to get back behind the pace car. So, they black-flagged us, and otherwise we would have won that race. As we were serving our black flag, what really hurt us was that Scott Sharp's car retired at the same time and brought the yellow out and bunched the field up. That put us to the back of the field, and we lost a lap essentially. We were a lap up on Scott Goodyear, who won that race, and it put Goodyear on the same lap as us. But these things happen in racing."

At New Hampshire International Speedway, Dobson put together a solid sixth-place run, while Sharp retired after completing just 12 laps. His car was launched into a frightening flip by PacWest's frequent sparring partner Mike Groff. "It looked worse than it was," Sharp related.

Both PacWest cars finished in the top 11 at the challenging Road America road course, but Dobson suffered another warm-up crash at Nazareth Speedway. Nazareth marked the first time Dobson's car ran with sponsorship from Bank of America. It carried one of six in-car cameras utilized for an experimental in-car-only broadcast shown on ESPN2 in parallel to the standard coverage on ESPN. When Dobson crashed in the Sunday morning warm-up, the team determined it would take less time to repair the damage to the primary car than to relocate the camera to the spare, resulting in a three-hour thrash for the teams of both cars.

Dobson ended the 1994 season 18th in the CART championship standings; Sharp was 21st, a distant second to Jacques Villeneuve among rookie drivers.

Russell Cameron (left, with John Anderson) joined PacWest in mid-1994 and quickly gained additional responsibilities.

Third-place finisher Dominic Dobson sprays race winner Scott Goodyear with champagne as they celebrate the result of the 1994 Michigan 500. Runner-up Arie Luyendyk (right) enjoys a drink and tries to stay dry.

Running flat-out at Nazareth Speedway, Dominic Dobson shows off the clean lines of the low-slung Lola T94/Ford-Cosworth. Bank of America joined PacWest late in the team's first full season in the PPG IndyCar World Series.

Scott Sharp had not raced on ovals prior to his rookie IndyCar season with PacWest and faced a steep learning curve. By the end of the 1994 campaign, the team decided to move forward with a more experienced driver lineup.

"We tried to do everything we could, and I don't think there was a lack of effort on anyone's part," observed Dobson. "But it was a lot to expect for a new, two-car team with one kind of journeyman driver who was probably more comfortable on the ovals than the road courses, and one rookie driver who was vice-versa. Although I had been around for a while, I just didn't have that many races under my belt relative to a lot of the other guys. We had the right people, but I don't think we had the right cars. In retrospect, with the experience I had at that point in my career, it might have been better for me with a seasoned pro that I could have learned from, rather than being the seasoned pro with the rookie as my teammate."

The ninth-place finish Sharp claimed in his second race with PacWest ended up being his best result of the season. At the end of the year he was released, despite having signed a three-year contract extension in May. The parting was difficult for both sides. Sharp was unhappy about the lack of stability and support at PacWest, while the team believed he didn't develop as a driver as quickly as he should have.

"At first, we were only going to run six CART races," Sharp said. "I took a chance by doing that instead of doing a full year of Trans-Am and whatever else might have come through Chevrolet. After things went fairly well in the first few races, they said they wanted me to do the full season and to sign a three-year deal. I thought, 'Great!' and they made a big deal out of having me sign when I got out of the car after qualifying at Indy. That was sort of fun. We all had agreed to that, but all of a sudden at the end of the year, Bruce hadn't found nearly the amount of sponsorship they had expected.

"At the end of the day, we didn't really have anybody that could help me make that transition," he continued. "I think I drove that car like a Trans-Am car for probably the first half of the year because I didn't know any different. There wasn't anyone experienced engineering-wise, or driver/teammate-wise, or coach-wise, or anybody that could say, 'Hey, change this!' or 'Use this part of the car to your benefit.' I just wasn't thinking along those lines because I hadn't been exposed to it. That part made it tough, and we didn't do a lot of testing. With those two things it was hard to excel, but it was an eye-opening experience."

Sharp believes that had he been given additional time to develop at PacWest, he and the team could have grown together. "My dad always said that you can get a flat tire when you roll the car onto the trailer or you can get one with two laps to go. And that was one of those years," Sharp commented. "We had some races where we really ran pretty well, but there were a lot of factions within the team, and now that I've been around enough to look back on it, I can see it was the new-team blues. The team was put together in a hurry, late, and without a lot of testing. With so many unknowns, maybe it just wasn't a recipe for success. But it was a bit contentious. I felt that at the end of the day, I didn't think there was a whole lot more that could have been expected out of me as a rookie. I felt it was obvious I needed another year to learn from a veteran and to show what I could do.

"So, I didn't have the best feelings, but that's the reality of the sport," he concluded. "It changed me as a person and woke me up to what the sport is all about. That has probably helped me weather some of the challenges I've gone through since then with a much stiffer backbone than I would have."

PacWest struggled to find consistent corporate sponsorship throughout 1994. The team did manage to sell race-by-race packages to a number of companies, including Rain-X, Bank of America, Columbia Helicopters, and the Vancouver Grizzlies NBA franchise, an organization Bruce McCaw and his brother John were instrumental in forming. Like everything else about the team's entry into Indy car racing, PacWest was extremely ambitious in terms of creating a new business model for sponsorship (see Chapter 5).

The team anticipated Sharp would bring a considerable amount of sponsorship to the table, but that never materialized. The PacWest principal also had an uneasy relationship with Bob Sharp, who McCaw had first met at the 1970 SCCA Runoffs.

"I think Scott would have been a lot better off if his dad hadn't hung around at the races, but Bob came to all the races," McCaw said. "I had a lot of respect for Bob; we had only met a couple of times, but I knew who he was. I once had a Trans-Am spec Datsun 510 as a street car, and had some friends with Datsun, and of course he was running the 240Zs. I thought they were pretty cool cars, so I paid some attention to him.

"In Bob's mind, Scott could never do anything wrong, but that sort of led to Scott never listening to what people were telling him," McCaw added. "Instead of Scott having to start dealing with stuff, he had dad sitting there saying what was wrong. And it was always the team's fault. I think his dad was one of the biggest problems because he sometimes failed to understand how much Scott needed to learn. That was a challenge all the way through."

Like his father, Scott Sharp had done his training in production-based sports cars that depended almost exclusively on mechanical grip rather than downforce generated by wings or the floor of the car. He wasn't the first driver, and certainly not the last, who struggled to adapt quickly to a radically new discipline.

RaceSport Management became involved in the ownership of the Vancouver Canucks NHL team and the foundation of the Vancouver Grizzlies NBA franchise. PacWest occasionally ran Grizzlies logos on Dominic Dobson's car during the 1994 season.

Scott Sharp leads Jacques Villeneuve, another rookie driver from the PPG IndyCar Series class of '94. Villeneuve went on to win the 1995 Indianapolis 500 and CART championship on the way to a successful Formula 1 career.

The solution McCaw offered was to have Sharp take a step back to Indy Lights and run the 1995 season in a PacWest-prepared car. McCaw actually purchased an Indy Lights chassis and agreed to run it for Sharp, with or without sponsorship, so that he could develop his skills in open-wheel cars. McCaw also committed to bring Sharp back to the PacWest Indy car team in 1996. Bruce remains convinced that was the best thing Sharp could have done at the time.

“We had this meeting at Armstrong’s house, and Tom and I were at strong odds about this,” McCaw said. “He liked Scott, and he liked hanging around with Scott’s parents and with his in-laws. They were all buddy-buddy, but the fact is it was not a recipe for success, and it was not going to get any better the next year. We couldn’t get anybody really interested in Scott. Pat Wall was trying to sell sponsorship and he was saying all the time I needed to get a driver with a name. The problem was Sharp wasn’t coming up with the money he was supposed to. He didn’t come up with one nickel.

“Bob Sharp, I’ll never forget it, he said, ‘We’re not going backwards,’” McCaw continued. “I said, ‘Bob, listen to what I’m saying: Your son is not at this level. He needs some experience in these cars and I’m trying to help him.’ Bob and I really got into it that day and I think I finally just walked out of the meeting and said, ‘We’re finished.’ But to me, it was the decision I had to make. Going forward it was not going to work.”

Despite the challenges he encountered during his rookie season with PacWest, Sharp went on to compile a solid career in the Indy Racing League. He won nine IRL sanctioned races between 1996 and 2005 and was the co-champion for the IRL’s brief three-race inaugural season. He later moved into sports cars, building a successful team called Extreme Speed Motorsports, in partnership with tequila magnate Ed Brown.

Wall believes PacWest’s difficulty in attracting a title sponsor in 1994 was typical for a start-up racing team. “Finding sponsorship anywhere, in any year, is a real challenge—I don’t care what you race or where you’re racing,” he said. “In that case, and in so many cases with start-up teams, you don’t have a hell of a lot to sell. The first year with PacWest there wasn’t much there, but we worked hard at establishing a PacWest brand. I was always big on PR and we had a PacWest fax-based newsletter before the internet was really established. It was all about building a brand of significance so you could go pitch somebody that you had a recognized presence.”

PacWest’s inability to quickly forge a commercial partnership with a corporate backer had a direct effect on Dominic Dobson’s career. Toward the end of 1994, the team shifted

Tom Armstrong (right) listens in as Dominic Dobson discusses his race car with crew member Paul “Ziggy” Harcus. Armstrong was usually PacWest’s owner representative at the track during the 1994 season.

Bruce McCaw was content to remain in the background for much of PacWest's first full season of IndyCar racing, leaving the day-to-day management of the team to Tom Armstrong.

some of its sponsorship goals to other drivers. "It was not an easy decision to put Dominic on the sidelines," McCaw said. "In a perfect world, I'd have liked to have just kept him in the car—he'd have done a very good job. But we were sitting there facing some very serious issues as far as revenue and we felt we had to change our whole strategy. In trying to position ourselves with some sponsors and listening to what some of the sponsors were looking for, we just had to make some changes."

Dobson admits that the minority owner/driver role he fulfilled in 1994 was difficult on him. "It was interesting to be involved in ownership and by virtue of that, the management of the team, and also being one of the drivers," he said. "I was involved in marketing, sponsorship, and figuring out budgets. I wasn't hands-on management except in the sense that I was the owner's representative who would go back to Indy on the most regular basis to deal with issues and help solve problems. I ultimately sort of became the link between Galmer and PacWest as well, which was frankly not the easiest thing to do. To be that liaison and be the driver as well probably didn't serve me very well from the driver's standpoint.

"We tested as much as we could, but there's no substitute for running a team for a year and gaining the experience and the trust in each other," Dobson continued. "While building an organization, it's tough to do all of those things. I think we bit off a lot. We never got any real sponsorship, though there was a lot of effort and a lot of my time put into trying to find sponsorship, all while managing the team, driving the cars, and testing. I found that to be challenging and sometimes overwhelming. It was just hard to put the helmet on and forget everything else. There were days when I wished I was just a driver or just an owner. It's tough to do both."

Dobson believes he did a good enough job under the circumstances as a driver in 1994 to be retained for 1995. Had he been able to continue as a driver, he thinks he could have shared in the success the team subsequently enjoyed.

"There were mistakes made," Dobson said. "Certainly, we crashed some cars and that set us back, but we had some highlights during the year. I think if we would have kept that team together for the next year, we would have made some real progress. But from the team's standpoint, they had to look at it business-wise and the deal that I had made going in was that if we could get some sponsorship in '94, then I would keep my drive. We didn't, so I didn't. It was matter of fact and I don't harbor any ill feelings about that at all. We made the deal at the beginning of the season and that was the deal that stood. As I look back, I wish it would have turned out differently, but hindsight is cheap."

Still, most within PacWest viewed the team's initial full-time campaign as generally successful. Most importantly, PacWest demonstrated the stability and commitment necessary to secure a pair of CART franchises for 1995 and beyond.

"That first season was a shaggy year for results, but it was a new deal and we expected that," said Anderson. "But it was a great year for the effort that went in and the start we made with no equipment. It was bloody hard work, but you could see that with the caliber of people we had that it was going to develop pretty quickly."

The difficulty the PacWest management team had in making and executing major decisions in the second half of 1994 convinced Bruce McCaw that the time was right for him to assume full control of the organization.

"I just basically told Tom Armstrong at the end of the season that I was going to run the team," McCaw said. "There were several decisions, like Scott Sharp, that Tom just didn't like. But I told him I was going to call the shots. I said, 'I'm the major owner here and that's what I'm going to do. You can have all the opinions you want, but the fact is I am going to make the decisions. One person has to.' From that point, the end of '94 forward, I pretty much made all the decisions about what we were doing."

Repairing damage was a way of life for the PacWest crew in 1994. Here Dobson's car is returned to the pits at Milwaukee after he crashed in the pre-race warmup.

Mauricio Gugelmin makes a pit stop during the 1995 Indianapolis 500.

3

REGROUPING FOR SUCCESS

THE SEEDS FOR PacWest Racing's 1995 Indy car campaign were sowed when Danny Sullivan tested one of the team's Lola/Ford-Cosworths in August 1994, the day after the CART series race at Mid-Ohio Sports Car Course. Though he didn't have a regular ride during the 1994 season, Sullivan's impressive lap times and feedback convinced PacWest that the 44-year old veteran still had some competitive races left in him.

Sullivan had developed his craft in England after Dr. Frank Falkner gifted him with a trip to the Jim Russell Driving School for his 21st birthday. Falkner, an internationally renowned pediatrician and child health specialist, was closely involved in auto racing for decades through his friendships with John Cooper and Ken Tyrrell. With additional backing from Brown-Forman spirits magnate Garvin Brown, Sullivan rose through the European open-wheel formula car ranks before returning to America to race in the SCCA Can-Am Series in the early 1980s.

After a couple of promising Indy car outings at the end of the 1982 season, Falkner helped Sullivan land a Formula 1 ride with Tyrrell. But despite posting a fifth-place finish in the 1983 Monaco Grand Prix, he lost the seat at the end of the season. Back in America, he won three CART races in 1984 for Doug Shierson Racing. That attracted the attention of Roger Penske, and Sullivan soon became a household name with his famous "spin and win" victory driving for Team Penske in the 1985 Indianapolis 500. He went on to win the 1988 CART championship for Penske, then joined Galles Racing in 1992 and scored the first win for the Galmer chassis in the Long Beach Grand Prix. Despite winning again at the 1993 Detroit GP, Danny felt he was not given the opportunity to compete on equal terms with Al Unser Jr., whose relationship with team owner Rick Galles dated to 1981. Sullivan ended up on the sidelines in 1994 when rookie Adrian Fernandez brought the team a lucrative Mexican sponsorship package.

Sullivan's best days on the track may have been behind him by 1995, but he was still a major star out of the car, thanks to his appearances on *Miami Vice* and other television shows. That, not to mention his 17-race winning pedigree, was why PacWest came calling. Bruce McCaw was intrigued by the notion of pursuing a recognizable name driver

PacWest signed 1988 CART champion Danny Sullivan for the 1995 season hoping to take advantage of his vast experience and star power. But Sullivan's best days were behind him and a pair of fifth-place finishes were his best results for the team.

Sullivan (center) parlayed his success at Indianapolis into numerous television appearances, most famously in a 1986 episode of *Miami Vice* alongside series stars Philip Michael Thomas and Don Johnson.

like Sullivan, not only in terms of improving his team's on-track performance, but more importantly, for potentially attracting additional interest from sponsors. But he encountered some hurdles he didn't expect.

"That was an interesting relationship and it became my first experience at trying to manage a 'star-quality' driver," McCaw said. "Danny and I started talking, but then he got to be a prima donna and tried putting me with this Hollywood lawyer who was calling me and telling me what was going on. I called Danny back and said, 'Danny, you can talk to any lawyer you want, but you and I are going to negotiate this deal and if you don't like that, we're going to stop talking.' Finally, he backed down, but a week later his PR firm—and I had never dealt with a driver who had a PR firm—got into the act and we had some issues there too. We came so close to not coming together."

For 1995, McCaw took on a much more hands-on role with the team, assuming many of the 'big picture' general manager duties from Tom Armstrong. "I had planned all along to work full-time for one year," commented Armstrong. "I'm still actively involved with the team, managing a few projects (including the construction of a new race shop in Indianapolis) and overseeing the financials."

The second driver PacWest hired for the 1995 season had a much longer and stronger impact on the organization. Mauricio Gugelmin, a native of Curitiba, Brazil, followed his friend and countryman Ayrton Senna to race in Europe in the mid-1980s, almost in his wheel tracks. Gugelmin duplicated Senna's Formula Ford 2000 and British Formula 3 championships, eventually landing in Formula 1 with the Leyton House/March team in 1988. He raced for Leyton House through 1991, building a strong work relationship and friendship with his race engineer, Andy Brown.

Following a less than satisfactory 1992 season with the Jordan-Yamaha F1 team, Gugelmin took half a year off to sail his boat and contemplate his future. He landed sponsorship from Hollywood cigarettes to run the last three races of the 1993 CART season with Dick Simon Racing. Hollywood was the flagship brand of Souza Cruz, the South American division of British American Tobacco. That led to driving a second car for Chip Ganassi Racing, with Hollywood backing, in Reynard's first year in Indy cars. Gugelmin did a sound job during the 1994 campaign, outqualifying his celebrated teammate Michael Andretti six times and earning a season-best fifth-place finish at Vancouver.

Brown was Gugelmin's first contact with PacWest. The engineer rated the driver highly and wasn't hesitant to recommend him to McCaw. "I felt we needed Mauricio in the car because he was a known quantity to me from working with him in Formula 1 for three years," Brown commented. "I knew he could sort the car for us, and he was very popular with Reynard, too. If a manufacturer sees you have a driver capable of delivering results, they tend to push a little more and help you a little bit extra."

Making the decision easier for McCaw, he instantly fell into an easy friendship with the 31-year-old Brazilian. Ironically, the relationship also began at the Mid-Ohio race in 1994 when Gugelmin approached the PacWest timing stand in a gaudy Ganassi fire suit. McCaw said, "He looked like Spider Man or something out of Flash Gordon. I felt so bad for him and thought I would never put a driver out in a ridiculous driving suit like that. But Mauricio and I really clicked. He was obviously very frustrated at Chip's because they were running him out of the back door of the parts department at Reynard North America. Michael got everything and Mauricio's engineer was not even allowed to talk to Michael's. It was pretty amazing how they were running the program, but Mauricio obviously had a relationship with at least one major sponsor he felt he could deliver on. We agreed he would take over Scott Sharp's car."

Danny Sullivan poses for a publicity shot with members of his 1995 crew: (left to right) Casey Eason, Ron Endres, Roy Wilkerson, Doug Conrad and Paul "Ziggy" Harcus.

After the tribulations of running a second-string effort for Ganassi, Gugelmin was eager to move to a team where his influence could be felt, and he saw huge potential at PacWest. "Of course, life with Chip Ganassi is not very consistent, to say the least," Mauricio said. "I really enjoyed (Ganassi team manager) Tom Anderson's company, but Chip has his off days. That didn't go over very well with me and from the middle of 1994, I knew I wasn't very keen to stay at Ganassi's. Andy Brown kept saying, 'You've got to come over here and drive for us,' so I kept in touch. I started paying more attention to PacWest and I eventually met Bruce. I could see they were serious about the business; the cars always looked well-prepared and neat."

In contrast to his dealings with Sullivan, McCaw found it was easy to negotiate a contract directly with Gugelmin. "Mauricio and I largely came to terms on the phone over the Christmas holiday, and while we hadn't actually signed a contract, we had an agreement on all the important things and the paperwork was done," he said.

But before the final paperwork was signed, the deal was threatened when Souza Cruz informed the driver it was withdrawing from motorsport. 'Hollywood Rock' was a multi-day rock music festival staged in Rio de Janeiro and São Paulo seven times between 1988 and 1996. The 1995 edition went over budget when it was modified to include promotion of the Rolling Stones' Brazilian concerts.

GUGELMIN AND SENNA: BRAZILIANS ABROAD

After working his way through the karting and junior ranks in Brazil, Mauricio Gugelmin followed his good friend Ayrton Senna to England to race for Ralph Firman's Van Diemen Formula Ford team. Senna was a couple years ahead of Gugelmin on his career path, but the two Brazilians remained extremely close.

Senna and Gugelmin shared a house in the UK during the 1982 season until Mauricio married his wife, Stella. The Gugelmins later shared a larger house with Senna, who had graduated to Formula 1 with the Toleman team by 1984. They all lived together through the end of 1987.

Gugelmin shared some memories of his friendship with the man many consider one of the greatest drivers and international sportsmen in history:

"I called Senna at the end of 1981, when he was in England driving Formula Ford 1600 for Van Diemen. I told him I was thinking about coming to England and asked him if he would introduce me to [Van Diemen marque founder] Ralph Firman. A few days later, he called me back and told me I was the works driver for '82! So, I went over. But at the end of the year, Senna decided to give up racing. His family was always against it, and his dad had some kind of aftermarket accessory business for cars, so he used that as an excuse—he said he [Senna's dad] needed help running the business. Ayrton had just gotten married, and I think deep down he just didn't want his son living so far away. Senna went back to Brazil before the 1981 season was even over—he was already the champion, but after a few months back there he realized he couldn't stay away from racing. He convinced his dad to let him go back, and he called me in England and asked if he could live with me. He was coming back to run Formula Ford 2000 and was coming on his own. He used to have long calls with his wife on the phone, but I could sense that things weren't going well in the marriage. But his racing was doing great, and so was mine.

"The first year in England was great. We shared everything, and my cousin Zeca was there to help us out. We went everywhere together and just lived motor racing. We were at Van Diemen every day from 8 a.m. to 10 p.m., and we really learned a lot from Ralph. We used to hate the pubs because of the smoke, but it's funny how much you can get out of an English guy after a few beers! We learned to appreciate that. We found a little Chinese restaurant called Forum in Shepperton and we would go there all the time for the Aromatic Crispy Duck. Then, after Senna started making it big in F1 with Lotus, Stella and I basically lived with him when I was in Formula 3 and Formula 3000. We shared all the expenses, but he didn't charge me any rent, which was good. And there was always a nice Mercedes or Renault for us, whatever he was driving at the time. But that's when the English government kindly asked him to leave or pay taxes. He chose to leave in a hurry.

"Ayrton was a great guy, nothing like what came across on camera. He had a great sense of humor, but you couldn't cross him. You couldn't even let him get the feeling that you were trying to get one up on him. He would just go nuts. But he was a very genuine person who enjoyed life. He was the ultimate practical joker—he used to play some very strong practical jokes that would make even me think twice. But he would just do it. Sometimes he could be like a little kid, and that side of him was dangerous. When eating next to him, you had to be as focused as on the starting grid of a race. If you relaxed for just one second, you could end up with a plate soaked in vinegar or a glass of milk full of pepper.

"I remember one time Stella and I had dinner with Ayrton, his girlfriend at the time, and Gerhard Berger and his girlfriend at a restaurant in London. He somehow found out that Berger only had credit cards—he didn't have any cash. So Ayrton chose a restaurant where you could only pay cash, and before the dinner was over, he told Stella and me to disappear, and he took off as well, leaving Berger there with the bill. There was always something like that going on, and it's a pity it couldn't have lasted until now.

"The last trick I played on him was the year he died. We were down at an island off Brazil where he had his beach house. I went there with my boat, and he had his 36-foot boat docked next to mine. We had a swim, and then he and a bunch of his friends had kind of ambushed me on the beach. At the

"Ayrton was a great guy…he had a great sense of humor, but you couldn't cross him."

Mauricio Gugelmin

end of the day, I was on the second level of my boat, and as he was getting aboard his boat, I threw a champagne bucket full of ice water on him. That was the last joke I pulled on him, and two months later, he died. I think I got the last laugh."

Senna was tragically killed on May 1, 1994, at the San Marino Grand Prix at Imola. That day, Gugelmin was participating in the Rookie Orientation Program at the Indianapolis Motor Speedway for Ganassi Racing when he got the news.

"You can imagine the wave after that with all the Brazilian press and pressure from the family," Mauricio said. "It was tough because it was the month of May, my rookie season at Indianapolis, and you're running every single day. There is lots of wall there, as you know, and it was character-building, for sure, to go through that. But I was enjoying so much the revival of my career in the United States that it came and went away."

Ayrton Senna and Mauricio Gugelmin leave Silverstone after a 1992 Formula 1 test. "About 90 minutes after that we were caught on the M25 doing 126 mph," Gugelmin recalled. "Ayrton lost the ability to drive in the UK for six months, which was funny at the time!"

Senna (left) and Gugelmin shared a passion for building and flying model aircraft.

Steve Swope/RMA

Mauricio Gugelmin led the 1995 Miami Grand Prix in his PacWest Racing debut en route to a second-place finish.

"Souza Cruz called me to Rio to tell me this news, and I couldn't believe it," Gugelmin recalled. "I walked out of the office not knowing where I was and I jumped into a taxi, which was the rustiest VW Beetle I had ever seen. I was afraid to put my feet down because I don't think there was a floor there! But on my way to the airport, I realized I had to tell Bruce—and at that point, I didn't know him very well. I always thought the best way to deal with a problem is to do it immediately. So I called Bruce and told him, 'I'm sorry, but everything I promised is not going to happen.' I felt like such a stupid guy because I hate to promise anything to anyone that I can't fulfill."

While disappointed by the setback, McCaw was still determined to reach an agreement with Gugelmin. "Mo called me up around New Year's when Hollywood said they were backing out," McCaw said. "They had a huge problem, because they had committed unequivocally that we had a deal. Mo was really in the dumps because he assumed that was the end of the road for us. But I told him we had come far enough and that I wanted to go forward. I said we'd figure out a way to make it work."

McCaw thought it was a pity, but asked Gugelmin to join them at Sebring the next week anyway to run the car. Mauricio said, "I was expecting him to swear and kick me in the ass and call me all kinds of bad words, but he didn't. That made me think, 'This is a nice guy in racing, and that's unusual.'"

The Sebring test was also important because it would be PacWest's first run with a Reynard chassis. Reynard Racing Cars was founded in 1973 when Adrian Reynard, an engineering student and aspiring race car driver, self-built a Formula Ford car as his final project at Cranfield University. Within a couple years, he was producing a limited number of copies that he sold to competitors, including fellow Englishman Rick Gorne. Gorne quickly became a friend but retired from driving after a bad accident in 1979. He joined Reynard as sales and development director in 1982. His commercial savvy helped the company grow quickly as it advanced into Formula 3 (1985), Formula 3000 (1988), and Formula Atlantic (1989), winning its first race in every series it entered.

After spurning a couple of opportunities to advance into Formula 1, Reynard instead entered Indy car competition in 1994. "Initially when we came in, we were partners with Chip Ganassi," explained Gorne. "Chip funded the prototype and he believed in us."

Gorne had a memorable first encounter with Bruce McCaw at Portland in 1994, discussing the team's potential move from Lola to Reynard for '95. "I remember meeting with him and Tom Armstrong, and they were playing with me," Gorne laughs. "They were just

"I was expecting [McCaw] to swear and kick me in the ass and call me all kinds of bad words, but he didn't."

Mauricio Gugelmin

Bruce McCaw (right) took a more direct role in PacWest's management in 1995 while Tom Armstrong focused on the construction of a new race shop in Indianapolis.

trying to get the best deal they could out of me, and I was just trying to stand firm and believe in what we had. But for them, it was fun, it was a game. I could see it, so I just had to dig my heels in and stand firm. There was a retail price, and that was it. That's what we stuck by. There was no wiggle room for discounts or anything—that was the price, and that's what they had to pay.

"But I immediately took a liking to Bruce and how he operated. I never found him intimidating, but he was definitely tough—probably one of the toughest negotiators that I had to deal with. From that moment on, we've been good friends."

In addition to Reynard's proximity to Galmer, the company distinguished itself with a higher level of customer service than Indy car teams were used to. Reynard opened a dedicated North American parts facility and embedded an engineer with each of its teams.

"We set the bar for quality," asserted Gorne. "We did things differently, and it really worked. We slowly took the marketplace over."

PacWest was joined by Walker Racing and Tasman Motorsports in switching to Reynard for 1995. "I think at that stage the Reynard was more aerodynamically advanced and it was my perception that they gave their teams much more support than Lola," observed Andy Brown. "Reynard was also just around the corner in the same industrial estate from Galmer, which was a big advantage to us. If we needed any help with the wind tunnel program or model parts, it's not like they were across the country in Cambridge like Lola was."

Preseason road course testing with the new Reynard/Ford-Cosworth combination went well, validating McCaw's decision to stick with Gugelmin even though the Hollywood sponsorship seemed to have fallen through. For his part, Gugelmin thought the deal could still be rescued as PacWest headed into the 1995 season opener on a new street course in downtown Miami.

"I told Bruce before the weekend that I was going to drive my ass off, and that Hollywood would be back," Gugelmin laughed. "He said, 'Be careful,' because I was talking so much he thought I was going to kill myself. But Andy and I were both motivated and pissed off because of being left high and dry at the last minute."

Brown also offered a clear recollection of Gugelmin's motivation. "Watching Mauricio as he came around the final turn to begin his last qualifying run, I turned to Russ Cameron and said, 'Mo's either going to be on pole or we're not going to see him again!'" he said.

"Miami was a typically bumpy street track, and that car was dancing. We witnessed total Commitment—with a capital C—that day."

Mauricio was good to his word. He ran third quickest in the first practice session and repeated that result in provisional qualifying. He improved to second in final qualifying to earn his and PacWest's first front row starting spot in the CART series. Pole position was taken by Gugelmin's former teammate Andretti, driving for Newman/Haas Racing.

Race day produced PacWest's best team performance yet. From sixth on the grid, Sullivan moved up to third place behind Gugelmin. The Brazilian held second through the first round of pit stops, then pressured Andretti into crashing on the 50th lap, just past half distance. That elevated Gugelmin into the lead, closely pursued by Jacques Villeneuve and Bobby Rahal.

On Lap 55, the yellow flag was shown when Eric Bachelart clipped a wall and stopped on course. Led by Gugelmin, the top cars pitted for what would be the final stop of the afternoon. PacWest executed a clean pit stop, but Villeneuve's Team Green Reynard exited the pits just ahead of Gugelmin's No. 18 car.

In retrospect, McCaw believes a simple strategic decision cost Gugelmin and the team victory in the 1995 season opener. "That was the time I really learned about pit layouts," he said. "You have to put the fastest car in front. Danny boxed Mauricio in just long enough for Villeneuve to get around us. I'll never forget looking up and seeing that blue car flash by just as Mo started to pull out."

"Danny was running behind me. But during the stops, he was pitted in front of me and he left the back end of the car halfway across the pit lane," Gugelmin said. "For me to get out, I had to move a little bit and that's why we got beaten in the pits and finished second. Barry Green's group with Jacques were a bit more prepared than us. We didn't give the better pit to the guy who qualified ahead."

Villeneuve drove the final 35 laps mistake-free to cross the line 1.022 second ahead of Gugelmin, with Rahal on his rear wing. Sullivan finished ninth. While disappointed with second place, it still marked a career best finish in the CART series for Gugelmin and PacWest. More importantly, the high-profile result rekindled Hollywood's interest in sponsoring the driver and his new team. "Hollywood called right away," McCaw said. Before the second race of the season in Surfers Paradise, Australia, McCaw announced that Hollywood and PacWest had come to terms on a two-year agreement as title sponsor of Gugelmin's car.

Gugelmin leads Jacques Villeneuve during the 1995 Miami Grand Prix. A faster final pit stop during a full-course caution would prove to be the key factor in Villeneuve's victory in the season opening race.

Strategic gaffe: Gugelmin was blocked from making a quick pit exit at the 1995 Miami Grand Prix by teammate Danny Sullivan, potentially losing PacWest its first Indy car race win. Villeneuve emerged from the pits first and led to the finish.

Sullivan was a popular favorite who was at ease interacting with fans.

"Sure enough, I got a call Monday morning," Gugelmin said. "Hollywood said they had a re-think about everything and they were coming back. From that day, my relationship with Bruce was just different because there was a great understanding that whatever we said, we fulfilled. We didn't have to have contracts or anything, though the business required that."

Gugelmin backed up his Miami performance by running fourth in provisional qualifying on the Surfers Paradise street circuit. He dropped to tenth on the final grid, but came home fourth on race day immediately ahead of Sullivan. It marked the first time that PacWest had two cars finish in the top five in the same race. Gugelmin added another fifth-place finish at Long Beach.

However, the 200-miler at Phoenix International Raceway revealed PacWest still had a lot to learn about the intricacies of setting a car up for short ovals. And questions about Sullivan's commitment were raised when he qualified 21st, then parked the car after completing only 21 laps. Gugelmin finished 13th, six laps down.

"Danny started out well at Miami, but he really started getting distracted quickly and I think at Phoenix he scared himself," McCaw said. "He didn't like short ovals anyway, and at Phoenix the car had evil handling and he just he parked it. I walked over to him and I said, 'Danny, if you do that one more time, you're history. I'll just set fire to your contract.' I could tell he had reached a point in his life where he had a new girlfriend and money in the bank and he didn't want to end up in a wheelchair or something else for the rest of his life, which is understandable."

Ziggy Harcus had a history of working with Sullivan at Galles Racing. He thought that even in 1995 the veteran driver still had some competitive runs left in the tank. "I always enjoyed working with him and when he joined PacWest it was like going back to the old family," Harcus said. "I think Danny was one of those guys that if he could smell the front of the field, he was there, whether it was an oval, or a road course, or whatever. If you gave him a good car, the guy could definitely pedal it. But when we ran bad, we ran bad. When you're fighting from 15th to 12th, is it worth putting your life on the line?"

The month of May got off to a delayed start for PacWest as the team waited on superspeedway parts from Reynard. But once he got on the track, Gugelmin made his presence known. "As soon as they unloaded my car, I couldn't believe how balanced it was from day one," he said. "I think on the first day I did half a dozen laps and I was doing 227s, P3 or P4 on the day. From that moment, I realized, 'This is going to be fun. It's going to be a great month.'"

Mauricio Gugelmin celebrates on the Miami podium with winner Jacques Villeneuve. "I looked like a doctor on the podium in my plain white overalls with nothing on them," Gugelmin said.

Crew chief Russell Cameron (left) and engineer Andy Brown confer with Mauricio Gugelmin during practice for the 1995 Indianapolis 500. The meticulous Gugelmin's temperament was perfectly suited to Indy's month-long grind.

Danny Sullivan at speed in 1995. Sullivan finished ninth in his final Indianapolis 500 appearance.

Gugelmin surprised many observers by regularly running in the top five in Indy's daily practices before qualifying sixth at 227.923 mph. But if anything, he and the team were disappointed.

"I'm not sure it was a surprise to us," reckoned race engineer Brown. "Road racers who come to the States normally do well at Indy because it's four 90-degree corners rather than long 180-degree corners where you have to get your entry speed exactly right. Indy has definitely got the entry, mid-corner, and exit they are used to. Mauricio took to the track like a duck to water and was very impressive.

"The USAC popoff valves used at Indianapolis were rather tricky, and our valve blew in qualifying. Otherwise I think we would have been higher up the grid and perhaps even on pole. I remember that car coming down pit lane after qualifying with methanol just streaming down the outside of the engine cover. We had lost a lot of boost."

Gugelmin acquired the popular nickname of "Big Mo" in May 1995 during an appearance on the BOB & TOM Show, a nationally syndicated radio program based in Indianapolis. Hosts Bob Kevoian and Tom Griswold were playfully having trouble pronouncing the name "Mauricio" when they came up with the memorable tag. Saxophonist Bud Shank, a longtime friend of McCaw's, later composed and recorded a jazz song called "Big Mo" inspired by the driver.

Though he never won at Indianapolis, Michael Andretti frequently set the race day pace. In 1995, he led 45 of the first 77 laps before he tapped the Turn 4 wall hard enough to bend his Lola/Ford-Cosworth's front suspension. He was attempting to pass third-place runner Gugelmin at the time and said he was taken by surprise when the PacWest car slowed to enter the pits.

Two laps later, Gugelmin took the lead when Scott Goodyear pitted. In all, Mauricio led 59 laps of the 1995 Indianapolis 500, more than any other driver in the field, and he was well positioned for the critical 50-lap final sprint. But that's when PacWest's relative youth as a top-line Indy car team again showed and Gugelmin faded to sixth place in the final quarter of the race with handling problems.

"What gave it away was our lack of experience," Gugelmin lamented. "At Indy, we were fast and all we had to do at the last pit stop was beat Robby Gordon out of the pits. Because it was close, the team didn't do a front wing adjustment that I asked for. We also put a soft set of Goodyear tires on the car that we had never run on the car before.

"If you think about it," he said, "it's absolutely crazy to run a month there, then on the last stint, the most important one, to throw something different that you have never run on the car. That's totally crazy! But we found ourselves running well, almost too soon. We were in a position to win something big, and we thought that we had something that was quicker, so let's go ahead and throw that in. But that's Indy. How many times have you heard that story, that the circuit changes and the car isn't right for the conditions?"

Alan Mertens surveys the action at Indianapolis. Acquiring Mertens' Galmer Engineering company gave PacWest the ability to design and produce its own parts, but the relationship dissolved by 1998.

Gugelmin noted that mistake was part of a trend at PacWest toward 'over-engineering' the cars. "That was very strange because when we started really well, everyone was hungry and the engineers were focusing on running the car fast rather than reinventing the wheel," he said. "Then we went a little bit in the wrong direction by trying to make a complicated science out of something simple. We started growing more, hiring more engineers, and at that time we still had the Galmer facility in England. That was a pattern and there was a lot of confusion. We would get a car from Reynard, the car goes through a lot of tests, and suddenly everything is wrong. You have to modify this, modify that. I think the next year we didn't even run the car before we put a different gearbox on the back of it! When before you even develop a car you start changing things, it turns into a bad pattern."

Adding to the problem was a simmering feud between Sullivan and Galmer's managing director Alan Mertens, stemming from their work together at Galles Racing in 1992 and 1993. "Mo was solidly out in front most of the time, which bothered Danny," observed McCaw. "Then Danny and Mertens started getting into it. One of the things I didn't realize until mid-season was that Mertens always blamed Danny for convincing Rick Galles to drop the Galmer chassis project. That was a dynamic I didn't see until probably the middle of the summer. Finally, it came out one day and I said, 'You guys have to get over this.' If they both got up on the right side of the bed, they could go well together. But you never knew from one day to the next, so it was unfortunate."

Sullivan believed his relationship with Mertens was compromised by the designer's close working relationship with Al Unser Jr. when both drivers were teamed together at Galles. "Over at Galles, it was 'Al this' and 'Al that' and there was no support there, but that wasn't the issue," Sullivan explained. "It came down to the same thing I went through at Penske with Alan Jenkins, who was a brilliant engineer. But the PC15 and the PC16 chassis he produced were disastrous cars. Even though the Galmer won Indianapolis, that car was terrible.

"From a racer's point of view, if I'm not stepping up and doing my job, they're going to get rid of me. Well, what if Alan Mertens is not stepping up—and he's dictating what

Indianapolis Motor Speedway

Despite winning the 1992 Long Beach Grand Prix in a Galmer, Danny Sullivan lost confidence in the car and designer Alan Mertens.

Danny Sullivan leads a pack of cars at Michigan Speedway in what would be his last Indy car race.

happens to my career and dictating what happens to the team? What if I don't believe in the guy and think that he's any good, since I'd already had those years with him? Why do I want to be out there just to be driving around? He had a vested interest because he wanted to make stuff for his company."

Andy Brown, who played a key role in the Galmer chassis program, stood up in defense of the car rather than its main detractor. "If the Galmer did have a bad reputation, it was down to Danny Sullivan, I have to say," Brown remarked. "He couldn't match (Unser) Junior's pace and it was easy for him to rubbish the car knowing there were not any other Galmers out there competing. Unfortunately, with his high profile, the criticism stuck and I wasn't too impressed with his testing abilities.

"When he ran for us at Mid-Ohio in 1994, it achieved our goals, because we felt our setup decisions had been vindicated," Brown added. "But long term, it did backfire on us. Both Alan and I had seen how poisonous Danny could be with his inter-team politics at Galles and it soon cost us [engineer] Will Phillips. Danny shouldn't have taken the drive in 1995—his heart just wasn't in it."

For the event on the Portland International Raceway road course, Galmer developed modifications for the front suspension that made the car very difficult to steer. It made Gugelmin's seventh place finish look downright heroic. "Mauricio used to joke, 'I almost had to sweat today,' but at Portland, it took two of us to get him out of the car and they had to give him an IV for dehydration, he was so beaten up," McCaw remembered. "It was almost a 100-degree day and Andy had run these packers that basically made it a car without suspension." This challenging mid-season period for Gugelmin also included a fairly heavy crash while testing at Road America.

After the team's strong performance at Indianapolis, PacWest had high hopes for the year's other superspeedway event at Michigan International Speedway. Gugelmin qualified sixth, but lost many laps in the race to a wheel bearing problem encountered by several Reynard runners. But Sullivan was not so fortunate. He suffered a fractured pelvis after being swept into Lyn St. James' accident three-quarters of the way into the race while he was running seventh. Danny underwent successful surgery in Indianapolis by Dr. Terry Trammell, but his season—and indeed, his Indy car racing career—was over.

Although he subsequently ran a few stock car and sports car races, Sullivan insists his retirement from full-time competition was not a direct result of the Michigan crash. "I don't remember anything of the accident because I was unconscious for 11 minutes, so I have no bad memories. I have some metal in my body from it and so forth," he said. "But lying in my hospital bed I thought about it all. I was 45 years old, I was racing against a bunch of young guys, and I wasn't as competitive as I had been. Then ABC TV came to see me, offered me a lucrative commentary contract. That helped me make up my mind to stop Indy car. But I still did some sports cars.

"I had a three-year contract with PacWest, but I really stopped because I didn't like where the team was going, particularly with Alan Mertens," Sullivan added. "He had a vested interest because he had his manufacturing division over there, and the proof was in the pudding when Mark Blundell later had his accident in Brazil. I didn't want to be in a situation like that."

Although Bruce McCaw's relationship with Sullivan was occasionally strained, he remains positive about Danny's time with PacWest. "Danny was a very talented and capable race driver and he had an extraordinary personality," McCaw commented. "His ability with sponsors was absolutely amazing. He'd have them eating out of his hand. Everybody loved him. He knew everybody and it was sometimes a challenge when he would bring his movie star friends to the races. Of course, dealing with celebrities can be good or bad. He did not like short ovals, but he was strong at Indianapolis and Michigan, and he was a great road racing driver, and a very smart guy. He remains a good friend and I think very highly of him."

McCaw considered running just one car for Gugelmin for the remainder of the season because there were few qualified drivers available. But PacWest still had to field the No. 17 car to comply with CART franchise rules. Instead, he approached racing legend Dan Gurney about hiring IMSA sports car champion Juan Fangio II, the nephew of five-time Formula 1 World Champion Juan Manuel Fangio. Their creative solution was to put Juan in the car for the remainder of the 1995 season as a precursor to Fangio's planned entry into Indy cars in 1996 with Gurney's Toyota-backed All American Racers team.

Fangio drove for AAR from 1990-1997, winning the IMSA GTP prototype class championship in 1992 and 1993. He posted a total of 21 IMSA race wins, including a series-record 19 solo victories. He also won the 1992 Jerry Titus Driver of the Year award presented by the American Auto Racing Writers and Broadcasters Association (AARWBA). With the demise of IMSA's GTP category, and Toyota's Indy car engine program lagging behind schedule, Fangio was essentially sitting idle in the summer of 1995 when PacWest came calling.

"I called Dan because we were looking around for a driver and there was nobody really exciting on the sidelines," McCaw explained. "I thought maybe we could borrow Fangio

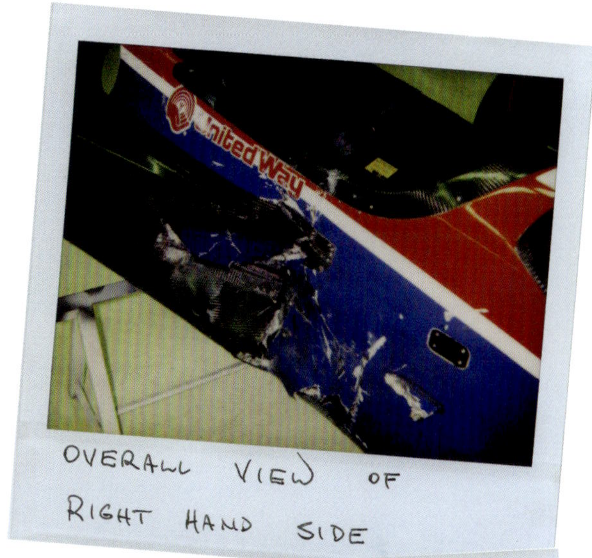

The team documented damage to Sullivan's wrecked chassis in a series of Polaroid photos annotated by John Anderson.

Juan Fangio II drove the last four races of the 1995 CART season for PacWest, replacing the injured Danny Sullivan. Fangio's debut for the team at Mid-Ohio Sports Car Course produced a promising seventh-place finish.

Bruce McCaw confers with Juan Fangio II on the grid at Laguna Seca. McCaw, an avid student of auto racing history, was thrilled to run a car for the nephew of the five-time F1 World Champion from Argentina.

from Dan, who thought it was a great idea." Gurney called Fangio's Indy car baptism with PacWest "an irreplaceable experience; it was a reality check in many ways, and a good one."

Fangio drove four races for the PacWest team, with his best result of seventh place coming in his debut at Mid-Ohio. "Getting Fangio in was a real treat," said McCaw. "Gurney told me a couple of stories later about Juan, and he and I connected from the beginning. I thought he was very special, and I really started seeing the depth of his talent. I'll never forget looking into his eyes and it was just like his uncle. You don't meet a lot of people where you sense that there is something extraordinary there. He just had this incredibly focused look in his eye that I will never forget. I can visualize the first time I met his uncle and I could see the same thing in him.

"That was still a high point in my life, getting to know Juan, and we have maintained a great friendship," McCaw continued. "I remember showing Juan his uncle's roadster (the No. 77 Dayton Steel Foundry Special that Juan Manuel Fangio drove in his Indianapolis 500 rookie test in 1958 shortly before he retired), and then later he drove it. When he first saw it, he had tears running down his face. He said nobody in the family had ever seen this car and it was very special when he drove it at Michigan. That was a real thrill. I cherish the friendship we have, and I got to know Dan Gurney a lot better in the process. He is one of the great people of all time. Gurney was very confident Juan could come up to speed quickly, and he did. That speaks a lot of his ability."

Fangio, who retired from racing after the 1997 season following two challenging years developing Gurney's Toyota-powered Indy cars, has extremely fond memories of his short tenure with PacWest.

"I remember my father had come to visit me in the US when I answered the phone, and Dan said, 'Fangio, next weekend you have to drive one of the PacWest cars!'" Fangio related. "I put the phone down and told my father, 'Sorry, I have to go!' But I was extremely pleased. It was a wonderful, wonderful experience. Something that I will never forget is how open everybody was. I was new in the team; I was coming in to replace Danny. You get there and you don't know anybody, but everybody was extremely open and that was great for me at the time.

"My goal was to drive Indy cars and I was under contract to Toyota," he added. "But because of Bruce, I was able to drive before then and I will always remember that. It worked out really nice. I had a great time in IMSA GTP, but I remember at the time, IndyCar had wonderful names, very good drivers. It was a very competitive class. I love the series when they are competitive, and I had the chance through Bruce to make it real."

Mauricio Gugelmin enjoyed his brief period as Fangio's teammate, but Guglemin's most vivid recollection is of the race at New Hampshire International Speedway. It was Fangio's first-ever appearance on an oval. "At Loudon, he was running really well," Gugelmin said. "He was running the car so loose, but he just kept his foot down. Juan was a nice guy who you could see really enjoyed driving. You could see it in his eyes and in his style. That was a really classy, classy guy, with a great personality, who was fast."

Bruce McCaw was delighted to build a strong friendship with racing legend Dan Gurney and his wife, Evi.

Fangio let out a hearty laugh when told of Gugelmin's description of his performance on the New Hampshire oval. "I remember Mauricio came to me and said, 'Juan, I saw the marks from the rear tires on the pavement behind your car!'" he recounted. "I said, 'I don't know what happened, Mauricio…the car is perfect for about nine laps, and then I lose the rear tires for some reason.' Every single time I changed tires the car came back to being perfect for seven, eight, nine laps and I was able to pass people everywhere. But after a few laps, again I was losing the rear tires. It was very strange and it never happened to me before. I was very loose, but I was lucky enough to make it to the end. But the balance was perfect on short runs and to qualify 12th out of 30 cars was great."

Fangio believes his brief experience driving Indy cars for PacWest was exactly what he needed in terms of his role as the chief development driver for Gurney's Toyota program debuting in 1996. "I found out it was possible to be competitive," he explained. "That's why it was so important for me to be able to drive the PacWest car for Bruce, especially mentally. When you are driving a car that is not completely developed, which happened to us with the Toyota car, then you start to think: 'Is it me, or is it the engine, or is it the car?' It doesn't matter if you have won races before in other categories. You always wake up with that question in your mind that maybe I am doing something wrong.

"But I was relaxed about that because I knew if we could get the car up to the point where it should be, we would be okay. And I was able to think like that because I drove for Bruce those few races. That was a very big help when we went through a heavy development with the Toyota car. We knew that if we did not have what we needed to have the result would not count. But if we do get to the point where the car is okay, the results will come. That's why I am so grateful about driving those races for Bruce. It gave me confidence in myself."

Mauricio Gugelmin enters the Keyhole at Mid-Ohio Sports Car Course. The Brazilian developed into a front-runner in 1995, leading several races and finishing ninth in the championship.

For his part, McCaw remains appreciative to Gurney for releasing Fangio to drive for PacWest in 1995. "It's a credit to our team that Dan would trust us with Juan's early development as an Indy car driver," McCaw said. "I have such huge respect for Dan, and what happened in 1995 was the catalyst of what became a great friendship with Dan and his wife Evi."

Gugelmin ended the season with another podium finish, coming from sixth on the grid to take third in the finale at Laguna Seca Raceway. He finished ninth in the CART series standings in 1995, and he still rates it as perhaps the most enjoyable single season in his distinguished career.

"That first year with PacWest was magic," he recalled with pleasure. "That whole year was incredible because the team was quite new. It was something we were building, and it was the first year of my relationship with Bruce as a friend and a team owner. But we were almost not ready for too much success."

Gugelmin is not the only PacWest team member who looks back fondly upon the 1995 season. "I still think of 1995 as one of the most enjoyable seasons of my whole racing career," remarked Russell Cameron, who served as Gugelmin's crew chief that year. "There were certainly more accomplishments in '97 in the record books, but boy, in '95, we were a tight, together little group. The energy was so strong between Andy, Mauricio, and the whole group. The team was maturing and Mauricio was ready to win, I think. We had good equipment and Andy was certainly a talented enough engineer to win.

"We just maybe weren't paying attention to the components of racing that would make us win," he added. "We built fast cars, but we didn't always produce the best pit stops or race strategies at that point. We weren't mature enough. It's a shame really, because we came out of the box strong enough in '95."

Juan Fangio II (left) drove the Dayton Steel Foundry Special at Michigan Speedway in 1996. The car was then owned by Bruce McCaw. Fangio's uncle, Juan Manuel Fangio, completed his Indianapolis rookie test in this car, but did not attempt to qualify for the race.

The elder Fangio poses with his rookie stripes after passing his rookie test at Indianapolis in the Kurtis-built and Offenhauser-powered Dayton Steel Foundry Special in 1958.

Mark Blundell leaves the Michigan International Speedway pits.

4

TOO MUCH, TOO FAST

IF THE 1995 season was PacWest Racing's coming out party in terms of race results, 1996 was the year when the organization went through some of its most rapid growth as a business entity. The change was most visible in the form of a brand new, purpose-built race shop at 4001 Methanol Lane in northwest Indianapolis. It went into operation on November 1, 1995.

During his tenure as mayor of Indianapolis from 1992 to 2000, Stephen Goldsmith was instrumental in creating financial incentives to attract teams participating in the PPG IndyCar World Series and other forms of racing to the Indiana capital. PacWest was one of several CART teams that took advantage of this climate. "This is a very important moment in the city's racing history," Goldsmith said. "We set out three or four years ago to try and get as many first-class teams to locate in Indianapolis as possible. Obviously, Indianapolis had a reputation as the motor sports capital of the world, but we really had not reached out to invite the best teams to locate in our marketplace. PacWest, in expanding their operation here, is great for the city. We think the city is great for PacWest as well."

Despite the tax incentives and other financial inducements, the state of Indiana was using to attract investment from the racing industry, it was still advantageous for PacWest to fall under ownership of Washington based RaceSport Management.

"For all the favorable atmosphere that Indiana was trying to provide, the property taxes were still punitive," related Bruce McCaw. "Teams were acquiring new chassis every year, and the old chassis would kill you in property taxes. We got a ruling from the IRS that allowed RaceSport to expense them every year. We could write off a chassis 100 percent annually as an expense, which is a big deal. We had to get the cars off the books of PacWest, or we would get killed by property taxes. So, PacWest would sell the cars to an entity in Oregon, which would take ownership. We got them off the books, and if needed, we could lease them back to the team as show cars."

By the end of 1995, PacWest was ready to burst out of its original home at 150 Gasoline Alley. From the end of 1994 to the end of 1996, the team's staff count nearly doubled

Construction on the new shop started in early 1995.

Indianapolis Mayor Stephen Goldsmith, Bruce McCaw, and Tom Armstrong cut a ceremonial ribbon at the public unveiling of the new shop in November, 1995.

in size from 25 to 47. So the christening of the new shop came just in time. Aside from providing more room to work, a total of 20,100 square feet, the new shop featured a top-grade Blowtherm paint booth and equipped the team with a modern, professional facility. The upgrade boosted PacWest's image for prospective sponsors.

"I think the new shop will cut down on our workload tremendously," said crew chief Ziggy Harcus. "Everything and everybody have a place in this shop, whereas before, there was so much scattered around that it was easier to make a mistake. It will make everyone work on a more professional level. You're forced to work a lot cleaner and and get rid of a lot of bad habits because those habits can be seen very easily in a new, state-of-the-art facility like we have now. I can't thank the owners enough for making our jobs easier."

The team was growing at such a rate that the shop underwent a major expansion less than two years later, including adding additional truck bays, a much larger engineering office, and an upgraded machine shop featuring cutting-edge Haas computer-controlled milling machines. A second expansion was completed in 1999, incorporating heavy duty flooring from Sika Corp.

Tom Armstrong was originally entrusted with management of the race shop build, but it quickly became apparent someone was needed on-site in Indianapolis observing and supervising the construction of the facility. To that end, Steve Fusek was hired in January 1995, launching a seven-year career with PacWest. Fusek grew up in West Allis, Wisconsin, within earshot of the Milwaukee Mile, and developed a love for Indy car racing at an early age. After graduating from the University of Northern Colorado with an accounting degree, Fusek worked as an auditor for Touche Ross & Co in Denver. On weekends, he got involved with Scott Atchison's Formula Super Vee team and by 1989, he parlayed that into a full-time job with Dick Simon Racing in the CART series. He joined Walker Racing in 1992, and his role in helping set up Walker's new race shop in Indianapolis—just two blocks from the site PacWest selected for its new base—was a key factor in his hire.

"They offered me a job to look after the building. It was a short-term project," Fusek said. "Right away I could see they were making some big mistakes. What they had done was said, 'OK, if Walker spent $1.2 million on his place, we're going to take three-quarters of that and build that,' not taking into account what was too small here or too big there. They just took three-quarters of everything. You had Tom designing it in Seattle not knowing what was needed or where it was going to go, and not understanding that the cheapest space you can build is truck bay space. If you don't fill them, you can use the area for storage."

With a greater knowledge of what a racing team required, Fusek and Anderson redrew the floorplan and persuaded McCaw to agree to the changes. Costs were reduced by trading sponsorship logo space on the PacWest race cars in exchange for materials needed for construction and furnishing of the shop, including Lista tool cabinets.

"We didn't add square footage, but we arranged it better," said Fusek. "There weren't enough parking spaces, the lunchroom was always too small, and the lobby didn't work from day one, but we tried to make it more practical. We told Tom that 40 parking spaces would never be enough for the season, and he replied, 'There's no way this team is ever going to have more than 40 people.' But you couldn't get there from here with him—he just didn't want to know."

McCaw noted that conflicts over the design and construction of Methanol Lane impacted his relationship with Armstrong. "Tom and I had a real falling out over that," he said. "Tom was so detailed, and he wanted an individual cupboard for every little tool. Ando and I went over the drawings and I thought if we ever needed to change anything, we were screwed. So, we took out about 80 percent of the interior shop walls from the plans and Tom was just livid about it. Part of the problem was Tom didn't want me involved in the building and he didn't want the team talking to me. He wanted to design the building."

While the new shop was in the final stages of construction, Anderson and the race team turned their attention to the 1996 season. PacWest was very pleased with the performance and service it received from Reynard in 1995. However, for the second year in a row, the team considered changing engine and tire suppliers before ultimately opting to remain with Ford-Cosworth and Goodyear. The lateness of PacWest's decision relegated the team to an upgraded 'Series II' development of the carryover Cosworth XB engine, rather than the all-new XD put into service by defending series champion Team Green, Newman/Haas Racing, Patrick Racing, and Walker Racing. PacWest paid $800,000 per car for its 1996 Series II XB engine lease package.

"We had a really good relationship with Ford-Cosworth," reflected McCaw. "From 1994 through '96, we worked well with them. We didn't agree with them on everything, and I think we managed their costs a lot harder than a lot of other people did because we looked at what was being done. We negotiated hard, but fairly, and I think that whatever we agreed on, we both did. But I think they respected us for that—Ian Bisco and Bernard Ferguson both. We had a very professional relationship."

Race Shop Manager Chris Griffis works in the shop's dedicated gearbox assembly area.

Armstrong was responsible for the initial planning for the new shop, but he and his wife, Susan, found their role with PacWest diminished after the project encountered problems.

REALITY CHECK IN BRAZIL

Indy car racing's popularity in Brazil was sparked by two-time Formula 1 World Champion Emerson Fittipaldi. Launching a second career in America in 1984, the Brazilian produced two Indianapolis 500 wins and the 1989 CART series championship. By the mid-1990s, the PPG IndyCar World Series featured half a dozen Brazilian drivers, including PacWest's Mauricio Gugelmin, and was attracting plenty of attention from fans and sponsors in the South American nation.

CART attempted to capitalize on the increased Brazilian interest by scheduling the second race of the 1996 season in Rio de Janeiro. The Jacarepagua road course that hosted the F1 Brazilian Grand Prix 10 times was converted into Emerson Fittipaldi Speedway, a trapezoid-shaped oval that required drivers to brake heavily for Turns 1 and 4. With an unusual trapezoidal layout that required the drivers to brake heavily for Turns 1 and 4, the track was dubbed a 'roval' by legendary Indy car driver Rick Mears. Hollywood cigarettes signed on as the title sponsor of the race, calling it the Hollywood Rio 400, and Mark Blundell's PacWest Racing entry carried a Hollywood livery for the Brazilian event similar to his teammate Gugelmin's car.

Blundell's transition to oval racing suffered a serious setback when his PacWest Reynard crashed heavily just 10 laps into the race due to a total brake failure. Maxed out at around 200 mph heading into Turn 4, Blundell tried to guide the car into the infield, but the Reynard-Ford continued straight on at unabated speed. Nearly clipping Gugelmin's car, it careened back across the track before striking the concrete wall at a 45-degree angle with a force of 122 G. The impact was severe enough to separate the engine from the chassis, and Blundell's seat belts were stretched by nearly five inches. The bent engine bulkhead now hangs on the wall of Ziggy Harcus' garage.

Blundell had deliberately aimed his stricken car at Gugelmin's ("I knew if I could hit him it would be better for me, if not him") and he tried so hard to intentionally spin the car that he bent the steering wheel. Then he braced for impact.

"I took my arms off the wheel and folded them across my chest, tucked myself down and said to myself, 'I am not coming away from this,'" Blundell remembered. "I was so aware of what was going on. Head-first into the wall at 198 miles per hour. The speed…I just could not believe that I would walk away. It was me and that concrete wall. What stays in my mind is that ferocious noise it made, hitting that concrete."

Although the car was heavily damaged, the cockpit remained intact. Almost unbelievably, Blundell managed to pull himself out of the wreckage to stagger a few steps before laying down on the track just as the CART Safety Team arrived on the scene. He sustained a fractured right foot, broken ribs, and multiple internal injuries along with a concussion.

"I had two days in hospital in Brazil, but they didn't give me anything like a brain scan—just a couple of paracetamols [Tylenol]," he related. "I flew home and by the time the plane landed, I had the worst headache I'd ever had in my life. Felt like my head was going to explode. My dad took me straight to hospital, they scanned me and found I had a blood clot on the brain. They said if the clot had burst in the air, I'd have been dead. But gradually, it dissipated on its own and I was racing seven weeks later."

The accident was caused by the failure of a part designed and manufactured by Galmer known as a brake hat or bell: a lightweight aluminum plate, attaching the rotor to the hub with a ring of 10 spring-loaded bobbins. The design allowed for a controlled amount of "float" to accommodate heat expansion between the two components. To solve a vibration issue, Galmer believed it could build a solid mounted brake rotor by making a bell with expansion joints between the mounting bobbins. The design would allow for the rotor's heat expansion and contraction.

"One of the drivers continuously complained about bad vibration through the brake pedal and pad knockoff even though we were running standard components—the same as all the other teams," noted Galmer co-founder and chief designer Alan Mertens. "We were under considerable pressure to find a solution even though, in light of other teams' experience, there was no obvious reason for it. A known alternative arrangement was to rigidly bolt the rotor onto a disc bell that had fingers machined in. These fingers allowed for the expansion and contraction of the assembly, but took out the 'rattle' of the floating system."

"I had a blood clot on the brain. They said if the clot had burst in the air, I'd have been dead."

Mark Blundell

The Galmer brake bells were briefly tested at Sebring International Raceway just before PacWest's cars and equipment were loaded onto cargo planes for the flight to Brazil. "We thought, 'Yes, this works. There was less pedal knock-back. Let's run them at Rio because we'll need it for braking into Turn 1,'" Cameron said. "But the load-up happened very quickly and parts weren't properly inspected afterward and crack-checked. We ran them and sure enough, one of those aluminum brake hats exploded."

Blundell's frightening incident at Rio in 1996 caused McCaw and PacWest to completely re-evaluate the team's methodology and led to major changes in the way Galmer was utilized. "I think it forced us to think about doing some things differently, changing our procedures and some of our disciplines," McCaw said. "We weren't doing anything too wrong, we just lacked some checks and balances, and perhaps some of the discipline that we needed. I think we emerged from that as a much better-focused team. It helped pull us all together.

"One of the things I think we discovered in '96 is that we were trying to do too much," he continued. "We were trying to do more things than we could do, and we just couldn't digest it all. So, one of the most important lessons we

This sequence of screen captures illustrates Mark Blundell's accident at Rio in 1996. The jarring crash caused PacWest to make major changes to its technical operations.

learned was when to say, 'No, we can't do that. Let's get the most out of what we have instead of trying to go after that last little increment and screwing up the whole works.'

"We went to Rio in '96 with two very competitive cars, but we got maybe a little too aggressive. We were trying to address some problems, but I think we had too much on our plate and we made a mistake that created an unsafe situation with our cars. Unfortunately, one of them crashed, and we were fortunate because it could have been both of them. That crash was the worst experience I've ever had." Indeed, Gugelmin's car suffered a similar brake failure on the 49th lap of the race, but it happened at a different point on the track and Mauricio was able to keep the car under control.

Like McCaw, Cameron believes that the unfortunate Rio episode was a catalyst for change and improvement within PacWest. Specifically, many engineering responsibilities were brought in-house to Indianapolis rather than assigned to Galmer in England.

"That was a turning point in the team that kind of made everybody wake up and realize that these were all good ideas, but we were not in control of our own destiny in terms of the car's development," Cameron stated. "We knew that to compete with the likes of Penske or Newman/Haas, and the front-running teams of the time, that we had to do more than just the status quo, which was finding a good driver and engineering a good car. You couldn't just buy a car and run it. That was the nature of the CART series at the time—it was a mini Formula 1 in a way. After Rio, it was decided that development would be done in-house with greater quality control. That's what brought us into the '97 season to become a stronger team."

"Brazil was a painful bloody experience," added John Anderson. "We could have lost two cars there and I saw the shadow of Mo's rear wing pass over the top of Mark's car. Thankfully, it wasn't as bad as it could have been. But Alan Mertens' attention had slipped from being the chief engineer, because it was a design problem with those brake bells that broke.

"I think if we had the chance to do it again, the resource of Galmer, given the right direction, would have been a big asset for the team," Ando continued. "Obviously I'd rather see stuff under the same roof, but with what was there as an established business, it was a great source. Shay Campbell was in charge of the day-to-day operations of Galmer and he was fantastic. It was great resource but unfortunately the focus had slipped from keeping these two groups together."

In late 1996, PacWest hired Allen McDonald as an in-house technical director. Galmer's engineering role diminished throughout 1997, though it still continued to manufacture parts for the team. "That pretty much put Galmer on its back foot," Mertens said. "We frankly had no choice but to put as much effort into finding an alternative source of income as we could. It came from two Formula 1 teams that contracted out surplus work, and from a pair of World Rally teams—Ford and Subaru. Prodrive, which ran the Subaru program, eventually bought Bruce's share and became a partner of Galmer."

As is often the case in racing, a serious incident like Blundell's crash led to important safety advancements. After analyzing the accident, the Brazilian organizers developed and installed an early version of soft wall technology, banding tires together and securing them with a composite material similar to what was used in conveyor belts. Ironically, Mauricio Gugelmin was the first driver to test the Brazilian soft wall during the 1997 Rio 400 when his car suffered a gearbox failure.

"The tire barrier did the job perfectly," he said. "It was a soft blow, like sitting down in a chair."

Around the same time, the Indianapolis Motor Speedway began trying to develop its own soft-wall solution. The first iteration, dubbed PEDS (Polyethylene Energy Dissipating System) debuted in May 1998 at IMS on a wall inside Turn 4 near the pit entrance. It was put to the test later that year when Arie Luyendyk had a huge impact in an IROC (International Race of Champions) stock car. Luyendyk walked away unscathed, but the huge foam debris field the crash created precluded further use. IMS persisted, commissioning research by Dr. Dean Sicking and the University of Nebraska-Lincoln. The result was the SAFER Barrier (Steel and Foam Energy Reduction). It was first put into use in 2002 and is now universally installed at oval tracks across America, arguably creating the biggest safety advance in the history of oval racing.

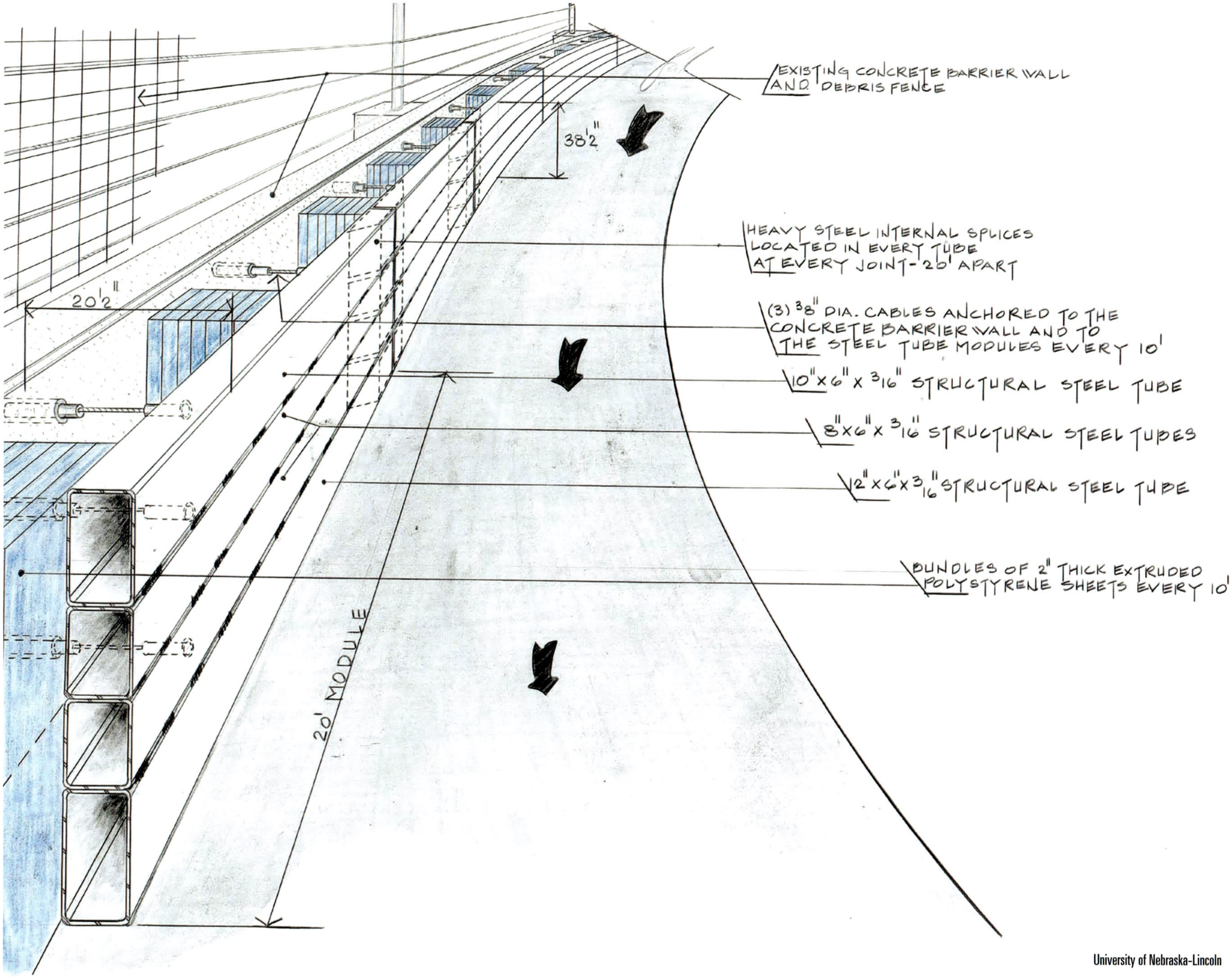

University of Nebraska-Lincoln

With support from the Indianapolis Motor Speedway, Dr. Dean Sicking of the University of Nebraska-Lincoln is credited with creating the SAFER Barrier now in common use at oval tracks. The SAFER Barrier uses a system of foam blocks and steel tubing to create a cushioned effect when a car crashes.

Allan McNish confers with Mauricio Gugelmin at PacWest's "shootout" test at Firebird Raceway.

Bisco, who served as Cosworth USA's vice-president and general manager, backed McCaw's remarks. "I will always have good memories of PacWest, from the very first time Bruce, Tom Armstrong, and Dominic Dobson came to see us in the motorhome at Laguna Seca at the last race of the 1993 season," he said. "These three previously unknown and very unlikely looking characters came in to ask us about an engine deal and we really did not take them too seriously at first. It was not until we got a heads up from Carl Haas about who they were that we really started to listen. From that point on we enjoyed working with them."

The final major decision to be made for 1996 was the driver of PacWest's second car as a teammate to Mauricio Gugelmin. The opening drew considerable interest. A diverse shortlist of a dozen interested applicants was compiled. It included Arie Luyendyk, Martin Brundle, Ivan Capelli, Perry McCarthy, Karl Wendlinger, Johnny O'Connell, Bertrand Gachot, Bryan Herta, Robbie Buhl, and Buddy Lazier. A 'shootout' test was organized at Firebird Raceway in December 1995. The five drivers included Dominic Dobson; Mike Groff, who drove for Bobby Rahal's CART team in 1994; Formula 3000 up-and-comer Alan McNish; and Formula 1 drivers Mark Blundell and JJ Lehto. Running one of PacWest's 1995 Reynards, McNish was quickest by a tenth of a second over Blundell.

John Anderson offered his recollection of the Firebird test: "I was really high on Lehto and felt he could have been good for the team," he said. "He was a bit 'Joe Cool,' but I enjoyed the guy socially. Very straight, but physically fit like you wouldn't believe. McNish, I really enjoyed, and it's a shame that no one picked him up at the time, or that we didn't. I think at the time we thought he was a skinny little weed. But as a team man, he would have done a fantastic job." Lehto and McNish both went on to enjoy successful careers in sports cars, scoring three outright wins each in the 24 Hours of Le Mans.

"I wasn't looking for somebody who could set the track record," Anderson added. "I was looking from the perspective of how he fitted in with the team. I think my choice was Lehto, McNish, and then Blundell and obviously, with their credentials, I'd have been happy with any of those three guys. I really feel the Brit got the job because of Galmer, and when it was decided he was the man, I didn't have any problems with that."

Blundell won British Formula Ford championships in the 1600 and 2000 cc classes, then defied convention by skipping Formula 3 to advance directly to Formula 3000. He bought a used Lola he affectionately named "The Shed" and enlisted the help of family and friends to run the car on a shoestring budget. Blundell switched to sports cars in 1990, claiming pole position at Le Mans by more than six seconds with one of the most memorable laps in the

"I wasn't looking for somebody who could set the track record. I was looking from the perspective of how he fitted in with the team."

John Anderson

Blundell ran car No. 21 in this VISA livery for the first race of the 1996 season at Homestead.

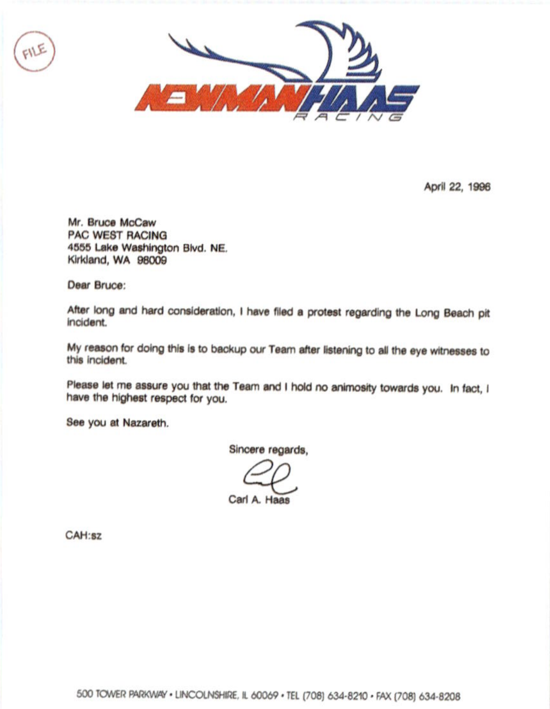

FILE

NEWMAN HAAS RACING

April 22, 1996

Mr. Bruce McCaw
PAC WEST RACING
4555 Lake Washington Blvd. NE.
Kirkland, WA 98009

Dear Bruce:

After long and hard consideration, I have filed a protest regarding the Long Beach pit incident.

My reason for doing this is to backup our Team after listening to all the eye witnesses to this incident.

Please let me assure you that the Team and I hold no animosity towards you. In fact, I have the highest respect for you.

See you at Nazareth.

Sincere regards,

Carl A. Haas

CAH:sz

500 TOWER PARKWAY • LINCOLNSHIRE, IL 60069 • TEL (708) 634-8210 • FAX (708) 634-8208

A letter from Carl Haas informing Bruce McCaw of a protest being filed against PacWest in regard to the post-race pit lane altercation between the teams' crews at Long Beach.

near century-long history of the race. He won the 24 Hours classic for Peugeot two years later, sandwiching a debut Formula 1 campaign with Brabham in 1991. Blundell returned to F1, driving for Ligier in 1993 and Tyrrell in 1994, then was drafted in at McLaren-Mercedes in 1995 when Nigel Mansell's F1 career came to a close four races into the season.

Andy Brown endorsed the hiring of Blundell. "He can thank me as well for his drive, just like Mauricio," Brown quipped. "I had worked with Mark at Brabham and was very impressed with him there. He was just a real hard charger, and that's what I thought he could bring to the team, and actually help Mauricio in that respect. Mauricio definitely had Danny covered; Danny was obviously in the twilight of his career, so Mauricio certainly didn't feel threatened by Danny. Bringing Mark on board solved that."

One disadvantage to hiring an F1 driver like Blundell was his complete lack of experience in oval racing. When Gugelmin joined PacWest in 1995, he had already completed a full season in the CART series and had half a dozen oval races under his belt. Despite some similarities in appearance, an Indy car is considerably different than a Formula 1 car and Blundell would be learning about that new car, and a totally foreign form of competition, on the fly. Plus, as Gugelmin could attest, oval racing looks deceptively simple, but it requires a different mindset and driving technique.

"Everything hit me over the head because it was such a big change," Blundell observed. "The Indy car was much heavier, the downforce level was slightly lower, the tires a bit harder, steel brakes, manual gearbox, sequential shift, clutch pedal…I hadn't used one of those in a while! Left-foot braking was the biggest other contention for me because I had never been brought up as a left-foot braking driver. Having to do it on the oval, to stabilize the car going into the corner and roll the throttle in at the same time, was something I had to learn as well. So, it was a big change in a lot of areas, but it's racing. It has four wheels and it goes fast. You can't let the differences control you—you have to control them. But the oval side was enjoyable and definitely one of the most thrilling experiences. When you had the car set up well on an oval, I don't think there's much to beat it."

Blundell's oval racing career got off to an auspicious start. He spun approaching the green flag for the opening race of the 1996 season at the new Homestead Speedway oval south of Miami. "We'll chalk this one up to experience," he said after recovering to record a 17th-place finish in his CART debut. "I definitely needed the experience, and that's what I got." But Blundell's desire to quickly gain additional Indy car seat time was put on hold when he sustained serious injuries in a crash during the second race of the season at Rio de Janeiro, Brazil. It forced him out of the car for seven weeks.

Teo Fabi temporarily took Blundell's place at Long Beach and Nazareth while Mark recuperated. The diminutive Italian was one of the first Formula 1 aspirants to switch to American open-wheel racing in the CART series. He took pole position for the Indianapolis 500 and scooped Rookie of the Year honors in 1983. He later raced for Brabham and Benetton in F1 before returning for a second stint in CART. As the lead driver for Porsche's Indy car effort from 1988 to 1990, he earned the German marque's only Indy car victory. Fabi then won the 1991 FIA World Sports car title for Jaguar before returning to America where he ran full-time for the Hall-VDS and Forsythe CART teams through the end of 1995. The two starts for PacWest in 1996 were the last races of his career at age 41.

Teo Fabi drove the No. 21 PacWest car at Long Beach and Nazareth in early 1996 while Mark Blundell recovered from injuries sustained in his Brazil crash.

"I liked Teo a lot," McCaw remarked. "He came in as a sub and recognized his role and respected it. I think he tried very hard just to support, and be accepted by, the team. I thought he was very professional about how he worked with us. Obviously, it was pretty brief. He wasn't really in top shape and had been enjoying the pasta, but I thought Teo was a very good solid capable driver and he tried to do the best he could for us."

At Long Beach, the PacWest pit crews got into a post-race altercation with crew members from Newman/Haas Racing. The spat was sparked by on-track contact between Gugelmin and Michael Andretti. Michael bumped Gugelmin into a wall while they were both attempting to put a lap on Adrian Fernandez. Andretti also clashed with Fabi earlier in the race. "He told me, 'I'm sorry, I didn't see you,'" Gugelmin related. "But that's the problem—he never sees anything!" It was the fifth time in a year that a PacWest car had been knocked out of a top-ten position by Andretti.

Along with fellow drivers Robby Gordon and Paul Tracy, Mauricio Gugelmin created a T-shirt for the "Michael Andretti Driving School for the Blind" after being rammed several times by the aggressive star.

At the next race, Gugelmin and several other drivers taunted Andretti by wearing T-shirts with a "Michael Andretti Driving School for the Blind" logo to the drivers' meeting. But it was no joking matter to officials, who placed Andretti on probation and fined PacWest and Newman/Haas $5,000 each for the fight.

Racing took a back seat to politics when the calendar turned to May. The simmering resentment and distrust between CART and the Indianapolis Motor Speedway turned into direct competition in 1996. When the newly created Indy Racing League decreed that 25 of the 33 starting spots in the Indy 500 field would be reserved for IRL regulars, CART made the decision to host its own marquee 500-mile race on Memorial Day weekend. CART leased Michigan International Speedway from Roger Penske and staged an event called the U.S. 500 on the very same day as the Indianapolis 500.

Associated Press

Mauricio Gugelmin's damaged car sits on the track after the first-lap accident that halted the U.S. 500. The PacWest crew repaired the car and Gugelmin finished second.

Blundell's return to action following his Brazilian crash, therefore, came on the fastest and arguably the most intimidating oval track on the CART schedule. "I do remember the first time back in the car again happened to be at a superspeedway, and that was jumping into the fire out of the frying pan," he observed. "That certainly gave me lots of things to think about, and one of those was whether I wanted to be doing that kind of stuff anymore. Still, one of the biggest regrets from that time, actually, was not being able to race at Indianapolis. Part and parcel of my contract when I went to America was Indianapolis was in there, but as we know now, the split took place and we never got to go there."

Unfortunately, the U.S. 500 turned out to be an embarrassment for CART. After months of promoting the race as featuring the true "Stars and Cars" of Indy car racing, front row starters Jimmy Vasser, Bryan Herta, and Adrian Fernandez triggered a 10-car accident. Both PacWest cars sustained damage in the debris field, but the race was red-flagged, giving the team the opportunity to make repairs during a 40-minute delay. It was a major undertaking; Gugelmin's car came in on a hook, with damaged front and rear suspension on the right side.

"The '96 U.S. 500 was a good example of our growth as a team," recalled Nigel Bloom. "Mauricio's car was pretty heavily damaged in the big crash, and we couldn't use the backup because the engine had mileaged out. It was all hands on deck and everyone jumped in to do what needed to be done to get the car back on the grid. Mark Moore and John Roof were over in the garage tearing parts off the spare car, and my wife and some of the other wives were carrying them out to the entrance to pit lane. I bolted the right rear corner onto that car, and I was the fueler and a tire man on the car, not a mechanic. It was an awesome testimony to the team. Nobody gave up and going through something like that meant a lot to all of us."

The efforts of the crew paid off because the U.S. 500 turned out to be PacWest's most competitive race in 1996. After being struck in the helmet by a flying wheel during the original start, Blundell overcame a splitting headache and produced his best finish of the season with fifth place. Mauricio Gugelmin ran even better, finishing second, some 11 seconds behind race-winner Vasser.

"I couldn't be happier with the team and our drivers," McCaw stated after the race. "The teamwork displayed by both crews was inspirational. It's truly amazing they were able to get the cars back in the field, let alone in a position to win the race. For Mark especially, faced with a 500-mile race as his first race back, he showed a tremendous amount of speed and ability. I'm pleased he finally had the opportunity to showcase his talent."

Drivers Frederik Ekblom, Adrian Fernandez, and Mauricio Gugelmin walk back to the pits after the first-lap U.S. 500 crash.

Mark Blundell leads Mauricio Gugelmin at Michigan International Speedway. PacWest produced four top-six finishes at the 2-mile superspeedway in 1996, setting the stage for an even more impressive performance in 1997.

At the same time that PacWest Racing entered Indy car competition on a full-time basis, Indianapolis Motor Speedway president Tony George announced the formation of the Indy Racing League. Over the next two years, team owners in the CART series grappled with the decision whether to remain loyal to CART or cast their lot with George and the IRL. Nearly a year prior to Indy car racing's 'day of infamy' when dueling 500-mile races were staged on May 26, 1996, Bruce McCaw wrote an essay for the PacWest *Reality Check* newsletter outlining the organization's position on the developing open-wheel war.

FAX RECEIVED JUN 22 1995

Reality from PacWest Racing Group

Wednesday, June 21, 1995 — Volume 2, Issue 15

Big Mo OK:

Mauricio Gugelmin was unhurt in a heavy crash while testing at Elkhart Lake. Mauricio went off exiting turn 3 and backed into a concrete barrier while still at high speed. He was briefly knocked unconscious, but released later the same day following an observation period and a CAT-scan. Fortunately, he is fine.

His car escaped with relatively light damage, destroying its gearbox and rear suspension, but leaving the engine and monocoque untouched. Both driver and car will be ready for the Portland race this weekend.

A Brief Pause and a Look Ahead:

As the 1995 Indy car season momentarily loosens its grip around the teams, sponsors and fans, providing the series with its first weekend off since late April, we have a chance for a quick glance at the upcoming year.

At Detroit, an exciting 1996 schedule of IndyCar sanctioned races was announced. Some highlights—Miami again will host the season opener on March 3, but at a new track. The Homestead Motorsports Complex is a state-of-the-art facility offering both a short oval (which we will race on) as well as a road course.

Next will be Rio de Janeiro. To accommodate our first race in South America, the Brazilians are building a new 1.3 mile oval on the site of the old Nelson Piquet Formula 1 track.

Australia will follow and the rest of the season will look familiar, culminating with Laguna Seca in September. Gone will be Phoenix and New Hampshire. As is traditional, the month of May is left open to run the Indy 500, our only USAC sanctioned event.

1996 IndyCar Schedule

March 3	Miami	June 30	Cleveland
March 16	Brazil	July 14	Toronto
March 31	Australia	July 28	M.I.S.
April 14	Long Beach	August 11	Mid-Ohio
April 28	Nazareth	August 18	Elkhart Lake
June 2	Milwaukee	September 1	Vancouver
June 9	Detroit	September 8	Laguna Seca
June 23	Portland		

Much Ado About...?

By Bruce R. McCaw

In response to some questions we have received about a new, and possibly, competing series, I would like to express our views on the topic.

As has been extensively documented elsewhere, our sanctioning body, Championship Auto Racing Teams, Inc. (CART) which is normally referred to as IndyCar, was formed by the car owners who withdrew from USAC in 1979 and began anew in hopes of moving the sport to the next level. Thus the Indianapolis 500 has remained the only USAC-sanctioned Indy car event on the calendar.

Under IndyCar's direction, the sport has risen dramatically in its presence and popularity. A few current statistics support this claim.

- Record attendance and complete sell-outs at Miami, Long Beach, Nazareth and Milwaukee this year.
- TV ratings up more than 25% over last year and audiences of typically 75 million people in 133 countries.
- Parity in a sport which has seen 13 different drivers make podium finishes in the eight races held so far this season, the top nine drivers representing eight different teams and fantastic finishes witnessed by the fact that the last three IndyCar sanctioned races have all been decided by less than one second. Competition is fierce, and the smaller teams are able to compete effectively with the larger, more established organizations.
- Competition among manufacturers—there will be four chassis manufacturers and four engine manufacturers next season as well as two tire suppliers.
- The growth of the Indy Lights series into a viable series which has proven to be a cost-effective training ground for drivers, engineers, mechanics and, even, sponsors.

For some reason the Indianapolis Motor Speedway wishes to start their own series sanctioned by their closely linked organization, USAC. The proposed series would be four oval races plus the Indianapolis 500. They currently have the same rules package that we are racing under this year. It is unclear at this time whether they will adopt CART's 1996

(continued on page 2)

chassis rules which reduces downforce and thus lowers speeds particularly at the super speedways. 1996 engine rules have not yet been put forth by either organization.

While the proposed series, known as the Indy Racing League (IRL), has published a schedule and discussed a few seemingly lofty goals, in my mind they have proposed little of substance and nothing beneficial.

Notwithstanding some very dedicated individuals, as we saw this May, USAC doesn't bring anything better to the party. Nor would expanding the calendar or adding additional events do any more than add costs to our program. The present six month long season is about max for our hard-working crews.

Much has been said about ovals being "American" and road courses being of European derivation. While ovals have never generated a huge following elsewhere in the world, I would argue that in the post WWII United States, road racing has been a major part of the racing scene here.

In our view, Indy car racing in its present format has become the United States racing "export" to the world. A unique blend of ovals, super speedways and road courses is our formula for success. It appeals to a broad spectrum of fans with its diversity of racing, challenging teams and drivers to expand on their talents and to be most adaptable.

We run on some magnificent courses in rural areas as well as taking our racing to the city streets which gives easier access to our customer, the racing fan.

The international flavor created by drivers from both Americas (North and South), Europe and Asia is enhanced by true world class competition, with top-level driving talent. Drivers from the U.S., Canada, Brazil and Italy are all in hot pursuit of the top ten championship positions.

Most of all, as we become ever more a part of a true global economy and population we must be global in our perspective to succeed. Indy cars are at the top level of open wheel racing in the world. Competition with other sports is intense for both sponsors and fans and thankfully we continue to grow both domestically and in the international marketplace.

Motor racing is one of the largest, if not the largest, spectator sports in the world. Yet, we continue to be amazed how little of the U.S. media covers racing, particularly newspapers and the sports coverage during broadcast news. We are given statistics ad nauseam on some stick and ball guy who has spent two years on injured reserve but to find a full list of all qualifiers or finishers, much less a "story" on a great race, is a minor miracle. Unfortunately, it is usually only a dramatic accident that will momentarily stir the "news media". When we compare the amount of coverage PacWest or IndyCar receives in other countries to what we receive in the Northwest, it amazes us. While specialized publications abound, dedicated reporters who cover automobile racing find their efforts stifled by editors who can't be bothered to learn what is really going on out there.

Automobile racing went through some lackluster times in the 70s and 80s, but it is very much on the upswing in the 90s. IndyCar is working diligently to better educate and support the mainstream media and to raise our overall visibility. Hopefully, the media will continue to respond as we are still a well kept secret.

When we added our name to the list of IndyCar franchised teams, we did so because we believed that IndyCar represented a tremendous opportunity to join a premier auto racing organization and we are proud to be a part of it today.

The IndyCar organization is the core of our series. Under the capable leadership of Andrew Craig, a very professional staff provides the planning, support and services necessary to make it all work for the teams, sponsors, race promoters, media and, most of all, the fans. It sets the technical direction to assure safety, fair competition, medical support and the practical application of new technology. IndyCar functions so effectively because every franchised team is required to run every race. PacWest remains fully committed to the entire IndyCar series and will field two cars at every event in 1996.

The Indianapolis 500 race is a wonderful event and an important and traditional part of our racing heritage. We hope and expect that the Indy 500 will remain part of our calendar next year and that the Speedway will not compromise the dignity, importance or quality of this event by inhibiting the participation of any team due to their affiliation.

In summary, we have no quarrel with any effort to expand automobile racing in the United States, but we firmly believe that the future of major league open wheel racing is best served by everyone working together furthering the positive momentum that IndyCar has generated.

Bruce McCaw instituted major changes in mid-1996, promoting Steve Fusek and John Anderson to Vice-President positions in charge of business and racing.

Mauricio Gugelmin's best races in 1996 occurred at Michigan International Speedway. The Brazilian finished on the podium in both Michigan events. This trophy is from his third-place finish at the summer Marlboro 500.

After the drama of his Brazilian crash, the top-five finish was exactly what Blundell needed to regain the confidence necessary to race wheel-to-wheel at 220 mph on a superspeedway. "I was pretty discouraged after qualifying," he said. "I'd been brought up in an environment where if the car wasn't working properly, you drove around the problem. Everyone kept telling me that if a car isn't working on an oval, forget it. But in the race, though, the car was fantastic. I was down the inside of people, over the top of people—it was great! I learned the art of drafting that day. At Michigan, you can come off Turn 4 and get a draft from some guy going into Turn 1. When you go by someone, it's literally like being in a light aircraft!"

During the course of the activities in Michigan, McCaw and PacWest announced a pair of key promotions: John Anderson to Vice-President of Racing Operations and Steve Fusek to Vice-President of Business Operations. As leader of the race team, Anderson's promotion was little more than a title change (and commensurate increase in salary), whereas Fusek's responsibilities grew considerably. He had quickly advanced from his role as the construction supervisor of the new shop to logistics manager for the traveling race team. His responsibilities now included overall management of marketing and hospitality.

"I think the professionalism of the team grew a lot between '95 and '96, mostly because Bruce started to say, 'We're going to do it this way. Now let's go win races,'" Fusek recalled. "Tom and Susan Armstrong were still fans playing around with it who didn't really rely on the professional people. I had a near punch-up with Tom at Rio in '96 over something I said to Susan, but Bruce found me afterwards and said, 'Stick with me, this is all changing.'

"By the time we got to the U.S. 500, he sat John and me down during the practice weekend and said, 'You're going to be Vice President of Race Operations, you're going to be Vice President of Business Operations. We're going to run it like a professional organization and we're here to win races.' That's when I feel he really switched gears and that was basically the end of Tom and Susan."

Armstrong's involvement diminished and by the start of 1997, PacWest was truly Bruce McCaw's team. "I was disappointed to see Tom go because he was instrumental in getting the program kicked off and running, getting the workshop built," Anderson remarked. "But by the same token, it seemed getting Bruce more closely involved was a step in the right direction. Tom was obviously a pretty successful businessman in his day as well, but you can't have a number of people running the same deal at the same time with the guy who was actually funding it playing second fiddle."

Blundell matched his Michigan finish a few weeks later in his Indy car road racing debut at the Detroit Grand Prix with another fifth-place run. But both PacWest drivers struggled for results throughout most of June and July. More drama occurred at the Grand Prix of Cleveland where Blundell's car was involved in a pit fire when the fuel hose nozzle malfunctioned during a routine stop. Safety personnel and onlookers were able to quickly extinguish the invisible methanol fire and Blundell returned to the race to finish 11th. But crew members Tim Douthat and Randy Smay suffered second degree burns to their faces. Douthat also sustained a sprained ankle and CART fined the team $1,000 for a safety violation.

PacWest held a press conference at the 1996 season finale to reveal changes to Mercedes-Benz and Firestone.

Constrained somewhat by the Cosworth Series II XB engine, PacWest's results in 1996 were not as good as they were the previous year. Gugelmin and Blundell were again very competitive when the CART series returned for a second 500-miler at Michigan, with the Brazilian earning another podium finish in third place and the Englishman finishing sixth. The nadir came at Road America, where both PacWest drivers were taken out in the same accident triggered by Andre Ribeiro. Gugelmin wound up 14th in the CART standings with Blundell 16th, but the team ended the season strongly with a top-five finish at Laguna Seca, where Gugelmin qualified third and Blundell fourth.

Despite PacWest achieving less impressive results in 1996 than it had a year earlier, Andy Brown looks back on the season with fondness. "I still remember that summer as my favorite time at PacWest," he said. "The things that we did and learned then, in trying to make an under-powered car with a tire disadvantage into a competitive option, really set us up for 1997. I feel proud of what the three of us in the engineering office, including Tim Neff and Mark Herd, achieved."

During the same September weekend at Laguna Seca where PacWest wrapped up the 1996 season on a high note, the team revealed it would change engine and tire suppliers in 1997 to Mercedes-Benz and Firestone, respectively. In December, at the team's annual Christmas party, McCaw announced PacWest had landed title sponsorship from the Automotive Energy and Controls division of Motorola for Blundell's car, making both cars fully funded. Clearly all the ingredients were now in place for success. Would that translate into race wins?

The collective corporate sponsorship of the CART field at its peak exceeded $250 million annually.

5

THE BUSINESS OF RACING

THE POST-WORLD WAR II auto racing industry saw many significant changes. One shift was in the underlying business model itself. Many consider the 1950s and 1960s the golden era for the Indianapolis 500. Car owners such as J.C. Agajanian, John Zink, John Mecom, and Al Dean were often wealthy businessmen or sportsmen who financed race teams out of their own pockets, more or less as a hobby. The USAC Championship Trail consisted of Indianapolis and a handful of other races at paved oval tracks such as Trenton and Milwaukee, with a few additional events contested on dirt tracks at state fairgrounds. It was far from a year-round endeavor. Only about a dozen drivers ran the majority of the races and competed for the USAC championship, and a team owner could easily recoup his investment through victory in the Indy 500, with a purse that dwarfed all others in motorsports.

For a new breed of car owners transforming the sport in the 1960s, racing became a business and a technical exercise as much as it was a sport. They needed their on-track exploits to at least be self-sustaining, if not profitable. Colin Chapman (Lotus), Dan Gurney (Eagle), Jim Hall (Chaparral), Jack Brabham, and Bruce McLaren revolutionized racing with their business and engineering savvy and the increasingly sophisticated racing cars they produced. These men were pure racers, drivers turned constructors/team owners, who were relentless in the pursuit of any advantage they could gain over their competition.

At roughly the same time, Roger Penske was among those instrumental in establishing the advent of corporate sponsorships to offset the rising costs. Prior to his remarkable 50-year run as the most successful team owner in the history of American auto racing, Penske was a talented road racer. He sold his first sponsorship to Dupont Corporation in the early 1960s and rechristened his Formula 1-based Cooper sports car the Zerex Special. When Penske won a series of high-profile races in the controversial car, Dupont and its Zerex anti-freeze brand gained far more value out of the sponsorship than the $5,000 invested. Strong corporate support and immaculate car preparation and presentation remain hallmarks of Team Penske to this day.

With race car technology advancing at an unprecedented rate in the 1960s and 1970s, and costs rising as a result, corporate sponsorship became an increasingly important factor.

Mario Andretti and Bobby Unser flank J.C. Agajanian, who fielded cars in the Indianapolis 500 for decades.

Seen here in the 1969 British Grand Prix, Bruce McLaren was one of a handful of drivers who began constructing their own cars.

Companies ranging from STP Oil Treatment, to First National City Travelers Checks, to Vita-Fresh Orange Juice, to Samsonite luggage got involved. Sponsorships expanded from specialty automotive to general consumer products. The most lucrative sponsorships came from tobacco companies as they looked for promotional opportunities in the wake of a federal ban on cigarette advertising on radio and television that went into effect in 1971; RJ Reynolds' title sponsorship of the NASCAR Winston Cup Series from 1971 to 2003 was a crucial factor in stock car racing's growth from a regional southeastern series into a national powerhouse.

Indy car racing failed to capitalize on the tobacco money as effectively as NASCAR. In 1971, Marlboro signed on as the title sponsor of the USAC Championship Trail, only to withdraw at the end of the year because USAC breached its contract by allowing rival cigarette brand Viceroy to enter the sport with its backing of the high-profile Vel's Parnelli Jones "Superteam" from 1972 to 1975. Marlboro and Philip Morris finally returned to Indy car racing in the mid-1980s, sponsoring Patrick Racing, and later Team Penske, until tobacco sponsorships were finally banned in 2010.

Fueled by decades of Indianapolis 500 history and hyperbole, the "rich car owner" became an idealized notion that some hold onto to this day. But by the late 1970s, racing was the primary form of business for the majority of team owners, and they found it difficult to survive financially in a USAC series that was poorly promoted and marketed outside of the newly built Interstate 465 beltway around Indianapolis. Spurred into action by Dan Gurney's 1978 "White Paper," the creation of Championship Auto Racing Teams (CART) in 1978 was an attempt to help the sport achieve its commercial potential and make Indy car racing a more credible business proposition for the team owners.

CART transformed Indy car racing in the 1980s with a higher overall level of professionalism than USAC demonstrated and an increased emphasis on road and street course racing. As CART became more successful, it attracted another new wave of team owners. Carl Haas, the US distributor for Lola racing cars, carried on the tradition of McLaren, Brabham, and Chapman, while former mechanics and managers, including Derrick Walker and Barry Green, graduated to team ownership. Meanwhile, yet another style of owner, one with little or no prior affiliation to professional racing, also arrived on the scene. Gerald Forsythe owned a company that produced steam power generators, Jim Trueman presided over the Red Roof Inn hotel chain, and Rick Galles was an Albuquerque car dealer, but they all took the plunge into operating Indy car teams. As did Bruce McCaw.

McCaw is a lifelong car enthusiast who participated in vintage car racing for pleasure, but when he made the decision to take PacWest Racing full-time, it was purely as a business. "I see a clear distinction. When someone else is driving, it's a business venture," he said in the early days of PacWest. "I'm not just in it to support racing; ultimately I expect a return. The more involved I got in the business of racing, the more interested I became in where it could go. I guess some of the knowledge and experience that I had garnered over the years helped me realize the potential that existed in an organization like CART. This used to be a seasonal business, but it's grown to a year-round professional series."

Roger Penske waits in his Zerex Special on the grid at the 1962 Puerto Rico Grand Prix.

Unlike many teams entering the sport, PacWest had an ownership group that was able and willing to contribute the considerable start-up costs to support a two-car effort. McCaw shouldered the majority of the financial burden to get the team off the ground, even though he remained in the background throughout most of 1994 while Tom Armstrong functioned as PacWest's front man. Like McCaw, Armstrong believed the solid financial footing of PacWest's ownership group gave the team the kind of security most new organizations would not initially be capable of providing. But both men also recognized the need for the team to quickly source an outside income stream.

"Obviously, the business doesn't work without big sponsorship," Armstrong said in 1994. "We're fortunate to have the financial base to do it different. Usually you stumble around until you find a sponsor. We've just come in and said we're going to make the commitment, and as we do it and do it well, we'll get the sponsorship."

The stability of the ownership group allowed PacWest to adopt a big-picture perspective that altered the team's initial approach to corporate sponsorship. Instead of trying to attract support from traditional racing sponsors like oil, beer, or cigarettes, PacWest attempted to build a more ambitious, business-to-business driven program anchored by the American Automobile Association. The modern AAA is a direct descendant of the very same organization that governed American auto racing up through 1955. AAA withdrew that year from all racing-related activities after the death of Bill Vukovich during the Indianapolis 500 and a tragic accident at the 24 Hours of Le Mans that killed more than 80 spectators.

McCaw envisioned a national program through AAA corporate, with varying participation from the individual clubs located around the country. Regions that hosted CART races would play a larger role and invest more into the national program. McCaw hoped to tie in other corporate partners, beginning with Cellular One for a low-cost emergency phone program. At the time, cell phones and airtime packages were still very expensive and the idea was to provide a phone that a club member could power up when needed

WINNING OVER MOTOROLA

John Creak had been on the job as PacWest's marketing director for only a few weeks in November 1996 when, as he put it, "We got lucky." At a post-season Drive Day function with Hollywood executives and other PacWest team partners at Sebring International Raceway, PacWest team photographer Dan Boyd tipped Creak and Vice President of Business Operations Steve Fusek about a potential commercial opportunity. After three mostly unsuccessful seasons with Rahal-Hogan Racing and Comptech Racing, the Automotive Energy and Controls Group (AECG) division of electronics/communications conglomerate Motorola was shopping for a new team to sponsor in the CART series. Creak and Fusek immediately sprang into action.

"We were late to the party, but Steve and I called [Motorola sponsorship manager] Tom Crawford from Orlando and set up a meeting in Chicago as soon as possible," Creak said. "Right there and then, we decided that we wouldn't send a proposal, we would hand deliver it. We had just a few days to get things done, so we headed straight back to Indianapolis. We had just installed an Apple Macintosh computer in the office so that we could generate proposals, and I set to work. We were also lucky enough that Motorola had a very specific brief for what they were looking for in a new team. It was clear that we ticked every box, from team structure, to engine manufacturer, to how the future of the program would look."

The creation of the Motorola proposal was not without problems; PacWest's new Mac froze, forcing Creak to complete much of the work at a Kinko's Copies shop. Fusek got sick and lost his voice. A snowstorm engulfed the eastern half of the country on November 30, the day Fusek and Creak were scheduled to fly to Chicago to present the proposal to Crawford. Many flights were cancelled.

"I literally spent the whole night at Kinko's getting it done; there was just me and the guy running the office and I had proposal documents all over the floor," Creak said. "Steve picked me up early in the morning and we decided to drive to Chicago—well, he drove, and I slept. We met Mark Blundell at O'Hare Airport—he had just flown in from a test session and had to change clothes in the car. We were all in suits and ties, and we presented them the proposal in metal briefcases that we had custom-made for the occasion. The presentation went well, although Tom told us that they couldn't keep the briefcases and would have to be left with an appropriate department at Motorola. But they did the job. Steve and I then dropped Mark off at O'Hare and drove back to Indianapolis. We were pretty tired, but buzzing, as we both thought we had hit every requirement that Motorola had laid out."

A few days later, Crawford called Fusek and arranged a site visit to PacWest's Indianapolis race shop. "That was a pretty short turnaround, so that was a good sign," Fusek said. "They hadn't really considered us at all and didn't see us as a serious player. The big question from them was, 'Can you guys win races?' Well, I guaranteed them that we would win races now that we had the right things—Firestone, Mercedes, and all the rest. They liked the Mercedes tie-in. We were up against Penske, Walker, and Green at the time, and I think getting Motorola was one of those things that made people think, 'Those PacWest guys are for real.'"

As a major vendor to McCaw Cellular, Motorola was certainly familiar with Bruce McCaw and the McCaw family, and after the initial contact from Fusek and Creak, McCaw himself sealed the Motorola deal, which was agreed on December 10, 1996.

"Clearly, when we found out that Motorola was available and that it was going to move, I felt that we had to get it," McCaw reflected. "Creak and Steve did a great job on the presentation. I had a personal business relationship with the company and the senior management, particularly with Keith Bane (then president of Motorola's Americas region), who was going to make the decision. I think above all we had by far the best concept for them.

"I literally spent the whole night at Kinko's... just me and the guy running the office and I had proposal documents all over the floor."

John Creak

"Motorola was a company that had largely been in a monopolistic situation," he added. "Their whole culture was based around radio and police and fire and municipal governments and things like that where they really didn't have a lot of competition, and they didn't always think well in competitive terms. Even in cell phones, they had a jump on that whole industry but ultimately they left the door open because they weren't listening (the company's share of the US wireless phone market dropped from 60 percent to 34 percent between 1994 and 1998). They were still in the Dark Ages. They finally built some pretty good small phones, but they were still never a company that had a strong marketing culture. So, we were trying to take the racing program and turn it into a marketing opportunity."

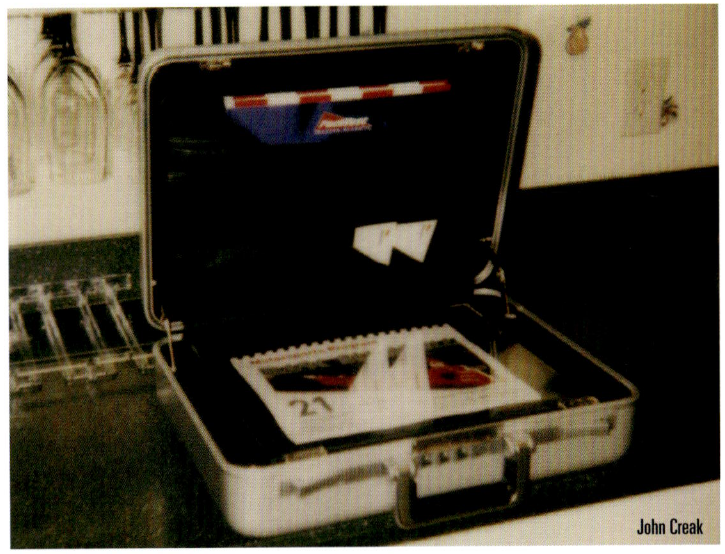

John Creak

PacWest presented its sponsorship proposal to Motorola executives in custom aluminum briefcases.

John Creak

The spiral bound presentation was simple but effective.

That was the key aspect of PacWest's pitch that convinced Motorola it was the right fit. "We met with many teams in CART, and I think we were approached by just about every team in every series," said Crawford. "The phone never stopped ringing. Some day we might like to diversify into another series, but right now, CART fits quite nicely with our marketing objectives and PacWest is a perfect match. You can be assured that sponsors only spend this kind of money if they can recoup their investment. CART's demographics really match the people we do business with."

PacWest and Blundell were featured on billboards and in print ads emphasizing the speed and reliability of the company's StarTac cell phones and electronic components, including computer processor chips and semiconductors. Motorola had production facilities dotted around the US, and Blundell frequently visited those plants for Q&A and autograph sessions, sometimes accompanied by a race car and a small group of PacWest crewmen who performed pit stop demonstrations.

Twenty years later, Fusek and Creak have differing thoughts about the sponsorship pitch they put together for Motorola. "If you look at the proposal now, it's comical," Fusek said with a laugh. "But at the time, we thought it was the best thing since sliced bread."

Creak takes a more charitable view of what was one of PacWest Racing's biggest business-related accomplishments. "The proposal looked great for 1996 and stands the test of time," he noted. "Clean, professional and succinct, printed and spiral-bound...I still have a copy for sentimental reasons. We stood out because we responded exactly to the brief. These days it would be done online, and we'd use video a lot more. However, I still get to see motorsport proposals that look very similar. At the end of the day it's all about the content and presenting that content in the best way."

"Sponsors only spend this kind of money if they can recoup their investment. CART's demographics really match the people we do business with."

Tom Crawford

McCaw looks back on the link-up with Motorola as the culmination of a four-year effort to build PacWest's business operations. "Adding Motorola was a huge breakthrough for us," he said. "We looked at how we were marketing ourselves and made some changes. John Creak really enhanced that side of our team. I think the reason we got Motorola was because we understood what they really wanted instead of trying to sell them what we had. We really tried to go out and create for them what they wanted, and I think that's why they selected us."

The Motorola-sponsored PacWest CART and Indy Lights entries line up at Gateway International Raceway with Derek Hill (No. 81) and the P1 Racing Formula Atlantic team.

Corporate branding extends far beyond logos on a race car.

with a one-touch feature that connected them to AAA and its towing and rescue service. Goodyear and Ford also expressed serious interest in joining the program. "The goal was a national program with AAA at the center and some really strong automotive partners," McCaw said.

"AAA was really amorphous, with a national organization, but several dozen individual clubs that sort of ran their own show," he continued. "They have an incredibly powerful brand and a hell of a network of people. But they were clearly in a situation where they had an aging membership that was going down at a fairly rapid rate, and they did very little to stimulate new members. We started looking at this and working with them at the franchise headquarters in Florida, putting together a racing package that could really work for the entire AAA brand."

McCaw made numerous trips to Orlando to meet AAA executives and a PacWest show car was put on display in the lobby of the company's corporate headquarters. What blunted the program's potential was the inability to get a significant number of the local AAA clubs to join a national promotion. "Some of these clubs were just run by old fuddie-duddies and they would have been more interested in doing a sewing machine program," McCaw said. "There was a level of guys who were intrigued and liked it a lot but didn't want to spend any money on it. Then there were some that thought you were trying to bring Satan into the organization. So, we spent a lot of energy pitching the national organization. The problem was there was not even a cohesive agreement on how they could use the brand, and the logo, and everything. It was very difficult to get this thing moving, but we started getting key pieces of it."

PacWest's top supporter within AAA was drag racing enthusiast Tom McKernan, the CEO of Auto Club of Southern California from 1991 until his retirement in 2012. Known to Californians simply as "the Auto Club," ACSC actually operates AAA motor clubs in 21 states, representing more than 30 percent of all AAA memberships. McKernan was credited for driving ACSC's growth; California membership grew by 70 percent during his tenure.

The "major associate" sponsor program PacWest created with ACSC was instrumental in sparking the club's modern-era presence in auto racing. Auto Club logos were prominent on PacWest cars from 1995 to 1997. The team also provided hospitality to hundreds of ACSC employees and club members at the Long Beach Grand Prix and California Speedway through the end of the decade.

Auto Club later sponsored the John Force Racing NHRA team and driver Robert Hight. It also established a long-running relationship with Team Penske, backing drivers Joey

"Some of these clubs were just run by old fuddie-duddies that would have been more interested in doing a sewing machine program."

Bruce McCaw

Auto Club Speedway

Tom McKernan (left) was responsible for growing Auto Club of Southern California's presence in auto racing.

Logano in NASCAR and Helio Castroneves in the IndyCar Series. In 2008, Auto Club signed a ten-year deal for naming rights at California Speedway (Auto Club Speedway) and the drag racing facility at the Pomona Fairplex (Auto Club Raceway) that hosts the NHRA Winternationals and the NHRA Finals. Auto Club is also the presenting sponsor of the Wally Parks NHRA Museum at Pomona and the annual California Hot Rod Reunion.

McCaw believes that a properly activated sponsorship with AAA on a national level could have been phenomenally effective for the organization of clubs. "In terms of trying to recreate an excitement about the brand, we felt that we had a huge opportunity, that AAA going into racing was a great story," he related. "The cross-marketing and the sales opportunities that existed with AAA were phenomenal. There was a huge opportunity for anyone in the travel or automotive industries in particular. It would have made Carl Haas's deal with K-mart or Chip Ganassi's package with Target look like child's play.

"I look back, and even more than 20 years later, I think what we were doing was absolutely the perfect deal for them," McCaw continued. "McKernan really got it. He sponsored us at Long Beach and later Fontana, and he of course ended up becoming a track sponsor at Fontana and Pomona. He loved drag racing, but he could always see that the CART fan base was his target customer. He was a good friend, but we never got the mass of the program that should have been. The structural problems within AAA kept us from getting a decent launch for a national program. If we had managed to pull that together and gotten AAA back into racing, it would have been huge. I think it would dramatically have changed AAA. We spent literally years trying to make a reality out of that and Tom's later programs were almost a by-product of what we were trying to do."

One of the co-branding opportunities that PacWest pursued during its pitch to AAA was a AAA-branded VISA card to be administered by Bank of America. The Bank of America efforts actually bore fruit before AAA as B of A logos appeared on PacWest's racing cars in late 1994 (including one of the first "branded" in-car cameras), followed by VISA in early 1995. For a period in late 1994 into 1995, it looked like Bank of America might become involved in the CART series at a significant level; in addition to sponsoring the PacWest cars in the 1994 season finale at Laguna Seca Raceway, it served as the title sponsor for the race itself (the Bank of America 300) and participated in the "Arrivederci, Mario!" promotion for Mario Andretti's final Indy car race.

"As an organization, we were working on building strong business-to-business stuff," McCaw explained. "I think we were somewhat on the leading edge of that, and Bank of America was going to really come out front. Like AAA, Bank of America was starting to go from being sort of a provincial bank to really wanting to step out and become a national organization. B of A was doing a lot of mortgage business from an office in Las Vegas and they thought a racing-themed program was a good way to build that business. We had a commitment with them to do a major launch and they were going to use us a lot in their leasing business. That was one of the reasons we brought Danny Sullivan in. They thought a high-profile guy like Danny was key to this.

In late 1994, it appeared Bank of America was prepared to make a significant commitment to auto racing with PacWest.

"But in 1995, Bank of America was closing a lot of branches and letting a lot of employees go," he continued. "It suddenly increased their sensitivity to employee reactions, so they ended up kind of retrenching and tried to use PacWest as more of a hospitality opportunity. Our original deal was to feature B of A on the car, but because of their sensitivity we ended up virtually taking them off the car and putting VISA on."

Logos from several sponsors and partners are clearly visible in this shot of Danny Sullivan at speed in 1995, including VISA, Best Buy, Auto Club of Southern California, and United Way.

VISA was featured as the title sponsor for the car driven by Danny Sullivan in 1995 and Mark Blundell in 1996. The largest consumer credit card brand in the world remained an associate sponsor of the team through the end of 1997. With some similarities to AAA, VISA appeared to be another potential avenue for successful business-to-business programs. The company structure allowed different banks to utilize VISA branding as part of their individual marketing budgets. But hopes for a more lucrative title sponsorship with VISA's national organization fell through when CEO Carl Pascarella abruptly shifted the corporate marketing budget to thoroughbred horse racing, sponsoring the VISA Triple Crown from 1996 to 2005.

"All of a sudden, Carl went out and spent all his money on horse racing and left us kind of holding the bag," said McCaw. "I think they had committed something like $10 million to us and I wrote Carl some pretty strong letters calling him out on the fact that he had really reneged on a program that we had spent close to a year to put together. At the end of the day we could have sued them, but I thought suing a new sponsor wasn't a good way to start the team. But it cost us a lot of money. VISA kept coming back to us with these onesie-twosie deals, but they never got into building a big program." VISA has no current presence in motorsports, but maintains corporate partnerships with the Olympic games, FIFA World Cup soccer, and the National Football League.

Up to that point, most sponsorship sales were instigated by Pat Wall, a commissioned consultant based out of Michigan. Wall believes the fact that McCaw was known to have considerable personal wealth often worked against PacWest's efforts as a business to attract outside sponsorship.

The author is seen with a Souza Cruz delivery van featuring Hollywood's racing sponsorship.

"The whole idea of raising money there was really difficult," Wall said. "Bruce had a retreat that he bought, called Caledon. I took the VISA guys there after a Vancouver race one time, and it was not the right thing to do because it put in their mind that Bruce had more money than God. They cut a cheap deal because they figured Bruce would pay the rest."

John Creak, PacWest Marketing Director from 1996 to 1999.

Wall did help PacWest land some powerful brand name sponsors at the associate level, which generally meant mid-sized logos placed on the front or rear wings. The No. 17 car driven by Sullivan and Juan Fangio II in 1995 ran with support from the Best Buy chain of electronic and appliance stores, while Taco Bell logos were featured on the front wings of Mark Blundell's No. 21 car in the second half of 1996. Neither deal panned out in the long-term, though Wall did deliver PacWest a key sponsorship from PPG Industries for its Touring Car program in 1997 (see Chapter 16).

The financial pressure was eased somewhat in 1995 when new driver Mauricio Gugelmin helped PacWest land a title sponsorship with Hollywood cigarettes (see Chapter 3). But the challenge of funding the second car continued throughout 1995 and 1996. Frustrated from falling just short of clinching major national programs with AAA, Bank of America, and VISA, McCaw orchestrated a major reorganization of PacWest in mid-1996, tabbing John Anderson and Steve Fusek for key managerial roles. As vice president of business operations, one of Fusek's tasks was to create an in-house marketing department. The team's racing operations had grown considerably since 1994; now it was time to expand personnel for sponsor procurement, client fulfillment, and public relations, and bring them all under one roof.

At the same time PacWest was looking to expand its commercial abilities, Englishman John Creak was taking an interest in the CART series after several years of working in marketing for the Arrows Formula 1 team. Creak interviewed with several CART teams in mid-1996, and in October he accepted an offer to move to the United States to establish PacWest's Indianapolis-based marketing efforts.

"What really struck home was the vision that Steve was presenting," Creak recalled. "After a fairly tumultuous 1996, Steve explained that Bruce wanted to set up a winning team by focusing on all of the required elements, both technical and non-technical. He charged Ando and Steve to put all of the elements in place. I really hit it off with Steve and I think we were both seeing exactly the same vision. From a marketing perspective, this really appealed." Creak quickly struck gold as PacWest beat out several other CART teams to land a highly sought-after title sponsorship with Motorola.

Hollywood pulled out all the stops in Brazil, including sending a PacWest show car to the top of Sugar Loaf Mountain attached to a gondola.

1,000 WORDS' WORTH

Associated Press

"Hey, buddy, can you give me a lift?"—The car of Brazil's Mauricio Gugelmin is carried by tram to the top of Sugar Loaf mountain in Rio de Janeiro to promote Sunday's CART Rio 400.

The publicity stunt gained worldwide attention, including placement in the *Los Angeles Times.*

With Hollywood and Motorola signed to multi-year contracts, the years 1997 to 1999 were PacWest's most successful from a business perspective. At the start of 1997, PacWest employed 47 people. By the end of the year, the team had grown to 65. The employee count jumped to 80 in 1999, with growth split between engineering/mechanical and marketing functions, as the team's hospitality and activation responsibilities increased.

Hollywood presented its share of challenges, starting with the obvious English/Portuguese language barrier. But PacWest and Hollywood generally enjoyed a harmonious relationship over five years and the team supported the tobacco company's ambitious promotional efforts with effort and enthusiasm.

On several occasions, PacWest show cars were carried by helicopter over the most famous beaches in Rio de Janeiro, including Copacabana, Ipanema, and Leblon. Prior to CART's 1997 race in Brazil, a helicopter was slated to carry a show car to the top of Rio's Sugar Loaf Mountain, but high winds scratched the plan. The car instead made the journey strapped to the bottom of the same cable car featured in the James Bond movie *Moonraker.* Photos of the cable car with a racing car dangling underneath were run by wire services around the world and appeared in many publications, including the *Los Angeles Times.*

In 1998, Souza Cruz performed a major re-launch of the Hollywood brand, with a new logo and pack design. As part of the rebranding, Hollywood unveiled a bold new look for Gugelmin's No. 17 car. The racing tie-in with PacWest was also a major element of Hollywood's Brazilian marketing program, with the Gugelmin car displayed on hundreds of billboards around the country.

Although tobacco advertising was banned on US television and radio in 1971, it was still legal in Brazil well into the 21st century except during primetime hours. Souza Cruz made the Hollywood/PacWest car the star of a television spot it unveiled in 1999. Edited to various lengths between 15 seconds and two minutes, the ad depicted a fantasy world where the Hollywood Indy car was helicoptered to Alaska for an ice race, complete with a pit stop from slicks to spikes. The car then raced across a desert, where its competition included a replica of the jet-powered Thrust SSC land speed record car that broke the sound barrier in October 1997. The ad concluded with the PacWest car making a perfect landing on the USS *Lexington* aircraft carrier.

PacWest provided the multi-million-dollar production with a customized 1995 Reynard powered by a motorcycle engine, a powertrain developed for the team's pit stop practice car. The team also provided support personnel, and Dominic Dobson came out of retirement to add "stunt driver" to his resume.

At the CART races in Brazil, more than 300 Hollywood banners lined the walls of the Emerson Fittipaldi Speedway, and Hollywood constructed an elaborate hospitality area at the track for guests. Souza Cruz always treated PacWest team members to a great time when they were in Brazil, with karting events and team dinners at the famous Porcao churrascaria restaurant. Hollywood also backed Indy car racing's first high-profile new car launch with a February 1998 event at the Planet Hollywood restaurant in Miami.

Brazilian culture also inspired the creation of Hollywood Happy Hour, which became a popular paddock social event at the PacWest Summit. On Friday afternoons when track activity was complete, PacWest hospitality often hosted media members and VIPs for hors d'oevurves and drinks, including the caipirinha, a Brazilian specialty cocktail made with fresh limes and a sugarcane derived alcohol called cachaça.

"In any business, you've got to understand your customer, and I think we went a long way with Hollywood," said McCaw. "That's a program we developed a lot, and they built virtually their entire identity around our team. We both learned a lot, and I think we helped give them some good guidance and recommendations along the way. I think we tried to steer them toward what was best for them, and if you can do that, you can build a pretty good relationship."

Mercedes-Benz became an increasingly important commercial partner to PacWest from 1998 to 2000. Prior to the 2000 season, McCaw brokered a deal that transferred the Hollywood sponsorship to the newly created Mo Nunn Racing team when Mercedes was short on entries. Nextel Communications served as title sponsor on Gugelmin's car in 2000 and 2001, but PacWest's inability to replace Motorola when it unexpectedly withdrew its support at the end of 2000, with a year remaining on its contract, was a crucial factor in the team's later difficulties.

By then, Creak had left PacWest. "The challenge for 1997 and 1998 was to set up the marketing department to look after the sponsorships," he remarked. "However, marketing-wise I think we lost a bit of focus after 1998. We became possibly more functionary than innovative. For me personally, my role had changed. which is why I ultimately decided to leave the team. Nevertheless, we did have the challenge of renewing the Hollywood sponsorship (achieved in 1998 at $5 million annually, tripling the initial 1995 commitment) and we kept looking for another big sponsor, which we were never to get."

Mauricio Gugelmin poses for a publicity photo with a Hollywood show car on Sugar Loaf mountain in Rio de Janeiro.

Hollywood extensively promoted the CART race in Brazil with billboards and banners.

Driver hero cards for Gugelmin and Blundell sported Motorola and Hollywood branding.

PacWest was successful in developing a group of Technology Partners, companies that traded out equipment in exchange for small signage on the car or hospitality access at races. Haas CNC provided the team with a pair of vertical milling machines that are still in use 20 years later. Other key Technology Partners included the Swiss firm Lista International, makers of the custom modular storage cabinets that equipped the PacWest shop, pit equipment and transporters; Everex computers; hardware and proprietary software providers DigiDyne and Autodesk; and Sika flooring.

"Support of a modern racing team involves more than an exchange of dollars and a few decals on a race car," said Jim Bowie, PacWest's business development manager from 1997 to 2000. "Technology Partners gain all the benefits associated with a racing sponsorship, but they also have the pride of knowing the product or service they provide is an integral part of putting a winning car on the track."

One common denominator among PacWest's key corporate partners over the years was a willingness to extend their sponsorship beyond the team level. In addition to Hollywood's activities, Bank of America was the title sponsor for the 1994 CART season finale at Laguna Seca Raceway, and Motorola served as title sponsor for several races at Gateway International Raceway and Road America. Motorola was also an official corporate partner of CART and provider of radio transmitters and other equipment to race officials and the Safety Team, as well as all of the radio equipment fitted to race cars and helmets allowing teams and drivers to communicate.

"Putting your name on the car is one thing, but the key is what we do with it," said Crawford, who managed Motorola's sports marketing programs from 1990 to 2007. "Indy car racing gives us the best and harshest test lab we can have, with the most adverse conditions."

McCaw maintains that the four-year partnership between PacWest and Motorola was beneficial for CART as a whole, in addition to the opportunities it provided the sponsor and the team. "I believe very strongly that to do a good job for a sponsor, you didn't just put signage on the car. You had to get them involved with the sanctioning body and the racetracks," he said. "I think we were perhaps one of the most active teams of anybody in terms of trying to get our sponsors to spend money with the racetrack owners and with CART. Most teams wanted every nickel for themselves. They couldn't figure out why sponsors left because they didn't get the results they wanted."

Andy Castleman

G.I. Joe's billboard featuring the Motorola car to promote Motorola pagers.

Pole winner Mauricio Gugelmin leads the field at the start of the 1997 Hollywood Rio 400.

6

INCHING CLOSER TO SUCCESS

WHILE PACWEST RACING'S hopes for 1996 were pinned on a cautious and conservative approach, the team made a number of aggressive changes prior to the 1997 season. Mauricio Gugelmin and Mark Blundell remained as the drivers, but Ford-Cosworth engines were exchanged for Mercedes-Benz power units designed and built by Ilmor Engineering. Goodyear tires made way for Firestone. The only constant in the technical package was the Reynard chassis, which itself was an all-new design because of CART rule changes that mandated a wider cockpit with higher sides and a removable padded horseshoe collar to improve driver head protection.

Ilmor was formed in 1983 as a partnership between Roger Penske and two former Cosworth employees, Mario Illien and Paul Morgan. Penske attracted corporate backing from General Motors to complete the ownership group, and the Chevrolet-badged Ilmor engine debuted in 1986. It endured a difficult opening season marked by reliability problems, but Mario Andretti broke through to win the 1987 CART season opener. Between 1987 and 1992, Ilmor engines won 77 of 94 CART races, including a stretch of 41 consecutive wins. Chevrolet withdrew its support for 1994, and a year later, Mercedes-Benz bought out GM's quarter share of Ilmor, taking over badging of the company's Indy car and Formula 1 engines.

Meanwhile, Firestone returned to American open-wheel racing in 1995 after a 21-year absence. By the end of that season, Firestone's tires already looked superior to Goodyear's product. Scott Pruett claimed the first race win of Firestone's comeback at the 1995 Michigan 500. Just a few weeks later, Andre Ribeiro won on Firestones at New Hampshire International Speedway in what was the first victory for the Honda Indy car engine program.

PacWest had been approached by Firestone in 1994 to become its lead test team, offering substantial technical and financial support; Patrick Racing and Pruett eventually assumed the responsibilities. "Unfortunately, at the time, as tempting as the offer was, we felt it was simply too big of a risk," recalled McCaw. "We also believed that Goodyear, under the direction of Leo Mehl and Stu Grant, would be the better choice in the long term. I don't believe that we fully understood everything that was going on inside Goodyear."

Firestone made a successful return to Indy car racing in the 1990s after a 20-year absence and quickly gained the upper hand over longtime rival Goodyear.

The Mercedes-Benz IC108D engine was probably the best overall powerplant in the CART series in 1997, mixing plenty of horsepower with smooth drivability and excellent fuel mileage.

In hindsight, moving to Firestone sooner would likely have been a better choice. For the 1996 season, Target/Ganassi Racing switched to Honda power and Firestone tires. Its drivers Jimmy Vasser and rookie Alex Zanardi took seven race wins to finish first and third in the CART standings. Firestone's only weakness appeared to be its rain tire, but a new design was promised by mid-1997.

PacWest came close to making the move to Firestone in 1996 but ultimately put it off for a year. Andy Brown pushed hard to make the switch. "I would say that if it is possible to change this year, go for it!" he wrote in an August 12, 1996, memo. "The Firestones are at least a second a lap quicker in testing at Mid-Ohio."

Prior to the 1997 season, John Anderson visited all of the relevant chassis, engine, and tire manufacturers, and coordinated the research effort ultimately leading to the technical changes. "It's a hard deal when you've had a good relationship with a company to pull your support, or to pull your relationship apart, to go with someone else," Anderson said. "We hadn't seen much of the Firestone guys, and we had been around Goodyear for a number of years, and had a good relationship with them. But the wheel had turned.

"I got quite a few good lessons about doing what you think is going to be best for your team," he added. "Whether it's crew members, drivers, tires, or engines, you've got to pick the best components. If you want to finish on the podium, what do you need? You look at your options, you kick it around, give it a lot of thought, and then you bloody go with it."

The decision to change engine suppliers was more difficult. Honda won 11 of 16 races in 1996, the only interloper being Michael Andretti's five victories for Newman/Haas Racing using Ford-Cosworth power. Mercedes was shut out in 1996, but in retrospect, that could be put down to the fact that the lead Mercedes teams (Team Penske and Team Rahal) were handicapped by their Goodyear tires. While the Goodyears were relatively competitive with Newman/Haas' Lola chassis, they tended to wear quickly when mounted to a Penske or a Reynard. Toyota entered the CART series in 1996 and was clearly not yet competitive in terms of speed or reliability.

The Ford/Cosworth XD developed into a very competitive engine in 1996 and Cosworth tried hard to retain PacWest. "I regret that at the end of 1995 we were not able to give them the new XD engine due to manufacturing and support concerns, and PacWest was forced to use the proven reliable, but less powerful, XB engine for 1996," recalled Cosworth USA vice president and general manager Ian Bisco. "They did a great job with the XB, but that inevitably pushed them away for 1997."

Both of the PacWest drivers had prior experience working with Ilmor in Formula 1. Gugelmin led the development of Ilmor's first V-10 F1 engine when he was with the Leyton House/March team from 1988 to 1991, while Blundell ran an updated version of the Ilmor powerplant (by then badged as a Mercedes-Benz) during his 1995 campaign with McLaren. Their endorsements, along with Anderson's research, led McCaw to sign a contract with Ilmor in September 1996. It called for the team to pay $1.8 million per car for a fully-serviced, turn-key engine lease package that guaranteed parity with the other Mercedes-Benz teams: Penske, Player's/Forsythe Racing, Bettenhausen Motorsports, and Hogan Racing. At the same time PacWest moved to Mercedes, Team Rahal switched from Mercedes to Ford-Cosworth.

PacWest always provided its drivers with the safest possible cars. John Simmonds of Profile Seating Systems (Pro-Seat) measures out a custom-molded seat for Mark Blundell.

"What was important for me was to get the engine that had the top spec for a given race, which we didn't have previously," Gugelmin said, recalling PacWest's experience running the Cosworth XB Series II engine in 1996. At the time, teams like Newman/Haas and Team Green were using the newer and more powerful XD. "We had always been a step behind some other teams with the same brand. For 1997, we had a proven package, so we knew we had something solid when we went testing. Everyone was focused; it was a new thing. We had changed tires and engines and we all thought, 'This is going to make the difference.' And it did."

For the most part, preseason testing went remarkably well. Already enjoying a close relationship with Reynard, McCaw negotiated for PacWest to receive Reynard 97I chassis 001, which permitted Gugelmin to shake down the new car at Sebring in November 1996. The early delivery of chassis 008 meant the team had two cars on track prior to the new year. Gugelmin frequently set the offseason testing pace, but complications arose for PacWest at CART's Spring Training open test in January. Blundell suffered a big accident on the Homestead-Miami Speedway oval. The Englishman was unable to explain why the Reynard-Mercedes snapped away from him into a thunderous rearward impact with the concrete wall in Turn 1, leaving him sore and bruised, but otherwise uninjured. The car, on the other hand, was severely damaged; the gearbox—the likely cause of the accident—was reduced to hundreds of pieces of shrapnel and the machined aluminum bulkhead at the back of the tub was bent by the force of the crash.

Mauricio Gugelmin prepares for another race.

"When the car let go, I thought to myself, 'I'll never survive this one,'" Blundell related. "The impact was terrifying. The rear of the car just exploded, and my knees bent the half-inch steering column 45 degrees. At first, I thought I'd broken my back—I had pins and needles in my arms and I really couldn't feel my hands. I wish they would stop using me as a crash dummy!"

Corporate work: Bruce McCaw and Mark Blundell pause for a photo opportunity in the Surfers Paradise pit lane with former F1 World Champion Alan Jones (left), whose Australian V-8 Supercar team was also sponsored by Motorola.

Blundell's was the first major crash of a 1997-specification car and the newly mandated safety enhancements performed well in the impact. In addition, PacWest always contracted with Pro-Seat for seats custom molded to each driver's body for maximum comfort, stability, and safety. CART Medical Director Dr. Steve Olvey compared Blundell's Homestead 1997 incident to the July 1996 Indy car crash at Michigan International Speedway that essentially ended Emerson Fittipaldi's racing career. Olvey said that the impact "would have caused significant injuries in any other year."

While dismayed by Blundell's crash, PacWest was buoyed by Gugelmin's performance. The Brazilian ran the third fastest lap of the two-day meeting. When the team returned to Homestead in March for the 1997 season opener, Mauricio qualified on the front row, just 0.025 second off pole man Zanardi. Perhaps more impressively, Blundell put his Spring Training crash behind him and qualified fifth fastest. But handling difficulties relegated them to 6th (Gugelmin) and 14th (Blundell) at the checkered flag.

Gugelmin threw away a potential solid haul of points at Surfers Paradise, Australia, where he spun out while trying to pass Jimmy Vasser late in the race for second place. "I was running pretty strong and going for a win. I was trying everything since I had a good car," Gugelmin said. "But as I was passing Jimmy, the back end just locked up and that was it. I T-boned him and it was my mistake. When you're going for it, these things happen." Blundell finished eighth after again qualifying fifth.

However, a podium finish was just a week away when Mauricio qualified third and finished second at Long Beach, crossing the line less than four seconds behind Zanardi and matching PacWest's best-ever finish on a road or street course. Blundell looked set for a top-six result until a slipping clutch led to a long second pit stop, and ultimately a 13th-place finish.

"Alex was just a little quicker today, so P2 has to be good enough," Gugelmin commented after the race. "But I'm very encouraged that all the hard work the PacWest team has put in is starting to pay off. I think we finished with about a half a gallon of fuel left and my only problem was with the backmarkers. Some guys made it really tough to get by."

Though the next race, at Nazareth Speedway in eastern Pennsylvania, did not result in a podium finish, it demonstrated PacWest was making consistent performance progress week to week. The team had often struggled to balance its cars on short ovals, but Gugelmin qualified third on the tricky Nazareth tri-oval and only unlucky timing for a full-course caution prevented him from matching that result in the race.

"At first, I thought I'd broken my back...I really couldn't feel my hands. I wish they would stop using me as a crash dummy!"

Mark Blundell

Gugelmin heads toward second place in the 1997 Long Beach Grand Prix. The CART field would become accustomed to the sight of the No. 17 car's rear wing by the end of the season.

The man nicknamed "Big Mo" won the $10,000 Marlboro Pole Award three times during the 1997 season, including here at Brazil. The pole at Rio was the first in Indy cars for PacWest.

"I don't think our finishing position gives any indication of how competitive we were," he said after taking the flag in ninth. "I'm convinced we had at least a third or a fourth place in the bag." Meanwhile, Blundell had a much less happy weekend. He qualified on the eighth row and crashed late in the race. "I'm pretty disappointed in myself for that one," he admitted. "I tried a move a couple of others had pulled, and the front of the car just got into the marbles and pushed out into the wall. That was a learning experience."

Gugelmin proved his strong oval qualifying performances at Homestead and Nazareth were not a fluke by earning PacWest's first pole position on the unique semi-oval at Rio de Janeiro, Brazil, for the Hollywood Rio 400. Mauricio was helped to the pole by a special Mercedes-Benz qualifying engine and a chassis setup conceived by Andy Brown. "I asked Firestone if they would make a zero rear stagger option for us, and we ran a standard differential. Result was much reduced tire scrub on the straights. Sometimes we engineers got it right!" But Gugelmin crashed on the 57th lap of the race. After qualifying a season-low 20th, Blundell advanced to an eighth-place finish at the site of the frightening accident he'd had the year before.

The mid-season run of four consecutive oval races did not work to Blundell's advantage. He continued to struggle for pace in qualifying for the inaugural Motorola 300 at Gateway International Raceway just outside of St. Louis. Things went from bad to worse on race day as an early engine failure left Mark watching the action from Motorola's suite with corporate executives and guests. Meanwhile, Gugelmin's side of the team continued to function smoothly, notching another top-six finish at Gateway.

The performance disparity between the two PacWest cars led to a major mid-season change. Technical Director Allen McDonald took over as Blundell's race engineer starting with the Milwaukee race in early June, replacing Jim Hamilton. Hamilton had joined PacWest from Dan Gurney's All American Racers in December 1996. Hamilton admitted six months later to author Paul Haney that he was baffled by how difficult it was to create a dynamic working relationship with Blundell.

"We were trying to get ourselves acquainted with the Reynard, the Firestone tires, and Mark and myself working together," Hamilton said. "He needs the rear of the car nailed. He doesn't like to feel any movement back there. He's making me look into this stuff deeper than I ever have, and some of the classical fixes seem to work backwards from how it's supposed to work."

The effect of the engineering change on Blundell's confidence was immediate and remarkable. "With Mark, what I could do was speak his language," observed McDonald. "Obviously we're both English, we've both sort of grown up in the same environment. He did have some great qualifying runs early in the year, but I think he was never able to communicate just what he wanted out of the racecar.

"Mo was very smooth, and he needed a loose car," McDonald continued. "In sort of a contradiction, Mark throws a car around, and because he drives a car so sideways, he needs a very, very understeery car. I think people just had trouble understanding that. The way I approached it, the way Mark threw a car around, there was no way he would be able to do that unless he felt the rear was there. I just worked from the premise that the rear had to be planted and then if we could get rid of the understeer, fine. If not, at least we would be halfway competitive. But if the rear wasn't there for him, we might as well just stay at the hotel and go down to the swimming pool."

After more than a year together as teammates, the team understood that Gugelmin and Blundell's driving styles were so different that they really couldn't share a common chassis setup. PacWest's baseline setup was largely developed by Gugelmin and engineer Andy Brown, whose working relationship dated to 1988.

"Of course, I had a jump start with the team because I was here earlier," remarked Gugelmin. "Mark and I had different styles and we couldn't really use much of the same setups, which was a little bit difficult in some ways. He can drive a car sideways and get away with it all the time. When the car is right, he gives 110 percent and he delivers. And that was a great push for the team."

It was a measure of PacWest's progress on short ovals that after again qualifying on the front row at Milwaukee, Gugelmin was thoroughly disappointed with a fifth-place finish. Greg Moore won the race by making only two pit stops and nursing his final tank of fuel more than 90 laps. Mauricio was second among those drivers who used a standard three-stop strategy. Meanwhile Blundell was much happier in his first race with McDonald engineering his car despite starting 11th and finishing 12th.

"The engineering change was a key factor because we struggled a bit early in the season," Blundell recalled. "Mauricio will be the first to tell you that the relationship between driver and engineer is very important and it takes a while to get that going. I think it was just a matter of two people getting an understanding and sort of getting a second thought process going. I can read Allen as well as he reads me, in a certain way."

Jim Hamilton started the 1997 season as Mark Blundell's race engineer, but the pair did not communicate effectively.

Blundell's season took a turn for the better when Technical Director Allen McDonald took over the No. 18 car's race engineering.

REYNARD AND AUTO RESEARCH CENTER

During the 1997 season, PacWest Racing got a new neighbor. After three years in partnership with Chip Ganassi, Reynard North America gained independence and broke ground on a new US headquarters on the northwest side of Indianapolis, just a few hundred yards from PacWest's base at 4001 Methanol Lane. In addition to administrative offices, the new RNA facility included a 7-post vehicle-dynamics test rig and an advanced rolling-plane wind tunnel, along with a model shop to create components for wind tunnel testing.

Although informally known as the Reynard wind tunnel, the tunnel and other testing services and facilities operated as a separate company called Auto Research Center. Since PacWest's switch from Lola chassis to Reynard in 1995, Bruce McCaw had forged a strong relationship with Reynard principals Dr. Adrian Reynard and Rick Gorne. When they shared the vision for ARC with McCaw, RaceSport Management became a partner in the venture.

Reynard experienced rapid growth in the 1980s and McCaw was impressed by what Adrian and his commercial director Gorne had achieved. Reynard constructed his first Formula Ford car as the final project for his studies at Oxford Polytechnic University and when the car proved successful, he began selling copies to competitors, including Gorne. He hired Gorne in 1982 and sales took off, allowing Reynard to advance into Formula 3 and Formula 3000 on the way to displacing March, Ralt, and Lola as the world's leading producer of customer racing cars.

An unfinished Reynard design formed the basis of the 1992 Benetton F1 chassis in which seven-time World Champion Michael Schumacher won his first Grand Prix. Following that failed attempt to break into Formula 1, Reynard Motorsport looked into the CART series. Reynard North America was formed in partnership with Ganassi, who funded the prototype and guaranteed a production run of 12 cars. Thirteen were sold prior to the first race of the 1994 season. That race was won by Michael Andretti in Ganassi Racing's Ford-Cosworth-powered entry, continuing Reynard's remarkable tradition of winning the first event in every category it entered.

By the time PacWest entered full-time competition in 1994, a team's success was heavily dependent upon choosing the right "package" of chassis, engine, and tires. PacWest campaigned the proven Lola chassis in 1994 but, impressed with the quality of Reynard's product and service, switched to Reynard in 1995. The move proved prescient; Reynard dominated the CART series through the end of the decade, and from 1997 to 1999, Reynard won 49 of 56 races.

Reynard and Gorne fostered a youthful, 'can-do' culture. Many of the firm's top engineers came straight from college and worked their way through the ranks. Malcolm Oastler, for example, joined Reynard in 1985, designed the 1987 Formula Ford car, the 1988 F3000 car, and subsequent developments, and finally the Reynard Indy cars from 1994 to 1998. Reynard assigned a dedicated engineer to each customer team and was also the first chassis constructor to align itself with drivers. Reynard was responsible for bringing Alex Zanardi and Gil de Ferran to America to race in the CART series, and along with Mercedes-Benz, the company played a role in helping Mark Blundell land his ride with PacWest.

Adrian Reynard has fond memories of his early meetings with McCaw. "Bruce is a highly discerning and serious team owner," Reynard reflected. "He has an immense amount of enthusiasm and he showed detailed interest in the structure of his team—the types of cars he was choosing, the staff he was employing, the strategies he wanted to go forward. Obviously as someone new on the Indy car scene, which we were, Bruce took a bit of convincing. He was listening carefully and trying to assess, because we came along and sort of changed the rules, really. Bruce picked up on that pretty soon and I did enjoy my meetings with him because he's got a very dry sense of humor. He made some big decisions and he became one of our biggest customers. He didn't short-change his team. He bought a lot of cars every year. He wanted to know the terms and he was quite hard in negotiations with my partner Rick, but they developed a very good relationship and Rick respected Bruce a lot. I think it was that mutual respect that in the end created a good bond between us. With ARC, there was no question with Bruce. I explained it to him, and it was like a switch went on. I remember he said, 'Yes, I'm in!' and that was that."

> “[McCaw] has an immense amount of enthusiasm and he showed detailed interest in the structure of his team.”
>
> Adrian Reynard

As the CART series began to lose traction around the turn of the century, it had an adverse effect on Reynard's largest source of revenue. The company's attempt to go public with a stock offering on the NASDAQ Exchange fell through, and an ill-fated attempt to take over car builder Riley & Scott to gain a foothold in the IRL chassis market resulted in a $10 million loss.

With sponsorship becoming increasingly hard to find, especially after the events of September 11, 2001, teams no longer had the resources to buy a half-dozen brand new $500,000 race cars every year. CART's business model changed to the extent that by 2003, it had essentially become a spec series where all competitors utilized the same chassis, engine, and tires, with a vastly reduced scope of development for teams.

Lola was the chassis that prevailed; the Reynard saga came to a sad end in early 2002 when the company went into receivership, the English equivalent to bankruptcy. In partnership with Bruce McCaw, Adrian Reynard maintained majority ownership in Auto Racing Center.

A Forsythe Racing Indy car on the 7-post shaker at Auto Research Center.

ARC's custom-built facility in Indianapolis was a stone's throw from the PacWest Racing shop.

Since opening in 1998, it had become an unlikely profit center for Reynard Motorsport.

"Reynard North America built a stand-alone wind tunnel because Reynard as a whole needed a tunnel," explained Gorne. "We started out using the tunnel at Shrivenham and then went to Southampton University in the UK. Reynard's Indianapolis facility was just a tunnel at the start, and nothing else.

"From there, we built a bunch of wind tunnel models for the CART teams, because in those days there was unlimited testing and no set rules or regulations with regard to teams doing their own development or having their own bits made," he continued. "Those were the days when cost was no object. You'd buy a model, get an aerodynamicist—PacWest had a really good guy in Andy Brown—and work your own development program."

"Suddenly team owners like Bruce were coming to us and saying, 'Hey! Can you build us a wind tunnel model?'" added Reynard. "We built a model for Bruce, and PacWest enhanced their performance. Then another team came along and by 1999 we were building our most profitable race car ever—a Reynard Indy car wind tunnel model! We made a production run of, I think, ten in one year. We made them for about £10,000, and I think we sold them for $100,000. Never in the history of Reynard Motorsport did we make such a high margin of profit on a race car! Then, of course, there was this virtuous circle where we ended up having just about all of our teams developing our cars, using their own technical resources and aerodynamicists. The technical side was growing in Indy car at that time, so they had their own clever people looking at the aerodynamics, coming to our wind tunnel facility, paying us good money to test there and improve our product. It was just incredible! I'd like to say it was meant that way from the beginning, but it was just one of those virtuous circles that happened."

When CART became a Lola-based spec series in 2003, ARC maintained its client base by creating a Lola wind tunnel model for CART teams that wanted to develop their chassis. ARC also attracted NASCAR teams and manufacturers by constructing a stock car model. The facility acquired a driveline dynamometer test rig, added 3-D laser scanning technology, and developed rapid prototyping capabilities. ARC underwent another expansion in 2008 and the firm soon began attracting business from the trucking industry for aerodynamic research to improve fuel efficiency. ARC also diversified into computational fluid dynamics (CFD) and developed its own CFD software. ARC continues to be one of the top transportation research facilities in the United States. The company now employs more than 50 people and has opened a second facility in North Carolina, primarily to service the NASCAR industry.

In recent years, with an assist from Rick Gorne, ARC Indianapolis also returned to its racing roots. Honda Performance Development owns a share of the company, and the majority of aerodynamic and vehicle dynamics research for Honda's modern Indy car program is done at ARC.

"ARC needed to get back into motorsport—that's where the company started and that's where it should be," said Gorne.

Adrian Reynard credits Bruce McCaw with continuing to challenge him to find new avenues of relevance for ARC. "He understands our business because he is infectiously enthusiastic about it, and he has the wisdom to apply in a very understandable way," Reynard observed. "He's still incredibly enthusiastic about cars and anything that moves. Whether it's the racing side or OEMs, he knows a lot of people and they respect him. He has made some fantastic introductions for ARC. Whether they are in aerospace, OEMs, or trucking, he's been a great asset to be able to make contact with these companies at the top. When you get an introduction to a company from the top down, the credibility of that introduction is far greater than if you just call the head of aerodynamics and say 'Hey, we've got a good idea we think can help you.' That has been huge, and I cannot say how much that has affected the business and the profitability of ARC in the past. That has been a huge factor.

"Bruce has always been honest about where I can improve, whether it's communicating or this or that," he added. "And he's always absolutely correct on his assessments. He thinks carefully about it and he cares about the business. He's become a very good partner and friend, and I really appreciate him. He's highly respected in the business, in everything we do."

JUNE 1997

PacWest Racing Group

upfront

Volume 1, Number 3

The Official Newsletter of PacWest Racing Group

Mo's Rio Pole Tops Big Month for PacWest

May 1997 was the busiest month ever for PacWest Racing Group. The CART team celebrated its first pole position at the Hollywood Rio 400 - fifth round of the PPG CART World Series - along with a raucous Brazilian crowd roaring approval for local hero Mauricio Gugelmin. To the disappointment of almost everyone, Gugelmin's day ended early with a crash, though Mark Blundell took eighth place after a storming drive.

The following weekend, PacWest was the only CART team to demonstrate Indy cars at the inaugural Dixie Crystals Grand Prix for Indy Lights cars at the new Savannah Harbor circuit. David Donohue took a pair of podiums for PacWest Touring Car Group at Savannah, while twin fourth place finishes for Dominic Dobson left him and Donohue a joint second in the Super Touring Championship standings. Robby Unser had his share of troubles in the Indy Lights headliner, his day ending early after a tangle with Cristiano DaMatta.

It was on to the brand new Gateway International Raceway in Madison, Illinois (just outside St. Louis) just six days later for the inaugural Motorola 300. Gugelmin was again splendid in qualifying, lining the Hollywood PacWest Mercedes-Benz third and missing out on his second consecutive pole by only 0.05 seconds. Mauricio was competitive all day long en route to sixth place in the 300 miler, while Blundell was eliminated early by an engine problem, a huge disappointment to the large group of Motorola employees on hand. Unser took seventh in Lights.

Back-to-back races immediately followed the Motorola 300, at Milwaukee and Detroit. When including the Savannah demonstration, PacWest's CART team is therefore in the midst of five straight weeks on the road!

MILESTONE: Mauricio Gugelmin claimed PacWest's first pole at the Hollywood Rio 400 to great fanfare from the Brazilian crowd. 'Big Mo' broke the track record by more than 5 mph.

The PacWest newsletter got a new name and a colorful new look in 1997.

PacWest attempted to complete the Detroit Grand Prix with a single pit stop. The strategy almost paid off with a 1-2 finish.

A series of four consecutive road races kicked off with the ITT Automotive Detroit Grand Prix on June 18th. Bruce McCaw brought his helmet to Detroit and competed in the accompanying Dodge Neon Celebrity Challenge race. He qualified on the pole but spun after leading more than half the race to finish third. Meanwhile, Gugelmin caught a lucky break when his car's throttle cable snapped on the final lap of the 30-minute Sunday morning practice session; it was replaced in time for the race.

Gugelmin and Blundell had qualified eighth and tenth, but PacWest potentially had a trick up its sleeve: If certain circumstances fell the team's way, strategists believed, the 77-lap race could be completed with just one pit stop.

"In the last five years here, there have been an average of 21½ laps run under a full-course yellow," said John Anderson in the team's pre-race briefing. "If we have a lot of yellow flags early in the race and then get a yellow with 42 laps to go, we figure we can go all the way to the finish, though we may need a few laps of yellow near the end to do that."

As predicted, there were several early incidents and full-course cautions, prompting most of the field to commit to a two-stop strategy. By not stopping early, the PacWest cars were promoted up the order and after the first stint, they ran together on the track in third and fourth place. On the 32nd lap, Richie Hearn spun into a tire wall, bringing out the pace car. PacWest had no choice: The team had to bring Gugelmin and Blundell into the pits under yellow on Lap 34 of 77, one lap outside the team's window for making the finish using a one-stop strategy. Clearly, PacWest needed as many laps run slowly behind the pace car as possible.

But the rest of the race was frustratingly clean. Michel Jourdain's crash on Lap 43 was initially handled by a local yellow. Finally, the pace car was dispatched on Lap 51 so Jourdain's car could be removed, and everyone other than Gugelmin and Blundell pitted under yellow. That elevated the PacWest duo to the front of the field. But the caution period lasted only two laps; would Mauricio and Mark have enough fuel to make the finish?

For 25 laps, Gugelmin led the race, pacing the field as slowly as possible in an effort to conserve fuel. "I was making a lot of calculations at that time," he said. "I kept in touch with the pits and they gave me the strategy on fuel map, then I started backing off way before the corners. I just coasted through the corners and tried not use the throttle, while trying to be as quick as possible, which is really difficult to do."

Gugelmin leads Blundell and Jimmy Vasser at the Detroit Grand Prix.

The No. 18 crew nervously watches as the laps tick down at Detroit.

Jolene McCaw shows the tension of the closing laps, while husband Bruce appeared to remain calm.

RMA/Steve Swope

Blundell bunched up the field and tried to act as a buffer for race leader Gugelmin.

Blundell ran immediately behind, trying to hold off the rest of the snarling pack while also practicing fuel-saving techniques. "It was actually a tremendous race from my end," he said. "Not only was I being defensive in terms of keeping Moore at bay, I was also the buffer for Mauricio while still keeping pressure applied, in case he had a mishap, though I wasn't prepared to jeopardize the team's chances of winning."

While Bruce McCaw sat calmly on the timing stand, the tension was almost unbearable for the rest of the team. And once the decision was taken to pursue the one-stop strategy, there was no turning back.

"To have pulled in one car really wouldn't have accomplished anything, particularly late in the race," McCaw said. "We took a calculated risk, but one we thought the odds were very much in our favor. We thought that we had a pair of top-six finishes pretty comfortably in hand, so this was a gamble worth taking. We decided to go all the way for it."

The PacWest cars led into the final lap, but Gugelmin's leading car ran dry halfway around. Blundell swerved past into a lead that lasted a few hundred yards before his car coughed and coasted to a stop two corners short of the flag. A surprised and delighted Greg Moore claimed his second consecutive race win as a potential 1-2 finish for PacWest turned into 16th and 17th place in a matter of seconds.

"At Milwaukee, I said we may have to give one away before we get one," remarked a crestfallen Gugelmin. "We gave one away today, so we better get one soon! We just didn't have the yellow that normally comes at this place. But that's racing."

"I honestly thought I had it," Blundell added. "The more I think about it now, the more I know I was that close, but so far. I just couldn't believe it. I thought I was home and dry, but unfortunately I was only dry!"

McCaw and everyone pulling for PacWest fully supported the gamble to try to finish the 77-lap contest with only one fuel stop. As the drama ratcheted up late in the race, ABC's cameras focused as much on the team principal and his wife, Jolene, as they did on the on-track action.

"I don't think there's anything that gives you quite the highs and the lows that racing can do in a very short order, but I don't probably get the yo-yo of emotions perhaps that some people get when you have moments like that," McCaw told reporters after the Detroit race. "I know I didn't breathe the last lap. I knew it was too early to celebrate. It's pretty draining. That last lap seemed like it took half an hour.

"We took our chances and we were right on the ragged edge," he added. "We just needed a couple laps of yellow and it never happened. The entire team made the decision and I'm proud of the decision we made. You know, our time will come. We expect to keep running at the front. When we win the first one, I'm sure the next one will be right behind it. I'm really proud of our team and I think the weekend showed how well everybody is pulling together and working as a cohesive unit. It's just great teamwork. I'm really proud of our drivers and the entire PacWest organization."

Though PacWest didn't win the 1997 Detroit Grand Prix, it was certainly the event that thrust the team into the public spotlight as a serious race-winning threat. As such, it ranks as one of the most significant moments in the history of the team.

"Detroit was a very important race for all of us because it gave us the capability to say we could run out front," said Blundell. "The gamble we played just didn't pay off, but I still think it was the right call and I still stand by it."

"Detroit was the one where people realized that we lost a race," noted Gugelmin. "It was the first race where they saw, 'Hey, these guys really are in the picture.' At the same time, we showed a lot of maturity by doing what we did. We made a lot of people pay attention and I think that was the biggest turning point. From then, we were regarded as a top runner."

The results from Detroit were bitterly disappointing, but also highly motivating. "There were some tears on pit lane, but it brought the team together," observed Steve Fusek. "We got 20 percent of the TV coverage and a lot of positive feedback from Hollywood and Motorola. After the Milwaukee race, the Motorola guys wondered why Greg Moore won and we talked a lot about fuel strategy. Fred Tucker and Bob Schaul sat in on our pre-race meeting at Detroit and they knew exactly what we were planning. The only negative was that we didn't win. We were all pleased with what happened, our sponsors were pleased, and we got a ton of attention."

The clock never stops in auto racing, and fortunately, PacWest didn't have to wait long to experience the team's first victory in the CART series.

Grand Prix drivers come up empty in computer test

The PacWest Racing Group saw both its cars run out of gas on the final lap of the Detroit Grand Prix.

Out of gas and out of luck

BY MIKE BRENNAN

The pits were full of high-tech gadgetry at the ITT Automotive Detroit Grand Prix on Belle Isle, where racing teams used computers last weekend to measure every nuance of how these Indy cars performed.

But more than $300,000 worth of computers and communications gear couldn't prevent PacWest Racing Group from suffering the embarrassment of having both its cars run out of gas on the final lap — one less than a quarter-mile from the finish line.

PacWest drivers Mark Blundell and Mauricio Gugelmin had been running first and second when their cars sputtered to a halt, gas tanks empty. It would have been team owner Bruce McCaw's first victory on the CART circuit.

■ Birmingham firm cures laptop glare. See Page 2E.

PacWest had invited the Free Press to watch the race from the pits to see how on-board computers beamed vital race information to the pits. Once the data is evaluated, team members tell drivers which switches to throw depending on whether they want fuel economy or more speed.

The tone of the two-way conversations turned frantic late in the race when it became obvious both cars might not have enough gas to finish.

As Blundell and Gugelmin sped by the pits on the final lap, John Anderson, vice president of PacWest racing operations, uttered over the radio, "Everybody pray."

But PacWest's prayers weren't answered. Canadian Greg Moore passed Gugelmin, then Blundell to win the race.

"We were maybe a pint short of fuel on Mark and maybe a half-gallon short on Mauricio," said PacWest Technical Director Allen McDonald after the race.

"The telemetry was in and out a lot today," McDonald said, referring to transmission of data about the cars —

Please see GADGETS Page 2E

Detroit Free Press business reporters were embedded with PacWest to capture the thrilling finish.

Mark Blundell flashes past Gil de Ferran at the line to win at Portland International Raceway, earning PacWest Racing's first victory in the CART series. De Ferran raises his fist, believing he won.

Allsport USA

7

VICTORY AT LAST

SINCE THE PPG CART World Series did not travel to Seattle or the state of Washington, PacWest Racing treated the events in Portland, Oregon, and Vancouver, British Columbia, as its "home" races. Generally staged in late June, Portland also offered PacWest the opportunity to celebrate Bruce McCaw's birthday. In the lead-up to the 1997 race, PacWest staged a charity event at the Pacific Science Center in Seattle (see Chapter 16), and a couple of days later, many of the team's Washington-based friends and supporters made the 160-mile drive south to Portland International Raceway.

As was the case throughout 1997, Mauricio Gugelmin was right on the pace in qualifying for the Budweiser/G.I. Joe's 200, earning a spot on the outside of the second row. Mark Blundell's qualifying lap was just 0.3 second slower than Gugelmin's, but it was enough of a difference to relegate the Englishman to 11th on the grid.

However, PacWest and its drivers had another concern on race morning: rain. In 1996, in marked contrast to its standard dry weather slicks, Firestone's rain tires were notably inferior to Goodyear on the few occasions they were needed. Firestone tested 40 different new wet weather compounds and promised that its 1997 rain tires were substantially improved. But the wet race at Portland would be everyone's first experience using the redesigned treaded tires in racing conditions.

Gugelmin immediately found the new Firestone wets to his liking. He passed pole qualifier Scott Pruett for the lead on the fifth lap and proceeded to pull away at the rate of almost two seconds a lap until a full-course caution eliminated 'Big Mo's' 12-second advantage at the end of Lap 11. At that point, Blundell had already worked up to fifth place as the Goodyear-equipped drivers struggled in the wettest conditions.

Mauricio lost the lead to Alex Zanardi when Zanardi short-fueled during a round of yellow flag pit stops on Lap 31. The Italian held the top spot in his Ganassi Reynard/Honda until he again pitted for a fresh set of rain tires on the 55th tour, leaving PacWest's Gugelmin and Blundell again running 1-2. By then it was obvious that the race would be run to a two-hour time limit rather than the full, 98-lap scheduled distance. In addition,

Mauricio Gugelmin leads the field during the race at Portland. Gugelmin led the most laps but an untimely spin relegated him to a sixth-place finish.

Dan Boyd's shot from early in the 1997 Portland race shows just how challenging the wet conditions were for the drivers.

the rain had stopped; now the calculations began, not only in terms of how many laps would actually be run, but at what point slick tires would prove to be faster than wets in the changing conditions.

Paul Tracy pitted for slicks on the 62nd lap and almost immediately spun off. But he was driving a Penske on Goodyears, so there was no direct comparison. However, as soon as Raul Boesel's Reynard on Firestone slicks turned a quicker lap than race leader Gugelmin, PacWest brought the No. 17 car and changed tires at the end of the 65th lap. Desperate to get back up to speed quickly, Gugelmin ran off the track during his out lap and lost valuable time.

"I feel we pitted for slicks at the right time," Gugelmin commented. "But when I came out, I got caught behind a lot of slower cars. I got off the dry line trying to get by and had a small off-track excursion. It didn't hurt the car, but I lost positions to the guys who finished ahead of me in the end."

Blundell came in for slicks at the end of his 67th lap and resumed in fifth place, just in front of Boesel, and 31 seconds behind leader Gil de Ferran. "I actually wanted to switch to slicks about five laps earlier and was shouting my head off inside the car, but John Anderson was reluctant to put me on slicks too early," Blundell said. "We saw Tracy and [Bryan] Herta change and then spin right off. The first couple laps were pretty tricky until the temps were up, but once we got some heat into the tires, the slicks were much quicker."

Only 14 minutes remained in the race—time for maybe a dozen laps. At the front of the field, de Ferran and Christian Fittipaldi ran at a snail's pace, trying to nurse their fading Goodyear wet tires to the finish on a rapidly drying track. Zanardi and Greg Moore were likewise running a conservative pace on their Firestone rain tires, while Blundell and Boesel reeled them in at the amazing rate of up to six seconds a lap on their fresh dry-weather Firestones.

On the 75th lap, Zanardi was unable to defend third place any longer and he slid through the complex of turns known as the Festival Chicane. Blundell took advantage and nipped past both Zanardi and Moore and set off after Fittipaldi and de Ferran. Judging the conditions and the grip level to perfection, Blundell caught Fittipaldi on the 77th lap and slipped past with a risky move into the fast chicane on the back side of the course.

"John Anderson came on the radio to tell me 'Six seconds to the leader,' but I didn't know who the leader was," Blundell related. "Christian made it a little difficult, but I was able to get by him going into the back straight chicane. Then I caught Gil on the last lap and tried to go around him a few times. He knew I was there, and he did what I would have done to protect his position. I got up onto the curbs and, for a few seconds, I thought it would end in tears."

De Ferran's Goodyears were worn down to the cords. "I was trying to make my tires live, looking for wet parts of the track to keep them cool because I knew the guys on slicks were catching up," he said. "With three laps to go, [team owner] Derrick Walker got on the radio and told me that Mark was up to third behind Christian. I hoped Christian would delay him a little bit because it was getting quite difficult."

Starter Jim Swintal waved the white flag at the end of the 77th lap signifying one lap to go. De Ferran kept Blundell at bay into the Festival Chicane and through the long, sweeping corners that make up the first half of a lap of PIR. Blundell purposely held the Motorola car back through the fast chicane, and he was able to carry much more speed as they braked for the final corner.

"Gil got off the gas a bit early and tried to slow the pace down, but I jumped off mine a little bit too," said Blundell. "I got the turbo boost rolling and just came off the turn a bit quicker. With slicks up to temperature, that made all the difference. From there it was a drag race to the line."

The worn wet-weather tires compromised de Ferran's acceleration off the final turn. "I had a lot of wheelspin and going into the last corner I tried to stop the car as much as possible to get good traction off the corner," de Ferran said. "But the rear wheels continued to spin, and Mark just got off the corner better than me. I still thought I had won the race."

De Ferran mistakenly raised his arm in triumph as he took the checkered flag, unaware of the PacWest car streaking past to his right. In fact, the victor was Blundell, by the margin of 0.027 second. Making the finish even more exciting, Boesel was closing quickly on the lead duo and the three Reynards crossed the line in a cluster separated by just 0.055 second.

While the PacWest crew celebrated in the pits, the winning driver was unaware of what he had just achieved. "To be honest, when we crossed the line, I didn't have a clue who won," Blundell said. "Normally the guys get on the radio right afterward and say 'Good job' or whatever. So, after about three turns, I got on and asked where we ended up. Right then I saw No. 18 on top of on the scoreboard and I gave the biggest 'Yahoo!' you've ever heard."

Winning pit stop: With the track rapidly drying and time running out in the 1997 Grand Prix of Portland, Mark Blundell chose exactly the right moment to change to slick tires. Pat Patrick and his team observe from behind.

Blundell is met by his jubilant crew and pit reporter Gary Gerould at Victory Circle.

Dear Brúce,

Sitting at the airport. in Portland the Monday morning after the race, we were of course reading all the local papers. The photo enclosed showed the joy a certain racing team felt about its first victory. We were quite touched because we remembered the feeling... In a business which is so much dominated by money, sponsors, politics and relentless hard work, it is moving to see moments of such sincere human happiness.

All the best to you and Jolene in the coming year. It will of course be extra special for the two (three) of you.

Dan & Evi

In the days following the Portland win, McCaw recieved a newspaper clipping and a note from Dan Gurney congratulating him on the victory.

At the time of writing more than 20 years later, Blundell's win over de Ferran at Portland in 1997 remains the closest road racing finish in the century-plus history of Indy car racing. Replays of the last-lap sprint to the flag are a staple of open-wheel racing highlight reels.

"Making the change to slicks when we did was the key because it made all the difference at the end of the race." Blundell recounted. "We made good decisions and when it came to the crunch, we kept it on the black stuff and that's what it's all about. We had already seen from Detroit that both cars were strong. To actually win was fantastic—it gave everybody the boost they needed, the whole team. Not just my side of the team, not just me as an individual, everybody. The fact that it was one of the closest races in history makes it even sweeter."

Champagne flowed and an impromptu party soon broke out in the team's hospitality area. "I was thrilled," said an energized Bruce McCaw. "From the first lap on slicks, I knew Mark had a shot at it. He was fast enough to catch everyone, and he had just enough to race to the end. It was a brilliant drive by Mark, although we really thought Mauricio was the guy who was going to get the first win.

"We couldn't ask for a better place to win than Portland and the great thing about that first win was that it was so dramatic for the entire race," added the team principal. "In a lot of ways, it was a lot more fulfilling than Detroit would have been."

Gugelmin was deeply disappointed that he was not the man who delivered the first Indy car victory to PacWest. Mauricio led a race-high 38 of 78 laps at Portland, but sixth place—just 3.04 seconds adrift of his victorious teammate—was scant reward after a stirring drive.

"Portland was such an open race," recalled the Brazilian. "I spoke with Tracy, Michael Andretti, Gil, Greg Moore, and everybody said, 'If I hadn't done this or done that it was my race.' Everybody had that race won but at the end of the day, Mark crossed the line first.

"As a driver, your strongest competition is your teammate," he noted. "It drives you to be better and better and as long as that is kept in a healthy way, it's fine. I knew I had to just keep working the same way I was and then it would come together pretty soon."

For Bruce McCaw, not only had the victory come in what was a "home" event, it produced a special bonus. "A few days later, Dan Gurney sent me the front page from *The Oregonian* newspaper with coverage of the race, with a little note that said, 'There's nothing like the first time,'" he said. "That's something I'll always treasure."

"Making the change to slicks when we did was the key because it made all the difference at the end of the race."

Mark Blundell

Mark Blundell led the 1997 Molson Indy Toronto from start to finish. Here at the start, Blundell is seen passing pole man Dario Franchitti, whose race would end quickly when he was spun out by Bobby Rahal at the first corner.

Blundell carried the momentum from his Portland victory into Cleveland, where he outqualified Gugelmin for the first time in 1997, third to Mauricio's sixth. But poor pit stop strategy and communication added up to a ninth-place finish for Blundell as PacWest's best result on a day when Alex Zanardi claimed one of the most remarkable wins of his Indy car career.

Blundell's mid-season surge continued at Toronto, where the Englishman qualified on the front row for the first time in his CART career. A first corner accident, triggered by Bobby Rahal, eliminated pole man Dario Franchitti. That left Blundell defending the lead from an aggressive Zanardi. In the pits, Butch Winkle and the No. 18 crew provided Blundell with two perfect green flag stops that kept him ahead of the defending CART series champion. Not that it was easy for Blundell on the racetrack. On at least two occasions, he had trouble downshifting for the tight right-hander at the end of the back straight, and he had to summon all of his skills to keep the car from spinning. After 95 laps of intense pressure, Blundell crossed the line 0.659 second ahead of Zanardi.

"I would have to say that was one of the best races of my life," Blundell related. "We started on the front row, led from the beginning, made no mistakes, and stayed there until the very end. The team did a fantastic job in the pits and it was a great day. We deserved it and we earned it from the beginning."

"Mark drove a very good race," assessed Zanardi. "I caught him, but on this kind of track, when you get behind another car, you lose a bit of downforce and it's very difficult to overtake. And at the end, Mark made no mistakes."

Next up was the U.S. 500 at Michigan International Speedway, a track where PacWest had always excelled. Gugelmin was fastest in practice with a 236.453-mph lap, but he had to settle for second best in qualifying as Scott Pruett took the pole at 233.857 mph. Gugelmin ran 233.493 mph on his own, while Blundell qualified 11th fastest at 229.358 mph.

In the race, Mauricio took the lead on the second lap and appeared to have the legs of the field. But a faulty component in the ignition system caused a misfire and the Brazilian lost five laps having it replaced. The sixth-place finish matched his results from Portland and Toronto. "I've got to get this monkey off my shoulders soon," sighed Gugelmin. Meanwhile, Blundell's superb form continued as he finished second in the 500-miler to Zanardi. It was the best oval finish to date in Blundell's American racing career.

The Miller 200 at Mid-Ohio Sports Car Course was PacWest's least satisfying race in the second half of 1997. Gugelmin qualified sixth and led nine laps, but the team's aggressive pit stop strategy only netted a ninth-place finish. An electrical misfire caused Blundell's engine to stutter and he was subsequently pushed off the track by a closely following Al Unser Jr.

The following weekend at Road America, Gugelmin and Blundell scored another milestone for PacWest by sweeping the front row in qualifying. The 4.0-mile road course near Elkhart Lake, Wisconsin, was always Gugelmin's favorite track in America; he loved the fast and flowing corners and he set a pole position lap with a record average speed of more than 142 mph.

Race day dawned rainy and it stayed that way until late afternoon, delaying the green flag by nearly two hours and denying PacWest the opportunity for a commemorative front row photo. Based on the form he showed in the wet at Portland, Gugelmin started the Elkhart Lake race as a heavy favorite and he led the first eight laps in soaking conditions. But the rain stopped and the track dried faster than expected; Blundell, whose car featured more of a dry setup, passed his teammate for the lead on Lap 9 and held it through the first round of pit stops. "I just overworked the tires and the car went very loose," explained Gugelmin.

Blundell was back in front from Lap 20 to 35, but Zanardi emerged in the lead following the final round of pit stops. Challenging Zanardi for the lead, Blundell was right on the Target car's gearbox when his Mercedes-Benz engine expired with just three laps to go. Gugelmin was left to pick up the pieces, finishing second some six seconds behind winner Zanardi. "I had a car that was miles too stiff for the conditions," commented Gugelmin. "I'm disappointed for Mark because he was very strong. It would have been a great result for the PacWest team to put both cars on the podium."

Mauricio's long wait to taste victory would finally end before the month of August drew to a close. Fittingly, the win came at McCaw's second "home" race, the Molson Indy Vancouver, just 140 miles north of Seattle across the Canadian border. That very morning, both Gugelmin and Blundell had publicly confirmed they'd signed contract extensions to remain PacWest teammates through the 1999 season.

Big Mo served notice by pacing both practice sessions on the Vancouver street course, but he was disappointed to qualify fifth. Early in the 100-lap race, pole starter Zanardi dropped back with brake problems and Rahal dropped out with a blown engine. Zanardi would remain a factor as he aggressively fought back through the field. Once pit stop strategies were worked out, the race boiled down to a two-man fight between Gugelmin and 1996 CART champion Jimmy Vasser. PacWest's No. 17 crew, headed by Mark Moore, elevated their driver into the lead with a superior final pit stop and Gugelmin pulled away to

Mauricio Gugelmin and Bruce McCaw share a private moment on the Vancouver podium after Gugelmin's victory.

FONTANA 1997

On April 20, 1994, Roger Penske announced the construction of a new 2-mile superspeedway. It would be built on the site of an abandoned Kaiser Steel mill in Fontana, California, about 50 miles east of Los Angeles. One day later, CART revealed its intention to stage an annual 500-mile race at California Speedway, the first of which would be the 1997 PPG CART World Series finale. With strong corporate support from Philip Morris USA and Toyota, the Marlboro 500 took place before a capacity crowd of 75,000.

California Speedway (later renamed Auto Club Speedway) was a near clone of Michigan International Speedway, another Penske-owned track. Michigan was the site of several of PacWest Racing's most competitive outings. Dominic Dobson claimed the team's first podium finish with third place in the 1994 Marlboro 500 at MIS. In 1996, PacWest placed both of its cars in the top six in both 500-milers staged at Michigan, topped by Mauricio Gugelmin's second-place finish in the U.S. 500. The team's Michigan success continued in 1997 as Gugelmin qualified on the front row and Mark Blundell finished second in July.

Michigan was the fastest track on the CART schedule, with speeds generally a couple mph faster than those achieved at the Indianapolis Motor Speedway. Penske's new track in Fontana featured slightly lower banking than Michigan (14 degrees vs. 18), but with new asphalt, was expected to be even faster. With Gugelmin increasingly gaining a reputation as a superspeedway specialist, Ilmor/Mercedes engineers really stepped up their efforts for him at Fontana. They equipped the Brazilian with a special qualifying engine that produced in excess of 1000 horsepower. Big Mo rewarded them by turning a practice lap at 242.333 mph before qualifying on the pole with a world closed-course record speed of 240.942 mph, some seven mph faster than he ran two months earlier in Michigan.

Gugelmin and his engineer, Andy Brown, believed that a 240-mph lap was possible and put more effort than usual into qualifying.

"The 240 lap was huge," recalled Gugelmin with a grin. "Probably the nicest thing about that lap was to see Bruce McCaw's face when I jumped out of the car. He's a very settled gentleman, but that day you could see that he was pretty excited."

Steve Fusek added, "I remember being on the pit lane with Bruce when Mo set his record. We were standing just past the pylon, thinking, 'There's no way he's ever going to do 240.' I'll never forget it. I have never seen the guy so happy."

Gugelmin tended to excel at fast corners and many of his best moments in Indy cars happened at the CART series' fastest tracks, both road courses and ovals.

"When I first came over to CART, I felt that ovals were something that I really had to start to work with and I succeeded on that," Gugelmin said. "I felt as confident as you are probably going to get on an oval track, and I understood what was going on with the car all the time. The superspeedways were probably my best tracks—not my favorite places, but probably where I ran the fastest compared to all the other drivers.

"The 240-mph lap was incredible because in places like Brazil and Japan, it calculated to almost 400 kilometers per hour (387.759)," he added "The fans love to see those numbers and the response from fans around the world was incredible. They often ask me, 'How does it feel?' Well, it feels fast, but it's hard to describe. It is almost like a different planet because you have to have your mind so far ahead of the car. At that speed, every single input had to be minute because it was very easy to lose control. You were basically on a wire and it was like flying a jet. It's amazing to look at the printout of the throttle traces and steering input because you hardly put any lock on the wheel. You had to be as smooth as you could and then just hold your breath for a couple of laps. But it was a great feeling."

The 500-mile race would provide even more excitement. Gugelmin led 66 laps and was the man to beat, but once again, a superspeedway win proved elusive as blistered rear tires relegated him to a fourth-place finish. "I was really sick about that, because that day, there was nothing even close to

"Every single input had to be minute because it was very easy to lose control...it was like flying a jet."

Mauricio Gugelmin

running with my car," Mauricio related. "Firestone apologized for that, but the way I used to leave my car so neutral on the ovals to be fast, the right rear just wouldn't take it. So we blistered tires and it was one of those things. Looking back, I can't believe we didn't win more races."

Fortunately for PacWest, Blundell was still running strongly, moving up to third place behind Greg Moore and Jimmy Vasser when Gugelmin pitted for tires with 15 laps remaining. Then Moore's engine blew in a massive cloud of smoke on the 240th of 250 laps. Anticipating a yellow flag, Vasser momentarily backed off. But Blundell's spotter Steve Fusek stayed calm and never called a yellow, the driver kept his foot on the throttle, and he zipped past Vasser into a lead he would not relinquish.

"I saw Greg's engine spit out some flames," Blundell related. "Jimmy backed off, and so did I. Out of Turn 2, I evaluated the situation quickly. John Anderson got on the radio and when it was obvious there was no yellow flag, I got back on the throttle and passed Jimmy. Then I drove flat out to the finish. It

Mauricio Gugelmin set a closed course record at California Speedway with his 240.942 mph qualifying lap for the 1997 Marlboro 500. Although Gil de Ferran raised the mark to 241.426 mph in 2000, Gugelmin's 242.333 mph practice lap from 1997 remains unofficially the fastest speed ever turned by an Indy car.

Flawless pit stops by the No. 18 team, led by crew chief Butch Winkle, contributed to Blundell's victory.

was a fantastic day. This is a marvelous finish to a great season. We won on a street course, a road course, and now a superspeedway."

On this occasion, Blundell's tendency to run a more conservative car setup worked to his advantage. Although he was also afflicted by degrading rear tires, he was able keep his Firestones intact in the sprint to the finish to claim PacWest's fourth win of the season after a dramatic shootout with Vasser. The margin of victory was 0.847 second.

Blundell is justifiably proud of his record in superspeedway races. "The big ovals were something I looked forward to," he said. "I think Mo was very good at putting that one lap together and just hanging it out there. That would make a statement and it was great for the team as well. But nine times out of ten I think we turned up with something that was a bit more user-friendly during the race. When it actually came to racing on a Sunday afternoon, from my side of things, that's where I feel I was at my strongest point because racing is exactly what it says it is: racing. And I don't mind going wheel-to-wheel with anybody at whatever level it is. The oval racing then, when the car was working well, was a very attractive proposition.

"I think at Fontana we drove well, we had a great car," he continued. "Yes, we were getting toward the end of the life on the tires; there were a couple of sensible-sized holes in them in terms of delamination by the end of that race. But that wasn't going to stop me. I'd sooner end up in the wall with a tire blowout than to not be in a position to win the race. That's the gamble we took, and it paid off. You have to capitalize on opportunities, and I think we did exactly that. We stuck it out."

McCaw's recollection of PacWest's only victory in a 500-mile race revealed his pride in winning the inaugural open-wheel contest at California Speedway, while at the same time expressed his disappointment that Gugelmin was not able to cash in on his record-setting pole position. "One of my favorite moments was when Roger Penske introduced me to Daimler-Benz CEO Jurgen Schrempp after we had just won the 500-mile race at Roger's new track," Bruce recalled. "Schrempp had had a fair amount of wine to drink and he was not at all careful with his words. He said, 'I'm certainly glad you've brought some pride to Mercedes-Benz. Obviously, Roger wasn't going to get it done for us.'

"I was so disappointed Mauricio didn't win that," McCaw added. "With his talent in the 500-mile races, to not have put more than one away is always a shame. That may reign as one of my great disappointments of things we didn't achieve because we were so good at the 500-mile races. We were always right there and the consistency we had in '95, '96 and '97...we were just so solid in those races. PacWest's speed and reliability in 500-mile contests is something to be really proud of."

One of the things that differentiated CART from other forms of racing was the diversity of tracks, with a near-equal mix of short ovals, superspeedways, street courses, and natural-terrain road courses. By the end of 1997, PacWest had become an acknowledged favorite on ultra-high-speed ovals and it's interesting to speculate how Gugelmin and Blundell would have fared in the Indianapolis 500 had PacWest and the other CART teams competed there in the late 1990s.

"I think Andy Brown has to take a huge amount of credit for PacWest's success on superspeedways," assessed Allen McDonald. "You can see what he later accomplished in the IRL with Sam Hornish at Panther Racing. He really pushed the aero program along very strongly and in a sensible way. His feel of the aero for superspeedways during that era was incredible...he knew what bits worked and what didn't. We had a damper program led by Tim Neff and that was a really good program. We also had some things in terms of ride height control and third springs that were very innovative for their time—even now. They definitely helped us.

"Mark and Mo drove completely different cars on the superspeedways," McDonald added. "Mo's ability to drive a very, very free car led up to that remarkable 240-mph lap at Fontana. That was unbelievable, really. Mark, in the race, because he had a more 'pushy' car, was the one who managed to make the rear tires live, and he won the race."

In mid-1997, Jolene McCaw commissioned noted artist Wally Thomason to create a painting commemorating PacWest's breakout season as a surprise anniversary present for her husband, Bruce. Thomason had the composition laid out and had nearly completed the painting by mid-September. When Mauricio Gugelmin starred and Mark Blundell won the season finale at California Speedway, Thomason took a picture of the winner's trophy from the television broadcast and incorporated it into the finished product. Bruce McCaw was surprised and delighted by the thoughtful gift, and a series of 500 prints signed by the artist, Bruce McCaw, and the PacWest drivers were presented to team members and supporters.

Blundell withstood intense pressure from two-time CART champion Alex Zanardi to win at Toronto.

defeat Vasser by 2.87 seconds. In his 65th start in the series, Gugelmin had finally won an Indy car race, and the victory gave PacWest Racing a clean sweep of the 1997 CART races in Canada.

"The team did a fabulous job," Gugelmin exclaimed. "It's something we worked so hard for and we came close so many times. It didn't feel like I had one black cloud over me, it felt like a whole monsoon! But we've done it now and it feels great. The hardest thing has been all the people asking, 'When are you going to win the first one?' That's not going to happen anymore!"

With the benefit of hindsight, Gugelmin was able to reflect on how frustrating it was to play second fiddle to Blundell when the Brazilian was generally perceived as the PacWest team leader. "It was difficult to deal with, even before Mark got his first wins," Mauricio noted. "If I knew at Miami in '95 that it would take so long to get my first win, there is no way I could have fathomed that. After we ran so close at Detroit, or after Portland, where Mark won after I made a mistake on the last set of tires when I led the most laps, I knew it was just around the corner. I was even more motivated and focused.

"After Vancouver, I felt great. I was relieved, but at the same time I felt anxious to go out again and drive without that extra pressure of having to get the first one. With my qualifying record that year (an average grid position of 4.2, best in the series) I knew it was just a matter of time. It came earlier for Mark. It was important for his side, and also for the team and for him. The team needed that win because then everyone knew we could do it."

Gugelmin and Blundell looked set to finish second and third in the penultimate race of the season at Laguna Seca Raceway, but Gugelmin's car suffered a brake failure on the last lap and he speared into the Turn 4 tire barrier. Blundell's second-place finish behind winner Vasser clinched the CART Manufacturer's Championship for Mercedes-Benz as PacWest scored more than 45 percent of Mercedes' point tally in 1997. The team capped the campaign with its strongest performance yet, with Gugelmin claiming pole position and Blundell the race win at California Speedway.

The season ended with Alex Zanardi as the CART champion, followed by de Ferran, Vasser, and Gugelmin. "Of course, it was a year we were very successful, but I wish I had won more races," commented Gugelmin. "We qualified really well, and looking back, you see reasons why, but the result is still there. Had a couple things gone the other way, we could have finished third or even second in the championship."

Tom Keene holds the pit board that tells race leader Mauricio Gugelmin 13 laps remain in the 1997 Molson Indy Vancouver.

With no other car in sight, Mauricio Gugelmin takes the checkered flag to win the 1997 Molson Indy Vancouver. Remarkably, it would be the Brazilian's only Indy car victory.

After a difficult start, Blundell ended the season sixth in the point standings and only Zanardi amassed more points in the second half of 1997. "I'm very happy with it," was the Englishman's takeaway. "Obviously the second half was very strong for us. My only frustration is that we weren't stronger at the beginning. I think if that had been the case, we could have been fighting for the championship. The next step is to get where, from race one, we're looking for the championship."

In December, Blundell was honored by *Autosport* magazine as British Competition Driver of the Year, while in Italy, Gugelmin was presented with *Autosprint* magazine's prestigious Caschi d'Oro (Golden Helmet) award in recognition of his 240-mph lap.

Mark Blundell was honored as "British Competition Driver of the Year" at the 1997 *Autosport* Awards.

"It was a great season in every respect," commented McCaw at the end of 1997. "From the time we got together with Mauricio and Mark, I believed in their capabilities, and this year, with help from Mercedes-Benz and Firestone, we gave them the equipment they needed to run at the front and win races. It was a breakthrough to get that first win. That was very important because it gave the team confidence and a foundation to build on and the remainder of the season was very successful. We had some good races in the first half of the season, notably with Mauricio, but from Detroit onward, we really had the confidence to go out and compete for wins every weekend. I always had confidence in the rest of the team and the quality of the people we had. Given those elements, what we needed was maturity as an organization to instill confidence in our abilities. We were clearly contenders for race wins in 1995 and 1996, but things just didn't come our way.

"I think four wins, three poles, and a world closed-course speed record of over 240 mph are achievements everyone at PacWest can be proud of," McCaw added. "The team is now perceived as a potential race winner at every venue and a championship favorite heading into 1998."

Postscript: On October 28, 2000, Gil de Ferran ran a qualifying lap of 241.426 mph at California Speedway to take over the world closed-course speed record from Mauricio Gugelmin. "CART was amazing then," de Ferran said. "Penske was Honda's number one team, and for that last race, they were throwing the kitchen sink at it to try and get the record. They came up with a qualifying engine with well over 1,000 horsepower that ran to 17,000 RPM and had a life of about 50 miles. The record was great, though at the time, it didn't seem very important to me because I was in a championship battle. But as the years have gone by, that's changed. As far as accomplishments go, that is one I am very proud of." Gugelmin retains the absolute record with his 242.333-mph practice lap in 1997.

Pit stop for Mauricio Gugelmin in the 1998 season opener at Homestead. The Brazilian finished 10th.

8

A FALL FROM GLORY

PACWEST'S SUCCESSFUL 1997 season raised expectations, both inside and outside the team. With four race wins and both drivers in the top six of the CART championship, confidence was high for everyone within the organization, including the drivers. Meanwhile, opposing teams and outside observers now viewed PacWest as a serious championship threat to the Indy car establishment of Penske Racing, Newman/Haas Racing, and Chip Ganassi Racing.

"The team was on a roll and everyone was going into '98 with an air of confidence," recalled Mark Blundell. "Many people looked at us to be the contenders fighting for race wins and a championship."

CART secured title sponsorship from Federal Express for its championship, which was rebranded the Fed Ex Championship Series. Part of the anticipation for the 1998 season revolved around the introduction of a new Mercedes-Benz engine. By the end of 1997, the Mercedes IC108D design had developed into perhaps the best all-around engine available. It demonstrated superior drivability and fuel mileage while sacrificing little on top-end power to the championship-winning Honda powerplant. Its success was evidenced by Mauricio Gugelmin's string of 240-mph laps at California Speedway.

In terms of manufacturer participation, CART was in the midst of its most bountiful period. There was still the potential to develop the IC108D for more power and efficiency, but Honda's rapid rise into a frontrunner throughout 1996 and 1997 convinced Ilmor Engineering that an all-new engine was necessary to remain competitive in the CART series. Ilmor set out to create the smallest and lightest engine the 2.65-liter turbocharged V-8 formula had ever seen. In that regard, certainly, the design known as the IC108E was a success. Compared to the outgoing IC108D, the 'E' engine weighed 50 pounds less and could fit inside a box smaller by one-third.

"For 1998, we decided a clean sheet of paper approach was the best because there was no way we could encompass all the new technology available to us in anything but an all-new design," explained Ilmor USA Vice President Paul Ray in his remarks introducing the new

The Ilmor/Mercedes IC108E engine (left) was much smaller than its predecessor the IC108D.

Designed to fit a much smaller Penske chassis, the new Mercedes-Benz IC108E engine was barely visible when installed in a Reynard. Did Ilmor go too far in its quest for packaging efficiency?

engine at the 1998 North American International Auto Show in Detroit. "The goal in designing the 'E' was to make it as small as physically possible given the 2.65-liter, eight-cylinder format mandated by CART rules, and in so doing, make the engine as light as possible by minimizing the number of parts. In order to accomplish the downsizing, it was necessary to package components much more densely and in much closer proximity to one another than we ever had before.

"We met, and in fact surpassed our goals, reducing the engine's height, width, length, and weight significantly," Ray added. "The chassis manufacturers, in turn, took advantage of the size reduction to improve the aerodynamic characteristics of the upper bodywork and maximize air flow to the rear wing, increasing downforce and stability."

One chassis manufacturer in particular was able to take advantage of the IC108E's compact dimensions: Penske Cars. It is clear that Ilmor's zeal to create an unusually small engine was driven by the company's co-founder and one-quarter shareholder, Roger Penske. After two unsuccessful years by Team Penske's standards (at least partly attributable to Goodyear's inability to build a tire that could consistently compete with Firestone), chief designer Nigel Bennett was reassigned. A new design team, headed by John Travis (ex-Lola), tried to create the 'unfair advantage' Penske's team often sought by building its own chassis.

With its high nose and tightly waisted rear aerodynamics, Travis' Penske PC27 chassis looked more like a Formula 1 car than a contemporary Reynard or Lola Indy car. The key to packaging such a neat and uncluttered rear end was a tiny engine—so Penske commissioned his own engine-building company to produce the 108E.

"What did they need a new engine for?" queried Andy Brown. "There was nothing wrong with the '97 engine. I mean, look what we were doing for lap times around Fontana. It was just Penske talking Ilmor into it so he could build a tiny car, which gave them bigger underwing tunnels. When you looked at that engine in a Reynard, it was lost."

Ray denied that the IC108E's radical packaging was dictated by Penske. "That's not true at all," he said. "The small package actually came from [Ilmor co-founder] Mario Illien. It was a Formula 1 concept. Right about then our Formula 1 program was getting going and we wanted to use a Formula 1 mentality so Ian Watson was sent to design the smallest and lightest engine he could to really steal a march on the other Indy car manufacturers."

But even Penske team members were forced to admit that the "E" engine was a step too far. "John Travis is a superb designer, but in retrospect I think he made an error in pushing Ilmor to make the 1998 engine as compact as possible in order to minimize the disruption of the airflow to the rear wing," said Nigel Beresford, a longtime Penske engineer. "Ilmor certainly achieved this target, but at the considerable expense of making the packaging of the induction system very tight indeed. At a time when it became apparent that Honda was making considerable gains by careful positioning of the injectors and increasing the plenum volume, Ilmor's hands were tied by the tight packaging imposed on them. They simply had no room to maneuver."

With a high nose and tight engine packaging, the Penske PC27 was heavily influenced by Formula 1 cars of the era. The car's potential was dulled by its Mercedes-Benz engine and Goodyear tires.

In terms of its packaging, Reynard, as a customer car builder, could not take full advantage of the IC108E's reduced physical size. The basic design of the 98I had to accommodate the dimensions of the larger Honda, Ford-Cosworth, and Toyota engines. Still, PacWest's new Reynard-Mercedes combination appeared fast out of the box, and Gugelmin maintained the team's high hopes for the new campaign by setting the fastest lap during the last of four test sessions at CART Spring Training at Homestead-Miami Speedway. Gugelmin's 210.682 mph lap was third quickest when all sessions were combined. "We weren't here to qualify, but it was nice to show we can do a quick time when we need to," summarized the Brazilian.

Mark Blundell and Mauricio Gugelmin pose with their cars prior to the 1998 season. The new Hollywood livery was designed by the Brazilian advertising agency DPZ.

Both PacWest cars sported a fresh look for the new season. The front two-thirds of the paint scheme for Blundell's No. 18 Motorola car was fairly similar, while the formerly white portion at the rear of both cars was now painted silver to represent PacWest's closer relationship with Mercedes-Benz. The team had renegotiated its contract so that it was effectively no longer paying for engines and service, working instead to cultivate a 'partner' relationship with Mercedes similar to a title sponsor like Hollywood or Motorola.

Meanwhile Gugelmin's No. 17 Hollywood car looked completely different. The main portion of the car was now painted Day-Glo orange, separated from green and blue bands at the car's nose by sharp zigzags, along with a silver section at the rear to acknowledge Mercedes-Benz. The design was adopted to reflect the "No Limits" theme of new packaging for Hollywood's three varieties of cigarettes (full-flavor, light, and menthol), including a redesigned font and delta logo.

The new design was unveiled at a reception at Planet Hollywood Miami that was attended by around 150 people. This marked the first time PacWest, or any other Indy car team, utilized a glitzy Formula 1-style launch. "We're really pleased with the new look for the Hollywood/PacWest/Mercedes-Benz," stated Felicio Ferraz, Hollywood's brand sponsorship manager. "We feel there are 'No Limits' to what the partnership between Hollywood and PacWest can achieve." Added Gugelmin, "If the new car runs as fast as it looks, we should be unbeatable!"

"E" FOR EXASPERATING

When all of the Mercedes-Benz powered teams encountered reliability problems and a lack of spare parts in testing prior to the 1998 CART season with the new Mercedes-Benz IC108E engine, PacWest tried a different approach. The team made a decision that seemed smart and conservative at the time: It entered updated 1997 Reynard chassis and the proven IC108D engine in the first three races of the championship.

"We know the 1998 car and engine package will ultimately prove superior, but in terms of speed, reliability, and raceability, we believe the '97 cars are the best option to start the season," said Racing Operations VP John Anderson. "We're fortunate to have the depth of organization to be able to make and execute a strategic decision like this."

The move didn't pan out. At Homestead, Mark Blundell qualified seventh and Mauricio Gugelmin tenth, a year after he had started that race in the same car from the front row. Gugelmin finished 10th and Blundell 12th, the last car on the lead lap. PacWest's pain was made more acute by the fact that Forsythe Racing's Greg Moore qualified his '98-spec Reynard/Mercedes on pole position and finished a close second to race winner Michael Andretti.

The 1997 car gamble continued to backfire for PacWest at the new Twin Ring Motegi oval in Japan. Qualifying was rained out, so Gugelmin lined up 11th based on practice times, marking the first time Big Mo started outside the top 10 since 1996. Mauricio's car was retired at three-quarters distance due to a wheel bearing failure, while Blundell finished 10th, two laps down to winner Adrian Fernandez.

At Long Beach, where Gugelmin had qualified on the front row and finished a close second to series champion Alex Zanardi a year before, the failure of the 1997 car experiment became clear. Rain on Saturday prevented PacWest from rebounding from a poor performance on Friday, leaving Gugelmin and Blundell 22nd and 23rd on the grid. The cars were much more competitive in the race, with Blundell taking 7th place and Gugelmin 10th. But 13th (Blundell) and 15th (Gugelmin) in the standings after three races was not the position PacWest was expecting to be in when it suspended development on its 1998 cars.

"We probably shot ourselves in the foot," Bruce McCaw admitted. "I can't blame everything just on the engine, but if I look back to '98, that was one of the decisions I probably helped push—and at the time it made all the sense in the world to me. Our '97 cars had been so good, which made it an easy decision. But clearly, we outsmarted ourselves at the time.

"When we showed up at Long Beach and we were a full two seconds slower than we had been the year before, that was stupid," McCaw continued. "I kept saying, 'How can we be so far off with these cars when the track has not changed and we're basically running the same tires and the same engine and the same drivers. How does Mauricio, who qualified on the front row, qualify 22nd? What has happened?'"

Gugelmin offered a theory. "Instead of going with what we knew we had that worked, we had '97½ cars that Allen McDonald threw a bunch of stuff on and we got lost," he said. "The cars were just terrible. We tried using '98 wings and put a bunch of things on the car that we just didn't understand. The way we put the car together, it wasn't sorted out right."

"We thought we could take advantage of our knowledge of the '97 cars to put us a step ahead and get some early points in the championship," added Anderson. "The points you miss at the start of the year can't be regained and they can win or lose a championship. But the three races with the '97s didn't pan out the way we thought they would."

In hindsight, Technical Director McDonald believes the approach taken—trying to update the 1997 cars rather than race them as they were—was wrong for several reasons.

"The '98 Reynard was very different for us from the '97 Reynard," McDonald said. "Suddenly our '97 setups just stopped working. We basically hadn't gotten any winter testing done so we were on a huge catch-up

“We basically hadn’t gotten any winter testing done so we were on a huge catch-up and we went down a lot of blind alleys.”

Allen McDonald

and we went down a lot of blind alleys. By the time we actually got the ’97 cars back out and started running them we were surprised because we weren’t as competitive as we’d imagined. We thought we would have solid cars, particularly at Long Beach. But things had moved on. Because the tire war was ending, the tires were changing, and I think that actually took us a long time to get to grips with the fact that the tires had just become a lot harder. From ’97 to ’98 there was sort of a transition and at Long Beach none of the old ’97 car setups worked.

“I don’t know if it was a mistake,” he added. “I think at the time it was quite a sensible thing to do. We’d gotten no testing done with the ’98 car and it seemed best to give Mercedes some time to take a breather because we had been breaking engines and giving them no time to sort the problems out because they were just kind of turning engines out to us. I thought we did the right thing.”

McCaw and Mark Blundell chat with Ilmor Engineering co-founder Paul Morgan and Norbert Haug, vice president of Mercedes-Benz Motorsports (left to right).

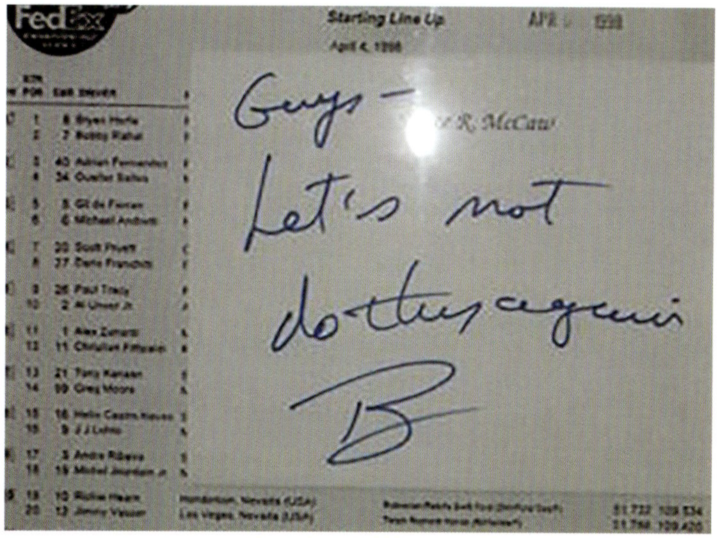

McCaw posted his reaction to PacWest’s Long Beach qualifying performance. Rain on Saturday prevented the team from moving up the grid after a difficult Friday.

Not confident in the power or reliability of the all-new Mercedes-Benz engine, PacWest campaigned 1997 equipment in the first three races of 1998, including here at Long Beach. In retrospect, the move was a mistake.

Behind the scenes, the outlook was not so rosy in the Mercedes camp. Although the new engine produced a competitive amount of power, reliability was a serious concern. Drivability—the smooth delivery of power, without turbo lag or wheelspin—was poor. And the problems were major. "It just seemed that the engine wasn't physically strong enough to cope with the demands that the chassis placed upon it," observed Brown. "We kept cracking blocks and cylinder liners, pressurizing the water system and blowing all the water out the exhaust pipes."

Those mechanical problems only surfaced when the engine had run long enough to overcome persistent issues with the new electronic fuel management system provided by the Italian firm Magneti Marelli. All of Ilmor's engines from 1986 to 1997 had featured engine electronics developed by Delco Remy. However, starting in 1997, Delco Remy withdrew from CART to align itself with General Motors and the Oldsmobile- and Chevrolet-branded engines used in the Indy Racing League.

Marelli came on board late and the program was problematic from the start. "I knew even the summer before that Ilmor was way behind on getting a new electronics supplier. I had been talking to Paul Ray and Paul Morgan, saying 'You've got to get this thing figured out!'" said Bruce McCaw. "They waited and waited and that was really starting to concern me. By the time they got Marelli on board, it was probably not the right choice to begin with. That was really a big mistake and it was all driven around trying to squeeze some extra dollars out of the thing. They ended up shooting themselves in the foot on it because when Marelli showed up, they didn't know anything about running a car on methanol, and they didn't have any spare parts. The fact that they were so strapped for electronic components was limiting our testing. At a test, you could only run one car and all these issues really hurt our winter test program."

Again, Ray was quick to defend Ilmor and its decision to contract Magneti Marelli for the fuel management electronics. "Much like the engine, we took a high-tech route and went after something that was a little bit better than anything we had seen in the pit lane prior to that time," he explained. "It took time to develop it. Those first six months from November '97 to April '98 where we had poor reliability with the fuel system and poor reliability with the engine meant that the teams had far fewer track miles than they should have had. It held everybody back, there is no doubt.

"You look back on those times and think it was a fundamental mistake," he added. "But at the time, we were all in a very highly competitive arena with four manufacturers spending vast sums of money to do the best they could."

"It just seemed that the engine wasn't physically strong enough to cope with the demands that the chassis placed upon it."

Andy Brown

Hollywood tried to promote a youthful, edgy image. Souza Cruz must have been pleased with the facial hair Gugelmin sported late in the 1998 season. John Anderson talks shop with the Brazilian.

PacWest's Motorola livery underwent only minor changes for 1998, adding silver to represent additional support from Mercedes-Benz. But the vivid, Brazilian-designed Hollywood paint scheme showed off the brand's new graphics.

Taking the reliability and parts shortage concerns into consideration, PacWest made a key decision to shelve the problematic 1998 equipment for the first three races of the season, reverting to the proven Reynard 97I chassis and Mercedes "D" engine with which it won four races in 1997. But that move did not produce the anticipated results and returning to the 1998 package for the fourth race of the season generally didn't improve matters—though late in the Bosch Spark Plug Grand Prix at Nazareth Speedway, Gugelmin appeared on the way to a fourth-place finish. Instead, a gear selection problem affecting both cars caused him to crash heavily and he sustained a badly bruised back, leaving his status for CART's race two weeks later in Brazil in question until the last minute.

Nazareth 1998 was a particularly bleak weekend for the entire PacWest team; Blundell crashed out of the Indy car race before Gugelmin, and Paul Morris' PacWest Lights entry was eliminated in an accident. There was also an incident in the pits that sent fueler Tim Douthat to the hospital.

"Mark crashed, Mauricio crashed, Paul Morris crashed, and we had a pit lane accident," McCaw recalled. "On my fourth trip to the hospital, I remember riding in the ambulance thinking, 'What on earth am I doing in this business?' Then I remember being in the emergency room seeing our guys side by side on four gurneys. I'll never forget that view."

PacWest continued to struggle with the 1998 cars in the oval races dominating the middle part of the season and the decision was taken to suspend the team's in-house shock absorber program run by Tim Neff. Neff subsequently left the team. Reynard specified stock Ohlins dampers, setting the team's road course chassis development program back even further, despite a brace of mid-season tests at Sebring, Road America, and Mid-Ohio.

"When we got the '98 car, it was just a very different beast for us and at Nazareth, we put both cars in the wall," noted McDonald. "We lost Tim Neff, which was a big problem at that time. We had to go to Ohlins shocks, which is a great product, but it was something totally different for us and it really meant we lost a lot of our development effort. We had already lost Jim Hamilton over the winter to Patrick Racing. He was a very wise person and I think he would have helped calm it all down. Unfortunately, it all unraveled."

Gugelmin finally notched a finish at Portland (7th) after a series of DNFs. But the bad luck seemed to transfer to Blundell's car. It was not until the mid-summer Michigan 500 that PacWest managed to get both cars to the finish line. Even so, the result was desultory by the team's high standard for superspeedways: Gugelmin was 13th and two laps down, while Blundell was several laps more in arrears in 17th place. His race was marred by a long pit stop caused by a sticking right rear wheel.

Gugelmin had his best race of the year at Mid-Ohio; he qualified fourth, then moved into the lead for 29 laps when front row starters Bryan Herta and Dario Franchitti crashed on the opening lap. Mauricio eventually finished fourth.

Then Blundell drove a storming race at Road America. It probably would have resulted in a podium finish had he not pitted on the parade lap to investigate a burning fuel overflow smell in the car. From the back of the field, he worked up to end in seventh place.

Gugelmin, meanwhile, saw his season reach its lowest point. "We've been through three engines, two turbos, and a throttle linkage and there's still a day to go," related Big Mo after qualifying. A brake problem took him out of the race the next day.

During this time, the drivers did the best they could to keep morale up within the team, often resorting to dark humor. "It's almost like crashing an airplane," Gugelmin joked. "You don't crash an airplane with one problem; but if you have a couple or maybe three problems, you stand a very high risk of doing so. It's the same thing to make a race car competitive. Everything has to be perfect. More than one problem, and you're not going to be on the pace."

Gugelmin took sixth at Vancouver, site of his victory the year before, and the PacWest cars were both more competitive in the season finale at California Speedway, taking fifth and sixth places. "That was the best race car I had all year and overall it was a good, solid performance," Blundell said. "It's a good way to put 1998 behind us and look ahead to 1999."

After entering the 1998 season as possible championship contenders, PacWest's Gugelmin and Blundell wound up 15th and 17th in the standings. While old guard teams Penske Racing and Newman/Haas Racing continued to struggle on Goodyear tires, Ganassi Racing won its third consecutive CART title with the Reynard/Honda/Firestone "package." Alex Zanardi earned his second consecutive CART championship, with a record points tally. Zanardi put together one of the most dominant seasons in the history of Indy car racing by winning 7 of the 18 races he started and finishing on the podium 15 times.

The post-mortem on PacWest's 1998 campaign started immediately. Blundell called it "definitely the most difficult year of my racing career." He added: "We felt we had a lot of momentum coming off the way we finished the '97 season with a win, but the '98

Gugelmin's best race of 1998 came at Mid-Ohio Sports Car Course, where he qualified and finished fourth in the Miller Lite 200. He led eventual winner Adrian Fernandez (left) and Greg Moore.

PacWest had one of its best qualifying performances of 1998 at Cleveland, where Blundell lined up 6th and Gugelmin 8th. They came 10th and 20th in the race.

program started late and progressed slowly. Once we got out testing, we were at least a month behind some of the others. Looking for positives, we had a group of guys who stuck together and kept their heads down despite some pretty dismal results."

Bruce McCaw was happy with the day-to-day effort put forth by the team despite the difficulties it faced. He said, "It was a very challenging time for everyone involved with PacWest, but what I had to be pleased about was the attitude and desire to move forward and learn from our experiences both bad and good from the past to get us back on track. I feel like we've done that pretty well.

"The drivers kept their heads down and never gave up despite some pretty tough situations," he added. "Everybody in the entire organization kind of just swallowed hard and got through the tough times and really did try to figure out how to make it right to go forward together. I think that says a lot about the individuals involved."

Mark Blundell started 1998 with Al Bodey as his race engineer, but he continued to struggle when working with anyone other than Allen McDonald.

PacWest lost one key team member at the end of 1998: After a short period working with the dedicated test team, Andy Brown left PacWest and accepted a position with Panther Racing in the Indy Racing League. The engineer would play a key role in developing driver Sam Hornish Jr. into an open-wheel racing star.

Brown had been a candidate for the PacWest technical director role that went to Allen McDonald in 1996 and, in some ways, Andy regretted not accepting that position when it was offered. Ironically, at the time, it was agreed that one person could not be the overall technical director while still race engineering a driver at the track, a dual role that Allen McDonald was thrust into with Blundell in 1997.

Brown expressed his frustration in a March 1999 letter to Bruce McCaw. "When that idea was reversed—for good reason where Mark's state of mind was concerned—I couldn't understand why, if we were to have a combined race engineer/technical director, why it would be Allen (with six months' Indy car experience) and not me (when I first worked on these cars back in 1984)," he wrote. "Anyway, I also believe that things happen for some good reason. You once likened the motor racing industry to the aircraft industry, in terms of the personalities and their character traits. I've concluded that sometimes those personalities are better off apart, and the time was definitely right for me to go. Strangely enough, I think that PacWest will also be better off for my move. With the personality clashes, and the corresponding difference in ideas removed, the team should now be able to move in one direction rather than plotting a zigzag course."

11/19/98

PacWest Racing Group
Damage Summary
1998 Crash Damage Year to Date

Race Track	Session	Driver	Chassis	Amount
Detroit	Race	Blundell	026	$ 48,199.13
Long Beach	Warm Up	Blundell	97 / #18	$ 11,358.02
Mid Ohio	Test	Gugelmin	035	$ 14,733.94
Motegi	Other	Gugelmin	97 / #17	$ 149.50
Nazareth	Race	Gugelmin	008	$ 165,088.20
Nazareth	Race	Blundell	016	$ 343,562.68
Nazareth	Race	Blundell / Gugelmin	008 / 016	$ 2,278.00
Cleveland		Blundell	016B	$ 661.57
Cleveland		Gugelmin	?	$ 650.00
Elkhart Lake	Race	Blundell	016B	$ 11,942.56
Mid Ohio Race	Race	Blundell	016B	$ 1,650.25
Michigan	Race	Blundell	026	$ 674.00
		Total Year To Date Crash Damage		$ 600,947.85

This snapshot illustrates a very painful and expensive year. Crash damage was always a significant part of the annual budget.

A few years later, McCaw was more candid and direct in his assessment of what went wrong in 1998. "If we had just stuck with the '98 cars and gotten them figured out, we should have at least been alongside Forsythe," he reasoned. "Penske was obviously lost. Of course, once we pulled the trigger on that, we were committed for three races—for Homestead, Long Beach, and Motegi.

"That was such a lesson to me, but I really didn't understand it for some time afterwards. And the window we had for the '98 stuff, we blew. I just didn't catch it. That got by me. The bottom line is we still performed better than Penske did with that engine on quite a few occasions. But as the engine developed, drivability issues began to set in, and we just got further and further behind."

Like many, McCaw believes Ilmor made a mistake in following Penske's direction in developing a super-compact engine. "Roger had obviously pushed it, looking for his unfair advantage, and forced Ilmor, being a shareholder, into making decisions that were not prudent for Mercedes-Benz," he said. "It was a bad concept. They packaged the engine so tightly, and while it was a brilliant engineering exercise, it really didn't lend itself to development. The minute they tried getting any more out of the engine than what they had, they would run into all sorts of problems because of the oil and fuel pump drives and locations. The engine was lost in a Reynard."

Even Ilmor's Ray now agrees that the IC108E was a step too far. "Hindsight is a beautiful thing, particularly in engineering," Ray said. "It was a big, big mistake on our part. It wasn't a bad engine, but it was unreliable, which was its biggest weakness. It was actually quite powerful, and it won its first race. Homestead was a high-power track, so it couldn't have been a terrible engine. But in hindsight, I think now we would have gone for a more conservative design and focused more on the performance elements rather than trying to get more out of the chassis."

PacWest's Office Manager Colleen Howerton put the difficult 1998 campaign into perspective. "I remember being extremely disappointed because we had such high expectations," she said. "I mean, we were going for the championship and thought we were going to be better than ever. I wanted to win as much as anybody. I always felt like I was part of the team, even though I didn't turn a wrench or anything. But I helped get it there.

"I cut out a *Peanuts* cartoon for Ando and he kept it in his book all that year," she added. "Charlie Brown said, 'We were the team to beat this year.' And Linus said, 'Yep, and everybody beat us!' Sadly, it was really true."

Late in the season, Blundell's car ran with associate sponsorship from Hollywood Video.

Showering gravel and spewing smoke, Mauricio Gugelmin pulls off track after another engine failure.

Roberto Moreno and Mauricio Gugelmin run side-by-side at Michigan Speedway. Moreno replaced the injured Mark Blundell for eight races and achieved PacWest's best results of the 1999 season.

9

STILL COMING UP SHORT

BY THE STANDARDS established with PacWest's four-win 1997 season, 1998 was a huge disappointment. But heading into 1999, there was still plenty of confidence within the walls of 4001 Methanol Lane. Much of that confidence was based upon PacWest's expanding relationship with Mercedes-Benz; by 1999, PacWest was a key Mercedes/Ilmor team, having advanced from the status of paying customer to that of a true partner.

Along with the other Mercedes-powered teams (Forsythe Racing, Bettenhausen Motorsports, Hogan Racing, and of course, Penske Racing) PacWest shared in the belief that the Mercedes-Benz engine program would rebound strongly in 1999. Ilmor Engineering had produced a major "Phase 3" revamp, that Paul Ray barely stopped short of calling a new engine, for the troublesome IC108E powerplant.

"It basically features a completely revised top end to allow higher revs, a much stronger bottom end to support the revs, and that whole package of course leads to more power," Ray said at the Mercedes-Benz media launch for the 1999 season. "The E3 from the outside looks almost identical, but I can assure you that there isn't a single major component on it that is similar to last year except for the crankshaft, and that's being worked on as we speak.

"We also knew that the engine couldn't possibly reach its full potential in one season," he continued. "The one thing that we did learn is it's not just about horsepower on the racetrack. A little term called 'drivability' reared its head fairly early in the season (the ability for a driver to accelerate smoothly from a low-speed corner without turbo lag or wheelspin), and it's something we've been working on ever since. It's one of those things that we definitely had to work very hard at to try to keep up with the competition. It also definitely takes more than one season to get the full potential out of the chassis with a smaller engine. This year we know the chassis designers have worked a lot harder to increase the benefits of this package over the competition."

PacWest also tried to maximize its relationship with its chosen chassis provider, Reynard Motorsport. Bruce McCaw made certain that PacWest got the earliest possible delivery

PacWest was the first team to receive a 1999 Reynard chassis and early tests of the car were encouraging.

Although engine reliability was somewhat better in 1999, the PacWest drivers (seen here with Technical Director Allen McDonald) continued to struggle for pace.

of its new cars, and in fact, the team received 99I chassis 001 and 008 in November 1998 and immediately commenced 2,500 miles of preseason testing.

Reynard's 99I was an update of the highly successful 1998 car which won 18 out of 19 races. Lola was shut out for the second year in a row, and the only other victory was a debut win for Swift, a California constructor that entered the CART series in partnership with Newman/Haas Racing. Thirteen of Reynard's 1998 wins were achieved with Honda power, along with three for Ford-Cosworth. Ilmor-Mercedes attained just two, those with Greg Moore. The 99I had improved rear aerodynamics, but as a customer car designed to accept four different engine installations, the Reynard was still not able to exploit the Mercedes engine's small size as well as the Penske chassis.

From the start, Maurico Gugelmin and Mark Blundell were pleased with the apparent progress of the new Reynard-Mercedes package. "It's very encouraging to have a successful first test. We did a lot of miles overall and had no problems whatsoever," Gugelmin reported after his sessions at Firebird and Sebring raceways. "The car was really reliable and I'm very optimistic because there's potentially a lot more to come. At least I know I have a car that I can use the brakes to attack the corners rather than a car that wants to attack me. One of the keys to our success in 1997 was getting the new car early and putting in a lot of miles to learn what it liked and didn't like. It's a tremendous advantage for us to be the first team out testing the '99 package. I'm very happy. I think we're in better shape than we were before 1997."

Blundell turned the fastest time in winter testing on the one-mile Phoenix oval. "We're back, and we're producing competitive lap times consistently," he said. "We went through a bunch of areas on the car, concentrating on where we went wrong last year, and I believe we have moved forward. I'm coming away very happy."

As usual, the season started at the Homestead-Miami Speedway oval, and the Mercedes engine looked more competitive as Homestead specialist Moore was victorious in his Forsythe Racing Reynard from pole position. Blundell finished eighth, two spots ahead of Gugelmin, who was a lap down. At Motegi, Japan, Mauricio qualified on the outside of the front row, and led 21 laps, but was a lapped seventh at the finish, while Blundell suffered his first DNF of the season. Road course pace hadn't improved much, however, as both cars ran in the midfield at Long Beach.

Blundell raised PacWest's hopes with a fifth-place qualifying run at Nazareth Speedway. Three days later, however, a mechanical failure caused Mark to crash while testing at

Gateway International Raceway. The injuries were less severe than those he sustained in his accident in Brazil in 1996—most significantly, a cracked vertebra—but the recovery was more difficult. Blundell was ultimately sidelined for three months.

"Before I knew it, it decided to drop itself into a lower gear and locked up and put me in backwards at 175 mph, I think," Blundell recalled. "It was a hard hit, and it was a transmission-related deal, the same thing that has happened to a few other guys. That was costly to me physically. I had some neck injuries and back injuries and so forth. I think the hardest thing for me to contend with is that mechanical problems caused both of the major accidents I've had—the one in '96 at Rio and my Gateway crash. My accident at Rio was probably bigger and scarier, but Gateway caused more problems."

To temporarily replace Blundell, PacWest called the driver who had affectionately become known as "Supersub"—Roberto Moreno. The epitome of a journeyman, Moreno bounced around between CART and Formula 1 throughout the 1980s and 1990s without ever latching onto a long-term home. But the 1999 season transformed his career. The happy-go-lucky Brazilian ultimately drove in eight races for PacWest, then finished out the season with Newman/Haas when an injury sidelined Christian Fittipaldi.

Moreno almost immediately lifted morale within PacWest by scoring a fourth-place finish in his first start for the team at Gateway International Raceway in late May. After starting 19th in the Motorola 300, the team quickly decided on an alternate pit strategy that allowed Moreno to lead 42 laps and put him in position to compete for a spot on the podium. "It was fantastic," Moreno said. "The Motorola PacWest team did a tremendous job because we came from nowhere to run up front. We took a couple of gambles that paid off, but here we are, happy as anything."

When the first yellow flew, John Anderson called Moreno in for a splash of fuel. After the rest of the field pitted for the first time on lap 36, the Motorola car led the Motorola 300. After the final round of pit stops, Moreno ran second to Michael Andretti, but he was passed by Helio Castroneves and Dario Franchitti in the closing laps. He was still very satisfied with the result.

"To get us from where we started this weekend on Thursday, to finish as competitive as we were, shows what a great job PacWest did," Moreno said. "In the past few years of my racing career, I've had to adapt to situations quickly and focus on solutions instead of worrying about problems. With another practice session, we could have run with the leaders."

Popular veteran Roberto Moreno was called on to replace Mark Blundell in mid-1999 when Blundell suffered a back injury while testing. Moreno quickly left his mark on the PacWest organization.

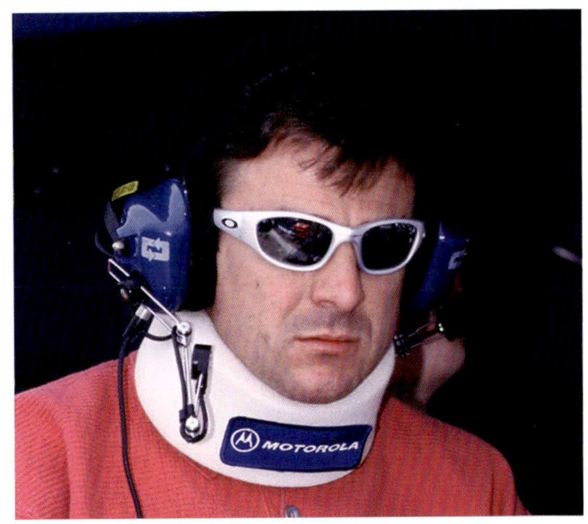

Mark Blundell continued to attend races while his injured back was healing, often wearing a Motorola-branded neck brace.

THE PACWEST SUMMIT

Steve Fusek and John Creak were hosted by the McLaren-Mercedes Formula 1 team at the 1997 Austrian Grand Prix. They were blown away by the quality of Formula 1 hospitality compared to what they were used to in the CART paddock.

Creak and Fusek tried to incorporate their experience into the PacWest Summit—a 53-foot Featherlite trailer outfitted as a leather-lined mobile office with two work rooms, two meeting rooms, 18 phone lines, computers, printers, and fax machines. Three overhanging awnings created a 4,000-square foot outdoor entertaining area with a seating capacity of 160. Chef Shane Azevedo prepared a breakfast and lunch buffet that provided guests (as well as PacWest crew members) many healthy options.

The Summit was visual proof of PacWest's ascension to the elite level among Indy car teams. "We wanted to develop a hospitality area for sponsors that had more of a permanent feel to it," Fusek said. "The Summit provides a very comfortable, restaurant-style environment that is the perfect place to develop business-to-business relationships. With the investments that our sponsors make in PacWest, we felt the need to raise our hospitality to a higher level. The Summit not only benefits PacWest and our sponsors, but also CART. It provides a fantastic opportunity to promote the FedEx Championship Series as a whole."

The Summit was not easy to set up or maintain; it took a crew of six at least a day and a half to get PacWest hospitality ready for guests at every race weekend and a similar amount of time to tear down. The manager initially in charge of The Summit was Laurence 'Laurie' Gerrish, a popular and experienced veteran mechanic who worked for the Brabham and Penske teams in F1 and Indy car.

"I find it interesting that for a while, hospitality in CART became a bigger operation than some race teams were only a few years ago," Gerrish observed. "Even in Formula 1, we used to work in sweatshirts and jeans. Now everything is made to measure. We have a trainer/nutritionist and more amenities than anyone can imagine. Most of the deals in racing happen in hospitality units, and racing became an industry, where it used to be a hobby or an interest.

"I found I really enjoyed the challenges that job presented—it's an interesting set of problems," he added. "Every race team and race car has a new set of problems. Instead of wishbones that crack on suspensions, you have wishbones that crack on chickens."

However, The Summit was symbolic of a schism between PacWest's rapidly growing marketing operations, headed by Fusek, and the racing side of the team, headed by John Anderson. The 'racers in the back of the building' felt that money being invested in things like The Summit—and the extra staff required to set it up and maintain it—would be better spent on developing the race cars.

"Unfortunately, the decisions made with the commercial side of the thing had nothing to do with me," Anderson said. "I was focused on what was going on inside the race team, and I think some of the decisions Steve made—like The Summit—we were trying to run before we could walk. Particularly with the expenditure for those things.

"We go down to Homestead and it takes three trucks, four dogs, and a bloody mule train to get everything associated up. It looked impressive when it was there, but you needed a cast of bloody thousands to put it up and tear it down. And the justification for that sort of deal, what we saw coming in the door with the decals on the cars, wasn't relating to what was being done outside."

Fusek believes Anderson's criticism of The Summit was not warranted. "The Summit was a total flyer, but it was built exactly on budget for $518,000," he noted. "That's still one of the cheapest motorhomes in the paddock. Yes, it was a pain in the ass to set up and we had some issues with it, but it certainly made an impact. Was it the right thing? I still don't know. I think we probably secured some sponsors. Invensys was a sponsor we got because of The Summit. They wanted to go to a professional team.

“It takes three trucks, four dogs, and a bloody mule train to get everything up.”

John Anderson

“My priority was to shift and put more emphasis into the commercial side because we needed to create dollars,” he added. “If we were investing in something, it was the commercial side, not the racing side. We worked a lot on the performance side and, frankly I think I was probably too complacent on the commercial side, thinking it was going to develop on its own. We had people previously who were incapable of getting it done.

“As much as The Summit looked like a big expenditure, it was cheaper than a new motorhome,” Fusek concluded. “The labor to maintain it was a factor, but most of the people involved in The Summit doing the work weren’t high paid people, so it was still cost effective and it got us a lot of attention. Was it perfect; did we get everything out of it? No. But it got us a new level of focus and was pretty cost effective. To try to create a profitable stand-alone company was my number one priority.”

With the benefit of hindsight, Russell Cameron backs up Fusek’s position. “When I look at some of the things that Steve was trying to create with marketing and hospitality and activation and some of the concepts to try to raise money, he had a hard job,” Cameron said. “I think if you look at The Summit and some of the things they were doing, Steve was trying to give the team a greater presence. It was just maybe a little too expensive in the way it was being done and they didn’t have as much return as they were hoping.”

With healthy food options and plenty of space to stretch out, The Summit was a popular hangout for PacWest guests.

Well-equipped work areas provided a productive environment for public relations and marketing team members.

At Michigan Speedway for his final race with PacWest, Moreno wore a new Bell helmet signed by every team member.

Andy Castleman

Crewmen from both of the team's cars share hugs of affection for Moreno who was well-loved by PacWest.

During the Gateway weekend, there was actually a substitute for the substitute driver in the No. 18 car. Prior to being hired by PacWest, Moreno had signed to compete in the Indianapolis 500, and he honored that commitment to Truscelli Racing. Roberto missed the first practice session at Gateway on Thursday due to Carburetion Day activities at Indy, so Gualter Salles was called in to shake down the Motorola car. Moreno ran as high as fifth at Indianapolis but was knocked out by a broken gearbox.

Blundell traveled to Road America in July believing he was ready to return to the cockpit, and his crew had even programmed the digital message center on the steering wheel of the No. 18 car to read "Welcome Back, Billy!" But shortly before the start of practice, he was advised to sit out another month by CART's orthopedic specialist Dr. Terry Trammell.

"It was kind of a tough deal because I got pumped up, then let down," Blundell told reporters. "The accident occurred as a result of a mechanical failure, something that could have happened to anybody. But you kind of start to feel a little down on yourself. It's frustrating, and frustration is something you can either get sucked down with, or you can rebel against it and move forward and take something from it. At this moment, I'm getting sucked down by it. I'm ready as far as I'm concerned, but it's not a case of me being in a race car for the next couple races, it's a case of looking at the next 50 years."

Moreno was on the road between Chicago and Road America when he got a call from John Anderson asking whether he could take Blundell's place for another three races. Supersub matched his fourth-place result from Gateway later in the summer at Toronto, and for his final PacWest race—the U.S. 500 at Michigan Speedway—he was presented with a helmet signed by all the team members. Moreno scored championship points in six of his eight starts for PacWest.

"Moreno left a big impact," McCaw said. "Of course, if anybody is experienced about subbing, it's him. He tried to fit in and make things work and do a good job. I thought he was very reasonable to work with and fun to be around. Roberto had some real strong moments and created some excitement. We had some disappointment that we didn't capture some opportunities, but he brought a spark to the team at a time when things weren't great and gave us something to look forward to."

Wearing a neck collar, Blundell attended as many races as he could during his enforced time out of the cockpit and did his best to assist and stay involved with the team and Motorola.

"The Moreno situation was acceptable," he said. "I'm old enough and big enough to understand that the team has to continue, and they needed someone else in the car. I don't think it matters who it would be, all of a sudden maybe there's a fresh approach or a fresh way of looking at things. You're no longer part and parcel of the everyday scenario and things may take a different slant. Don't get me wrong, I'm quite confident in my abilities, I'm quite confident in what I've achieved and what I can achieve, and what was achievable. That's only achievable when the whole package is working towards the same aim."

Though Moreno drove only a handful of races for PacWest, he recalls his brief stint with the team with fondness. Moreno's performance as a substitute for Blundell at PacWest and Fittipaldi at Newman/Haas Racing later in 1999 revitalized his career and helped him land a full-time ride in the CART series with Patrick Racing in 2000. He parlayed that into a pair of race wins and a career-best third place in the series standings.

"It's extremely difficult and very challenging because you always have to fit into a situation that is out there," said 'Supersub.' "It might not be ideal for you and might not be ideal for the team sometimes, but you just have to make it work. So you come in with that attitude and you get to know the engineers the best as you can; try to assimilate their needs and that is the way you fit in best. That is what I have been able to do. I must say that PacWest and Newman/Haas, they made my life very easy because they were ready for me. It was good, because after a couple of years out, [being with PacWest] took the rust out of me. I thought it was better for me to be around this scene and learn the racetracks, to get credibility, so I could get a ride with one of the top teams that had the budget. Unfortunately, I think people saw me as a back-of-the-grid runner, and I had a very hard time trying to get credibility in CART until I became "Supersub." But I can't complain about life at all. I'm just glad to achieve what came to me."

The U.S. 500 represented a milestone for PacWest as the team's 100th race in the CART series. A party was staged in the Michigan Speedway paddock at the PacWest Summit and Marketing Director John Creak created a commemorative T-shirt and poster with the theme "Time Flies."

"One hundred events is an important landmark in the continuing development of PacWest Racing Group, and it's particularly fitting that we celebrated this milestone at Michigan Speedway, where Dominic Dobson scored PacWest's first podium finish five years ago," McCaw remarked. "I'd like to thank all of the talented drivers and team members whose committed efforts made this event possible."

"[Moreno] brought a spark to the team at a time when things weren't great and gave us something to look forward to."

Bruce McCaw

PacWest organized a team photo to commemorate its 100th race in the CART series at Michigan in 1999.

Although they were not all with PacWest, Mauricio Gugelmin also celebrated a milestone at Michigan, having participated in one hundred consecutive CART races since Mid-Ohio 1993.

"One hundred races is a great achievement, but one hundred consecutive is even more significant," Gugelmin said. "Bruce McCaw started PacWest with the aim of winning races and championships, and he's done a remarkable job of developing a stable, highly-competitive team. He's not only very important to PacWest, but he is also an instrumental figure in the CART administration who plays a key role in the success of our series."

Blundell returned to action at the Detroit Grand Prix in August, just in time to debut a new paint scheme highlighting Motorola's Digital DNA branding. During practice for the Detroit race, Mauricio Gugelmin's car made contact with Patrick Carpentier's Forsythe Racing entry and made a complete rollover into a tire barrier; Big Mo was uninjured but his crew subsequently dubbed the car "Flipper."

Blundell matched his CART career best by qualifying second for the inaugural Target Grand Prix at Chicago Motor Speedway. But after falling through the field with an ill-handling race car, cooling system issues ended his day at two-thirds distance. During the Chicago weekend, PacWest announced contract extensions for Blundell and Motorola through the end of 2001. "We're very pleased to extend our relationship with a proven winner like Mark Blundell," stated McCaw. "Mark has been an excellent ambassador for Motorola and PacWest, and plays a major role in the continuing development of our organization."

The 1999 season certainly didn't live up to expectations within PacWest. There were 12 mechanical DNFs, including 7 for Gugelmin and the No. 17 car, though Mauricio's season did improve near the end with a fourth-place finish at Vancouver and sixths at Houston and Fontana. But PacWest and the other Mercedes-Benz runners were miles from the championship battle fought out between the Reynard-Hondas driven by Juan Pablo Montoya and Dario Franchitti.

The latter part of the 1999 CART season was marked by tragedy. First, rookie Gonzalo Rodriguez was killed in a freak accident at Laguna Seca Raceway. Observers at the scene of the accident speculated that the throttle in Rodriguez' Penske Racing Lola-Mercedes may have stuck open on the approach to The Corkscrew, a point where the drivers reach around 160 mph before braking hard over a brow for a tricky, blind left-hand turn. However, Ilmor Engineering Managing Director Paul Morgan said the throttle mechanism did not malfunction in Rodriguez' crash and the cause was never identified.

When Mark Blundell returned to action in the Detroit Grand Prix, the No. 18 car sported a new livery promoting Motorola's Digital DNA technology.

Blundell was delighted to get back in the car at Detroit.

Mauricio Gugelmin runs with Greg Moore in practice at California Speedway. Moore lost his life in a crash during the 1999 CART season finale.

Then, on the 10th lap of the season finale at California Speedway, Greg Moore crashed to his death as he attempted to aggressively race through the field after starting at the back. This was a stunning blow to the FedEx Championship Series. Just 24 years old, Moore was already one of CART's brightest stars, and would have undoubtedly only gotten better, having signed to drive for Penske Racing alongside Gil de Ferran for 2000 and beyond. That ride was subsequently claimed by Helio Castroneves in a series of events indirectly impacting PacWest (see Chapter 10).

At Road America, the PacWest cars carried a memorial to Bruce McCaw's friend Charles "Pete" Conrad, an Apollo 12 astronaut who was the third man to walk on the moon.

Moore's victory in the season opener was his last race win and the only triumph for the Mercedes engine in 1999. Yet, Ilmor's Paul Ray believes the E3 engine was an advance over its predecessor. "It improved enormously," Ray said. "We found lots of horsepower and we cured a big chunk of the reliability issues. It still wasn't as reliable as the 108D, but it got more and more powerful. As time went on, we did find many development areas that we could take advantage of. By that time, CART was changing the aero rules. They wanted wider bulkheads to protect the driver to a greater extent. So the advantages of the smaller engine were going away anyway. If you look at a '99 car, the engine is tiny, sat in a big hole. We really didn't get the advantages from it."

However, Ray conceded that all of the Ilmor/Mercedes cars failed to finish a satisfactory number of races. Carl Hogan's team, with Castroneves, suffered five engine failures during the Vancouver race weekend alone.

"The thing most apparent if you look back at Ilmor's history—or the history of any racing organization—is that reliability is the king," Ray said. "We all get tempted to push the envelope to get that last teeny tiny bit of performance, but sacrifice reliability in the process. It's the difference between a qualifying engine and a race engine. A team will always say, 'Let's race the qualifying engine!' because three or five extra horsepower is going to make all the difference in the world. Of course, the risk of failure is five times what it would be, but as racers, emotionally you will sacrifice it for the extra performance. That was the trap we were all in for '99."

Two weeks before the last race of the season, some external news broke that had a profound short- and long-term impact on PacWest Racing. Roger Penske, who co-founded Ilmor Engineering in 1983, revealed that his team would no longer use Ilmor's Mercedes-Benz branded engines in the CART series. Team Penske would instead switch to the dominant Honda powerplant, and replace its Penske chassis with the highly successful Reynard, to be enhanced by the capabilities of Penske Cars. Penske's team had not won a CART race since 1997, and coming from the company co-owner, the move to Honda wasn't exactly a ringing

Ilmor co-owner Roger Penske's late-1999 decision to switch from Mercedes-Benz to Honda engines would have huge implications for PacWest's direction.

Mauricio Gugelmin pauses for a photo op with actors (and spouses) Courteney Cox and David Arquette at California Speedway.

endorsement for the Ilmor CART program. In retrospect, much of the blame for Penske's problems could also be placed on Goodyear, which saw its tires win just six out of 56 races between 1997 and 1999.

"Obviously it was a difficult decision, but from an objective standpoint, one has to look at the future and look at the past," Penske remarked. "I had a long meeting with Paul Morgan about our results and what we needed to do to change the game. Quite honestly, when I look at my results over the last five years, we really haven't been able to meet the expectations of myself personally or as a team. Therefore, I felt a wholesale change was in order."

Penske did his best to put a positive spin on the situation from the Ilmor perspective. "Ilmor is in the business of selling engines to other teams," he said. "I certainly didn't have an exclusive arrangement, so they looked at our team as one of many. People think that we got some preferential treatment, but the answer to that is we couldn't sell engines to any other team if that was the case. In fact, I thought we brought quite a bit to the party from the standpoint of our transient dyno for durability testing."

Although he didn't announce it at the time, Penske had also already concluded a deal to race on Firestones in 2000; in November 1999, Goodyear revealed that it was pulling out of the CART series and the Indy Racing League altogether.

Penske-to-Honda wasn't the only major shake-up during the 1999-2000 offseason. Ilmor/Mercedes-Benz lost another strong team when Player's/Forsythe Racing made the switch to Ford-Cosworth power. At the same time, Toyota was showing signs of getting closer to victory lane, with Scott Pruett notching the Japanese manufacturer's first pole position at California Speedway. Toyota's intentions were made clear when it attracted four-time CART champion Chip Ganassi Racing into its ranks for 2000, reportedly with a large financial inducement. Ganassi also made a surprise late change from Reynard to Lola chassis.

Bruce McCaw obviously viewed Penske's abandonment of the Ilmor CART engine program as an area of concern. At the same time, he felt PacWest could benefit from the sudden opening at the top of the Mercedes depth chart. "One thing I learned early in this business is that it is very much a business of relationships," McCaw said. "You would ride up and down with some of your partners, but building strong relationships was still one of the fundamental keys to success in the business, whether it was chassis, tires, engines, sponsors… in all those things, the relationships were fundamentally critical to being successful.

"Obviously when Penske bailed out after '99 that was a concern," he continued. "Being a shareholder of Ilmor, at the time, he and Mercedes were having their feuds too. He told me personally that he still had confidence in Ilmor but that his sponsors had demanded that he go to Honda. It always left me wondering a bit because Roger usually doesn't succumb to anybody—he usually sets the demands himself.

"We looked at the fact that there was a real opportunity with Roger leaving to become the Number One Mercedes-Benz team," concluded McCaw. "I felt that was a huge opportunity, even though we still had concerns about the program and about the engine itself. That was an opportunity one looked at and said, 'This could be a great opportunity with one of the great names, if not the greatest name, in motorsports and the automobile world.' Those opportunities don't come often."

Mauricio Gugelmin prepares for a practice run. The PacWest veteran ended the 1999 season with three top-six finishes in the final five races.

Now sponsored by growing communications firm Nextel, Mauricio Gugelmin's car sported a new look for the 2000 season.

10

MERCEDES' SUDDEN EXIT

ROGER PENSKE'S DECISION to abandon the Ilmor/Mercedes-Benz engine program in late 1999 in favor of running customer Honda engines had a major impact on PacWest Racing. On the one hand, PacWest was now in position to become the flagship team in the CART FedEx Championship Series for one of the most prominent and prestigious automotive brands in the world; conversely, Penske's clear lack of confidence in a program in which he had an ownership stake was an ominous warning signal.

After two unsuccessful years with the extremely light and compact Mercedes IC108E engine, Ilmor was forced to admit defeat. The IC108F motor the company produced for the 2000 season was a somewhat more conservative package.

"It was a more conventional design; it was a little tiny bit bigger, but not much, and it was pretty much the same weight as the 'E' engine," commented Ilmor's Paul Ray. "We did a lot to keep the engines as light as possible. That was driven by Reynard as much as anything. They desperately wanted us to have the lightest engine. They could prove, as could Penske through their analysis, that taking weight out of the center of the car allowed you to move it fore and aft for an advantage at different tracks. But the 'F' engine was also late and not as reliable as it should have been early on."

The biggest change in Reynard's 2000 chassis, dubbed 2KI, was a brand-new gearbox to replace the design used since 1997. Indy Lights driver Tony Renna ran the initial shakedown test of PacWest's first 2KI at Putnam Park outside of Indianapolis. Then, Mauricio Gugelmin and Mark Blundell got down to the business of preparing for the 2000 CART championship. The team sometimes utilized Indy Lights drivers Renna and Didier Andre for the gearbox testing so they could gain seat time in an Indy car. PacWest played a key role in the development of the new gearbox during the second half of 1999, racking up 1,200 test miles.

Gugelmin's car sported a new look for the season to promote a new sponsor: Nextel Communications. Nextel, although a relatively recent arrival in the rapidly expanding American cell phone market, already boasted a significant international presence, particularly in Mexico and South America. Nextel logos were carried on the PacWest cars at

"Fireman" Mauricio Gugelmin prepares to unveil his 2000 car.

Michael Levitt/LAT USA

Mark Blundell's 2000 season started with a crash in qualifying at Homestead and never really improved.

selected races starting in 1997, but now the world's leading provider of all-digital wireless services stepped up to the level of title sponsorship.

Nextel was expanding into the US consumer market after providing products only to business clients. The key feature differentiating Nextel's service from other wireless phone companies was a unique 'push to talk' function, similar to a walkie-talkie—but with a range of thousands of miles.

In addition, almost all Nextel phones were produced by Motorola, creating a natural business-to-business relationship that PacWest could build upon. Motorola developed the iDEN (integrated digital enhanced network) technology behind Nextel's digital phones and participated in the manufacturing process.

"Clearly Nextel made a lot of sense," noted Bruce McCaw. "We previously did certain things with Motorola through Nextel of South America. Motorola was virtually their sole supplier, and there was a lot of synergy and great friendships there; Keith Bane, who was instrumental in helping us get Motorola in the first place, was on the Nextel board and we all thought this was a pretty sensible thing to do. It gave us two sponsors that had a lot of business together and a lot of promotional opportunities. I was very excited about it."

Hollywood, a PacWest partner since 1995, would still be indirectly involved with the team. McCaw orchestrated a transfer of that sponsorship to Mo Nunn Racing to bolster the rapidly dwindling Mercedes-Benz ranks. Tony Kanaan was hired to drive the Nunn car, satisfying Hollywood's desire for a young Brazilian driver.

Meanwhile, the PacWest/Nextel car, along with a re-liveried Motorola car for Blundell, was unveiled at an elaborate reception in February 2000 at the Firehouse Four nightclub in Miami. Before some 200 guests, a pair of large crates labelled "PacWest Racing" began emitting dry ice 'smoke' in front of the venue. On cue, a Miami fire engine arrived on the scene and a fleet of first responders began investigating the smoldering crates. Two of the 'firemen' turned out to be Gugelmin and Blundell, who pulled the wraps off their newly-liveried machines.

"This new arrangement takes our partnership with Nextel to a whole new level," McCaw stated at the launch. "We will be doing everything to be a leader out on the track this season. We have had success in the past and intend to taste the winner's champagne again this year."

The international nature of the CART series made it an attractive marketing platform for

Nextel which offered service in four of the five countries the FedEx Championship Series raced: USA, Canada, Japan, and Brazil.

"On behalf of our more than 4 million customers and 13,000 employees, I would like to thank Bruce McCaw for welcoming Nextel officially into the PacWest family and the exciting sport of Champ Car racing," stated Ben Banta, Nextel's vice president of corporate communications. "Nextel has enjoyed phenomenal success by focusing its unique wireless service offering solely to the business community. We are encouraged by the marketing synergy that this sport brings to our business. We see this sponsorship as a great opportunity to strengthen our existing customer relations while also providing a high-class sports venue to showcase our technology, draw attention to our company, and attract new customers."

Brett "Crusher" Murray gets quotes from Mark Blundell.

The high-profile, "Fire & Ice" themed launch was one of the first initiatives put together by PacWest's new communications director. Brett "Crusher" Murray was an Australian who had masterminded the promotional effort for the highly successful CART race in Surfers Paradise. Crusher's efforts earned PacWest a staggering amount of publicity in 2000, even though the team continued to struggle to run at the front of the field.

During the Nazareth snow-out, Mark Blundell and Mauricio Gugelmin tossed snowballs for photographers.

"I was approached by Steve Fusek and John Anderson after the success of the Australian race to come work with the team and it was a great opportunity," Murray remarked. "It had always been a dream of mine to come over to the States and work in big-time motor racing on the big stage. I'd had opportunities before, but they didn't involve my wife Trudi. This time Trudi was able to come over and she worked in hospitality for the team. We had a fantastic year."

Unfortunately, the Mercedes-Benz engine again failed to live up to expectations and, accordingly, PacWest suffered through another dismal season in terms of results. Blundell raised hopes by charging through the field to finish eighth at Long Beach and seventh at Brazil. Gugelmin lined up seventh at Motegi, Japan, and scored his best result since 1997, taking second place at Nazareth Speedway in late May. Originally scheduled for April 23, the race was postponed several weeks due to snow.

Halfway through the 2000 campaign, Gugelmin offered his assessment. "Things are improving; they're better than last year," he said. "But it still is a bit disappointing. We had one good show at Nazareth. We tend to have some highs and lows and, I think as a team, we are a lot more aware of what the problems are. We're working really closely with Mercedes, and they are improving. But we still need to work harder because it's a moving target. Everyone else is getting better too.

KEEPING MERCEDES-BENZ ON THE GRID

With Team Penske and Forsythe Racing changing engine suppliers for 2000, and the demise of Carl Hogan's team, Bruce McCaw's focus shifted to making sure that PacWest Racing was not the only Mercedes-Benz powered team on the CART series grid.

"I had enough fears about what Mercedes and Ilmor were likely to do that I became very concerned that the program was losing critical mass," McCaw recalled. "If we didn't have enough cars running, we simply wouldn't have a broad enough baseline. Further, frankly, I wanted another credible team so that if the engine failed, PacWest didn't get blamed for it. Not that I was looking for failure to occur; I could just see enough handwriting on the wall that if it didn't work, we needed to protect ourselves or it was going to wipe us out.

"I think our conduct through the entire process is well documented," he added. "We tried very hard to do the right thing for Mercedes to help them be successful in CART, both on and off the track. We used The Summit heavily to help support their brand and their image, we worked closely with their corporate people and we tried very hard to be a good partner. And we were obviously committed to winning."

By the time CART raced at Vancouver in September 1999, McCaw was fairly certain that Penske was leaving the Mercedes fold. McCaw had already been approached by Domingos Piedade of AMG, the German tuning firm closely associated with, and later owned by, Mercedes-Benz. Piedade had expressed interest in putting together a Mercedes-powered CART program for a German driver with sponsorship from Warsteiner beer. "They recognized that the learning curve would be too steep to do it on their own and, because of our relationship, they asked if we could basically give them a turn-key racing team," McCaw said.

Ilmor co-founder Paul Morgan suggested renowned engineer and former driver Morris Nunn as a potential partner. Nunn had previously owned the Ensign Formula 1 team in the 1970s before moving to America in the mid-1980s to work as an engineer for various Indy car teams. In 1993, he joined Chip Ganassi Racing and was generally credited for getting the most out of the Reynard/Honda/Firestone combination the Ganassi team adopted. The combination resulted in four consecutive CART championships from 1996 to 1999. Even more impressive, the last three of those championships were won by Alex Zanardi and Juan Pablo Montoya, drivers who previously had zero oval racing experience. Nunn, age 61, had been dropping hints about retirement for several years. But the prospect of having an ownership stake in a new team convinced him to remain active in the sport.

AMG eventually dropped out of the picture, but after a series of meetings in the late summer, a plan to form Mo Nunn Racing was nearly finalized. Bruce McCaw would be a partner in the new team; he offered Nunn use of the old PacWest shop at 150 Gasoline Alley and arranged for Hollywood cigarettes to transfer their sponsorship from PacWest to the new effort. The driver would be Helio Castroneves, who found himself looking for a ride for 2000 when Hogan announced he was shutting down his team.

Hollywood's level of support had grown significantly since it joined forces with PacWest in 1995. Hollywood paid PacWest $1.66 million plus bonuses in 1995 and 1996, but by 1999, the base figure grew to $5.25 million. "Hollywood was shopping around," McCaw said. "We had a superb relationship with Hollywood, but they wanted a different driver and I wasn't prepared to replace Mauricio at the time. I was pretty up front; I said, 'I know what you need, but I don't have a place to run what you need.' We didn't feel like we could take a third car in-house [at PacWest] at the time. Of course, Castroneves was perfect, so I went to Hollywood and said, 'We're going to start a team, I'm going to be a shareholder, and we want to put Castroneves in there. It's a perfect fit.'"

The plan suffered a tragic setback when Greg Moore was killed in the 1999 CART finale at California Speedway. Moore had signed a contract to drive for Penske Racing in 2000. Literally within hours of Moore's death, Roger Penske moved quickly to sign Castroneves, much to the chagrin of McCaw and Nunn.

"We tried very hard to do the right thing for Mercedes to help them be successful in CART...we used The Summit heavily to help support their brand and their image, and we tried very hard to be a good partner."

Bruce McCaw

The haste with which Penske acted was exposed a decade later when Castroneves was indicted on federal tax evasion charges and it emerged that attorneys, including the driver's agent and lawyer, Alan Miller, did little more than substitute the Brazilian's name for Moore's in a nearly identical contract. After a six-week trial and six days of jury deliberation, a federal jury acquitted Castroneves in April 2009 on six counts of tax

Souza Cruz President Flavio de Andrade (left) pushed hard to have Felipe Giaffone (right) drive the Mo Nunn Racing entry, but PacWest believed he was too inexperienced and Tony Kanaan got the nod.

Indianapolis Motor Speedway

Mo Nunn continually ignored the business and technical partnership agreements between Mo Nunn Racing and PacWest Racing. Ultimately, his move to Honda blocked PacWest and brought the relationship to an end.

evasion, but was hung on one count of conspiracy. The jury acquitted his sister, Katiucia Castroneves, on the tax evasion counts, but also hung on the conspiracy charge. Miller was acquitted on all three counts of tax evasion and one count of conspiracy.

"Mercedes actually held Castroneves' contract at Hogan's," McCaw commented. "But Mercedes just didn't have the nerve to stand up and tell Penske he couldn't do it. They had already forgiven a bunch of debt to Hogan in the assignment of the contract, and now here's a shareholder who goes out and goes around them. That was a bad deal and it left us at a critical time without a driver for the Nunn effort."

With Hollywood as the sponsor, a young and dynamic Brazilian driver was a necessary part of the equation. Now Castroneves, the number one choice, was no longer available. "Hollywood urged us to consider Felipe Giaffone, who they were sponsoring in Indy Lights," McCaw said. "We really liked Felipe and had a good relationship with him, but he simply did not have the level of experience to succeed in what was both a start-up and developmental program. Mo Nunn and I both agreed that would be a mistake. We finally got Tony Kanaan, who I think was a good selection and a guy who went on to accomplish a lot." Kanaan had a contract with Gerald Forsythe for 2000, which Souza Cruz reportedly bought out for $2 million.

Despite a renowned engineer and a talented young driver, Mo Nunn Racing failed to achieve success in 2000, suffering many of the same engine-related problems as PacWest. While that was certainly not what McCaw was hoping for, MNR's struggles validated PacWest's belief that the Mercedes engine was dragging the team down.

"Bruce's insight to help Mo Nunn get into business was really quite a wise decision to make sure there was another top-level team in the Mercedes camp with us," said Russell Cameron. "It wasn't inexpensive for him to pull that off and it was obviously good for the series to have another good team around. But Bruce did that as a level of protection to make sure that PacWest didn't get the finger pointed at them.

"That was a bad deal and it left us at a critical time without a driver for the Nunn effort."

Bruce McCaw

"We were all working harder than most people realized, with a wind tunnel program," he added. "Mercedes, and Paul Ray in particular, were really critical about our aero program. He felt like our aero program was what was causing our lack of performance, not really the engine. I just think that was wrong. Paul said this to divert attention from the engine problems. Mo Nunn wanted to use the development parts we were producing because he knew they worked. That was a very big endorsement for our aero program."

The Nunn-PacWest relationship ended in acrimony. In the immediate fallout of Mercedes' hasty and unexpected withdrawal from the CART series in September 2000, Nunn quickly aligned himself with Honda. He essentially ignored the three-year Technical Assistance Agreement contract between his team and PacWest, and the move blocked PacWest's chances of obtaining a supply of Honda engines. McCaw firmly believed Nunn used him as a source of seed money to start his own team. Two years later, he instigated legal proceedings that were eventually mediated by former CART CEO Andrew Craig. Represented by Alan Miller, Nunn was ordered to pay McCaw an undisclosed settlement. "Alan's advice cost Mo a great deal of time, money, and anguish," McCaw said.

Bruce McCaw helped form Mo Nunn Racing to strengthen the Mercedes ranks in 2000.

A crewman is ready with a fire extinguisher as Mauricio Gugelmin pulls out of the 2000 Rio 400.

"Mercedes hired one of the best guys in the business, Mo Nunn, and set him up with a team," Gugelmin continued. "I was glad they did that, because it was a good reference. When I look at it, it shows that we haven't been too far off for the last couple of years. It's good to have someone like Mo, because he has a lot of knowledge, and he's facing the same problems. I think we're on the right track, and we're really working hard to make those changes. I think races like Nazareth are going to happen more often this year, and maybe I can improve one place from what I did there. But it's not going to be without a bit of luck—we need to be creative."

A development engine helped Mauricio qualify third for the Grand Prix of Cleveland, but he could only manage 10th place in the race. A pair of seventh-place finishes were his best results in the second half of the season. Blundell, meanwhile, never finished better than 11th after his early season top-eight runs, and the PacWest drivers wound up a distant 17th (Gugelmin) and 21st (Blundell) in the final championship standings.

"I think there were some areas of concern with the engine," said Blundell. "It was definitely getting more powerful, but we were struggling with some reliability issues. And those reliability issues continued throughout the whole season, even until the last race at Fontana. I remember quite clearly taking the lead at the 500 and, within that lap, the engine blowing up. That kind of summed up the whole thing. There were so many other possibilities and directions that could have been looked at and were open, but things never quite went down those avenues. I think it was getting to a stage where serious reviews needed to take place within the organization, and with the partners, and it was something that needed to be addressed."

Reliability was still a major problem for both the No. 17 and No. 18 cars, as each managed to make it to the checkered flag only nine times in 20 races. By contrast, the top four championship contenders were all running at the finish 14 or more times. In an engine analysis memo written in August, John Anderson observed:

"The 'F' engine started life far too late to be a viable powerplant for 2000. From a race team's perspective, we are six months behind the curve. The problems we are having currently are problems we should have had in preseason testing, maybe carrying into the first few races as the manufacturer strives for reliability and drivability, not two-thirds of the way through the season. Our fuel mileage is abysmal, and we are forced to test new fuel mapping strategies during a race weekend as test days have already been used."

"I think there were some areas of concern with the engine. It was definitely getting more powerful, but we were struggling with some reliability issues."

Mark Blundell

Mark Blundell and Mauricio Gugelmin join the other Mercedes-Benz powered drivers for a photo op. The Mercedes ranks thinned considerably in 2000.

The magnitude of the difficulty Ilmor and Mercedes were facing to be competitive in the CART series can be measured by the struggles that Mo Nunn Racing endured during the 2000 season. After guiding Alex Zanardi and Juan Pablo Montoya to a combined 19 race wins and three consecutive championships from 1997-99 with Ganassi Racing, Nunn was celebrated as the best engineer in the CART series. Kanaan, the 1998 CART Rookie of the Year and winner of the 1999 U.S. 500, was one of the most promising young drivers in American open-wheel racing at the time. Yet he finished 19th in the 2000 standings with little more to show than a trio of eighth-place finishes. The Nunn team's problems were compounded when TK crashed during qualifying in Detroit, breaking his left arm and fracturing two ribs; Bryan Herta substituted for three races.

Kanaan would go on to establish himself as an enduring Indy car star, winning the 2004 IRL championship and the 2013 Indianapolis 500. But he holds little pleasure in looking back on his 2000 CART campaign with Mercedes-Benz power. TK finished only nine of the 16 races he started that year, and the Bettenhausen and Arciero Project teams suffered similarly poor reliability with their Mercedes powerplants.

"That was something that looked good on paper that didn't translate to real life," said Kanaan. "We had all the tools to work with, including plenty of information from PacWest. But the engine was uncompetitive and unreliable, and that's a bad combination. I missed a few races after I crashed in the middle of the year and we never put together any consistency."

Meanwhile, now utilizing Honda engines, Firestone tires, and its own highly developed version of the Reynard chassis, Penske Racing won a total of five races. Gil de Ferran ended the season as the 2000 CART champion, and Castroneves claimed three wins for Penske and emerged as a bright new star.

In Formula 1, after winning two consecutive championships with the McLaren team, Ilmor and Mercedes-Benz now found themselves struggling to keep up with Ferrari, as Michael Schumacher won the first of what would turn out to be five consecutive F1 world titles. Mercedes and Ilmor had increased their resource outlay to the F1 program in an effort to counter Ferrari's surge.

Ilmor USA's Paul Ray refused to concede that the Mercedes-Benz CART program was being compromised by the F1 effort. "No, they were totally separate and run by completely different groups of people and engineers," Ray said. "I can't say there was never an occasion where Formula 1 got more of its share and Indy car got less, but there were equally other occasions where we were stealing all the manufacturing resources and Formula 1 was beating the door down to try to get us out of the way so they could get their share.

"If anything, the error made was not recognizing that Formula 1 and Indy cars are totally different racing styles," he continued. "In Indy cars, you have to have a very strong engine that is completely reliable because you are dealing with a bunch of different teams, none of which are what I would call professional manufacturers. They don't make cars and they have very limited design capabilities and engineering. We probably had 10 times as many engineers as PacWest, maybe more than that.

"So, what you have to do in Indy cars is supply a package that is complete and finished so a team can put it in and somewhat abuse it," Ray concluded. "The mistake we probably made at the time was to build this high-tech beast that we put in an Indy car environment where it wasn't properly looked after. Any time you drift away from that you put yourself in peril of having more problems than you can deal with, having a limited number of people at the racetrack."

Perhaps not surprisingly, Ray also tried to deflect responsibility for the Mercedes brand's poor performance to anything but the engine itself. While placing the brunt of the blame for the lack of performance on the teams, particularly PacWest, Mercedes also conveyed its belief that PacWest's drivers, who were now both in their mid-thirties, bore their share of responsibility for the decline of the team's competitive level since 1997.

"Candidly, I think Mark and Mauricio were both demotivated by then and had perhaps lost some of the drive that they had," Ray commented. "None of us were squeaky clean when it came to reasons we weren't performing. But Mercedes was paying some sponsorship to PacWest, so we felt we had some ability to speak freely about team issues and performance issues that were occurring. Those conversations can be extremely difficult, particularly when there are people involved who are quite vocal. It's hard telling someone that you don't think their driver is going to work or that he's not doing the best job he could.

"The other side of that is when they think your engine is terrible after you just worked 72 hours straight just to make sure the engine gets to the racetrack. But you have to have those conversations when you are spending tens of millions of dollars trying to achieve things."

Russell Cameron believes it is impossible to accurately determine how much the declining engine program had on the fate of PacWest Racing. But he also has no doubt the team worked as hard it possibly could to regain winning form.

Michael Levitt/LAT USA

Hollywood also supported the Arciero Project car driven by Luis Garcia Jr.

Michael Levitt/LAT USA

Mark Blundell and Helio Castroneves were involved in a heavy crash in the delayed Nazareth race.

Mauricio Gugelmin receives the message that he is leading the 2000 Marlboro 500 at California Speedway.

Mark Blundell attacks a street course late in the 2000 season.

"I think that three-year span of running the Mercedes engine when it was a dead duck just kind of wore on everybody," Cameron recalled. "It was very difficult. The one thing I think all of us learned through it was how deep Bruce's loyalty runs in any relationship or agreement. He doesn't pull the plug on anything or anybody without giving it the right amount of effort. The information he was getting was telling him that there would be enough information or crossover from Formula 1 to help the Indy car program along, and he believed it.

"Obviously Bruce has got a lot of time for the Mercedes product and their history in motor racing," he added. "Business-wise, I think he's worldly enough to have realized the Germans will pull the rug out from under you as quickly as if they were Korean, Japanese, or Brazilian if the business side of the thing wasn't working. So, I was a little surprised that he wanted to hang on so long when the writing was on the wall a lot earlier than the announcement."

In retrospect, it came as no surprise in September 2000 when Mercedes-Benz confirmed its withdrawal from the CART series effective at the end of the season. But at the same time, PacWest's four-year relationship with Motorola was rapidly unraveling. Motorola was increasingly disenchanted with PacWest's lack of results and began putting pressure on McCaw to change engine suppliers. The ideal scenario from Motorola's perspective would have been for PacWest to switch to Honda power, because Motorola was a key electronics supplier for Honda's range of road cars built in the United States. But PacWest was locked into additional years in its contract with Mercedes-Benz.

Motorola, like Mercedes, was also keen to see PacWest make a driver change and was particularly enamored with Michael Andretti, then in the twilight of his long and successful Indy car racing career. In August 2000, despite McCaw's pleas for patience, Motorola exercised its option to decline an extension into 2002 of its sponsorship with PacWest. "Clearly the present level of performance is not acceptable to anyone," he wrote in a response to Motorola's Keith Bane. "We are committed to returning to a level of podium finishes. Given the well-known engine difficulties we have encountered, I think the team has continued to perform well and I am confident that renewed success is close at hand."

But McCaw was unable to persuade Motorola that the team would be able to reverse the three-year slide and, after a few weeks of intense negotiation, Motorola and PacWest reached a settlement to terminate the sponsorship contract one year early. Motorola took its support to Team Green, a Honda team that expanded to three cars to accommodate Andretti for the 2001 season. Andretti subsequently bought out Barry Green's majority ownership stake in the team in late 2002, and with Honda's support, the renamed Andretti Green Racing switched camps to the IRL for the 2003 season.

Bane made Motorola's split with PacWest official on September 8, 2000, in a letter to Bruce McCaw. "Despite the positive relationships we have developed, the performance of the PacWest Racing Team and the Motorola car have been unacceptable," Bane wrote. "This decision was not easy given the long-term relationship we have developed with PacWest Racing. Unfortunately, the team's continued inability to perform overshadowed such relationship and, accordingly, it was in the best interest of Motorola to exercise its option...to terminate this agreement."

Although Motorola was responsible for directly injecting more money into PacWest than Mercedes-Benz was, McCaw believes Motorola's departure as a sponsor was less critical to the team's well-being than the sudden and unexpected withdrawal of its engine supplier.

"Motorola came to me to buy themselves out of their contract so they could go to Team Green," he said. "We had another year on that contract, and they didn't have a legitimate exit and they knew it, but we had enough of a relationship where it didn't behoove either of us to go to court over it. So we negotiated a settlement. We tried to exit that as cleanly as we could, and tried to move forward the best we could, building on what we had with Nextel. We had already moved Hollywood over to Nunn's, so it was a big transition. Clearly making big changes like that all at once is not easy, and that's where we scrambled hard to go forward."

In the space of a few weeks, with little or no warning, PacWest learned its business relationships with two key commercial partners were coming to an end much earlier than anticipated. Yet those weren't the only major changes occurring within the PacWest organization—or within all of Championship Auto Racing Teams—in what had turned into a very troubled and turbulent period for American open-wheel racing.

Despite a lack of recent results, Mauricio Gugelmin claimed the September 2000 cover of *Championship Racing Magazine.*

MERCEDES PULLS THE PLUG ON CART

In May 2000, for the first time in the five years since the start of the CART/Indy Racing League war, one of the top CART teams broke ranks and entered the Indianapolis 500 with Juan Pablo Montoya scoring an easy victory for Chip Ganassi Racing. Shortly after that, Norbert Haug, the sporting director for Mercedes-Benz, made some extremely critical public comments about the CART series, a series locked in a political battle with the IRL for control of top-level American open-wheel racing.

In the summer of 2000, rumors began surfacing that Mercedes-Benz was contemplating an immediate withdrawal from the CART series. It had been nearly two years since the company's last race win in the FedEx Championship Series in the 1999 season opener. Ilmor Engineering was devoting a rapidly increasing amount of resources toward keeping up with Ferrari in a battle for supremacy in Formula 1.

Bruce McCaw recognized Mercedes was considering an immediate withdrawal from American racing and took steps to protect PacWest's position. "I had a meeting with Paul Morgan and Paul Ray after Norbert's comments in July 2000," McCaw recalled. "We were very emphatic—we had another two years with Mercedes, as contracted. In the meantime, I had written a couple of letters to Norbert, trying to be constructive. I had also sent a pretty strong letter to Professor [Jurgen] Hubbert, who was the president of Mercedes at the time under Jurgen Schrempp. It was positive, but it was strong, about what we needed to do.

"He had really chewed us out the year before, along with a couple of others, at Stars & Cars about our performance. It was embarrassing to be slightly lambasted in front of 3,000 people and being told the performance was not acceptable. Well, it wasn't acceptable to me either! Having gone from being the shining stars to taking a fair amount of heat on the stage of this event in the space of a couple of years was difficult. It was not quite the same as the year I carried the Engine Manufacturer's Trophy over to present to him. Our contributions to them receiving that award were substantial."

At a board meeting in New York on September 6th, DaimlerChrysler voted to end Mercedes-Benz' involvement in the CART series at the conclusion of the 2000 season. Three days later at the CART race weekend at Laguna Seca Raceway—and one day after PacWest received official confirmation that Motorola was terminating its sponsorship contract with the team a year early—Mercedes officials distributed a two-page press release confirming the withdrawal.

"We have had to re-evaluate our motorsport strategy from 2001 onwards in order to meet higher targets in the Formula One World Championship, where eight manufacturers will be competing beginning in 2002," stated Hubbert, the DaimlerChrysler board member responsible for Mercedes-Benz cars and motorsport activities. "We are also very keen to further develop the DTM Touring Car Series, especially in Germany. In order to concentrate our efforts on these two series we have to stop our CART program.

"We had a good time in CART," Hubbert's statement concluded. "We experienced highs in winning the 1994 Indianapolis 500 and the 1997 CART Manufacturer's Championship. Mercedes-Benz expresses its gratitude to its teams and wishes them all the best for the future."

The withdrawal had a huge impact on many fronts. Obviously, the most seriously affected parties were the Mercedes-powered teams: PacWest Racing, Mo Nunn Racing, and Arciero Project Racing. Apart from that, Ilmor USA, which the Mercedes teams were contracted to for engine supply and service, was left wondering about its future.

"We got to Laguna Seca, the announcement was made, and it was clearly quite a shock," said McCaw. "I really never thought they would exit the way that they did and as abruptly. Clearly, Ilmor was every bit as surprised as I was. It had come down from on high and perhaps could have been generated by my letter. That may have actually sparked the fuel. I've always wondered about that. But everything in my letter spoke about what we needed to do to make it work, not threatening to leave or anything like that.

"We have had to re-evaluate our motorsport strategy from 2001 onwards in order to meet higher targets in the Formula One World Championship, where eight manufacturers will be competing beginning in 2002."

Jurgen Hubbert

"From a psychological standpoint I would have to say there were a lot of people who were relieved," McCaw added. "They thought 'enough is enough,' and now we'll get a better engine. But from a business standpoint, I think it hurt us because we had built a lot on the relationship with Mercedes-Benz. That was a big blow, because it was a bit late in the year."

Mercedes-Benz executives Jurgen Hubbert and Norbert Haug in conversation with engine designer Mario Illien. Mercedes' withdrawal from CART stunned the series (left to right).

Paul Ray confirmed that Ilmor USA was given no indication that Mercedes was prepared to make such a radical move. "It wasn't until after the [DaimlerChrysler] board met that we got the word," he said. "Within hours we had to tell our teams because it would leak out into the media anyway; the Germans are notoriously bad at keeping secrets. Paul Morgan and I found out at pretty much the same time that Mercedes had decided that they wanted out at the end of the year. So, we had to unravel it all and it was a very difficult conversation with Bruce, naturally."

Of all the involved constituents, PacWest had the most to lose from the Mercedes withdrawal. At the time, McCaw estimated the lack of Mercedes engines and sponsorship support would cost the team in excess of $11.5 million toward its future budget, leaving the team in an extremely vulnerable position heading into 2001. Two weeks after the Mercedes announcement, McCaw met with Hubbert at the United States Grand Prix at the Indianapolis Motor Speedway in an attempt to get the decision reversed. He continued to state his case through the end of the year.

"The problem is simply that Mercedes-Benz has cancelled its commitment to PacWest and Ilmor when we still have one year remaining in our contract," he wrote in a December 28, 2000, letter to Norbert Haug. "Both this, as well as a terrible lack of engine performance and reliability, has caused great harm to PacWest...Unfortunately, most if not all of this loss could have been mitigated by simply giving us reasonable and adequate notice of Mercedes-Benz' desire to withdraw. Notice in June or even July would have made a world of difference, but we continued to receive assurance 2001 was fully committed. PacWest was constrained by its contractual commitment to Mercedes and Ilmor. We lost an important sponsor in Motorola due to our unwillingness to change engine supplier, as well as missing opportunities for competitive, no-cost engine supply."

Mercedes-Benz' focus and investment in Formula 1 paid off in the long run. Daimler AG increased its share in Ilmor Engineering to 55 percent in 2002 and, three years later, Daimler took over full ownership of the company. Now known as Mercedes AMG High Performance Powertrains, it's still based in the original Ilmor facilities in Brixton, England. Mercedes AMG became a full-fledged works F1 team in 2010, taking over the team started by Reynard as British American Racing in 1999 (known at various times as Honda and Brawn F1).

Mercedes AMG struggled for results in its first few years despite employing seven-time World Champion Michael Schumacher as lead driver, but the 'Silver Arrows' dominated F1 after new turbocharged V-6 engines with hybrid energy recovery systems were mandated. The team won six consecutive championships from 2014 to 2019.

"Unfortunately, most if not all of this loss could have been mitigated by simply giving us reasonable and adequate notice of Mercedes-Benz' desire to withdraw."

Bruce McCaw

Gugelmin and Blundell run together at 220 mph.

PacWest Racing's longest-running and most-successful driver pairing, Mauricio Gugelmin and Mark Blundell, were teammates from 1996 to 2000.

11

MAJOR CHANGES

DURING THEIR NEGOTIATIONS throughout the summer of 2000, Motorola executives made clear to Bruce McCaw that a change of engine suppliers was a prerequisite for the electronics giant to continue its sponsorship of PacWest Racing. Motorola also believed the time was right to make a driver change. Although Mark Blundell's contract still had a year remaining, McCaw and the PacWest management team independently reached the same conclusion. At the same Laguna Seca weekend where the Mercedes-Benz withdrawal was revealed, PacWest announced that it had bought out the final year of Blundell's contract.

"We understand it has been a frustrating couple of seasons for Mark and we have decided it would be in his best interests if he became a free agent at this stage," read McCaw's statement. "Mark is an extremely talented driver and it is unfortunate he has been unable to demonstrate his true ability recently. Mark is a professional on and off the track and I fully expect to see him in a Champ Car next season."

"I would like to thank Bruce McCaw, the PacWest team, and Motorola for their support during the last five seasons," said Blundell. "Special mention has to be made of my Motorola crew this year which has again worked tirelessly in what has been an enormously frustrating season."

McCaw was generally satisfied with Blundell's on-track performance over his five-year PacWest career and he will always treasure the race wins they achieved together. "Mark was a good racer," he observed. "Once the flag dropped, he really got all the BS behind him and he would just concentrate on passing whoever was in front of him. I think that was where his real skills were, just that aggression. He had to always be in front of the car ahead of him and he would do pretty much everything he could do to do that. He was very capable."

PacWest went to great lengths to create more harmony within Blundell's No. 18 Motorola team and hopefully achieve better results. Major changes were made during 1999 and 2000. Most notably, John Anderson and Russell Cameron swapped car strategy roles during races, with Cameron taking over Blundell's No. 18 car while Anderson moved to

Mark Blundell and Bruce McCaw share a laugh on a rainy day at Twin Ring Motegi in Japan. Their business relationship would deteriorate by the end of 2000.

John Anderson and Mauricio Gugelmin lifted PacWest's spirits in difficult times with their strong leadership.

Gugelmin and the No. 17 team. Although the results didn't show it, Cameron believed that Blundell was still capable of front-running performances at the end of his PacWest career.

"When Ando had some frustrations with Mark, I volunteered to work with Mark on the radio during the weekends and I think it helped a bit toward the end," Cameron said. "I certainly missed working with "Squirrel" [McDonald] and Mauricio, but I think it still worked well and calmed the situation down a little bit. It was just frustration with the engine and the performance. Everyone knew how hard we were working to produce, and Mark was a good racecar driver. He might not have always qualified well, but when the green flag fell, he could definitely race well. Rarely did he make big mistakes in races. I never felt Mark should be replaced. I thought his heart was in the right place, he was driving hard, and he had done a good job for the team."

John Anderson, who called the majority of Blundell's races at PacWest, added his own assessment. "I had a lot of good times with 'Billy,' particularly during races," he said. "He was one guy that you could wind up, and I really enjoyed the radio work with him. He needed a friend. He needed a buddy to pat him on the back and pull him along or give him some encouragement or abuse him if necessary. I did enjoy working with him, and the bastard could drive. But he was very temperamental. If things weren't going right, he would throw his dummy in the dirt.

"Looking back on our years together, there were times when we pissed it away a little bit where the team let him down, but there were others where he could have jumped in there and fought for it but didn't because he said he didn't have the car, so why bother? Overall, he was pretty determined and, when he was on his game, he was bloody good."

The departure of Mark Blundell was not the only major personnel change for PacWest Racing in late 2000. For the last four years, tension between the business and racing operations within the team had been increasing; Steve Fusek, vice president of business operations since 1996, desired more overall responsibility, but McCaw was hesitant to elevate Fusek's position in the company based on reports of his increasingly antagonistic relationship with Anderson, the vice president of racing operations.

Russell Cameron, who as team manager was Anderson's right-hand man, offered this analysis: "The general feeling throughout the camp was that Steve wanted to be the number one guy who not only raised money for the team, but led marketing and PR, and really had a hand on guiding race operations," Cameron said. "It wasn't a comfortable position for anybody, and I had discussions with Bruce about that a time or two.

"I think looking back, Bruce was between a rock and a hard place. Neither one of them (Fusek or Anderson) possessed both skills required to take the team forward in an overall view. I'm sure that was the hardest thing for Bruce to make a decision about—how to split up their duties and keep them from killing each other. He knew there were frustrations there. They displayed that openly. Looking back, John certainly had the operations side well under control and he was always pretty helpful in terms of providing marketing activation tools to Steve. But I think he didn't appreciate Steve's dabbling in some of the operational sides of the effort, whether it was a driver issue, a strategy issue, or a car preparation issue. And Ando didn't pull any punches when he gets an opinion about something like that."

Bruce McCaw installed Mike Lowry (left) as general manager in 2000 to oversee all aspects of the operation in Indianapolis.

Fusek maintains that he doesn't know if the friction he encountered when dealing with Anderson was directed at him personally, or just a result of the positions the two men occupied. "John wanted nothing to do with me and I still don't know why," Fusek said. "I thought we could be allies but he would just as soon not. I don't know if it was me personally, or anyone who would sit in that chair, because I never wrestled John for control. That was frustrating. I thought I was doing all the right stuff. I guess someone else could look at it and say it was all very selfish. Some folks don't want any marketing or advertising or sponsors or anything else."

Anderson also acknowledged the uneasiness that existed between himself and Fusek during the late 1990s. "Steve and I were never drinking buddies," Anderson said. "Maybe it was a function of having two guys running side by side with a sort of equal status or level of responsibility in different directions. If Bruce was in town, and not an absentee owner, maybe that would have made a bigger difference. Or if someone was in the position to say, 'Hey Steve,' or 'Hey Ando—that lathe isn't coming in the door because we cannot afford it.' Or, 'These are your options. This is the one I'd pick, go in that direction.' Unfortunately, we were looking at each other, the commercial side and the operations side, and weren't really fitting up together."

McCaw's solution was to create a general manager position, a level of management to oversee both racing and business operations. Four candidates interviewed for the job, which went to Mike Lowry, an economic analyst McCaw was familiar with from the aviation industry. Lowry's background included stints as chief financial officer for Horizon Air and Gates LearJet.

"There was more polarization occurring in Indy than I think I realized," McCaw commented. "I didn't realize how segregated Ando and Steve had become and that was a significant issue. I became increasingly aware of that fact, which was one of the reasons

SEARCHING FOR CHEMISTRY

With three Indy car race wins, including the 1997 Marlboro 500 at California Speedway, Mark Blundell was the most successful driver in the history of PacWest Racing. But he never seemed to foster the same kind of close-knit relationships within the team that Mauricio Gugelmin enjoyed. PacWest management sometimes found it difficult to work with Blundell, and the team was never able to find an enduring engineering match for the driver. After their success in 1997, Blundell wanted Allen McDonald to serve as his race engineer, but the team believed that diverted McDonald's focus from his main responsibilities as the team's technical director. This saga played out from 1997 through 2000.

Blundell is in full agreement that it was difficult for him to forge a satisfactory long-lasting relationship at PacWest with his race engineer. "The biggest problem at PacWest, if you look back, was that there were several people who were engineering my car," Blundell remarked. "First and foremost, I should have had somebody on my car who knew what they were up to in terms of depth of experience in Indy car racing or understanding of what was required. And somebody who was actually understanding of the European mentality. Someone who the pair of you get on outside the car as well as inside the car. That matters a great deal. Race drivers and engineers are as whole as a marriage in many respects, and if they don't get on and they don't work well together, that's the end of the marriage."

Blundell believed the answer was right there in front of them in the form of McDonald, who had successfully stepped into the race engineer role in mid-1997 when Mark struggled working with Jim Hamilton. The pairing of Blundell and McDonald was originally intended as a short-term experiment, but after the successful second half of the '97 campaign, Mark lobbied for it as a permanent solution.

"I think Allen understood what I needed, and I understood Allen," Blundell said. "If you look at the start of my Indy car career and the things that went on, I was very much behind the 8-ball and on my back foot. I didn't have the depth to dig down into the oval stuff especially, to try and give them some direction where I needed to go. I was on a learning curve. Just because I was coming out of Formula 1, it spells one thing in terms of credentials, but that doesn't mean to say it's instantly rolled over into Indy car racing. It wasn't really until we got into a situation where that relationship (with McDonald) got put together, then the results started to come. I always knew what I needed. It was just trying to get everybody to think along the same lines."

From 1997 onward, Blundell fought hard for McDonald to serve as his race engineer. But McDonald had been hired as PacWest's technical director, and he found himself torn between those responsibilities and the additional workload resulting from switching to race engineer mode for tests and event weekends. It is to McDonald's great credit that he was able to juggle those responsibilities, all while building a remarkable amount of depth into the team's engineering operations.

The team tried pairing Blundell with race engineers from a variety of backgrounds and skill sets, but the driver never achieved the comfort level he did when working with McDonald. And these were top-notch personnel; several of the engineers who worked with PacWest and Blundell in the late 1990s went on to illustrious careers with different teams in Indy car racing and other forms of motorsport, including:

- Matt Borland (race-winning crew chief for Team Penske in NASCAR)
- Roy McCauley (technical director for Team Penske in NASCAR)
- Guillaume Rocquelin (race engineer for four-time World Champion Sebastian Vettel with Red Bull Racing in Formula1)

What made the Blundell situation more frustrating is that, in 1998, PacWest had also broken up the Gugelmin/Andy Brown partnership, one that appeared to be the perfect example of a driver/engineer relationship. That led to a period of instability with the No. 17 car that finally ended when McDonald took over race engineering duties for Gugelmin in late 1999. It only added to Blundell's exasperation.

"Race drivers and engineers are as whole as a marriage in many respects, and if they don't get on and they don't work well together, that's the end of the marriage."

Mark Blundell

Though he wanted to travel less, Brown's unhappiness with a predominantly shop-based role, as well as his bubbling dissatisfaction over not being selected as technical director, eventually prompted him to leave PacWest.

"The challenge, not so much with the drivers as with engineering, was having the right guys in the right places," commented Russell Cameron. "Andy Brown was a smart guy who had a good relationship with Mo, but

Debrief: (left to right) Mauricio Gugelmin demonstrates how his car is handling to aerodynamicist Bernie Marcus, Mike Lowry and Mark Blundell.

Russell Cameron listens to Mark Blundell, while engineers Steve Clark and "Rocky" Rocquelin take notes.

we made a change there and unfortunately we lost Andy because of it. My take on it was, and I think Bruce agreed with it at the time and so did Mo, that every now and then you need a change of faces, a change of perspective to get that spark going again. Andy and Mo had got to know each other so well and worked together so long it needed a bit of spice thrown in to get another season or two out of a driver who was in his twilight years."

However, McCaw viewed the engineering turmoil that Blundell was constantly embroiled in as less of an issue than the way the driver sometimes tried to play politics between Motorola and PacWest. McCaw was also not pleased by the conduct of several Motorola executives, notably Fred Tucker.

"Later in '97, Motorola started doing separate promotional deals with Mark and they enhanced his income significantly," McCaw said. "I think because of that we lost a little control over him in ways I wasn't totally happy with. He started using Motorola as a way of communicating with the team, which I didn't appreciate at all, and I think that started a process that we could never really arrest. Mark sort of had two channels at that point. If he wasn't happy about something, instead of trying to resolve it within the team, he'd try to get Motorola to put pressure on me. Whether it was engineers or people on his crew, if he didn't like something, instead of trying to make it work, he'd try to force the changes. That began a pattern that was really not healthy and, coupled with all the difficulties we had with Mercedes, something we never really recovered from."

Blundell was not pleased by the way his career at PacWest concluded. "If I'm very honest, the relationship didn't end in a way that I would have liked and probably between myself and Bruce when we think back, there were different ways of going about how to finish," he said. "It's very easy to blame the drivers for many things if things are not going right and it's an easy switch just to take one out and plug another one in. Ultimately, the only people who understand the bottom line of our situation or our relationship are myself and Bruce. At the end of the day, what went on has been and done, and what went on with many things, will stay behind closed doors. I truthfully believe that's the way it should be."

The loss of the PacWest seat ended Blundell's full-time driving career; apart from a few occasional sports car races, he switched paths to embark on a successful broadcasting career. He went on to work as a studio analyst for Formula 1 coverage on ITV and BBC before creating the MB2 Sports Management company in partnership with former driver Martin Brundle. Renamed MB Partners after Brundle departed, Blundell now manages drivers Gary Paffett, Mike Conway, Jordan King, and Marino Franchitti, as well as a handful of up-and-coming golfers on the European Tour. He also made a racing comeback at age 53, competing full-time in the 2019 British Touring Car Championship.

"When Motorola decided to go with [Michael] Andretti, I don't think Mark ever realized how high and dry they had left him," McCaw explained. "All of a sudden it became my problem, but in fact he kind of painted himself into the Motorola camp in so many ways, and he had done it at the expense of many of his team relationships. I felt bad and I really tried to get him to understand. I said, 'Mark, you need to know what is happening.' But he had kind of poisoned himself in the pit lane because of his attitude, which people were becoming aware of. Nobody else wanted to deal with him, as talented as he was. What he needed to do was bite hard, say 'OK, I want to get back in it and go win some races.' I like Mark a lot and I have so much respect for him in so many ways, but we reached this point where we were always trying to unravel some deal he was doing. People started losing respect for him."

McCaw said he split the settlement he received from Motorola for the early contract termination equally with Blundell. "I tried like hell to give him a good send-off and I don't think he understood," McCaw revealed. "I fought very hard and probably did a lot of it at the expense of what the team should have been entitled to. I was always disappointed that not only was he not grateful, [but] that he continued to harbor so much resentment and anger over that. I don't think he ever understood what happened, never stopped and tried to look at it from a proper perspective. And I think that's sad because we had some great success together."

In 2000, Gugelmin was engineered by Roy McCauley (left), who went on to achive success with Team Penske in NASCAR.

"He patted me on the bloody back, and I didn't know him from a bar of soap."

John Anderson

why I felt the team needed to be run by somebody on-site. That was never going to be me, and neither Steve nor John had the ability to run the company. We needed to bring somebody in, and the question was who? I had worked closely with Mike at both Horizon and LearJet. I felt that, under the circumstances, Mike was the best and most credible person that I could come up with."

Lowry had been e-mailing McCaw with constructive critiques for the past couple of years. "I had an interest in Indy car racing, and I started to e-mail Bruce, not criticizing the team, but telling him what he could do better after each Sunday," Lowry remarked. "I think he decided to put my feet to the fire and shipping me back to Indy would be a good thing. He'd been at it hard since 1993 and they had an established team, so basically, my role was to go in and really provide some oversight for him. He wasn't there on a day-to-day basis, so anything that seemed to be outside of the norm, I was accountable for and really responsible for. I guess from a financial standpoint, I really tried to tighten it up a little bit on his behalf."

Despite Lowry's accounting background, he wasn't directly tasked with solving the financial quandary PacWest found itself in following the departure of key corporate partners Motorola and Mercedes-Benz. Instead, his main responsibility was to streamline the team and create greater synergy and harmony between racing and business operations. Ironically, for more than a year, Blundell had been pushing hard, imploring McCaw to hire such a person—albeit with greater racing industry experience.

"It is still my belief that the position of a general manager/team manager is needed to operate the team," he wrote in a memo to McCaw in September 1999. "That person needs to have the knowledge and experience of running a high-level international race team. The issue is one we have touched on many times and one where I have tried to help by making some introductions to possible candidates."

With PacWest's revenue declining and expenses rising, in many respects a person with Lowry's cost-cutting background was correct for the job. But as a racing outsider, he encountered significant resistance when he arrived on the scene in March 2000.

"We were testing down at Homestead and this guy was there with Bruce," recounted Anderson. "He comes up to me as I'm eating lunch and says, 'Hey Ando, Mike Lowry. You're doing a great job!' He patted me on the bloody back, and I didn't know him from a bar of soap. I thought, 'What the heck is this?' and the hair on the back of my neck reacted to this guy pissing in my pocket.

"The disappointing thing was being there that long, Bruce didn't so much as say, 'Hey Ando, I've got a guy coming in who's going to be general manager, or king of the hill,' or whatever. There was no communication from the boss what the deal was. I'm sure that made it difficult for Lowry as well. It was a head-butting contest that I wasn't going to win because he was there in that position."

Changing of the guard: After John Anderson's departure, Russell Cameron (left) assumed control of PacWest's racing operations, while Mike Lowry led the team's business operations.

While Lowry's presence provided a level of comfort to McCaw, Lowry may have underestimated or failed to recognize the schism between Anderson and Fusek, or Anderson's increasing unhappiness. Anderson had struggled to come to terms with the business aspects of his position as far back as 1997, when just a few weeks after PacWest's most successful season, he poured out his soul to McCaw in a faxed memo. "I have let the financial side of the team down very badly," he wrote. "I struggle to try to keep up with our expenditure, but I don't succeed. I seem to find every reason to be in the workshop to put off doing the paperwork…It seems the bigger and/or more efficient we become, the less I enjoy doing what's left over. Internally, here in Indy, we seem to be going in different directions sometimes. We're aware of our communication shortcomings. Steve and I have discussed and implemented ways to alleviate our problems which help in the short term, but we fall off the wagon after a while. Our priorities are different."

Lowry maintains he didn't identify or understand how strained the working relationship between Anderson and Fusek had become. "I'm really not aware of that conflict, except to understand that it existed," Lowry said. "I didn't really see it and quite frankly, when I came on board, Steve basically backed off, as did Ando. I guess my appointment separated the two, and that became less of an issue. No question they were upset with [an additional level of management between themselves and McCaw], but they didn't voice it, or their mannerisms didn't get more aggressive with me than they did with anybody else. Maybe I just chose to ignore it, but it was not really an issue, at least with respect to my role. I never picked that up."

Anderson never did warm up to Lowry when he started working out of PacWest's Indianapolis race shop. Ando submitted his resignation and left the organization in mid-November.

"I was there for seven years and leaving came down to one thing: Mike Lowry," Anderson reflected. "When it became evident that Bruce wanted him to be at the shop and keep an eye on what was going on, I tried to work with him. He was telling me he's a bit concerned about Steve (Fusek), but I think he was playing both sides against the middle. When I finally woke up to what he was about, I didn't involve him. But he didn't involve

'It's good to chase your dreams and take the nontraditional road not traveled.'

Photos courtesy PacWest Racing Group

Russell Cameron, left, talks with team driver Mauricio Gugelmin of Brazil.

Man lives dream on fast track

■ Former Custer resident now on a top team on the auto-racing circuit.

By Jim Holland
Journal Staff Writer

Russell Cameron's road to success happens to be one traveled at more than 200 mph.

From a humble start on the family horse ranch near Custer, Cameron, 36, oversees one of the top teams on the Championship Auto Racing Teams (CART) circuit.

"It's good to chase your dreams and take the nontraditional road not traveled," he said.

"That's where you find true happiness."

Now living in Indianapolis, Cameron is director of racing operations for the PacWest Racing team and drivers Mauricio Gugelmin and Scott Dixon.

Cameron credits the get-it-done work ethic learned in his early years for helping him make his way in professional auto racing.

"Showing and training horses is a lot like these race cars," he said. "It all takes a lot of preparation."

Cameron started by turning wrenches on farm tractors, and he fiddled with cars and motorcycles as his interest evolved from real horsepower to that of the mechanical variety.

Most of his formative years were spent in Custer.

The family later moved to Scottsdale, Ariz., where Cameron graduated from high school in 1983.

After high school, he built off-road machines for desert races,

See **CART,** Page B2

Former Custer resident Russell Cameron, left, talks with Mike Lowry and Bruce McCaw at a Championship Auto Racing Teams race earlier this season. Cameron is director of racing operations for the PacWest Racing team owned by McCaw. Lowry is team manager.

Cameron, a South Dakota native, was profiled in the *Rapid City Journal* in 2001.

me. I slowly developed an aversion to even talking to the guy. I think he was a sneaky bastard. I don't think he treated people well. He'd smile at you on one hand and stab you in the ass with the other. That's the way Bruce wanted to go, but there was no room for me there with Lowry there. I was disappointed with Bruce and I told him as much."

Lowry's arrival was also viewed with disdain from outside PacWest. "Where I think PacWest went wrong was when they brought in Mike Lowry," remarked Reynard commercial director Rick Gorne. "I think that was the PacWest turning point. The guy didn't understand motorsport. Bruce didn't go to the races as much and I think Lowry—how can I put it?—Lowry contributed to the PacWest downfall. We'd always dealt with Bruce and his people and they were a delight to deal with. Lowry's introduction cast a shadow on PacWest's operations because the team started to lose the key people that made the organization great."

For the most part, McCaw got what he hoped for out of Lowry during the 2000 season. "I really gave it a year to see how he was going to do," McCaw said. "And while I was probably pretty disappointed in some of the things he ended up doing, I personally felt that he had a pretty good read on the business and what the company needed. Throughout 2000 he would send me his observations from every race or test that he attended, without knowing how I really felt about things. I thought his observations and his recommendations were dead-on what we needed to be doing. He was well-spoken; he brought a higher level of stature to our sponsor work and things like that. He could present himself very well, and represent the company well, and he brought a higher-level executive presence."

Russell Cameron was the natural successor to Anderson in the role of running race operations, so that transition was not difficult. Cameron assumed the role of vice president of racing operations, while Lowry was assigned the new position of senior vice president of racing and business operations.

"I could have waited for a long time to step up or do that," Cameron said of his promotion. "I wasn't waiting in the wings trying to get anybody's job. I would have been glad working with or under Ando for a long time. When he left, a big part of the team left. I was flattered when Bruce asked me to step into that role when it happened, and some people asked me why I didn't leave, too."

Instead, Cameron stuck around to face the challenge of helping PacWest rebuild for the 2001 season. With the added disadvantage of a very late start, the team was shopping for a new engine supplier, looking to replace a departing major sponsor, and set to make a driver change for the first time in five years. Although it wasn't confirmed until January 2001, Indy Lights champion Scott Dixon was promoted from within the PacWest organization to bc the new driver of the No. 18 Champ Car.

Ironically, despite PacWest's poor run of results over the previous three years, Cameron believed the team itself was stronger than ever.

"When you look back at some of the things we were doing after '97—in '98, '99 and 2000—as bad as our performance was with that Ilmor engine at the time, the team was growing by leaps and bounds," he said. "That was forcing the team to become a more responsible party all the time. As much as we blamed the engine, we were always looking inside at ourselves for what we could do to make it better."

Lowry shared Cameron's belief that even if the results didn't always show it, PacWest was working harder and more efficiently than ever.

"I thought that there was always 100 percent effort," said Lowry. "Of course, I was on the floor walking around, and I made sure that everybody was committing to a solid eight or ten hours of work per day. I think their spirits remained fairly high. There was always the expectation that they were going to break through at the next race. They never got down in the dumps."

But these were tough times for any team in the CART series. By 2001, the tide was turning toward the IRL in the battle for control of American open-wheel racing. Chip Ganassi Racing entered the 2000 Indianapolis 500 and Juan Montoya easily won the race in his first attempt. Team Penske followed Ganassi to Indianapolis a year later, claiming a 1-2 finish led by Helio Castroneves. Roger Penske moved his operation from CART to the IRL at the end of the 2001 season, followed over the next three years by most of the sport's other top teams. In an environment where CART and the FedEx Championship Series were mired in uncertainty and instability, PacWest Racing set about rebuilding for the future.

Cameron co-produced and his wife, Molli, directed the highly acclaimed independent film *Lakota Girls*. Based on Molli Cameron's family history, the production drew considerable attention to Native Americans. *Lakota Girls* was screened at more than a dozen film festivals and won the People's Choice Award at the 2016 Black Hills Film Festival.

JOHN ANDERSON: 1945–2010

Bruce McCaw was the team principal of PacWest Racing. Mauricio Gugelmin and Mark Blundell were the public face of the team. But John Anderson was PacWest's heart and soul.

Few involved in racing don't have at least one enemy. Ando bucked that trend. Anderson was one of the sport's good guys, a larger-than-life character who made everyone he came in contact with smile or laugh. He died in Indianapolis, at age 65, in December 2010. He suffered a heart attack after a game of racquetball with his friend, and former PacWest engineer, Will Phillips.

Anderson was one of PacWest's first employees and helped build the team into a powerhouse within a few years. After leaving PacWest in 2000, Anderson joined Team Green. He memorably teamed with Paul Tracy prior to managing championship and Indy 500 winning campaigns for drivers Dan Wheldon (2005) and Dario Franchitti (2007). He also worked in an administrative role for CART.

He then led Gil de Ferran's successful start-up team in the ALMS sports car series and briefly moved to North Carolina to manage the USF1 Formula 1 team before that effort folded. But Anderson's heart was always in Indy cars, and it was almost impossible to find anyone he worked with in the sport who had a bad thing to say about him.

"Ando was an incredibly solid part of the team," said McCaw. "He had good focus and good discipline, and I think he was a very good judge of talent. He really understood the chemistry part of the dynamics between individuals, so I think he was a very solid leader and he was obviously likeable and fun. I give Ando a huge amount of credit for a lot of our success."

Mauricio Gugelmin also has positive recollections about his time working with Anderson. "John was always a great guy, a great personality to work with," said the Brazilian. "He was a real racer and an emotional guy who was down to earth and probably had the biggest heart I've seen in racing. He kept a lot of the fires under control at PacWest. As a person, he was one of the key team members.

"But it got to a point where even John wore himself out through the pressure of the engineers and performance and the whole system itself," he added. "He got tired of fighting for what he believed in. He was very efficient when you could count everybody with a couple pairs of hands. But when things got really big, I think he probably didn't enjoy it as much as he did before."

Anderson kept in close touch with racing people in his homeland and was responsible for bringing Scott Dixon to PacWest, initially to race in Indy Lights (where he won the championship in 2000) and eventually to the CART series. When Dixon won the 2001 CART race at Nazareth Speedway at age 20, he was the youngest ever winner of an Indy car race.

"Ando was a huge influence on me," Dixon remarked. "He was one of the great people at PacWest because he was such a straight shooter and he didn't beat around the bush. He was a huge part of that team and things kind of turned to junk after he left."

Throughout Anderson's tenure at PacWest, Office Manager Colleen Howerton was his "go-to" person, in charge of many of the behind-the-scenes administrative aspects of the team including payroll and travel.

"I have a lot of respect for Ando—always did, always will," she said. "He was a tremendous leader and all-around person. He was smart and had more passion in him than a lot of people I ever worked with or worked for. If you had the worst day in the world, he would come in and say, 'Hey mate!' and lift your spirits."

Russell Cameron succeeded Anderson as the leader of PacWest's racing operations but was sad to see his former boss go. "Ando is the true definition of a mentor in my opinion," Cameron related. "He wasn't the kind of guy who would selfishly hold on to something he created. He tried to make sure that there were people raised up through the organization. PacWest was really built by John Anderson. He had everybody's full respect, and that is one of the most important things. He was part of the group, one of the guys."

"He was a tremendous leader and all-around person. He was smart and had more passion in him than a lot of people I ever worked with or worked for."

Colleen Howerton

Though he ultimately achieved his greatest success elsewhere, Ando used to look back with extreme fondness on his seven years with PacWest.

"We jumped in at the deep end, obviously," he said in 2005. "There was nothing in that workshop when we got in there but some very willing people. It was like working in a phone box; you could touch one end of the shop and the other without moving your feet. The satisfying thing was not only to see it grow, but the people themselves and the commitment they had.

"In the position I was in at PacWest, it was always a growing process, but the thing you had to watch was that when things are good, you get fat. You have to keep questioning yourself: How can we be more efficient? Unfortunately, it got to the stage where we were spending a lot

John Anderson and Allen McDonald worked together at PacWest for almost five years. They continued their collaboration at Andretti Green Racing and won the 2007 Indy Racing League championship with driver Dario Franchitti.

Bruce McCaw was occasionally frustrated by Ando's dislike of cell phones.

of money and then it was very difficult to change direction and slice the expenses off. It's where you slice and how you plan for the deal, and it's a necessary thing to do. At PacWest, we had real good communications and operations, but where it fell on its head is how operations and the business side of the arrangement cooperated."

When Anderson joined Team Green, he was soon followed by PacWest engineering director Allen McDonald. The pair teamed up to lead Franchitti's 2007 championship-winning campaign.

"I had worked in Formula 1 for 12 years and was with Arrows in 1996 when this strange Australian bloke rang me up," McDonald recalled. "To be honest, when I went out there to interview in Indianapolis, I really didn't have any great intention of doing it. I couldn't see uprooting my family and the whole bit on almost like a whim. But John was such a great bloke and PacWest just seemed like such a nice organization with such nice people. I thought it had a decent chance of success, so I ended up saying, 'Ok, I'll do it.'

"I don't think I'll ever again feel the kind of attachment I felt toward that team," he added. "Maybe this was one of its faults, but it was very much a family. Everybody loved working there, and that was all down to John Anderson."

Nigel Bloom was one of Anderson's closest friends at PacWest and loved to share stories about his old mate. "One night he was leaving Gasoline Alley and he had just gotten a new green Jeep Grand Cherokee. Some guys in an old Oldsmobile were tailgating him on Interstate 465 and they actually ran into the back of him. He only had the car for a couple weeks and got rear-ended by somebody late at night.

"Another time he tried to pass a semi in St. Louis driving Lesley's white Cherokee and took out two of her wheels and tires when the lane ended. You can imagine how thrilled Lesley was with that. Ando was not one to piss off when he was driving, that's for sure.

"Everybody loved working there, and that was all down to John Anderson."

"One year, Ando said I didn't need to ride back in the truck from Mid-Ohio since it was such a short drive," Bloom continued. "He said I could ride in the team van with him and Tim Douthat. He insisted that Timmy drive, and not drive like an old lady. He had to promise Timmy he'd pay for a speeding ticket if we got pulled over, and sure enough, Timmy got nicked. Then a bit on up the road, we pulled up alongside one of the Team Green trucks and, being that it was one of Ando's old teams, he leaned out the window to haze the driver. The wind blew off his glasses, meaning he had to go home to Lesley and explain not only that he had lost a $300 pair of glasses, he was paying Timmy's speeding ticket as well. Good old Ando—that had to have been a $500 trip for John."

Anderson earned his pilot's license in 1989 and his tales from the skies were part of PacWest team folklore. By the late 1990s, Ando had his own plane, a single-engine, four-seat Cessna 182 Millennium Edition that he flew to races whenever possible, often accompanied by his wife, Lesley.

Anderson was such an ingrained part of PacWest lore that the team created a dictionary of "Ando-speak" to help newbies decipher his colorful Australian colloquialisms. He often referred to people as 'shag,' 'slug,' or 'slick.' When running under caution and tire temperature needed to be maintained, Ando implored his drivers to "Get some heat into those bags!" "As long as he didn't call you a ferret, you were okay!" laughed Howerton. "If you were a ferret, you were on the downhill slide!"

Clockwise from top left: 1. Ando was a man of many skills. 2. Even in down times, Anderson kept up the team's morale. 3. With Gugelmin, Jennifer Rinas and Ziggy as helpers, Ando was a great Santa Claus. 4. Flying was a passion for Ando, who loved to fly to races and often traveled with friends or his wife, Lesley.

The Lakeview Mountains provide the backdrop as Scott Dixon poses at California Speedway for preseason publicity photos.

12

A SHOT OF YOUTH

JOHN ANDERSON AND Paul "Ziggy" Harcus had lived and worked in America for many years, but they maintained close ties with key racing people in their homelands of Australia and New Zealand. Kenny Smith was a New Zealand racing legend, and beginning in late 1998, he started trying to help place a talented young Kiwi driver with a team in America. His name was Scott Dixon.

"Kenny lives and breathes motor racing and he can recognize talent," Anderson remarked. "He was a racer down to his bloody toenails. There were a couple of guys he kept an eye on, but Dixon was the first one he tried to get a drive for. We kept up that relationship and the chance came to get Dixon in an Indy Lights car."

Prior to the 1999 season, PacWest Racing gave Dixon his first test in an Indy Lights car. But the very next day, the young driver tested for Johansson Motorsports and he ended up competing in the 1999 Lights championship with that team. For 2000, Johansson had taken over management of Dixon's career and was shopping him to Indy Lights teams.

"Kenny actually called me in 1999 and asked if we could give Scott a test," confirmed Harcus. "I'd known Kenny from New Zealand and he had never asked me for anything. But he said, 'This guy is fantastic and you need to give him a run.' I spoke to Ando and he thought it was a good idea, so we agreed to it.

"We went and did a test at Sebring," he continued. "The first day, he ran for us and you could see straight away that he was good. Little known to me, the next day he was testing for Johansson! We thought, 'Man, he is good,' but he picked up a ride straight away with Johansson and we lost out."

Dixon's career rise was meteoric. Supported by his parents Ron and Glenys, both dirt car racers, Scott started racing karts in New Zealand when he was seven years old. He showed exceptional talent and gained a special dispensation permitting him to advance to cars at age 13. Dixon rewrote the record books, earning the New Zealand Formula Vee title, followed by both classes of the country's Formula Ford championship by age 16,

Scott Dixon was just 17 years old when he was named Australian Champion Driver after winning the Formula Holden title.

Dixon's parents Glenys and Ron (in white shirts) celebrate after Scott claimed the Denny Hulme Trophy at Terretonga in 1999.

all on his family's shoestring budget. The Dixons often camped at the racetrack, visiting friends and competitors staying in hotels for a shower and a barbecue.

Dixon was mentored and championed by Smith, assisted by businessman Christopher Wingate, who organized a company that sold shares in the young driver's career. Scott moved to Australia in 1997. He was named the country's champion driver after winning the 1998 Formula Holden championship in open-wheel cars, similar to Indy Lights. At that point, he had offers to take his career into the popular Australian V-8 Supercar series, but Dixon wanted to remain in open-wheel cars so Smith explored Indy Lights opportunities in America for him. That resulted in the 1999 ride with Johansson Motorsports.

"We tested him, and we were all quite impressed," Johansson said. "PacWest tested him first and kind of passed on him, but we were like, 'Whoa! This guy's a bit special.' So, I took a punt and kind of carried it [financially] through that first season. I sort of took it on me to carry a big portion of the season in exchange for a management deal, over I don't remember how many years at the time.

"He had barely turned 17 when he came to us, but you could tell the attitude was right," Johansson added. "He had this sort of quiet self-confidence. He knew what he had to do and got on with it."

Dixon's 1999 season in the Johansson Indy Lights car started strongly with a trio of top-four finishes prior to a mid-season slump that was perhaps not unexpected for a teenager living and competing on the other side of the world from his homeland. But the young driver regained his form in the latter part of the season, winning on the Chicago Motor Speedway oval from pole position and adding a second-place finish at Laguna Seca Raceway. He ended the year fifth in the standings, three places ahead of Didier Andre, who was PacWest's 1998 and 1999 Indy Lights driver.

With ginger complexion, chubby cheeks, and freckles, the Dixon of the late 1990s looked a lot like a young Paul Tracy. His performance in 1999 made him a hot commodity in the CART ladder system and Anderson and Harcus did not want to let him slip away twice. Johansson was subsequently able to complete a long-term agreement for the driver to join PacWest to compete in Indy Lights in 2000 before hopefully graduating to the CART series.

"I think they were keen on having him and we were keen to find a place for him," Johansson observed. "It kind of worked out on its own, really. It was a matter of getting him in a good car that we felt could win the Lights championship—which he did, of course."

NOV 14 '99 03:49PM PACWEST RACING GROUP P.1/1

PacWest Racing Group
4001 METHANOL LANE, INDIANAPOLIS, IN 46268 * 317-297-2500 FAX 317-297-2100

FAX RECEIVED
NOV 15 1999

14th November '99.

Dear Bruce,

An opportunity presented itself at the end of last week that I feel is of extreme importance to our long term future with regard to drivers.

There has been some conjecture as to whether Johansson can field a car for Scott Dixon next year in the Lights series as he is contracted to do. It now looks as if this will not happen due to lack of finances, and as a result, several teams are pursuing Dixon for 2000 and beyond.

Green and Haas are the two leading contenders with Barry having issued a formal proposal for Dixon's services to partner Johnnie Kane.

I've spoken to Vern Schuppan several times and last Friday he called with the above news. He also told me that he has resigned from Johansson Motorsports but he is still a partner with Stephan in a motorsport promotions venture. I assume this company holds Scotts contract. They are willing negotiate on several options, one of which is the complete sale of his services.

Scott is 19 years old and one of the best prospects I've seen in a long time. He was one of the candidates from Lights that we tested at Putnam where he and Phillip Peter achieved equal times. The guy is smooth as glass and mature beyond his years when you put him behind the wheel. He's a winner this season and in the right team he'll be next year's Lights champion.

He has no money to bring with him but the Lights car is part of his contract. He was financed by a group of New Zealanders to get a start in Lights and the car goes with the driver. I have some of the details of his 5 year contract with Johansson (unbeknown to Vern) and would like to explore the situation further before he gets away. Another test may be in order also to further evaluate his potential. We could coordinate something with a Y2K car test ??

Tony Renna and Scott Dixon would make a formidable team in 2000 but the longer term possibilities are fantastic. I feel this opportunity is too good to miss.

I know you've got more important things to occupy your attention right now but I'd like to discuss this further with you as soon as possible.

Give our best wishes to Jolene and hope all's well with both "J" and Wynn. By the way, there was a rumor circulating that you'd named him "Klaus". I don't know how that started !!

Regards,

Ando.

Fax from John Anderson urging Bruce McCaw to sign teenage phenom Scott Dixon.

JIM LEO: FROM PIT CREW TO FIT CREW

In 1993, Jim Leo was a young trainer working with Detroit Diesel Corporation in his home state of Michigan when he pitched DDC owner Roger Penske on working with Penske's Indy car team. Penske responded to Leo with a hand-written note that simply said, "Go for it!" Leo began working on fitness techniques with Penske's pit crew, which contributed to one of the most successful seasons in the history of the sport, with 12 wins out of 16 races.

Leo's gym was located in the same complex as Ilmor Engineering's U.S. base, and Ilmor's Paul Ray, Wayne Bennet, and Ian Hawkins frequently came over to work out. Ilmor introduced Leo to PacWest Racing's John Anderson in mid-1997. Before long, Leo was asked to work with PacWest as the team trainer and nutritionist. He contracted exclusively with PacWest through 2000, conducting strength and fitness work with the drivers while also refining the team's pit stop procedures. For several years, the drivers and over-the-wall pit crew also underwent a battery of strength and agility tests under the direction of Dr. Donald Chu at the United States Tennis Association facility in Key Biscayne, Florida.

What started out for Leo as general physical training has become a very specialized skill. Equipment and exercises have been developed to help drivers strengthen key muscles, and increased attention has been devoted to preparing for the mental aspects of racing. In recent years, Leo has utilized Senaptec Sensory Station software to assess visual and sensory skills with the goal of improving reaction times. More than a third of the drivers in the modern Indianapolis 500 field are Pit Fit clients.

"When I started with Penske, I didn't even really know what I was doing—I was just going to work with the pit crew and design a gym for them," Leo recalled. "One of the Mercedes guys was assigned to PacWest, and I pitched something to go test the crew's cholesterol or something like that, just to get a feel for it. The week after Mark Blundell won at Portland, Ando called me and that led to more communication and bouncing around of ideas.

"I don't think it was super well-received at first; I think Ando was the only one who believed in it, thank God. But I basically started making myself useful, whether it was smoking cessation programs or bringing food to the guys and working hospitality at the track. I just did whatever Russ Cameron asked me to do because I knew I had to justify what I was doing. I worked with [team chef] Shane Azevedo on a healthy menu and snacks—performance-based food instead of hamburgers and hot dogs or whatever. There was so much stuff to learn, but it gradually grew and grew and grew."

As time passed, the resistance Leo initially encountered began to subside. "It all came down to Ando's support," he said. "If I didn't have him on my side, battling the other powers at PacWest and guiding me like a father figure, I might have been cut loose much sooner or not utilized. Steve Fusek was not behind me at all; he saw it as a waste of money, and Russ Cameron, being super structured and organized, wanted to make sure I was on his program. That was hard because I wasn't used to having a thumb on me, but he was also usually right most of the time. I learned a lot from Russ about being organized and planning ahead, and the fear of disappointing Russ was just terrifying. He could come down on you hard and make you feel like an idiot, just by looking at you. His leadership helped me a ton. He really had his act together and he gave me other responsibilities that justified my salary. I helped run the pit stop practice. I'd videotape practice and go over things as well as I could with the guys, trying from a scientific standpoint to break down things they could do differently. Some people were more receptive than others."

Leo relocated to Indianapolis and opened PitFit Training, and over the last 20 years, he has worked with many top racers including Dario Franchitti, Sam Hornish Jr., and Will Power. But Leo's most notable success story is Scott Dixon, who was a pudgy teenager when he began taking fitness seriously during his 2000 campaign with PacWest. Nearly 20 years later, Dixon still trains with Leo and PitFit.

"In 1999 Tony Renna, and then Scott Dixon came on board," Leo said. "That was kind of the defining moment. Somebody sat me down and said, 'Your job is to make sure that Scott Dixon stays on the straight and narrow.' He had a bad reputation as a partier. So I focused on him and Tony

> "[Dixon] was just super focused on everything, and he was winning."
>
> **Jim Leo**

almost exclusively. I stayed on Scott all the time. I didn't let him drink, we ate the same foods, and everything was working. He obviously was doing well. He got to the point where he was so, so thin—down to 140 pounds. I probably should have had him eating a bit more, but he was just super focused on everything, and he was winning.

"Of course, Scott was the poster child who helped people see what we were accomplishing. It just became much more accepted and PitFit became well known. There's a whole slew of young trainers now, and I've helped many of them set their programs up. We share tons of information with people. Our name has grown through having such success. We oversaw the Formula BMW program and have been working with James Hinchcliffe since 2004. Robert Wickens and Alexander Rossi were in that program; Spencer Pigot came to us with his dad when he was 10. It's cool to see these drivers move up and continue in the sport while being a part of it.

"In the beginning, I think people looked at it like PacWest had a lot of money and were just doing it to spend money because it's out there," Leo concluded. "But people started understanding that this sport costs a lot of money and maybe there was an advantage to the pit crew being fit. There's no doubt that without John Anderson and PacWest Racing, PitFit would not be so established, and we probably wouldn't be having this conversation right now."

Jim Leo gives Scott Dixon an "adjustment" prior to an Indy Lights race in 2000.

PitFit founder Jim Leo (left) and Scott Dixon often train together and have competed in Ironman triathlon competitions.

Dixon demonstrated his talent with an Indy Lights win at Chicago Motor Speedway in 1999. Manager Stefan Johansson rests his hand on Dixon's shoulder.

Mauricio Gugelmin proved to be a perfect mentor for Scott Dixon, who displayed a maturity rarely seen from a 20-year-old.

Dixon delivered six victories on the way to winning the 2000 Indy Lights title for PacWest over Townsend Bell and Casey Mears (see Chapter 15). To some observers, he was almost unrecognizable to when he first arrived in America. His physique no longer resembled that of a young Tracy, thanks to a strict diet and training regimen organized by the PacWest team's nutritionist, Jim Leo. Dixon took another page out of Tracy's book and bleached his hair.

With PacWest's flagship Champ Car effort again struggling for results in 2000, and the team's relationship with Mark Blundell deteriorating, Dixon and his Lights teammate Tony Renna recognized the very real possibility that they could advance to the CART series in 2001. Not for the first time in his career, Dixon was in ideal position to capitalize on such an opportunity. He got the nod, while a disappointed Renna unsuccessfully attempted to sue PacWest and Bruce McCaw for breach of contract.

"Tony and I both knew that contractually, if you had a good year you had a chance to move up," Dixon said. "That was the big key to that. It was one of those right place/right time things where I got the opportunity to move up."

McCaw was pleased to give Dixon a chance to run Champ Cars. "We started looking at how Scott was coming along as probably the likely guy to move up," he noted. "He certainly had some talent and I think we were all excited that we had used our own internal ladder system successfully. Ziggy did a fabulous job with the Lights team and with hindsight, you could say that was a very good program. We felt the Lights team, fundamentally, was a people development program and it gave some opportunities to some very good people. I also thought Mauricio Gugelmin would be a great mentor for Scott."

The promotion was announced in January 2001, and Dixon immediately demonstrated his promise by qualifying faster than the more experienced Gugelmin for the first two races of the 2001 season. In fact, he scored the notable achievement of leading 17 laps in his debut CART race on a new circuit in Monterrey, Mexico; Dixon remained on track when most of the field pitted for the first time, then held station at the front of the pack despite pressure from veteran stars Bryan Herta, Kenny Bräck, and Cristiano da Matta. Even in his first race at the top level, Dixon showed the ability to maintain pace while stretching his fuel longer than the competition, a talent he would make the most of throughout his career.

Gugelmin's streak of 130 consecutive starts—the most in the CART series at the time—came to an end in April 2001 when PacWest withdrew the No. 17 car from the race at

Nazareth Speedway following the death of Mauricio's son Giuliano (see Chapter 13). Yet in the face of that tragedy, the team banded together and Dixon, still three months short of his 21st birthday, scored perhaps the most surprising of PacWest's five Indy car race wins. In doing so, he became the youngest driver to win a top-level race in the long history of American open-wheel racing. The mark was later eclipsed by Marco Andretti in 2006, Graham Rahal in 2008, and finally by Colton Herta in 2019. From 1984 to 2003, only six other drivers (Nigel Mansell, Jacques Villeneuve, Andre Ribeiro, Gil de Ferran, Alex Zanardi, and Juan Pablo Montoya) won CART-sanctioned Indy car races in their debut seasons. All but Ribeiro went on to win CART championships.

Dixon crosses the line to claim a surprising but much-needed victory for PacWest at Nazareth Speedway.

At Nazareth, Dixon kept his cool and used perfect pit stops and pit strategy from the PacWest team to take the lead. He then held off Bräck by 0.366 seconds, with Paul Tracy third. Dixon's run from 23rd to first was bettered in a CART-sanctioned race only once before when Mike Mosely drove to victory from 25th on the grid to win at the Milwaukee Mile in 1981.

Dixon's Toyota engine suffered fuel feed problems on Friday, and handling issues on Saturday hindered the young Kiwi's qualifying run. But the PacWest team, led by Russ Cameron, devised a strategy that brought Dixon into the pits on Lap 7 during a full-course caution after Helio Castroneves spun in Turn 1. Dixon gained six positions when he pitted with the field on lap 76, and he stopped for a third and final time on Lap 116. From there, he stretched his fuel over the final 109 laps, aided by a 22-lap caution for a crash involving de Ferran and Alex Tagliani.

Dixon exults in victory circle after his stunning victory for PacWest at Nazareth Speedway. Too young to legally drink the champagne, 20-year-old Dixon sprayed it instead.

"It was a total team effort," said Cameron. "The guys in the pits decided ahead of time to bring Scott in if there was an early yellow, and that put us in the race when the yellows fell our way later on. It was tough not having Mauricio here, but the Nextel guys pitched in on Scott's car and had a big hand in the win. Scott drove a hell of a race. He withstood a tremendous amount of pressure and did everything that was asked of him. This feels great."

In fact, Dixon's only mistake on the afternoon came on the cool-down lap; still concentrating intensely, his car touched wheels with the machine of Max Wilson. Victory Lane photos clearly show a chunk of the right-rear wheel missing from the winning No. 18 car.

"Our car was very good exiting the corners," Dixon commented. "There was a lot of radio communication with the team to see if I could go the distance on fuel. I saved fuel early in the run and was able to run full rich at the end. I think Kenny and Paul had to conserve a little, and I was able to build a cushion.

Bruce McCaw and Scott Dixon display the modest trophies won at Nazareth.

Dixon clipped a backmarker on his cool-down lap, damaging his car's right rear rim.

"It's hard to know what to expect out of this," he added. "There has been a lot of down times with the team, even this weekend with Mauricio not being here. I was definitely feeling a little down starting back in 23rd. This hasn't really hit me yet, but hopefully in a few days it will."

Bräck, who won the 1998 IRL championship and the 1999 Indianapolis 500 driving for A.J. Foyt, was gracious in defeat despite missing out on his first CART series victory. "I'm still a little surprised where we ended up, but Scott drove a good race," remarked Bräck. "Scott's car was better off of Turns 2 and 3, but mine was quicker all around. But you can't drive through people and I couldn't get a run on him through the corners because the straights are so short. At the end, Scott had no one in front of him, so he had a clear run. He did a great job, because I tried everything."

After three winless seasons, the Nazareth triumph was a huge emotional boost for the entire team. Car No. 18 Crew Chief Daryl Fox was delighted to capture PacWest's first Champ Car win since Mark Blundell's victory in the 1997 season finale at California Speedway. "After we brought Scott in for a top-up very early, our boys gained him six spots in the first 'real' pit stop," Fox said. "We annihilated the rest on that stop, and it kind of made Scott say, 'Wow! I can really get a good result here.' The stops were perfect. These days, the team that makes the fewest mistakes wins the race, so I'm really proud of the whole team effort.

"For a rookie, Scott drove a very mature race," Fox added. "He passed [Alex] Zanardi when he had to, and then he handled a lot of pressure from Bräck and kept from going a lap down. That gave us the yellow we needed, and Scott took it from there. I think he and Bräck were the only guys on the track who were really passing people."

When Dixon, Fox, and the rest of the PacWest crew got back to Indianapolis that Sunday evening, they found a party waiting for them. Receptionists Mindy Koup and Valerie Selman gathered the team's shop-based personnel and their families and were waiting on hand at the airport to greet the charter flight with coolers full of champagne and beer—for everyone except for the 20-year-old Dixon, who had to make do with Sprite.

The impromptu celebration meant the world to the tired crew when they piled off the plane. "That was awesome to come back to that, a huge surprise," said Fox. "But this was a full team effort. There are a lot of people back at the shop who put in a huge effort to help make all of this possible. There aren't too many people that are still here from when we won the last one with Blundell in 1997. For some of the guys, this win came in their third race. But it was especially great for the guys who have been here for the long haul through the tough times."

"It definitely helped out, and everybody is really pumped up," noted Charlie Guilinger, a shop-based machinist who had been part of Blundell's race winning over-the-wall crew in 1997. "It was a bit hard for me on Sunday, because the last time we won, I was right there at the track. This was a long time coming, but it was worth it. A lot of people left after the last couple of years, but a lot of good people stayed. This was worth the heartache for the people who stayed, and when I watched on TV, I thought it was the most energetic I've ever seen Bruce McCaw. He looked over the moon."

Mike Lowry, who experienced his first Indy car win as a member of the PacWest management team, echoed that observation. "We didn't see much of Bruce in 2001, so it was nice that he was at Nazareth for that race," Lowry said. "I don't ever recall seeing him show that much emotion, and his passion returned as the season went on. Actually, I don't know that he ever lost the passion, but this has been a long three years for him.

"It was amazing how it lifted everyone's spirits," Lowry continued. "I wasn't here in 1997, so I didn't know what it felt like to win. But to see the spirits of this team raised was just a remarkable thing and it carried through the entire season. It brought the expectation that this team could win on any weekend. We clearly began to have more confidence in ourselves. It erased the doubts that we were doing the right thing and that we could win. Even with the difficulties we had in seasons past, the cars were being prepared well. All Scott did was demonstrate to the team that they were doing the right things."

Years later, Dixon looked back on his historic Nazareth triumph with some reservation. "It was a big moment, but very shocking too," he reflected. "It was definitely a strategy call. We qualified near last and it was also a rough weekend because Mauricio's boy had just died, and it was just myself at the track. It was good in that sense, but it was a fuel strategy win. You still have to take every win you can, but I don't think we won it straight out."

By mid-2001, Dixon had established himself as PacWest's lead runner, and he continued the team's resurgence with a mature drive to a podium finish in early June at the Milwaukee Mile. Dixon's run to third place on the historic oval was in some ways more impressive than his victory at Nazareth. At Milwaukee, he started eighth, and after losing positions during the first lap confusion triggered by a clash between Helio Castroneves and eventual race winner Bräck, he raced competitively to another excellent

"These days, the team that makes the fewest mistakes wins the race, so I'm really proud of the whole team effort."

Daryl Fox

Dixon's victory at Nazareth earned the cover of *Championship Racing Magazine.*

result. Dixon was tactically boosted by a fuel-only second pit stop and he pressured second-place finisher Michael Andretti all the way to the checkered flag.

"At the end, we were hoping it wouldn't go yellow because we had plenty of fuel in hand," Dixon said. "Michael was getting high in Turn 1 and 2 and I thought I could catch him. Unfortunately, the last yellow came and after the restart we didn't have anything for him."

Once again, Dixon's ability to extract speed from a car while conserving fuel was a vital skill as fuel strategy was becoming an increasingly important tool in Indy car racing. "Scott is one of the very best at being able to go fast while saving fuel, and I think Mauricio Gugelmin deserves a lot of credit for helping develop that skill," observed McCaw. "Even in the years since PacWest, he remains one of the best in the business at managing a race that way. Not only is he very quick, his ability to be fast and efficient at the same time gives the team many more options with their strategy."

The roller-coaster 2001 campaign produced another high at Wisconsin's fabled Road America circuit as Dixon and his crew produced another memorable PacWest moment. After qualifying a season-best third, Dixon dropped back from his second-row grid position and collided with Andretti early in the race, requiring the replacement of a toe link during a red flag brought out by a heavy downpour. Following the restart, Scott got caught in the debris from Memo Gidley's huge accident. A chunk put a gash in Dixon's helmet and tore the rear wing off his car.

Dixon pitted each time around during the lengthy caution period to clean up the track so the No. 18 crew could do a little more work on the damaged rear end of his car. After five such stops, aided by the fact that each yellow-flag lap of the 4-mile long road course took some four minutes behind the pace car, he rejoined the race still on the lead lap. Driving flat-out, Dixon was elevated to fourth place as others saved fuel or had to make splash-and-go stops. He maintained the position when the race was controversially flagged early due to CART's two-hour race limit.

Dixon drove a total of seven laps without a rear wing as repairs were affected to his crippled Reynard. "The crew did an unbelievable job keeping me on the lead lap," he said. "Every time we came in for more repair, we topped off the fuel. So, I knew I could race the rest of the way."

Lowry paid heed to the effort he saw that afternoon in Wisconsin's Kettle Moraine country. "There's a quote by Teddy Roosevelt on the shop wall that says, 'Only those who try are the ones who have the opportunity to succeed or fail. The worst thing is not to have tried at all,'" Lowry said. "Elkhart Lake falls under that category. Sometimes the achievement doesn't come in the form of a win, and what I saw at Elkhart Lake was remarkable. There were literally piles of bodies on top of each other and tools being thrown everywhere. Russ Cameron was timing it to the second when they had to leave the pits to stay ahead of the pace car, and Scott had to run 180 mph down the straight without a rear wing to catch up with the pack. To finish fourth was remarkable."

Scott Dixon earned another trip to the podium by finishing third at the Milwaukee Mile.

Perhaps the most impressive performance of Dixon's rookie season came at Laguna Seca Raceway, where he matched his season best by qualifying third, then finished fourth in another race that was thrown into disarray by CART's timed-race rule. Despite starting 25th and passing only one car throughout the two-hour contest, brilliant strategy by Scott Roembke put Team Rahal's Max Papis at the front of the field when the checkered flag fell seven laps short of the scheduled 83-lap distance. Had the race been run to full length, third-place finisher and pole-qualifier Gil de Ferran would have been the likely winner. Dixon gave the 2000 and 2001 CART champion all the pressure he could handle.

The No. 18 crew works on Dixon's car during one of several stops needed to repair crash damage at Road America.

"All credit to Dixon," de Ferran remarked after their race-long duel. "He's in his rookie season, but he has a fantastic head on his shoulders. He's a tremendous driver. He really drove extremely well all year long. He was very strong, mature and fast, all in one package."

Russell Cameron also paid tribute to PacWest's young star. "Dixon's performance at Laguna Seca in 2001 was memorable because we were really battling Penske head to head," he noted. "I felt good about that because I really thought the team at that point had graduated away from some of the mistakes. We had grown from '98 to 2000 but we had gotten sort of top-heavy with all our programs. We had less money to spend so we were deleting some of our programs and were simplifying our effort. Dixon and the team did a great job and Scott was battling Gil de Ferran. That's no small accomplishment for a rookie and those Penske Reynards were awesome cars."

Dixon finished the season ranked eighth in the CART championship and won the series' Rookie of the Year honors, besting Ganassi Racing's Bruno Junqueira. Although he didn't win the overall championship in his first effort—as Mansell and Montoya accomplished—Dixon's rookie Champ Car season was certainly on par with Villeneuve, who had won one race and finished sixth in the standings in 1994.

But PacWest's young driver wasn't completely satisfied with the result.

Dixon's fourth-place drive at Laguna Seca was praised by two-time CART champion Gil de Ferran.

"The rookie award was what we were working towards all year long, so it was good to get it accomplished," said Dixon. "But in retrospect, it's actually disappointing we finished as far back in the overall points as we did, because we let some good results slip away. We started out a little slow and the hardest thing was the one-day tests. You basically get up to speed on the first day, you spend a lot of time baselining things and you don't really get around to most of your testing options. The last few tests, we've had back-to-back days and it's really shown. We're right there on times now. We still have a lot of work to do on the car, but the Toyota engine has definitely helped. It's definitely a nicer package than the Mercedes engine I tried last year."

Dixon garnered accolades from within the PacWest team as well. "Scott was great," observed Cameron. "He was so dedicated, so committed, so talented. One of the great memories from 2001 was winning the race at Nazareth. We weren't a great qualifier, but he did a good job in the race and saved fuel when he was supposed to. Rocky [Race Engineer Guillaume Rocquelin] had a really good fuel strategy and the guys did a great job. We could have won Milwaukee the same way, but we had a refueling problem that cost us four or five positions in the pits. We still finished on the podium, but we really had a chance to win that one."

From an upper-level management position, Dixon was a dream come true for Mike Lowry. "In terms of his driving this year, Scott exceeded our expectations," Lowry remarked. "He never put a wheel off the track in preseason testing, and I think he was fairly cautious, which led to some concerns from the engineering group that he didn't have the speed. But that was just a measure of Scott's maturity. He knew how far he could go, and he slowly built up that speed, and by the time we got to Laguna Seca, he was ready to race.

"We had a huge crash damage budget for Scott," Lowry added with a laugh. "We had a very little one for Mauricio, and while it wasn't Mo's fault, Mo ended up having the bad luck and Scott was great. The No. 18 team was exceptional and Russ Cameron was superb. What's funny is that our sales and marketing people were always bitching about the fact that he was so young and not very good in front of the camera. They would teach him over and over again how to be more relaxed and presentable and verbal to whatever interviewer he happened to have. That was aside from his driving, which was really, really good. It was amazing how much he matured both in and out of the car in later years."

Looking exclusively at Dixon's development and the success of the No. 18 team, the 2001 season was highly positive for PacWest. But Mauricio Gugelmin suffered two major crashes and continued to struggle for results, and CART itself was starting to show signs of being in deep trouble. By the end of the 2001 campaign, the future of both the team and the sanctioning body were very much in question.

Mauricio Gugelmin drives out of the pits as the cars roll off for the American Memorial 500 at Eurospeedway Lausitz. Staged just a few days after the 9/11/01 terrorist acts, this race is remembered for the accident that cost two-time CART series champion Alex Zanardi his legs.

13

DIFFICULT TIMES

WHILE SCOTT DIXON'S promotion to the Champ Car team in 2001 gave PacWest Racing an emotional lift and helped the team run more competitively on the track than it had since 1997, behind the scenes the organization was working through difficult business circumstances.

The departure of Motorola and Mercedes-Benz left PacWest in a precarious position. The United States economy was not in good shape and CART was suffering in the American marketplace as the open-wheel war with the Indy Racing League waged on. CART lurched from disaster to disaster throughout 2000 and 2001, creating an unstable environment for any participating team.

Making matters still more difficult, the terrorist event of September 11, 2001, made an already volatile American economy even more unstable and uncertain. In light of world events, many companies took a far more conservative approach toward spending, especially in terms of corporate sponsorships.

"I remember Bruce McCaw telling me afterwards, 'Mike, everything has changed,'" recalled Mike Lowry, vice president of business and racing operations. "I didn't recognize it at the time, but he ended up being right. It really lent credence to the business savvy Bruce had. The whole business climate changed. I'm not aware of his personal situation, but certainly from a team standpoint, it was turned upside down."

In retrospect, CART's public downfall started with the saga of the Hawaiian Super Prix, a proposed non-championship race to be run in November 1999, on a 1.67-mile temporary track at Barber's Point Naval Air Station in Oahu, Hawaii. Touted as "The Super Bowl of Auto Racing," the HSP promised to pay the winning team and driver $5 million from a $10 million purse and was set to be broadcast via pay-per-view by Showtime. PacWest sent a car and Mauricio Gugelmin to Hawaii to run a few publicity laps in June. Financing failed to materialize and the event never came close to happening. CART recouped its financial investment via a surety bond, but the cancellation was highly embarrassing for the organization.

Mauricio Gugelmin was the only driver to turn laps of the proposed Hawaiian Super Prix circuit in a racing car. PacWest sent a Motorola-liveried car to promote the stillborn event.

Mike Levitt / LAT

Bobby Rahal green-lighted CART's race at Texas Motor Speedway during his brief tenure as the series CEO.

The failure of the HSP turned up the heat on CART CEO Andrew Craig and in June 2000, under pressure from several team owners, Craig abruptly and unexpectedly resigned from his position—much to the displeasure of Bruce McCaw. Craig was made a scapegoat as CART's performance in the American sports marketplace declined, mainly due to the confusion and animosity related to the seemingly unresolvable CART-IRL conflict.

Craig was instrumental in leading CART through a successful Initial Public Offering in 1998, which saw the opening stock price of $16 rise to $35 (and spawn a release of additional stock in 1999) before hitting a steep decline to the $20 range at the time of his ouster. By that time, the organization faced a number of critical issues in addition to its diminished share price, including declining television ratings and attendance, a problematic relationship with the Indianapolis Motor Speedway and several other key promoters, and a perceived overall lack of 'American-ness.' None of these problems could be directly attributed to Craig, but his departure was clearly viewed by some as the first step on the path to recovery.

McCaw offered his perspective on Craig's ouster. "As sorry as I was to see Andrew go, it was clear he did not have the support of enough board members for his contract to be renewed. It would not be until later that several board members would realize what a mistake this would be. For Andrew's sake, it was better that he left immediately, which both allowed him a severance that I believe he richly deserved, and the ability to move on with his life. But it was a pivotal error for CART."

Bobby Rahal, the former driver-turned-team owner, was named CART's interim CEO. However, Rahal's time in the seat would be extremely short-lived; within three months, he announced plans to move to England to serve as team principal for the Ford-owned Jaguar Formula 1 team. This left CART without a leader as it struggled to make critical decisions about its future engine and chassis formula. In December 2000, CART announced that it had identified its new full-time CEO. Joe Heitzler boasted a strong and varied background in the broadcast communication industry and he was the unanimous choice of CART's expanded nine-man board of directors. But it was soon revealed that Heitzler's résumé was deceptive and his marketing cliché-laden vocabulary quickly gained him the nickname 'Jargon Joe.' His single year on the job was a study in crisis management from the very beginning, starting with the cancellation of CART's race in Brazil scheduled for March 25.

In this turbulent environment, PacWest was attempting to secure major commercial partnerships, including a new engine supplier. The team faced several key problems.

There was much more movement than usual between teams and engine manufacturers during the 2000-01 "silly season," and PacWest was one of the last teams to enter the market. In addition, the three consecutive uncompetitive seasons with Mercedes power had adversely affected the team's reputation and Toyota and Honda were not willing to offer PacWest the kind of incentives they were now paying some teams, including Ganassi, Newman/Haas, Penske and Green. PacWest ended up contracting to use Toyota engines for 2001, but the lateness of the team's arrival into the engine marketplace left them far down the manufacturer's pecking order.

"Toyota seemed quite keen to take us on, but it became apparent later that Toyota was trying to take advantage of the situation," said McCaw. "We ended up with a decent engine; probably not the engine of choice, but that's where we were, and we scrambled hard to go forward."

PacWest also took a hard look at switching to the Lola chassis for the 2001 season but eventually decided to remain faithful to Reynard. Following its disastrous period in the late 1990s, Lola rebounded strongly in 2000 with a new car that featured heavily revised aerodynamics helped by a slender longitudinal gearbox. Lola won seven of 20 events in 2000, including Toyota's first victory in the series after four years of trying.

By 2001, Rick Gorne had left Reynard after a disagreement with Adrian Reynard, and the general consensus was that Reynard's entry into Formula 1 (in partnership with British American Tobacco) was adversely affecting the Indy car program in a manner similar to the Ilmor/Mercedes situation. The challenges that all CART teams were facing also contributed to Reynard's troubles and the company's failed initial public offering on the NASDAQ stock exchange.

"Formula 1 sucked myself, Adrian, (chief designer) Malcolm Oastler, and a few engineers out of Reynard," admitted Gorne. "That wasn't a bad thing, because we had good engineers and we were struggling for them to grow, while Malcolm and a couple of other guys were at the top. It allowed new, young talent to come to the fore. But that was the start of the demise—the brain-drain, as such.

"Then Lola became more aggressive in the way they dealt, so we lost a couple of customers," Gorne continued. "When I left, we had 100 percent of the CART grid, but Lola became more aggressive commercially and that sort of upset the on-track balance a little and they got a bit of a foothold back into the marketplace. Then, with the slow demise of CART, it became more difficult."

Mike Levitt / LAT

Chip Ganassi with Toyota Racing Development President Lee White. Toyota's introduction of financial inducement to teams including Chip Ganassi Racing and Newman/Haas Racing was a key element in CART's downfall.

Mike Levitt / LAT

By 2001, the engine manufacturers were the driving force behind CART, including Toyota's Jim Aust and Honda's Robert Clarke.

There was also the matter of sponsorship. Nextel was committed to continue as sponsor of Gugelmin's car, but Dixon's car started the season with 'PacWest' on a plain blue and white car, reminiscent of 1994. With the team's relatively poor on-track record over the last three years, and CART in a state of decline, PacWest found it increasingly difficult to find a corporate partner to replace Motorola.

"We kept trying to fund it with smoke and mirrors," recalled Steve Fusek. "I think that was the beginning of the end of CART as well. The value was decreasing, the IRL's strength was growing, and a concern was growing about what was going to happen in the long run for the series. We couldn't fund anything. We had a lot of small deals but there wasn't any serious money behind it."

Even the Nextel sponsorship wasn't bringing PacWest the level of income it should have been generating. "In 2000, it was actually a pretty good deal," explained McCaw. "It created a lot of excitement; we did a lot of promotional stuff with Motorola and Nextel, and we encouraged both of them to really get in and try to make this work as a way to really help leverage it. Unfortunately, for a couple of reasons, it didn't materialize into all that we had really expected.

"In 2001, Nextel had really kind of overcommitted," McCaw continued. "I actually ended up in January that year getting hurt by my brother diving into the America's Cup; Nextel, at the same time, decided to put a lot of money into the America's Cup. We had several structures to the relationship that would have worked well, and we had reached a point where we were pretty much committed for the season, but it wasn't generating the money it needed to. That became a difficult situation; the financial markets were melting down and everything else. It was a pretty challenging time."

PacWest's fortunes—and the credibility of CART as a whole—received a serious blow at the third scheduled event of the season. Built by Speedway Motorsports Inc., Texas Motor Speedway opened in 1997 and rapidly developed a reputation as one of the most notorious circuits in America. The high-banked 1.5-mile oval outside Fort Worth annually hosted NASCAR and the Indy Racing League. Spurred on by interim CART CEO Bobby Rahal, who enjoyed a longtime friendship with TMS President Eddie Gossage, the FedEx Championship Series race was scheduled for April 28, 2001.

In some respects, Texas was the track that put the IRL on the map, thanks to the League's low-power, high-downforce cars that created extremely close pack racing that was spectacular, but downright frightening at times—like NASCAR restrictor plate racing at Daytona or Talladega, but with open-wheel cars. After seeing the pack racing that was common in the IRL's two annual races at Texas, many constituents within the FedEx Championship Series were vehemently against racing on such a high-banked speedway. Among them were former CART Chief Steward Wally Dallenbach and Mauricio Gugelmin, who had been elected president of the Championship Drivers Association in 2000.

Despite well-publicized concerns, plans with the race continued, pushed forward by Rahal. In fact, Team Rahal was chosen to handle the initial pre-race testing because driver Kenny Bräck had competed numerous times at TMS in IRL cars. Bräck barely topped 220 mph in testing, about the same speeds achieved at that time by the IRL cars.

Team Rahal Technical Director Don Halliday ran Bräck's Texas test in partnership with CART's Kirk Russell. "No problem at all," Halliday remarked. "All the hype and subjective comment we've heard was not for real. The car behaved like a normal race car. The maximum lateral G spikes we saw were 4.5 for a tenth of a second or so, which is normal for tracks like that. It was no big deal—everything was A-OK."

Still, many remained convinced the track was not suitable for the CART-specification cars, with more sophisticated aerodynamics and an additional 200 horsepower compared to the normally aspirated IRL machines. The drivers and several teams shared a two-page list of concerns and recommendations with CART and TMS officials, but played down talk of a boycott.

"From what I understand, they are all being taken care of," CDA President Gugelmin said in the run-up to the Texas event. "As long as the race is on the calendar, the drivers will go; there is no question of the drivers not participating in the event. But we are not the only ones who have raised concerns about the place. I went testing there and I really had to think why we were even contemplating going there."

No one was prepared for what happened when the CART teams showed up for the race weekend and actually tried to go fast. Speeds immediately exceeded 230 mph, with Team Green's Paul Tracy topping the charts with a 236.678-mph clocking. CART used a different track measurement than the IRL (1.482 miles vs. 1.500) so published speeds between series were not directly comparable—at the IRL track length, Tracy's lap calculated out to 239.553 mph. But ignoring speeds, Tracy's lap time of 22.542 seconds was more than a second under the IRL record of 23.896 seconds set by Billy Boat in 1998.

During the Saturday morning practice session, Gugelmin was involved in an enormous accident. His PacWest Reynard-Toyota snapped loose exiting the Turn 2 banking and

"We kept trying to fund it with smoke and mirrors. I think that was the beginning of the end of CART as well."

Steve Fusek

FedEx Championship Series Race No. 3
Firestone Firehawk 600 Presented by Pioneer
Texas Motor Speedway
Fort Worth, Texas
Combined Practice Report (After Saturday AM Session)

April 28, 2001

TrackLength 1.482 Miles

Pos	Driver	Car#	Engine/Chassis/Tire	Lap Time	Speed Mph	Speed Kph	B. Leader	B. Next
1	Paul Tracy	26	Honda/Reynard/Firestone	22.542	236.678	380.886		
2	Tony Kanaan	55	Honda/Reynard/Firestone	22.556	236.531	380.650	0.014	
3	Max Papis	7	Ford-Cosworth/Lola/Firestone	22.604	236.029	379.842	0.062	0.048
4	Bryan Herta	77	Ford-Cosworth/Reynard/Firestone	22.605	236.019	379.825	0.063	0.001
5	Kenny Brack	8	Ford-Cosworth/Lola/Firestone	22.624	235.820	379.506	0.082	0.019
6	Alex Zanardi	66	Honda/Reynard/Firestone	22.685	235.186	378.485	0.143	0.061
7	Michael Andretti	39	Honda/Reynard/Firestone	22.692	235.114	378.368	0.150	0.007
8	Patrick Carpentier	32	Ford-Cosworth/Reynard/Firestone	22.709	234.938	378.085	0.167	0.017
9	Gil de Ferran	1	Honda/Reynard/Firestone	22.751	234.504	377.387	0.209	0.042
10	Oriol Servia	22	Ford-Cosworth/Lola/Firestone	22.777	234.236	376.956	0.235	0.026
11	Dario Franchitti	27	Honda/Reynard/Firestone	22.794	234.062	376.675	0.252	0.017
12	Alex Tagliani	33	Ford-Cosworth/Reynard/Firestone	22.805	233.949	376.494	0.263	0.011
13	Cristiano da Matta	6	Toyota/Lola/Firestone	22.840	233.590	375.917	0.298	0.035
14	Michel Jourdain Jr.	16	Ford-Cosworth/Lola/Firestone	22.882	233.161	375.227	0.340	0.042
15	Scott Dixon (R)	18	Toyota/Reynard/Firestone	22.917	232.805	374.654	0.375	0.035
16	Helio Castroneves	3	Honda/Reynard/Firestone	22.953	232.440	374.066	0.411	0.036
17	Bruno Junqueira (R)	4	Toyota/Lola/Firestone	22.975	232.218	373.708	0.433	0.022
18	Christian Fittipaldi	11	Toyota/Lola/Firestone	23.001	231.955	373.285	0.459	0.026
19	Shinji Nakano	52	Honda/Reynard/Firestone	23.063	231.332	372.282	0.521	0.062
20	Roberto Moreno	20	Toyota/Reynard/Firestone	23.100	230.961	371.686	0.558	0.037
21	Jimmy Vasser	40	Toyota/Reynard/Firestone	23.116	230.801	371.428	0.574	0.016
22	Nicolas Minassian (R)	12	Toyota/Lola/Firestone	23.144	230.522	370.979	0.602	0.028
23	Alex Zanardi	66X	Honda/Reynard/Firestone	23.165	230.313	370.643	0.623	0.021
24	Adrian Fernandez	51	Honda/Reynard/Firestone	23.247	229.501	369.335	0.705	0.082
25	Cristiano da Matta	6X	Toyota/Lola/Firestone	23.321	228.772	368.163	0.779	0.074
26	Adrian Fernandez	51X	Honda/Reynard/Firestone	23.343	228.557	367.816	0.801	0.022
27	Toranosuke Takagi (R)	5	Toyota/Reynard/Firestone	23.366	228.332	367.454	0.824	0.023
28	Mauricio Gugelmin	17	Toyota/Reynard/Firestone	23.386	228.136	367.140	0.844	0.020
29	Kenny Brack	8X	Ford-Cosworth/Lola/Firestone	23.395	228.049	366.999	0.853	0.009
30	Toranosuke Takagi (R)	5X	Toyota/Reynard/Firestone	23.558	226.471	364.460	1.016	0.163
31	Jimmy Vasser	40X	Toyota/Reynard/Firestone	23.634	225.743	363.288	1.092	0.076
32	Nicolas Minassian (R)	12X	Toyota/Lola/Firestone	23.684	225.266	362.521	1.142	0.050
33	Patrick Carpentier	32X	Ford-Cosworth/Reynard/Firestone	23.702	225.095	362.245	1.160	0.018
34	Max Papis	7X	Ford-Cosworth/Lola/Firestone	23.768	224.470	361.239	1.226	0.066
35	Michael Andretti	39X	Honda/Reynard/Firestone	23.792	224.243	360.875	1.250	0.024
36	Bruno Junqueira (R)	4X	Toyota/Lola/Firestone	23.810	224.074	360.602	1.268	0.018
37	Scott Dixon (R)	18X	Toyota/Reynard/Firestone	23.873	223.483	359.651	1.331	0.063
38	Dario Franchitti	27X	Honda/Reynard/Firestone	23.900	223.230	359.244	1.358	0.027
39	Max Wilson (R)	25	Phoenix/Lola/Firestone	24.065	221.700	356.781	1.523	0.165
40	Michel Jourdain Jr.	16X	Ford-Cosworth/Lola/Firestone	24.109	221.295	356.130	1.567	0.044
41	Mauricio Gugelmin	17X	Toyota/Reynard/Firestone	24.231	220.181	354.337	1.689	0.122
42	Paul Tracy	26X	Honda/Reynard/Firestone	24.338	219.213	352.779	1.796	0.107
43	Bryan Herta	77X	Ford-Cosworth/Reynard/Firestone	24.451	218.200	351.149	1.909	0.113
44	Tony Kanaan	55X	Honda/Reynard/Firestone	24.859 *	214.618	345.385	2.317	0.408
45	Roberto Moreno	20X	Toyota/Reynard/Firestone	25.267 *	211.153	339.808	2.725	0.408
46	Shinji Nakano	52X	Honda/Reynard/Firestone	25.656 *	207.951	334.656	3.114	0.389
47	Christian Fittipaldi	11X	Toyota/Lola/Firestone	26.200 *	203.634	327.708	3.658	0.544
48	Gil de Ferran	1X	Honda/Reynard/Firestone	26.314 *	202.751	326.288	3.772	0.114
49	Oriol Servia	22X	Ford-Cosworth/Lola/Firestone	26.611 *	200.489	322.646	4.069	0.297

* Lap time exceeds 110% of the average of the 2 fastest drivers best practice times
(R): Designates the driver as a series rookie

Printed:April 28, 2001 11:16 am

Page 1 of 1

When the CART cars ran faster than expected at Texas Motor Speedway, the G-forces caused some drivers to become dizzy or nauseous.

speared head-on into an inner retaining wall with a 66-G impact that lasted an unusually long 0.1-second. The Brazilian's right foot got wedged between the brake and throttle pedals, powering the crashed car down the back straight with a series of smaller impacts, shedding parts all the while. Some six seconds after the initial frontal impact, the crippled machine then spun around and clouted the outer Turn 3 wall backwards with a 113-G impact before rolling to a stop at the entrance to Turn 4. The accident unfolded over roughly half a mile.

Gugelmin was taken from the car on a backboard, but he remained awake and alert throughout the crash and the rescue operation. Dallenbach, who had retired as Chief Steward but was on hand as an advisor to CART, shook the driver's hand as he was wheeled to an ambulance. Gugelmin was later taken to North Hills Hospital for precautionary X-rays. Remarkably, he suffered no major injuries.

"I had been running a few laps behind another car and I could feel a slight turn from the rear of my car coming out of Turn 2," Gugelmin said. "I was able to correct the first twitch, but then the back end came around again and I lost it. I remember heading towards the wall, then the next thing I remember is letting go of the wheel and I became a passenger. Then, when I finally stopped, I could see daylight by my feet and Dr. [Terry] Trammell greeting me at my car."

Dr. Steve Olvey, who responded with Trammell to the accident, described the situation in his book *Rapid Response*:

His car still hadn't stopped after the second impact and was headed for a third impact with its nose cone totally removed. At this juncture, his feet were completely exposed and if he hit a third time he would never walk again. Luckily, the car came to a stop and when the Safety Team arrived, Gugelmin was awake and appeared to be uninjured. A double impact of this magnitude would have been fatal just a few years earlier. Thankfully, he was wearing his HANS Device. Without it he likely would have been killed. We found that the HANS Device was badly fractured...we had not seen that before. Without it, those fractures would have been in his neck. The scary thing about the crash was that the usually very analytical Gugelmin was dumbfounded as to why he crashed, and his crew could find nothing broken in the car. The observers reported a normal racing line before he lost control, and telemetry had not registered any malfunctions in any of the car's systems. The cause remained a mystery.

Developed by Dr. Robert Hubbard of Michigan State University, in conjunction with racing driver Jim Downing, the HANS (Head and Neck Support) Device is designed to

The CART Safety Team treats Mauricio Gugelmin at the scene of the Brazilian's crash at Texas Motor Speedway.

The Reynard chassis withstood two huge impacts and protected Gugelmin from serious injury.

Fans express their displeasure after CART cancelled the 2001 Texas race just hours before the scheduled start time.

keep a driver's head from suffering from a whiplash effect in an accident—the leading cause of basilar skull fractures. The HANS consists of a U-shaped carbon frame with a flange serving as a headrest, custom fitted to a driver's shoulders, to which the helmet is attached by straps. In an accident, the HANS keeps the head from whipping forwards and backwards while also preventing excessive rotational movement as a secondary protection. "It basically fastens your head to your neck," said Dr. Trammell.

CART made use of the HANS Device mandatory at oval tracks in 1999 and expanded the rule to include all tracks after driver Gonzalo Rodriguez was killed at Laguna Seca Raceway late in the 1999 season. As was often the case, CART was an industry leader in mandating an important safety advance.

"The car did the job," Gugelmin said. "The seat collapsed, which it was supposed to do in a situation like that, and the head restraint broke—again, by design. I didn't expect or want to be the guy to test the HANS Device, but the truth is that it probably saved my life. I had two major accidents in the space of about six seconds, and I walked out of the hospital a few hours later. That wouldn't have been possible just a few years ago, and it shows just how seriously CART takes the safety issue."

Cristiano da Matta of Newman/Haas Racing also suffered a big accident that he could not explain. By Saturday evening, more serious problems had been revealed when it emerged during the routine pre-race driver's meeting that most of the drivers had been experiencing dizziness and nausea after just a few laps of the high-banked speedway. Olvey, who served as CART's Medical Affairs director, suspected the high G-loads generated by the CART cars at Texas were causing some drivers to experience dizziness or even temporarily black out.

Olvey consulted with Dr. Richard Jennings, a former flight director at NASA who specialized in aerospace medicine at the University of Texas. After procuring telemetry printouts from several teams, and sharing the information with Jennings, Olvey knew there was a serious problem. Jennings told Olvey that the sustained G levels being recorded in the CART cars were above a threshold where pilots are required to wear a G-suit. On Sunday morning, just two hours before the scheduled starting time, CART made the uncomfortable yet necessary decision to cancel the race.

"All in all, we found the limit of our bodies," noted Gugelmin. "We had a new situation, with vertical and lateral G's. The speed was not a surprise, but the physical effects were. It's all about safety. I'm very impressed with the way Joe Heitzler handled the situation

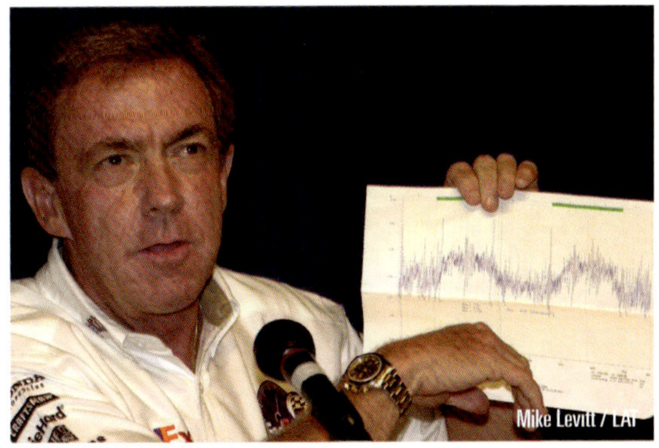

Mike Levitt / LAT

Dr. Steve Olvey determined that forces exerted on the CART drivers at Texas were similar to those of fighter jet pilots.

Phil Sedgwick / LAT

Texas Motor Speedway President Eddie Gossage was understandably upset by the last-minute cancellation.

Mauricio Gugelmin was joined by his wife Stella and 6-year-old son Bernardo for the pre-race parade lap at California Speedway. The Gugelmins tragically suffered the loss of Bernardo's twin brother Giuliano in 2001.

and the way he stood behind the drivers. The track did what it could to improve things and they did a fantastic job, but these cars are just too fast. I only felt dizzy after a 25-lap run, but it wasn't a factor in my accident."

The eleventh-hour cancellation was a public relations disaster for CART and TMS boss Gossage was furious. "The bottom-line point is CART should have known," he said. "It wasn't until Saturday night, 18 hours before the green flag was set to fall, that CART expressed this problem to us. Texas Motor Speedway and its fans have suffered tremendously. This racetrack was ready to race in the fashion that CART told us it needed to be in, and I'm just frustrated that it didn't happen."

Within the PacWest team, Gugelmin's big accident in practice for the aborted race was quickly forgotten because the Brazilian and his wife Stella were soon affected by a much more tragic event: the death of their six-year-old son, Giuliano, who had been afflicted by cerebral palsy since birth. Giuliano was rendered a quadriplegic by the crippling disease due to complications during the birthing process. He required 24-hour care throughout his life, and the twin brother of Bernardo finally succumbed peacefully to respiratory complications on May 3, 2001.

Gugelmin withdrew from the race at Nazareth Speedway. "Our family has been blessed with three wonderful children, and this morning God decided to take one of them to a better life," Mauricio said in a statement. "Giuliano was a brave young boy who battled his way since he was born. He blessed and enriched our lives and made us appreciate just how fortunate we are to have enjoyed him for six years. We are comfortable in knowing that he will be with us forever and will always remain in our thoughts and hearts."

Scott Dixon's victory in the race at Nazareth lifted the PacWest team, and the entire CART community rallied around the Gugelmin family (see Chapter 12). "Mauricio always maintained a positive attitude throughout some difficult times with Giuliano," remarked John Anderson. "He never looked at Giuliano's situation as tragic, but rather as an opportunity to contribute to learning about cerebral palsy and helping others. Mauricio frequently said he felt lucky that he was able to provide Giuliano with the kind of care and facilities he needed. He's always been a wonderful father to all of his kids, and it's just unfortunate the way life tests people sometimes."

By then a father of two, Bruce McCaw was deeply moved by the affection that Gugelmin demonstrated toward his children, in particular Giuliano. "That was a very difficult challenge, and yet Mauricio and Stella just did everything possible to make Giuliano's life as normal as it could possibly be," McCaw observed. "Their dedication was extraordinary. A lot of people would have said it's costing too much money or it's too much aggravation. Of course, it's great that Mauricio was able to do what he could, both financially as well as with the household support. But most of all, the love and devotion in their family was incredibly special. They never complained and the way they spoke of Giuliano, you would never know of the difficulties he faced."

A popoff valve with the controversial spacer installed.

CART's troubles intensified in June at Detroit, exactly one year after dismissing Andrew Craig. It suffered a major blow to its credibility when a controversial fight broke out between the series' engine suppliers. Toyota tipped CART to its belief that Honda and Ford-Cosworth were directing the air flow in the plenum chamber to manipulate the manifold pressure relief valve (also known as the popoff valve), providing as much as three extra inches of turbo boost, an advantage worth about 75 horsepower. The plenum chamber designs in dispute had been submitted in advance and approved as legal by CART's Technical Committee. Toyota is also believed to have recommended a solution to CART: a ¾-inch spacer at the base of the popoff valve to negate the advantage being gained. Additional pressure was put on CART by Toyota announcing its intention to build normally aspirated engines to Indy Racing League specifications beginning in 2003.

When CART implemented the spacer without prior warning at Detroit, Honda and Ford-Cosworth held their cars out of Friday practice. Honda persisted, and after a series of protests and appeals over the next six weeks, CART eventually ruled in favor of Honda. But the appearance of collusion with Toyota was obvious and the 'Valvegate' controversy upset Honda to such an extent that, in September 2001, it announced it would exit the CART series at the end of the 2002 season—another crippling blow to the beleaguered sanctioning body.

The high point of Gugelmin's 2001 campaign came in early July at the Grand Prix of Cleveland, where the Brazilian claimed the fourth pole position of his CART career, and the first since the 1997 season finale at California Speedway. Circumstances contributed to Gugelmin's success; with the 26-car field split into two qualifying groups to create less crowded track conditions, the first group qualified in perfect conditions, whereas the second (and theoretically faster) group had to take to a wet track after a sudden shower between sessions. Gugelmin's qualifying lap during the first group was the fastest lap of the Cleveland weekend by 0.6 seconds. "I think my lap was pretty decent," Mauricio noted. "It would have taken a big effort on someone's part to beat it. But we need to come up with a system that's more equal for everyone."

Mauricio Gugelmin took advantage of changing conditions at the Grand Prix of Cleveland to earn the fourth pole position of his career.

Mauricio was unable to maintain his pole-winning pace in the race, slipping to a tenth-place finish. A seventh-place run at in the Molson Indy Toronto a week later would be the best result of remainder of the season for the 38-year-old veteran.

At Chicago Motor Speedway, Gugelmin was lucky to survive another heavy crash. Big Mo had been fourth fastest in the Friday morning practice, but during the afternoon session, his Reynard/Toyota snapped out of control in Turn 1 and thumped the wall backwards with an impact measured at 123G. It was the greatest impact to date since CART began measuring G-loads in crashes. Gugelmin was taken to the CART Medical Center complaining of pain between his shoulders and in his knee, but he was released later that afternoon and competed in the race two days later.

"I downshifted approaching Turn 1 and the rear of my car got loose," Gugelmin reported, speculating that high brake temperatures might have caused a rear caliper to catch. "I walked away with really just cuts and bruises, so I'm very fortunate to have been wearing the HANS Device and thankful these cars are so safe today."

CART Director of Medical Affairs Dr. Steve Olvey was again stunned by the ferocity of the accident. "The impact was even larger than his crash in Texas and it completely used up his headrest and cracked the HANS Device," Olvey said. "But that's better than his neck cracking and instead of being knocked out or finding himself in a hospital for the night, Mauricio was back in the car on Saturday."

As August rolled in, PacWest's star-crossed 2001 season nearly came to a grinding halt at Mid-Ohio Sports Car Course's Miller Lite 200. Toyota put itself at the center of another political storm when it refused to supply PacWest with key electronic components for Friday's test sessions due to an ongoing dispute between manufacturer and team over the terms of its engine supply lease.

Toyota had aggressively pursued new partners in 2001 and forged deals with Newman/Haas Racing, Patrick Racing, and Walker Racing, while continuing to supply Chip Ganassi Racing. All those deals were completed before PacWest even entered the 2001 engine market. Newman/Haas and Patrick broke existing contracts with Ford-Cosworth when they accepted Toyota's offer and, in a compromised position, PacWest was ultimately the only Toyota team that was required to pay for its engine lease.

After a successful start to the relationship that included a victory for rookie Dixon at Nazareth Speedway and several other impressive performances, PacWest believed it was

Three-wide into the first corner at Cleveland, with Gugelmin to the inside of Michael Andretti and Gil de Ferran.

Gugelmin suffered another big crash in practice at Chicago Motor Speedway, but he was able to start the race.

PacWest did not enjoy the most harmonious relationship with Toyota and executives Lee White and Jim Aust.

in position to re-negotiate its contract with Toyota. But the engine supplier refused and instead demanded the outstanding balance due from the team to secure the release of the team's engines for the Mid-Ohio event.

McCaw offered his perspective on the dispute with Toyota. "I met with Jim Aust and Lee White in November 2000 and March 2001 and told them that I felt the team was going to need relief on the engine costs, and that PacWest was indeed the only team that was paying a significant cost for engines," he recalled. "I said that in the current environment, that wasn't going to work. They said, 'Well, you have to make it work.' I said, 'No, I don't.' I told them straight up that I wasn't personally going to bankroll the engine program. Some of this happened even when we signed the contract. They were looking for assurances, and I said, 'Look, this is an organization. This is not me. You need to tell the difference and if you can't, then maybe we shouldn't do this.' They were very excited to get Scott, but for a long time, I don't think they were listening to what I was saying. Either that or they listened, and they didn't believe me."

A contingency plan was drawn up for PacWest to borrow and run a Ford-Cosworth powered car from Dale Coyne Racing to keep the team from defaulting on its franchise commitments to the CART series. But it wasn't necessary, because it was reported that Mike Lowry negotiated a compromise that released the engines and put the PacWest cars on track for Saturday practice and qualifying.

"They threw Lowry an ultimatum, but he went in and stared Toyota down and they caved in," McCaw said. "They decided they had more to lose."

However, Russell Cameron recently revealed that even McCaw did not know the true story of why Toyota capitulated. "The 2001 Mid-Ohio engine negotiation success had very little to do with Mike," Cameron said. "In fact, he was an obstacle to the team's final year. I never told Bruce or any other team member, but I was asked by the CART management and the Toyota leadership to a meeting in the CART office trailer. At this meeting, Lee White said he trusted me, so they would step up on TRD support of the team."

By the end of the 2001 season, Lowry had succeeded in renegotiating the team's Toyota contract without any cash outlay. Toyota credited PacWest the sum of $2.675 million, contingent upon the team fielding at least one Toyota-powered entry for Dixon in the 2002 CART series, with engines to be supplied at no cost to PacWest. In effect, Dixon was used as collateral for PacWest's engine supply.

"We were a team that was by all means really struggling to stay afloat," Cameron recalled. "We had every right to negotiate a better deal for the team's engine supply, whether it was Mike's belief or Bruce's belief that it was wrong for us to be paying for engines when everyone else was getting free Toyota engines. We were providing so much information and so much to their championship hopes that a standoff was necessary to make them realize what we were all about.

"I was really proud of the team that day," he added. "When we were told we weren't running, we pulled the team together in the trailer and told them to keep it amongst ourselves and not really speak to the press. They did a great job, showed a lot of maturity and demonstrated that they were really behind the effort."

PacWest worked diligently to sign a title sponsor for Dixon's car throughout 2001. Enron Corporation signed on for the Grand Prix of Houston in September, but hopes of a long-term commitment were dashed when Enron subsequently filed for bankruptcy.

Finances remained the team's most pressing issue. For the Grand Prix of Houston, Dixon's car raced with sponsorship from Enron, and PacWest believed they were on the brink of clinching a lucrative future sponsorship worth as much as $25 million from the energy and commodities conglomerate. However, within weeks Enron's stock became virtually worthless and by the end of 2001 the company had filed for bankruptcy. That was the latest near-miss in PacWest's attempts to find a suitable replacement for Motorola.

"Enron appeared to be the perfect sponsor to assure the team's long-term future and on my last trip to Houston to meet with their senior executives, they assured me that we had a deal," McCaw said. "I was fascinated by this company that had come out of nowhere and suddenly was one of the hottest companies around. Their headquarters were impressive, and their trading facility was just amazing. However, I remember making a comment to our marketing group that I still didn't quite understand what these guys do. When the company virtually evaporated overnight, it became clear that it was really just a shell game of massive proportions. We still had some other very strong prospects for a successful program, but this was a huge blow."

While Dixon's impressive rookie campaign helped improve PacWest's results in 2001 compared to the prior three seasons, there was still a great degree of unrest behind the scenes. By the end of the season, Steve Fusek and Allen McDonald had departed from the team. Fusek struggled to come to terms with reporting to Lowry after working so hard to establish a close working relationship with Bruce McCaw. By late in the season his unhappiness was apparent, and he departed immediately prior to the Vancouver race.

"Bruce gave me an awesome opportunity, but in the end, it changed a lot," Fusek said. "Obviously the Lowry days totally changed things. I tried to play along with it for a while, but it

MAURICIO GUGELMIN RETIRES

With the death of his son, Giuliano, and two of the biggest accidents of his career, 2001 was a very hard year for Mauricio Gugelmin. In early 2002, the Brazilian quietly announced his retirement from driving after competing in 128 races for PacWest Racing.

"At the end of the season I just had to sit down and look back at all this, combined with a lot of absurdity in the sport itself," he reflected at the time. "The family was not demanding more of my presence, but you could see they were getting more tense about racing. My older son started to understand more about it, especially when the car hits the wall. I thought, 'Well, why not do this a little bit earlier than planned?'

"I talked with Bruce McCaw quite a lot because he's been very instrumental to my career here in the USA," Mauricio continued. "I have a lot of respect for him and the team. Then it got to a point where I felt it was definitely the right decision. The time is right, I feel fortunate to be in one piece, and fortunate enough to have done so many races and raced in so many different series all over the world. The most important thing was to build up so many friendships and learn about different cultures and so on. It will be interesting to see the perspective of all this from a different angle."

Russ Cameron led the tributes to the driver most closely associated with the organization. "I think Mauricio was the heart of the team," Cameron said. "He spoiled all of us—that's the easiest way to say it. He's a typical Brazilian driver in the way he treats everyone so well. I can't remember a morning when Mauricio walked into the tent and walked by anybody—the entire staff—without saying good morning. At Christmas, he never forgot anybody on the team. He didn't pick and choose; he knew that everybody was looking to him for some leadership and I think he did that better than anybody I have ever seen.

"But it wasn't just that he was a gentleman who treated people well—he was fast," Cameron continued. "He was very talented and I've apologized to him on a couple of occasions because we weren't ready to win races in 1995 as a team. His career would have been a different career if he had won a few races in '95. He could have won the Indy 500 in '95. I think Mauricio looks back and he enjoyed his whole career, but it could have been a bit more colorful with a few more wins and poles. He was well respected by the drivers in the driver's meetings and I don't think any of the drivers ever tried a stupid move on him or put him in any jeopardy. He was a good guy to a fault, almost."

McCaw continued on that theme. "To begin with, Mauricio impressed me not only as a very capable driver but also just a really solid human being. He really had everything in balance mentally—his family, the way he interacted with the team members. At the end of the day, the driver needs to be a great cheerleader and Mauricio was all that. He was always just a solid facet to the team because he could rally people and he could focus them.

"I think what always impressed me about Mauricio was how aware he was of everything going on around him. He could be sitting in the car and not only pick out a good-looking gal walking 50 feet away in his mirror, but if somebody did something wrong to the car, he'd see it. He'd watch every car that went by and look for changes. He had an incredible sort of awareness of what was happening."

Gugelmin was responsible for sparking PacWest's five-year commercial partnership with Souza Cruz, and his savvy in terms of working with the media and sponsors was an important factor throughout his career.

"Obviously he was terrific with sponsors," observed McCaw. "Hollywood loved him; he did what he should and he understood what that meant. He presented himself impeccably at all times. You never had to worry about anything with him even when he was out having a good time. I think he was a guy of incredible integrity, which I think was not always highly visible either in the sport or particularly in the driver community. Obviously,

"I think Mauricio was the heart of the team. He spoiled all of us—that's the easiest way to say it."

Russ Cameron

he was humorous and fun to be around but also a guy of deep faith and understanding. I think he was sincere about the friendships he made, beyond any shadow of a doubt. He kept his ego well under control, which I think was a challenge for most drivers. They either had superiority complexes or inferiority complexes; there were very few drivers who had a sort of fundamental balance in terms of who they were and what they were all about.

"He was obviously respected and a great leader in the Championship Drivers Association and he had respect from both the CART executive and the CART technical staff. If Mauricio brought up an issue with a track, they took it seriously. If he saw something—and he was a guy that was always looking—he knew he either had to avoid it or get it fixed. A lot of drivers never stop to think about some of those things, but he just had such an expansive approach in looking at everything around him. I think he was respected highly for very good reasons by everybody around as a quality guy and just one of those people who doesn't come around every day."

Pictured with son Bernardo by his side, Mauricio Gugelmin retired from racing after the 2001 season.

A big accident at Texas Motor Speedway gave Mauricio Gugelmin cause for reflection.

Steve Fusek addresses guests touring the PacWest race shop. Fusek left the team in 2001 after struggling to find a role under General Manager Mike Lowry.

Fusek has served as Takuma Sato's U.S. manager since 2012.

was too big of a change. I didn't want to give up any control or decision-making. It got complicated and the enjoyment was definitely leaving it. The whole Toyota thing definitely left a sour taste. You didn't know what was going on. We didn't call any sponsors and obviously my phone was ringing off the hook with people saying, 'What the heck is going on?'"

Fusek later served as Marketing Director for CART during Chris Pook's tenure as CEO. He left the motorsport industry to open a hardware store and mail order business in downtown Indianapolis. But like many bitten by the racing bug, he couldn't stay away. Since 2012, he has served as the US manager for Takuma Sato, Japan's most successful racing driver and the winner of several IndyCar races, including the 2017 Indianapolis 500. Though he was driving for Andretti Autosport, Sato's Indy victory had a very PacWest flavor; in addition to the presence of Business Manager Fusek, Sato's car was run by Ziggy Harcus and engineered by Garrett Mothershead, who apprenticed as a data engineer with PacWest in 2000 and '01.

Over the years, Fusek hosted dozens of race car drivers and team personnel at his home. That's how he established a link with Sato. "Matthew Winter (who worked in a marketing capacity for PacWest from 1999 to 2000) was managing Takuma, and he called and asked if they could stay with me when they were finalizing their contract with KV Racing in January 2010. I figured it would be a day or two, but it ended up being three. Matthew went home, but they asked if Takuma could stay until after the first test. Then they were testing regularly, so he asked if he could stay until after the first race. Then it was Indy and it turned into the whole year. Takuma decided he was going to make a management change and he asked me if I would do it. I couldn't really commit to it and I told him no two or three times, but I told him what I could commit to and we worked it out. Now he's part of the family."

McDonald had been unhappy with his diminishing influence at PacWest over the last couple of years, and he landed a race engineering position at Team Green, working alongside his former colleague John Anderson. McDonald went on to engineer Dario Franchitti's successful 2007 IRL campaign in which the Scotsman won the Indianapolis 500 and the IndyCar Series championship. McDonald's career later took him to Schmidt-Peterson Motorsports, Ed Carpenter Racing, and Rahal Letterman Lanigan Racing.

"I think I wasn't really happy with the direction or uncertainty of where the engineering was going and I got bad tempered about it enough that they decided they'd had enough of me," McDonald admitted. "The lovely thing about PacWest was that everybody who worked there loved working there, and loved Ando and Bruce, despite the frustration of him being a very distant team boss. A really great man to work for, and certainly in my case, I wanted it more than anything to be successful for them. When Ando left, he left for all the wrong reasons, mostly because of Mike Lowry. I didn't work very well with Mike because I remembered the old PacWest. So most of it was my attitude problem, if you like, that kind of ended my tenure there."

While McCaw was pleased with the effort and leadership McDonald put into growing PacWest's engineering operations, he believes that ultimately the technical director may have been placed in the wrong capacity.

"I think Allen did a good job and I probably didn't spend as much time with him as I should have," McCaw said. "We were trying to get a more practical mindset to engineering and be more hands-on. Somebody had to be in charge of engineering and I still think Allen was the right guy to put in charge because we were trying to take a different course. Andy Brown would have been the only other choice and I don't think Andy is much of a manager. He was a very capable engineer, but—as I think Mauricio commented—he didn't listen well. He had his mind made up going into something and that was it. Allen was maybe in some ways the opposite of Andy. You had to pry stuff out of him; he was not forthcoming. I don't think he ever really took strong control. Maybe he didn't feel comfortable. Obviously when Allen started engineering Mark in mid-1997, that probably diluted some of his technical director role. But he did a good job with Mark and was at least a reasonably open-minded guy."

Allen McDonald was a key team member for five years, serving as technical director as well as engineering Mark Blundell and Mauricio Gugelmin.

Russell Cameron believed that by the end of 2001, PacWest had returned to the level of 1997 even if there were not as many race wins on the board to show for it. As head of racing operations, he was pleased with the direction the team was headed in.

"I think PacWest has had the tools for a while, but we've certainly been handicapped by our engine package the past few years," he said. "It's taught us a lot of things. We really looked at ourselves every time we had a failure inside of our own four walls. That time was so valuable. I can't think of a team I've ever been with that has more policies and procedures and that's just through time and failure that we've kept looking at everything we could to try to make sense of it, and never let it happen again.

"Certainly, we've simplified our effort," he said in a post-season interview. "We don't produce a lot of the parts and the trick bits that we used to. My feeling about CART racing right now is that it's more of a game of reliability and doing the best you can with the basic package, and really just producing quick pit stops and putting a lot of pressure on our drivers. We had a very good, reliable package this year with the Reynard/Toyota."

At England's Rockingham Speedway, Mauricio Gugelmin's car carries the 'lowline' engine cover that PacWest developed for the 2001 Reynard chassis.

Despite a general upturn in its fortunes on the racetrack, PacWest was not a stable organization at the end of the 2001 season. The lack of title sponsorship for one car, and the reduced level of commitment by Nextel for the other, had left the team in serious financial straits, and McCaw had made it clear that he would not bail out PacWest using his personal resources. In conjunction with the unease created by the major changes in the management team over the previous 12 months, not to mention the rapid decline of the CART series under Joe Heitzler's tumultuous single year in power, PacWest's future was still decidedly shaky heading into 2002.

The Nextel sponsorship generated plenty of attention but failed to achieve the financial goals that PacWest hoped for.

CART had a superb on-track product, but the open-wheel split created confusion in the marketplace and crushed the series' momentum.

14

THE END FOR PACWEST

BY 2001, BRUCE McCAW was increasingly focused on his family life, as well as growing the Talaris Institute, an organization he and his wife, Jolene, founded in 2000. Talaris' goal was to stimulate and direct research about the brain in infants to support parents and caregivers in raising socially and emotionally healthy children. Inspired by their experiences as parents, Jolene and Bruce maintained the McCaw family tradition of philanthropy by supporting Talaris and other organizations that focused on the healthy growth and development of children and the important role of families and other caring adults in children's lives.

It was, therefore, not a surprise to those who knew McCaw well when he gradually began to decrease his direct involvement with PacWest Racing as his own family expanded. By 2001, he had installed Mike Lowry as the overall day-to-day manager of the team, and he was traveling to fewer and fewer race events.

"The family was clearly first and foremost," McCaw said. "Coming from the West Coast, you lose a day for every eastern race—that travel time really starts to add up. Plus, one of the real difficulties was I couldn't do Mondays in the shop in Indianapolis because that was the day that everybody was off. It was very hard for me to build the synergy of being efficient traveling across the country twice a week. We were getting 18 or 19 races by then and I was just getting worn out. I wanted to spend time with my family and Jolene couldn't travel with me anymore. We took Skye (the McCaw's daughter, born in 1998) to a number of races, but all of a sudden with a second child, you get pretty anchored. You're not very portable.

"The thing that people on the outside didn't realize was that I was really committed to stepping back my involvement with the team and set 2001 to be a transitional year for the team," he continued. "By the end of the 2000 season, I was pretty much mentally doing that, not to the detriment of the team, but as a way to help them grow. My goal had always been for the team to be not only self-sustaining, but self-managing. It was really the way to allow everyone to grow and play a greater role in their own destiny. Even at the end of '99 I was starting to try and make that transition."

Bruce and Jolene McCaw were married in 1996, but after the birth of their children, Jolene attended fewer races with husband.

Future racer? Sixteen-month old Skye McCaw sat in the 1997 Portland winner at a PacWest Racing party at the same venue in 1999. Bruce McCaw's desire to spend more time with his growing family was a key factor in his decision to step away from PacWest.

This was nothing new for McCaw; in the past, he had built up several businesses and worked out a plan for the employees to take over ownership. "That was really my style," he said. "My insurance business, which I started as a one-man show, is still a very successful company. We went through a merger and a de-merger along the way and I finally sold it to my employees. It was a remarkably similar deal to PacWest. I told them, 'December 31, 1993, will be my last day, and one of two things is going to happen: You're going to buy the company from me, and I will structure it and finance it and support it; or I'm going to sell the business to someone else. Either way, on January 1, I'm no longer going to be in the insurance business.' But I wanted to see the company sustain itself as an independent entity, which it still does today.

"One day, the three gals that bought it called me up and said we need to get drunk over lunch," he added. "They had made their final payment to pay off the loan and now they own a successful company that's worth millions of dollars. And I'm really proud of them. That is somewhat indicative of how I have always looked at things and done things is to try and build something. I have more fun building something than I do running something. So, a lot of this was predestined for a long time. Even back when I started giving Steve [Fusek] and Ando greater responsibility and greater authority in 1996, I was really trying to groom them and the whole company up to replace me. That was the goal from long ago."

McCaw has a long history of deeply immersing himself in whatever industry he chooses to participate in, and auto racing was no exception. As he would in any of his other businesses, Bruce took the roles and responsibilities of being a team owner and shareholder in Championship Auto Racing Teams Inc. very seriously. Following its initial public offering in 1998, CART established two boards of directors: the Franchise Board, made up of 17 team owners comprising 24 votes; and the Delaware Board, a more traditional five-member board of directors. McCaw served on both boards, and he was a strong proponent of Andrew Craig, CART's CEO from 1994 to 2000.

"Overall, I think Andrew put together and ran a pretty effective organization," McCaw reflected. "But one of the challenges that CART had was they never let the management manage. When you have a public company that relies on others, you have to have a level of consistency and you have to let management run the company. I think we should have controlled the [Franchise] board better. The way the world works in a democracy is the majority make the decision and the rest really need to go along with the decision that got made. In CART, that really didn't happen. We had quarterly meetings of the public board where we set out objectives, and when we would get to the next meeting of the Franchise

At Nazareth Speedway in one of his final public appearances as CART CEO, Andrew Craig acknowledges Roger Penske's 100th Indy car race win.

AFTER PACWEST

When PWR Championship Racing withdrew from CART competition in May 2002, Russell Cameron maintained control of key assets of the PWR 17 and PWR 18 holding companies, including equipment and a lease on the race shop owned by Bruce McCaw at 4001 Methanol Lane in Indianapolis. In August, he formed Horizon Motorsports, employing a skeleton crew of former PacWest team members while he looked for an opportunity to get the team back on the racetrack.

What Cameron did not have was financial backing. That soon changed when he was introduced to venture capitalist Kevin Kalkhoven and Craig Pollock, who managed the career of driver Jacques Villeneuve prior to serving as the team principal of the British American Racing (nee Reynard) Formula 1 team from 1999 to 2001. Ousted at BAR after three mostly unsuccessful seasons, Pollock teamed up with Kalkhoven and attempted to acquire the Arrows F1 team. When that transaction fell through, he set his sights on fielding a car in CART, resulting in the formation of PK Racing.

"It actually happened through my lawyer," Pollock explained. "We had been dealing with Kevin on something else and it put the two of us together. We got along immediately, which is extremely unusual in motorsports, and we started looking into buying a Formula 1 team. That didn't work out, but we kept in touch and Kevin thought it might be a good idea to start up a CART team. We couldn't have done it if Russ hadn't provided the infrastructure."

Kalkhoven was looking for opportunities after a successful career in the fiber optics industry. Between 1993 and 2000, he led the growth of JDS Uniphase from a $35 million company to a $100 billion enterprise as the world's first independent merchant supplier of optical components for the telecommunication industry. The Australian native's laid-back style was perfect for Silicon Valley; known to his employees as "the Kevster," he made *Worth* magazine's list of the Top 50 CEOs in 1998. He walked away two years later, citing burnout.

A longtime racing enthusiast, Kalkhoven looked at team ownership and liked what he saw in CART. "Venture capitalists invest in start-ups, and to me, some significant proportion of this is that it is a start-up," he remarked. "It's at a time when the market is down, which is always a good time to get in, and I believe it's going to be successful and make money. I'm not doing this entirely for altruistic reasons—it's for business reasons. But I believe it will be a successful business among other things."

"It's exactly the right time to get involved," Pollock added. "Everything goes in peaks and troughs, and CART fell down into a trough last year. It's going to go back up, and the reason it will go back up is the vision behind it."

Cameron saw his staff at Horizon dwindle from 14 to five between August and December 2002 and was struggling to keep his hopes of running a team alive. "I had a few contracts and some deals going to basically fund the team with, and Bruce McCaw leased me the building, so I had a facility to do business in," he related. "But it was very tough trying to look for sponsorship for the future. My background as an operational person made it a challenge. I told everybody if they had opportunities they wanted to pursue I wouldn't hold it against them. They had families to consider. In the end, there were five of us left. Colleen Howerton was one of the original PacWest employees and she stayed. Tim Love, a great gearbox guy, is another, as well as Jeff Horton, who will manage our shop and handle our international shipping, and Mike Andres, a truck driver who had been with us for years.

"When Craig approached me with this scenario, I was incredibly interested because it was exactly what I wanted," Cameron added. "As soon as this deal came about, we went after it."

By the start of the 2003 season, PK Racing boasted 30 employees and was set to field a car for rookie Patrick Lemarie in the revamped CART championship. But it was a thrash that rivaled PacWest's full-time entry into Indy car racing in 1994.

"We had a good head start because of the acquisition of all the old equipment," Cameron said. "Getting the people in the door, the cars, then

"We got along immediately, which is extremely unusual in motorsports...Kevin thought it might be a good idea to start up a CART team."

Craig Pollock

engines, the tires, then making the schedule and getting it all to gel in an incredibly short period of time, with a limited test schedule, was definitely a challenge. But I pulled back some of the people that I knew from before who really liked working for us, and some good names that were out there came in to fill some key positions."

Lemarie rode his friend Villeneuve's coattails into a development driver role for BAR, but he sorely lacked racing experience and failed to crack the top 10 in six CART starts for PK Racing in an 18-car field. For what turned out to be Lemarie's final race, at the Milwaukee Mile, Cameron brought in Mauricio Gugelmin (who had relocated with his family to Brazil after his retirement from competition) as a driver coach and advisor. But Lemarie crashed out on the first lap. He was replaced by Bryan Herta at Laguna Seca and then Max Papis took over for the next seven races.

Mike Levitt/LAT USA

PacWest Racing ceased to exist at the end of 2001, but much of the team carried on as PWR Championship Racing into early 2002.

Phil Abbott/LAT USA

Scott Dixon finished ninth at Twin Ring Motegi in his last start for PWR Championship Racing. He made a mid-season switch to Chip Ganassi Racing.

"Obviously I have a great interest in PK Racing," Gugelmin said. "It's a nice group, with a lot of the best guys from when I was at PacWest—and it's an opportunity to help them get some success sooner. There's nothing missing in terms of people, engineers, and equipment. Craig and Kevin are really serious team owners, and I think pretty soon we'll get them up to speed. This group wants to succeed, and it is really behind CART.

"There are a few areas where I can help," Mauricio added. "I can help create better communication between the driver and the engineers because I know almost all of the tracks and I know how the car should behave. I can watch from trackside and see things that the engineers and the spotters can't see. The other thing is to give an opinion to Craig and Kevin about things that are important to the team. Craig's focus has been mainly Formula 1 and Kevin is fairly new to racing, so I can be another head to bounce opinions off of.

"Russ Cameron is a very good team manager, and I've gotten along well with him since my early days with PacWest," he concluded. "He's come a long way since then. He kept a good group of people together, he knows how to run a business, and he knows how to get results on the track."

Papis claimed a fourth-place finish at Road America, while Mika Salo earned the team's first podium by finishing third at Miami during the four races he drove to wrap up the initial campaign. For 2004, the team underwent a revamp, renamed PKV Racing with 1996 CART champion Jimmy Vasser joining as a driver and minority owner. In addition, Pollock stepped aside, with his stake in the team (and the 'P' in PKV) taken over by Dan Pettit, an associate of Kalkhoven's at JDS Uniphase and a partner in KPLJ Ventures. Kalkhoven attracted sponsorship from Gulfstream Aerospace—he was a long-term customer who traveled in a G550 jet—while the second car was driven by Roberto Gonzalez with support from Nextel of Mexico. Along with Gerald Forsythe and Paul Gentilozzi, Kalkhoven was also part of the ownership group that acquired the assets of CART following its bankruptcy, and from 2004 until early 2008, he would function as the front man and driving force behind the rebranded Champ Car World Series.

More changes arrived in 2005 as Jim McGee, the most successful crew chief/team manager in the history of Indy car racing, took over running the team, and 2002 CART champion Cristiano da Matta was tabbed to drive the second car alongside Vasser. At the same time, Cameron departed the organization, taking the fall after PKV failed to achieve satisfactory results for its owners following the expansion into a two-car team.

"Although we had a good manager that organized it well, I think we came to the conclusion that we needed a 'super-manager' with a lot of experience and a lot of knowledge," said Pettit. "We just didn't have the guy that could run it to the peak that it needed to be. As Jim came on the radar screens, we knew we had to have him. We're just thrilled that he was happy enough to come with us."

The arrival of McGee and da Matta failed to transform the team into a regular frontrunner, though da Matta claimed the team's first victory at Portland International Raceway. At the end of 2005, Pettit expanded his racing interests to become a co-owner of RuSPORT Racing, taking da Matta with him. PKV's 2006 drivers were Servia and Katherine Legge, the first female driver to win a race in Formula Atlantic. PKV contested the 2007 season with Servia and Neel Jani; renamed KV Racing Technology, the team was one of the few that were able to make the transition from Champ Car into the Indy Racing League when the two series merged in 2008. KVRT actually won the last Indy car race run under Champ Car sanction—the 2008 Long Beach Grand Prix—with driver Will Power, who later would emerge as one of the top drivers in the IndyCar Series after he joined Team Penske.

Bruce McCaw believes that Kalkhoven failed to adequately utilize him as a resource as the Australian expanded his presence in American open-wheel racing. "I have always been disappointed that Kevin didn't pick my brain more," he said. "When we first met, we had dinner at Vancouver. We had a great evening, drank a bunch of wine and got to know each other. I said, without preaching, 'I think there are a lot of things I can maybe help you avoid that you probably don't need to learn all over again.' But he never took advantage of that, though I pushed him several times.

"Kevin had some good instincts, though I think he got sold a bill of goods with Vasser," McCaw continued. "The way they overhauled the team to satisfy Jimmy... you could see where the problem was, and that was the loose nut behind the wheel. They spent a lot of money bringing Jim McGee in there, and what are you going to get for it? I don't believe you could have found a more honest or dedicated guy than Russ. Russ certainly needed some help in areas from sponsors right on down and I think he knew the right things to do, but sometimes he just needed support to do them."

KVRT generally ran a single car in 2009 before re-expanding into a two-car operation a year later, fielding drivers Takuma Sato and EJ Viso. With support from Lotus, KVRT ran three cars in 2011 and 2012, taking on 2004 IRL champion Tony Kanaan and his countryman Rubens Barrichello. In 2013, Kanaan won the Indianapolis 500 for KVRT and the team also fielded a car for female star Simona de Silvestro. Sebastien Bourdais, the four-time champion of the Champ Car World Series, was KVRT's lead driver from 2014-16, earning four race wins before the team ceased operations prior to the 2017 season.

"I want to thank all of those who have written to express their appreciation of the efforts of KV Racing Technology during the last 14 years," Kalkhoven stated. "However, as I approach 73, I feel I can no longer give the team the effort and support it and the team members deserve. I have really enjoyed my time in the series, helping with reunification and of course winning the greatest spectacle in racing—the Indianapolis 500. I remain committed to help in any way I can, particularly in encouraging new owners and sponsors."

With the closure of KVRT, PacWest Racing's distant ties to Indy car racing were finally severed.

CART CEO Chris Pook is flanked by Craig Pollock and Kevin Kalkhoven at the January 2003 announcement of PK Racing.

PK Racing team manager Russell Cameron reached out to Mauricio Gugelmin when the team struggled in early 2003.

Mike Levitt/LAT USA

Craig weathered a series of crises as CART's CEO, most notably the open-wheel split with the Indy Racing League.

Paul Webb

CART raced in front of packed grandstands all over the world, but was unable to sustain itself as a profitable business entity after Andrew Craig's departure.

Board, it would get voted out. It was like you just threw away three months of time and opportunity and it was very draining."

Over time, McCaw was increasingly disenchanted with the frequent management changes at CART and by how much of his time he was forced to dedicate to the direction of the company. He resigned his position on the Delaware Board in March 2001.

"I really viewed where I could bring the most value, both to PacWest and to CART, was to spend time trying to build the CART organization with sort of a rising tide theory—if it would help the sport it would help the team," McCaw said. "Once we became a public company it was a serious responsibility. But you couple those board meetings, often in the eastern half of the country, with races, and I was just getting worn out. I felt like I was becoming ineffective. Every time I traveled, I would travel with foot lockers full of stuff to read, phone calls to return, and everything else. It was time for me to shift gears, and it was clearly a time when I felt the team needed to be financially self-sustaining."

Regarding his decision to leave the CART board, McCaw said, "I had flown down to Naples, Florida, for a board meeting, and I spent three days there. By the time we left, I think we had unraveled everything we had done the last two meetings. I remember leaving on a Friday night and I was finished. I was so worn out from all of the BS. From the airplane, I called my attorney David Koopmans, who was still in his office at about 7 or 7:30 at night and told him I wanted him to write a letter resigning me from the board of CART, today. He said legally he couldn't do it, which I understood. But I said I wanted to be on the record that today is my last day, that I am resigning from the board, so that if something happens over the weekend, it doesn't become the reason why I can't resign. Pat Patrick called me Sunday morning at home and said, 'You can't resign from this.' Pat was pissed because I beat him to the door! He said, 'We really need you. I want to see you stay on the board.' I told him: 'I appreciate that, but I'm done. I am not going to spend my time unproductively. It's too precious to me and I'm not willing to do it.' Monday morning, I sent another letter that affirmed it and that was it."

Although he absolved himself of responsibilities in the CART organization, McCaw continued to provide guidance to PacWest throughout 2001, albeit much more at arms-length than up to that point. "I continued to talk to the team to try to help give them some direction, but I didn't do much traveling," he said. "I'd show up from time to time. Above all, I wanted to see the team succeed. It had always been my goal for the team to become completely self-sustaining in terms of both management and money.

“By 2001…a better decision might have been to just close the doors,” he added. “We had a lot of things going against us, though we also had a lot of things going for us. I think we structurally had the pieces there, but the fact was that additional sponsorship was going to be needed, and that market had really collapsed. The financial markets had collapsed. That was kind of a double whammy, and part of what the team had to operate on in 2001 was its CART stock. I had relinquished that as part of the plan, and when the stock went down, it shrank the value.”

Chief Steward Wally Dallenbach with Pat Patrick. Bruce McCaw's frustration with Patrick and other team owners led to his resignation from the CART board of directors.

That plan included setting up new companies called PWR 17 and PWR 18 that would lease certain assets of PacWest Racing so that the new organization could continue into 2002 with a minimal impact on personnel. But the PWR nomenclature did little more than create confusion, especially at a time when McCaw was putting distance between himself and PacWest.

“I was really opposed to them using PWR as the name because it wasn't making as clear a distinction as it should have,” he said. “From their perspective, they saw it as a bonus; from my perspective, I saw it as a negative. Part of what I wanted was that whatever company went forward was not just seen to be a continuation of the same. PWR 17 and PWR 18 were really just place-marker names to file as a corporation. They weren't ever designed to be an entity. Right at that time Lowry was quite confident Gateway Computers was going to be coming on board as a major sponsor and it was going to become Gateway Racing or something like that. I didn't really fight it very hard at the time because I didn't think it was going to stick. But the fact that it did stick, and the fact that they continued doing business that way, led to some confusion—though there were some people who claimed to be confused who clearly really weren't.”

CART CEO Joe Heitzler (left) greets Jolene McCaw (right) on the grid at Long Beach. CART suffered through a disastrous year with Heitzler at the helm from December 2000 to December 2001.

With Bruce McCaw and the PacWest Racing name officially out of the picture, Lowry and Russell Cameron managed to continue into 2002 under the name PWR Championship Racing. The staff was cut from 63 to 33, and a supply of Lola chassis and Toyota engines were secured to enter cars for Scott Dixon and Oriol Servia in the CART series. Servia was the 1999 Indy Lights series champion and had made 40 previous Champ Car starts. But after just three races, the last netting a pair of top-ten finishes at Twin Ring Motegi, the team disbanded. By then, Dixon's manager Stefan Johansson had already started the process of negotiating the driver's transfer to Chip Ganassi Racing.

“I could see the writing on the wall,” Johansson reflected. “I've been there before in Formula 1 and other categories where you can kind of see which direction it's going to go. I went to Lee White at Toyota and said, ‘Look, I don't think this is going to survive much

Mike Levitt/LAT USA

Gerald Forsythe (left) was among Heitzler's strongest defenders and the driving force behind the group that acquired the assets from CART in a 2004 bankruptcy auction.

Lesley Ann Miller/LAT

CART's appointment of Long Beach Grand Prix founder Chris Pook failed to reverse the company's slide.

longer. Is there anything you can do? We need to make something happen.' He said, 'Well, we've got a little bit of a slush fund, let's say. We'll see if we can get him into a third car with Chip.' Lee approached Chip, and between the two of them, they sort of managed to make it work for the rest of the year. Of course, lo and behold, one race later, or maybe even before the move to Chip happened, [PWR] folded."

Even though the move to championship-leading Ganassi undoubtedly featured a number of positives for Dixon, it also carried some risk because of the team owner's well-known lack of patience with drivers. In addition, Dixon would be taking a significant pay cut for the rest of the season, though in theory he had the security of a contract that carried through the end of 2004.

Johansson related, "It was tough for Scott to kind of put that out of his mind and go and drive for Chip for basically nothing at first. I said, 'Get in the car, get the job done, and everything is going to work out fine.' That's kind of what happened."

According to Lowry, the effort to keep PWR running remained intense to the very end. "At the time, we were really pretty excited that there were going to be sponsors on board, both Gateway and Enron. It just didn't turn out that way," he said. "In fact, if anything, as things started to wind down and it was apparent that we were on a shorter leash, I think our energy level was raised at that point to push sales and marketing, as well as myself, to try and get these elusive sponsors. It was post 9/11, and at least in Indianapolis, we were somewhat distracted because obviously there was a sense that things weren't right. But credit to Bruce—he never really communicated that outright, we just kind of sensed it. We just kept on working, trying to make it work. Obviously, we never got there, but clearly, we thought there was another leg to go.

"It was all so glamorous when I was just e-mailing Bruce, but the glamour went away when you got on the inside," Lowry added. "It was a lot of work. It was dollars and cents. When that car hit the wall, you were looking at the bill, as opposed to just the simple act of repairing the car. It's a legitimate business and, on the inside, I began to recognize that very quickly—which gives me more respect for Bruce, in fact, for being able to create the team that he did."

Naturally, there were some bitter feelings. Colleen Howerton was one of many who were disappointed by the way things came to a conclusion. The longtime office manager was one of four team members—along with Tim Love, Mark Moore, and Nigel Bloom—who remained with PacWest from the start in 1993 to the bitter end.

"In my mind, Mike Lowry ruined nine years of Bruce McCaw's built-up respect in one year," Howerton commented. "And that is a tragedy because I think Bruce is a very good person who did a lot for the sport and a lot for all of us as employees. I think Lowry tried to bring his business experience and tried to run a race team like a business, which you have to do to a certain extent. But I think racing is different and not like your normal business where you are taking Learjet out of the red. Yes, it needs to be run like a business to keep in business, but not with the business ethics Lowry had. He was very damaging. He took all of our passion that we had, not only for PacWest, but for racing, and squished it and wrung it out like a wet rag and just drained everybody of emotion. I think that's horrible because the one thing we all had was a lot of passion for what we were doing."

PWR shut its doors in mid-2002 and CART as a whole didn't last much longer. Joe Heitzler's reign as CEO lasted exactly one year. In December 2001, he was dismissed in favor of Long Beach Grand Prix founder Chris Pook, the charismatic front man many believed could be the series' savior. But Pook couldn't save a sinking ship. Despite creating a low-cost spec engine program with Cosworth for 2003 (Honda and Toyota both switched from CART to the IRL at the end of the 2002 season), and providing the remaining teams with millions of dollars of support, all Pook succeeded in was delaying the inevitable while burning through the $100 million CART had accumulated through its stock offering.

By June 2003, the company admitted in delayed public guidance that it would not have enough money to stage a 2004 season; in October, CART's stock was de-listed, and in December the company filed for Chapter 11 bankruptcy as part of a plan spearheaded by team owners Gerald Forsythe and Kevin Kalkhoven. Despite an 11th-hour counter-offer from Tony George and the Indy Racing League, United States Bankruptcy Judge Frank J. Otte ordered CART's assets—chiefly its contracts to stage races—to be sold to the Forsythe/Kalkhoven group in January 2004. The re-branded Champ Car World Series (Bridgestone Presents The Champ Car World Series Powered By Ford, to use its full corporate title) operated in opposition to the IRL until early 2008, when they were merged into a unified IndyCar Series.

In retrospect, PacWest Racing was formed just in time to catch the end of CART's glory days in the 1990s. But the decline of the series, the Indy car split, and the slumping global economy in the early 21st century, doomed the team's chances of achieving long-term stability.

Russell Cameron offered his own perspective on the final days of PacWest. "It was unfortunate that the team truly ended at the end of the 2001 season as PacWest because I

"When that car hit the wall, you were looking at the bill, as opposed to just the simple act of repairing the car."

Mike Lowry

SCOTT DIXON: INDYCAR LEGEND

Perhaps the saddest aspect of PacWest Racing's demise is that the team did not get to share in, and contribute to, Scott Dixon's subsequent success. Although he did not win a race in 2002 for Chip Ganassi Racing, Dixon was incredibly consistent, finishing nine of his 16 starts for the team in seventh or better, topped by second place in a Coors Light-liveried car in the Grand Prix of Denver.

Ganassi withdrew his team from the 2003 CART series and followed his engine supplier, Toyota, to the all-oval Indy Racing League. This was not what Dixon was expecting or hoping for, yet in what would become a hallmark of his Indy car career, he adapted quickly to the bigger, heavier IRL cars. Though the IRL chose to not classify him as a rookie for his first year in the series, the 22-year-old claimed five poles, scored three race wins (including his IRL debut at Homestead-Miami Speedway), and led more laps than any other driver on the way to clinching the 2003 IRL championship.

"I probably wouldn't have picked it and it was a hard move to come over to the IRL, with the all-oval experience," Dixon said. "But it's one of those things and with motorsport, it's hard to determine what you are going to do from one day to the next. I was definitely surprised, but I totally and thoroughly enjoyed this year. Life takes different steps and I am sure if you asked Tony Kanaan and Helio Castroneves, they would say they didn't expect to be here either."

Dixon's performances in America attracted the attention of the BMW-Williams Formula 1 team, which had tested Dixon in 2004. Williams offered a test contract but did not want to field an F1 rookie in races. Instead, Johansson negotiated a new three-year contract with Ganassi, a cycle that has repeated itself several times in the years since. During Dixon's seventeen-year tenure with Chip Ganassi Racing in the No. 9 car, he has had no fewer than 20 teammates from mid-2002 to the present.

That long association with the Ganassi team helped Dixon become one of the most successful drivers in the history of Indy car racing. By the end of 2019, he had amassed 46 race wins, a number exceeded by only A.J. Foyt (67) and Mario Andretti (52). Dixon's tally of five Indy car championships (2003, 2008, 2013, 2015, and 2018) is second only to Foyt's winning of seven, in four distinct specifications of car. Dixon also triumphed in the biggest race of all, winning the 2008 Indianapolis 500 after leading 115 of 200 laps. Queen Elizabeth II named Dixon a Companion to the New Zealand Order of Merit in 2019 for services to motorsport.

In 2018, director Matthew Metcalfe produced the documentary *Scott Dixon: Born Racer*, focusing on Dixon's 2017 season with Ganassi Racing. It was a somewhat turbulent campaign for the driver and team, notable for a huge airborne accident during the Indianapolis 500. Dixon was fortunate to escape from with nothing worse than a fractured foot. Through interviews with engineers Chris Simmons and Kate Gundlach, the film does a nice job of explaining the team effort that goes into putting a winning car on the grid. *Born Racer* also reveals a great deal of insight into Dixon's family life and his relationship with his wife, Emma, and daughters Poppy and Tilly.

Indeed, Dixon's reputation as a race car driver is exceeded by his reputation as an outstanding person outside the cockpit. Dixon had become close friends with PacWest Lights alumnus Dan Wheldon when they were teamed together at Ganassi Racing from 2006 to 2008. When Wheldon was killed in the 2011 IndyCar Series finale at Las Vegas Motor Speedway, Dixon and his family temporarily relocated to Florida for several months to support Wheldon's wife and children.

"That's the extraordinary part," said Stefan Johansson, Dixon's longtime manager. "He doesn't have the big ego that sort of comes with success a lot of times. He's just developed into an extraordinary human being. You pick the people you surround yourself with, but he's created a circle of people around him—starting with his wife—who are just really good people. It's incredible to have been part of it from the beginning and see now not only as a racing driver, but as a human being, how he has developed into an amazing person."

Chip Ganassi also paid tribute to the most accomplished driver in the history of his highly successful organization. "Scott and I have been together a long time; he was pretty shy at the start and I think 'Yes' and

“He knows how to win…and how to win championships.”

Chip Ganassi

‘Okay’ were the first 37 things he said to me,” Ganassi related. “I was thinking, ‘This kid is good, but can he string together a sentence?’ But people confuse that quietness with not caring about things. It’s a relief to know that really wasn’t what it is. It’s a quiet confidence that is sort of his trademark and that is a very powerful tool.

“He knows how to win, and more importantly, he knows how to win championships,” Ganassi continued. “He’s proven that he’s not just a normal run-of-the-mill driver in any sense and where he is in the overall win column speaks for itself. He’s the kind of driver that any team would want to have as their lead driver. He has the same desire to win today as he did when he came to our team, and I think that’s impressive. He’s a team player. He’s always pushing the limits, and he likes to get the most out of any situation.

“Probably the nicest thing is that I don’t think anybody could have grown into a better person than Scott Dixon, whether he’s a racing driver, a family man, a husband, a father, son, friend—whatever you want to call him.”

Although Dixon achieved the majority of his success with Chip Ganassi’s team, everyone involved with PacWest Racing remains fiercely proud that the organization gave the young driver his big break in Indy car racing. Dixon, for his part, rarely fails to mention that he scored his first top-level race win with PacWest. By grooming a future champion with its internal ladder system, Dixon represents everything PacWest Racing set out to achieve. But the team ceased operation before it was able to reap the ultimate rewards.

Dan Helrigel/IMS

Dixon’s most important individual race win came in the 2008 Indianapolis 500.

INDYCAR

Dixon has remained with Ganassi since mid-2002. He earned his fifth Indy car championship in 2018.

Lesley Ann Miller/LAT

Oriol Servia receives service in the 2002 season opener, with his PWR crew still wearing 2001 PacWest/Nextel firesuits.

think it was a good team to go forward with—a lot better than people gave it credit for," he said. "It was maturing, it was simplifying, and it understood the mistakes from '95 when it wasn't ready to win. Now it had good pit strategy and stops, and we were producing all the right things—good reliable cars, we had good engineers that were producing good setups, and we had two good guys in the seat with Oriol and Dixon. I think we were positioned really well.

"But the series was flaming out. When you're in the trenches, you don't always realize what's going on around you, and the company CART was really in trouble. You're kind of living in your own world and you don't always recognize that."

Bruce McCaw confers with Roger Penske. McCaw took a strong behind-the-scenes role trying to help CART through a difficult time.

PacWest's first open-wheel champion, Scott Dixon, is flanked by Bruce McCaw and Indy Lights team manager Paul "Ziggy" Harcus at Long Beach, 2000.

15

PACWEST INDY LIGHTS

THE DEVELOPMENT OF top-level Indy car drivers has gone through a major transformation over the years. Up through the 1960s, that path generally consisted of USAC-sanctioned Midgets and Sprint Cars on dirt and paved ovals, with the ultimate goal of graduation to what were then called 'Championship Cars' at the Indianapolis 500.

USAC attempted to expand into formula car racing in the 1970s, sanctioning a "Mini Indy" series from 1977 to 1980 and using the same Volkswagen-powered Super Vee cars that were campaigned in that era by the Sports Car Club of America. The SCCA phased out its Super Vee championship when it took over sanction of Formula Atlantic in the United States in 1980.

Believing there was a need for a performance level between the 240-horsepower Atlantic cars and the 700-horsepower cars of the PPG/CART IndyCar World Series, team owner (and CART co-founder) U.E. "Pat" Patrick created the American Racing Series. The ARS featured a spec March chassis similar to the company's Formula 3000 car mated to a 425-horsepower Buick V-6. The series was renamed Indy Lights in 1991, followed by the introduction of new Lola chassis in 1993 and 1997.

Formula Atlantic and Indy Lights shared an uneasy coexistence in a loosely defined CART Ladder system in the 1980s and 1990s, the series often battling each other to attract the most promising young talent. Atlantic, despite its smaller cars and lack of horsepower, was a fertile training ground, producing star drivers including the Villeneuve brothers, Gilles and Jacques, and later Gilles' son Jacques Jr. and Michael Andretti. Led by a series of dynamic young titlists, including Paul Tracy, Bryan Herta, and Greg Moore, winning the Indy Lights championship emerged as the more effective route to Indy cars by the mid-1990s.

One of the goals of Indy Lights was to encourage CART teams to use the series to develop next-generation drivers, mechanics, and engineers. But few of them actually did. PacWest started exploring the feasibility of running an Indy Lights program during Scott Sharp's difficult rookie Indy car season in 1994. Bruce McCaw wanted Sharp to take a step back to Lights and run the 1995 season in a PacWest-supported car (see Chapter 2).

With less travel and a lower stress level, the formation of PacWest Lights in 1997 came at the perfect time for Ziggy Harcus, seen here with Indy Lights president Roger Bailey.

Motorola provided some support for the Lights team, and the car was presented in a livery similar to Mark Blundell's entry in the CART series.

Though McCaw actually bought a car and lent support to David Donohue (son of the late champion racer Mark Donohue), plans for an in-house PacWest Lights effort remained on the back burner. Donohue contested a handful of Lights races in 1995. "Bruce had a car that they had gotten for Scott Sharp or somebody, and that didn't work out," Donohue recalled. "But like every day, it was all about where the money was going to come from. That was run by Alastair McNeil, and it was really always a last-minute thing. I mean, I went to Long Beach and it was there that I learned I was going to drive. They were bolting blocks to the pedals the morning of the race so that I could reach them! It was that kind of effort, not exactly the level of quality you would expect with those teams. But that at least got me a little bit of a relationship with PacWest." A year later, Donohue was tabbed to drive for PacWest in the North American Touring Car Championship (see Chapter 16).

PacWest then purchased one of the new 1997 Lola Indy Lights chassis. Thoughts of contracting an outside organization to run it changed markedly in early 1997 when Ziggy Harcus approached John Anderson to tell him he was resigning and relocating to New Mexico.

"I was still enjoying the Indy car team, but my twin boys were still back in Albuquerque," Harcus explained. "With the workload we had, I had no time to see them. Galles Racing called me up and offered me a job back there on their IRL team. It was two years guaranteed, with half the number of races, so my wife and I discussed it and we decided it would be a good idea to go back.

"I went to Ando and told him, 'I'm leaving,'" Harcus continued. "He just laughed at me and said, 'I'll see you tomorrow morning!' I said, 'I'm not here to negotiate. I'm telling you I'm done. I've already signed to go back to Galles and I'm going to go back to see my kids.' I had already rented my house in Indianapolis out, and they were two weeks away from being here. I came home to [wife] Nicki and said, 'I don't know what happened—I quit, and they didn't even listen to me!'"

The next day, Anderson and Harcus sat together for a conference call with McCaw, who indicated that PacWest was willing to work hard to keep Harcus on board. McCaw offered to help the Harcus twins relocate to Indianapolis, or to fly them from Albuquerque to Indianapolis several times a year to spend time with their father.

"There were some very generous offers on his part, but I still said no because I knew what the workload would be," Harcus said. "Even if they were back here, I would be working a lot of hours and couldn't do it. That's when the Indy Lights deal came up."

With a 13-race schedule, far less international travel, and a lower sense of urgency, running an Indy Lights program not only offered Harcus the opportunity to reduce the number of hours spent in the shop or on the road, he would also gain valuable managerial experience. It was a win-win situation for the team and for Harcus.

"I was very happy with where it went and it actually led me down a different path in life as well because I was going from "mechanic-ing" to learning how to be a manager and that was a huge step," he said.

For Anderson, a solution that allowed him to keep Harcus on board was a huge relief. Harcus had been a contender for the assistant team manager position in 1996 when it went to Russell Cameron.

"Those are two guys who, one or the other, could have been on my right shoulder, and I chose Russ," said Anderson. "That was the hardest decision I had to make, and the only reason is that I saw Russ possibly as being a little more maybe ruthless than Zig. Some people have said, 'Look out for Russ,' but if the guy's ambitious, that's the guy you want because you know you're going to get the job done. Zig's a great guy but Russ was probably removed that little bit more personally to be able to make a decision that wasn't done so much with his heart.

"I was so thankful when we decided to go with the Indy Lights team," he added. "Zig was looking for another position and I think he was very affected by my decision to have Russ take over as the team manager. I was thankful that we had a way to hold onto Zig."

The decision to establish PacWest Lights in-house wasn't made until the calendar turned to 1997, so recruiting experienced mechanics and engineers was a challenge. "Wow! It was desperate," Harcus recalled. "It got put together extremely late, so when we did get going, it was difficult to find people because they had already signed for other teams. It was a bit of a rag-tag sort of group; we had a truck driver, I think we had two mechanics, an engineer, and a gearbox guy."

Motorola agreed to provide some sponsorship support, and the chosen driver was Robby Unser, the youngest son of three-time Indianapolis 500 winner Bobby Unser. Robby Unser had a year of Indy Lights experience under his belt in 1996 with a best finish of fourth place at Michigan, and he brought some sponsorship from a consortium led by ADT Automotive. But the 29-year-old failed to improve on that result during the 1997 season with PacWest. He started the season reasonably well, with top-ten finishes in five of the

PacWest Lights' first driver was Robby Unser, the youngest son of three-time USAC champion Bobby Unser.

Unser confers with engineer Roberto Trevisan. Unser went on to make 21 starts in the Indy Racing League, scoring a pair of second-place finishes.

PacWest Lights expanded to two cars in 1998, running Frenchman Didier André and Australian Paul Morris. Lights team manager Ziggy Harcus ducks out of the rain to chat with André at Long Beach.

first six races, capped by sixth at the Milwaukee Mile. Results faltered in the second half of the campaign, with a seventh at Toronto as the only top-ten.

"I like Robby a lot and there was some speed there, but I think he struggled to put all of the corners together," recalled Harcus. "The more corners on the track, the further off we were. He'd get Turn 4 and 6 right one time, but without changes to the car he'd mess them up the next time out. Really nice guy to work with. Great guy. He just wasn't the guy that was going to lead the Lights team going forward."

Unser landed a ride in the Indy Racing League in 1998 and finished fifth in the Indianapolis 500 on his IRL debut. He later added a pair of second-place finishes in a 21-race Indy car career.

Despite the difficult first season, plans were made to expand PacWest Lights to a two-car effort in 1998. In addition, Motorola and PacWest provided support for P1 Racing to field a car in the CART Formula Atlantic Championship for Derek Hill, the defending Barber Dodge Pro Series champion and son of 1961 F1 World Champion Phil Hill.

PacWest's Indy Lights drivers for 1998 were 23-year-old Frenchman Didier André and Paul Morris, a 30-year-old Australian who had spent the previous five years racing sedans in his homeland. Morris had a joking personality belying the serious businessman at his core. He took a unique, carefree approach and almost treated the campaign like a summer holiday, driving to and from races with his girlfriend in a pick-up truck and towing a camper caravan. Morris returned to a successful career in Australia following his one-off Indy Lights season in America, compiling an enviable record with victories in all three major races at the Mount Panorama circuit in Bathurst.

"Paul Morris was the 'Dude from Down Under' in the Terry 2," chuckled Harcus. "Fantastic guy, but I don't know whether his commitment here was as strong as it needed to be. He was a big guy, so in a Lights car he had a penalty working against him right then and there. He was good in places and others not so good. Hell, he won the Bathurst 1,000 twice!"

The 1998 season continued to challenge the young team. But André developed into a Lights frontrunner, culminating in the first Indy Lights race win for the team at Laguna Seca. That breakthrough secured Didier second place in the final championship standings. In a year when the Indy car team struggled, Andre's victory provided a valuable morale boost for everyone at 4001 Methanol Lane—and a much-needed bit of levity. "Hollywood had invited a bunch of guests from Brazil, and we had some girls dressed

"I like Robby a lot and there was some speed there, but I think he struggled to put all of the corners together. The more corners on the track, the further off we were."

Ziggy Harcus

A last-minute decision resulted in PacWest running a second car in 1998 for Paul Morris, who enjoyed a long career in Australian motorsport, including a Bathurst 1000 victory.

in Hollywood dresses, as ambassadors for the brand," recalled Harcus. "We hadn't won a race all year, so I told Didier if he won the Lights race, I'd wear one of those dresses. Well, he goes and wins the race, so I had to wear the dress."

Overall, the 1998 campaign represented a step forward for the Lights team. "We seemed to get involved in a few accidents that year," Harcus recounted. "I remember crashing in places where we shouldn't have, and that was a struggle with that whole program that year. "You've got to look back and ask whether the team was as good as it could have been at that stage," he continued. "Well, maybe not. I was still learning and the other teams that had been in the Lights series were doing a better job on their engines. They knew what they had and what to do. There was a lot that I had to learn."

André returned for 1999 with the expectation that he would be a strong contender for the Indy Lights championship. But prior to the season, he had an unproductive test at Homestead-Miami Speedway that badly affected his confidence on ovals. Even on road courses, the season as a whole was a struggle, typified by the Cleveland weekend where André claimed pole position, only to be swept into a first corner crash. André won at Laguna Seca for the second year in a row, but he finished a disappointing eighth in the Indy Lights championship.

André's struggles on the ovals in 1999 came as a mystery to him and to Harcus because he had some good runs in 1998, including a second-place finish at Nazareth Speedway on a day when Morris and PacWest Champ Car drivers Mark Blundell and Mauricio Gugelmin all visited a local hospital after crashing.

"We had some problems early, but we fought back as a team and we were strong in the second half of the season," said André. "I've had the opportunity to test a Champ Car for PacWest, and I was very pleased at how well that went. I'm putting all of my efforts into finding a Champ Car ride for next year. I'm ready."

"Didier struggled to get on top of the ovals, and I don't know what it was," Harcus related. "Believe it or not, he went off and did a two- or three-day course at some sprint car place in Illinois where you just throw the car around to get a feel for the way it slides. We were trying to get him up to speed and just could not, and I think that's how Tony Renna got involved."

Renna was a 21-year-old American who jumped straight into Indy Lights in 1998 despite having run only a handful of F2000 races in his career. He scored a victory at Michigan

Speedway and finished third in the season finale at California Speedway, earning a reputation as an oval specialist. He was also without a ride in early 1999, leading to an audition with PacWest Lights.

"Tony kept coming around and he was just a great little guy," said Harcus. "I knew that he was fast on ovals so I called Bruce up and asked him whether I could put him in a car to try and get Didier better. Bruce agreed, and we went up to Milwaukee, if I recall correctly. It was an open test, and Tony was P1 on the first day and the car was really good. The next day, I just took the drivers out of the cars, left the crews with the cars, swapped the drivers only. I wanted to prove to Didier that the car was good, that what we had to fix was his feeling that the car was always loose and ready to come around on him.

"But I think that's just the way the old Indy Lights cars felt, with a big old engine out the back," Harcus added. "That didn't help much, and Didier wasn't happy, but I love Dids and I told him, 'We've got to point to the problem. If we don't do that, we're wasting our time.'"

PacWest ended up running a second Lights car for Renna at Milwaukee, where he drove to a third-place finish. Meanwhile, André failed to finish higher than 12th in the year's first five ovals before ending his Indy Lights career with a third place run at California Speedway. His lack of competitive form on ovals would always remain a mystery and, with André believing he was ready to step up to Indy cars, PacWest went in another direction for its 2000 Lights program. André ended up competing in the all-oval IRL IndyCar Series championship for Galles Racing in 2001 before returning to Europe to focus on a successful sports car career. He netted a class win in the 2003 24 Hours of Le Mans. André now runs a driving school and development program in his native France.

Three years into its existence, the PacWest Lights team was achieving its goals of developing personnel. "We're still learning about how to make that program complimentary, but it has clearly been the right thing for us to do and I think it's necessary for our overall organization," McCaw observed at the time. "This business isn't going to get any simpler. You've got to be able to bring people in, and at this level, you don't have time to train. You can't give up test days in a CART program to do driver training or evaluation, or crew training or evaluation either. You have to find other ways to do it, and I think the Lights series is the best way to do that. It's a great compliment to CART."

Though the third place in his first start at Milwaukee would be the best of Renna's results in his partial 1999 campaign, he was brought back as half of PacWest Lights' strengthened attack for 2000. Eighteen-year-old Scott Dixon was hired on a longterm contract for the other seat.

PacWest retained Tony Renna in mid-1999 to give the team guidance with its oval program. He qualified on the front row and finished third on his debut at Milwaukee.

FORMULA ATLANTIC WITH DEREK HILL

PacWest Racing never assembled a full-fledged entry in the CART Toyota Atlantic Championship. But the team did partner with P-1 Racing in 1998 to field a car for most of the season for Derek Hill, the 23-year-old son of 1961 Formula 1 World Champion Phil Hill. Bruce McCaw was acquainted with Phil and his wife Alma through common interests in classic cars; in addition to his career as a champion F1 and sports car driver, Phil Hill was a noted collector and world-class restorer of Packards and other classic autos. "Hill & Vaughn had the reputation of being one of the premier automotive restorers in the world," marveled McCaw. "When you see something Phil restored, it is just perfection."

As Derek's racing career came into shape, McCaw took a keen interest in trying to assist the younger Hill. Meanwhile, P-1 owner Bill Fickling was trying to reestablish a presence in a rejuvenated Formula Atlantic, which at the time was being relaunched under CART ownership with backing from Toyota and a new spec chassis produced in California by Swift Engineering. Fickling was the first dealer for Swift racing cars, and P-1 would run Hill's car out of its San Clemente workshop with sponsorship from Motorola and a livery almost identical to Mark Blundell's PacWest entry in the CART FedEx Championship Series.

"Bruce was very enthusiastic about it all and to have my car in the same livery as the Indy cars that Mark Blundell was driving was just very cool," recalled Hill. "It was all in all like feeling a big boost in my career to be able to do all that. I'll never forget being at St. Louis [Gateway International Raceway] on the banking and having all the Motorola cars lined up for a photograph, being able to feel like I was a real racing driver."

Like his father, Derek Hill started racing fairly late in life compared to many of his competitors. His open-wheel career started in the Barber Dodge Pro Series, where he took Rookie of the Year honors in 1996 before winning the championship a year later. At the time, Barber Dodge had a scholarship program to Indy Lights, but CART was in the process of revamping its ladder system and Barber Dodge was being pushed out of the rotation. Hill chose to pursue the PacWest/P-1 Atlantic option. "I remember it didn't go over well with the Barber Dodge people when I decided to do Atlantics, because I guess of the deal with IndyCar and the ladder they had in place," he said.

Hill drove the majority of the 1998 season in the P-1/PacWest car, achieving a best finish of fourth place at Long Beach. "The best thing about doing the Toyota Atlantic deal is I had a funded season in racing... what could be better than that?" Hill said. "When we were running, we were running pretty well, so no complaints there. We just had a lot of problems with that car, with the Swift. I know we were in the first year of development with that chassis and as the politics of racing go, there wasn't a whole lot of development we could do on the car. But what can I say? I thought it was very cool to be part of a satellite operation to an established Indy car team and it was thrilling to watch Mark and Mauricio run well when they did.

"I can look back with hindsight and say that is something I would have love to have stuck with, maybe doing another year of Toyota Atlantics and developing that relationship further with the PacWest team," Hill added. "But as it goes, I made those decisions to move on after that season. I just had such a string of DNFs and things going wrong that year that it's a tough one to look back and say, yes, that we achieved everything we wanted to that year."

He pursued an open-wheel career in Europe and reached Formula 3000, and compiled an accomplished career in sports cars that included class wins in the 12 Hours of Sebring and Daytona 24 Hours. He also served as the front man for a Cadillac television advertising campaign and performed stunt driving duties in the acclaimed racing movie *Ford vs. Ferrari.*

McCaw and Hill maintained a friendship over the years as they often came in contact in classic car and vintage racing circles. Aside from occasionally driving in vintage events, Hill started serving as the Master of Ceremonies for the Pebble Beach Concours d'Elegance in 2015. In that role, he presented McCaw with the Best in Show award in 2017 when McCaw's

"Bruce was very enthusiastic about it all and to have my car in the same livery as the Indy cars that Mark Blundell was driving was just very cool."

Derek Hill

1929 Mercedes-Benz S Barker Tourer claimed the prestigious honor. "Derek has undertaken the task of fully organizing his father's archive and photographs into an extraordinary resource," noted McCaw. "The first product of this is a truly amazing three-volume set of books of Phil's photographs curated with Doug Nye, Steve Dawson, and others."

Derek Hill, the 23-year-old son of legendary driver Phil Hill, raced a Formula Atlantic car with PacWest's support in 1998.

Hill's first race was his best, finishing fourth at Long Beach.

PacWest's pairing of Tony Renna and Scott Dixon in 2000 was arguably among the strongest in the history of the Indy Lights championship.

With two aggressive young guns on board as paid drivers, expectations for PacWest Lights rose in 2000. Harcus and his team delivered, with Dixon scoring six race wins and earning the Indy Lights championship crown for PacWest. Renna ended the year fifth in the standings.

"That was actually when the Lights team changed into being top notch," Harcus said. "Before that we had been a middle of the road team. You've got to have that driver in there. I look back and wonder, is there a huge amount I changed on the cars? No. The crews were the same; we did a little bit more with the engines; we'd dyno them and figure out which ones had the best top end for an oval and which were better for a road course. But realistically, it was drivers that were pushing each other.

"Dixon and Renna were fantastic friends," he added. "Renna was really funny because he could never figure out how Dixon could go so quick on his out lap. It used to drive him nuts. That was a really good year, to me one of the best years because they were great drivers and great guys and it just makes your life easy."

Dixon started the season in the best possible way by scoring a dramatic win at Long Beach. The New Zealander ran second for most of the race, then took advantage of a late caution to pressure pole man Jonny Kane into a mistake with just four laps remaining. A shocked Dixon cruised to the finish to win by 3.753 seconds over Jason Bright.

To some observers, Dixon was almost unrecognizable on the podium. His physique no longer resembled that of a young Paul Tracy, thanks to bleached hair, and a strict diet and training regimen organized by the PacWest team's nutritionist, Jim Leo.

"I've lost 15-20 pounds," Dixon confirmed. "We're training pretty much seven days a week, two hours a day. The training has helped me a lot. I'm a lot fitter, and that makes my job a lot easier. The whole PacWest outfit is so organized, it makes it easy."

Dixon added a dominant win from the pole at Milwaukee, where Renna got the jump from fourth on the grid to lead the first 34 laps before he dropped out with a duff engine.

"Two out of two for Scott was fantastic, but it could certainly have been a 1-2 for PacWest," said Harcus. "Tony made a tremendous start and was doing everything right before a trail of smoke started to appear. We had a major oil leak of some sort."

Perhaps even more impressive than Dixon's pair of season-opening wins was his cool drive to fourth at Detroit. Scott had to cope with poor handling all weekend, and his race

Peroxide alert! Scott Dixon and Tony Renna confer with PacWest Lights team manager Ziggy Harcus in the Milwaukee pits.

At the height of PacWest's investment in young driver development, Bruce McCaw celebrates a 1-3 Indy Lights finish with Tony Renna and race winner Scott Dixon at Chicago Motor Speedway in 2000.

Now four-strong following the birth of son Wynn, the McCaw family helped Dixon celebrate another victory at Vancouver.

pace was slowed by high engine temperatures. But the Kiwi was able to drag his stricken car to the finish for valuable championship points.

Dixon had a less happy day in Portland, losing the front wing of the No. 17 car at the first corner. He pitted for a new nose and was able to stay on the lead lap, but the race ran green from start to finish, forcing Dixon to work hard for 11th place. At Michigan, he had a late-race clash with championship rival Townsend Bell, who recovered to finish fourth.

At that stage of the season, Bright led the point standings, but Dixon regained the top spot by leading 70 of 97 laps to win for the second year in a row at Chicagoland Speedway. Renna earned his first podium of the season with third place. "I'm happy to be back on the podium after a brief absence," Dixon said. "We had a couple bad races at Portland and Michigan, but I guess that's how it goes in racing."

Bell won at Mid-Ohio over Dixon to move up to second in the standings, 13 points behind the PacWest driver. Dixon then extended the gap to 42 points by winning at Vancouver and Laguna Seca. The tables turned at Gateway International Raceway when Dixon crashed early in the race and Bell won, knocking 20 points off Dixon's advantage heading into the last two races of the season.

Another incident on the Houston street course, coupled with a second-place finish from Bell, meant that Dixon entered the championship finale at California Speedway only four points to the good. But there was little drama at Fontana, because although Bell again finished second, Dixon led 99 of the 100 laps to claim his sixth win of the season. He won the Indy Lights title by 11 points over Bell.

Dixon immediately jumped into the lead at the start, and Renna latched onto his PacWest teammate's gearbox. "I owe a lot to Tony for covering my back and helping me stay out front until the end," commented Dixon. "These superspeedway races are a bit of a lottery because it's so easy to get hung out to dry if you don't have anyone working with you.

"Midway through the race, I was hoping Tony and I could stay together for the entire race. But Bell got past, and then all Tony could do was put pressure on him from behind to keep him occupied."

"I knew what I needed to do to help Scott and really I was just a buffer in third place," said Renna. "It was certainly pretty tight out there at times, but it worked out great for all of us in the end. We got a great start and held on to first and second for most of the race, then when Townsend got ahead of me, I knew that I just needed to make sure Scott finished second in order to help PacWest win their first championship."

Bell piled pressure on Dixon in the closing laps, but the Kiwi never cracked. Bell made a final lunge down the inside as the pair headed toward the checkered flag, almost running onto the grass, but Dixon aggressively defended the position and held on across the line.

"What a great feeling!" Dixon exclaimed. "This is definitely the biggest championship I've won in my career. We didn't figure on having to fight it out in the final event, but I finally had some luck after two bad races. My team was incredible all year and it paid off in spades."

"Scott has been consistently fast and won the championship as a result," said McCaw. "They say the first championship is the hardest one to get, so hopefully we can go on to a lot more success in the future. It really was a strong season for us and today we won the trophy we have been after for four years now."

It was widely believed at the time that Dixon and Renna were racing for the opportunity to graduate to a PacWest drive in the CART series for 2001. In January, Dixon was confirmed as Mauricio Gugelmin's teammate. That did not sit well with Renna, who believed his PacWest Lights contract stipulated he would move up to the Champ Car series if he finished fifth or better in the 2000 Indy Lights standings.

Renna unsuccessfully sued PacWest for breach of contract and, without options in the CART series, he pursued a career in the IRL. Renna made six starts for Kelley Racing in 2002, earning top-ten finishes in four, and ran the 2003 Indianapolis 500, finishing seventh. In late 2003, he landed what looked like his big career break: an IRL seat alongside his old friend and teammate Dixon at Chip Ganassi Racing. And Ganassi wasn't the only IRL team that was competing for Renna at the time.

"Kyle Moyer called me because Andretti Green was also looking at Tony," recalled Harcus. "I told him as an oval racer, Tony was fantastic. He was at one with the car, very at ease with it and always quick. As a road course racer, he wasn't bad either. He was a good all-rounder. I told Kyle I'd hire him in a heartbeat, especially back then when the IRL was all ovals. I think he had a huge amount of talent and was easy to work with. He was going to win races and possibly a championship."

Tight racing in the championship finale, as Dixon and Renna dice with Townsend Bell.

Dixon celebrates his Indy Lights championship with his parents and mentor Kenny Smith (left).

Running the number 1 earned by Dixon, PacWest's lead Lights driver for 2001 was 22-year-old Dan Wheldon.

Wheldon posted consecutive wins for PacWest at Gateway and Road Atlanta, the latter causing some acrimony with teammate Dominguez.

Unfortunately, Renna's life came to a tragic end before he ever ran a race in the Target colors. He died in a violent single-car testing crash at the Indianapolis Motor Speedway in October of 2003. No video exists of the accident and the cause remains a mystery.

In 2001, PacWest Lights ran cars for two more drivers who went on to successful Indy car careers. Mario Dominguez earned two wins in Champ Car sanctioned competition, while Dan Wheldon developed into one of the best drivers of his generation, claiming 16 IRL race wins including the 2005 Indianapolis 500 and the 2005 IndyCar Series championship. Wheldon would also team with fellow PacWest Lights alumnus Dixon at Chip Ganassi Racing from 2006 to 2008.

The 2001 Lights championship was dominated by Townsend Bell, who won six races. Wheldon won twice for PacWest and finished second to Bell in the points chase, while Dominguez claimed fourth in the overall standings.

"Both of those guys were good racers—you couldn't complain about either one of those two," recalled Harcus. "Dan was very good at the IRL formula. I don't know how instrumental Ando was in getting him over to Andretti Green, but he [Dan] won a championship and an Indy 500 with Ando. I'm sure Ando must have thought about that because we knew he [Dan] was a pretty good racer when he was running for us."

One aspect that Wheldon appreciated about his year with PacWest was the opportunity to get to know Dixon. "We weren't pure teammates because he was running CART and I was doing Indy Lights, but he was somebody that I would ask questions and he's obviously someone I respected a lot," Wheldon said in 2006, when he joined Dixon on the Ganassi IRL team. "You could see the impact he had on the organization at PacWest, which was pretty impressive because they had some pretty big names there before. He's one of those guys you can level with because he always says it like it is. That small history we had together will definitely help speed up our learning curve. You have to have a good relationship to succeed and we both understand our mission is to help the team advance."

Unlike the harmonious pairing of Renna and Dixon, Wheldon and Dominguez did not get along famously as teammates. Much was made of the chemistry that Wheldon later shared with his Andretti Green teammates Dario Franchitti, Tony Kanaan, and Bryan Herta, but it's a fair argument that Wheldon did not become a true team player until he was paired with Dixon at Ganassi.

Harcus remembers one particularly tense exchange between the 2001 PacWest Lights teammates. “Wheldon ran Dominguez off the road during the race at Road Atlanta and went on to win the race,” Harcus said. “We might have been first and third or something like that, but Dominguez was really upset and said he was going to write a letter to the series and demand that they remove Dan as the race winner. Then we all had to drive back to the airport together. A 45-minute drive with the two of them in the car...it wasn't pretty.”

PacWest Lights ended its five-year run with a total of 10 race wins and one Indy Lights Series championship. It helped advance six drivers to Indy cars, including Dixon and Wheldon, who developed into two of the finest champions of their generation. Wheldon, sadly, died in late 2011 after an Indy car career that produced two Indianapolis 500 victories and the 2005 IRL series championship.

Ziggy Harcus also enjoyed a successful career post-PacWest; as a team manager at Andretti Autosport, he managed three Indianapolis 500 winning teams with drivers Ryan Hunter-Reay (2014), Alexander Rossi (2016), and Takuma Sato (2017).

“We felt the Lights team, fundamentally, was a people development program and it gave some opportunities to some very good people like Ziggy, who needed a new challenge,” said McCaw. “He was doing things on the management side that he had never done before in his life, and he's gone on to have a lot of success at the Indy car level.”

Harcus credits McCaw's flexibility and desire to keep him part of the PacWest team for transforming his career. “Bruce gave me an opportunity to get into management side of it through the Indy Lights program, and if it wasn't for that, I'd still be bent over with my back broken under a race car,” he said. “Bruce sort of forced me to take the step that led me in another direction and led to other opportunities. I'm very grateful and appreciative.”

Dominguez took three second-place finishes during his year with PacWest. He went on to a solid career in the Champ Car World Series, scoring a pair of race wins.

PacWest achieved great success in the North American Super Touring Championship in 1996 and 1997.

16

PACWEST TOURING CAR GROUP

IN THE 1990s, a common form of production-based automobile racing known as Super Touring gained widespread popularity around the world. BMW, Alfa-Romeo, Vauxhall (a twin of Opel, the European division of General Motors), Ford, Audi, Volvo, and Renault all supported factory efforts for mass-produced 2-liter sedans in various national championships. Led by CART team owner Gerald Forsythe, the first North American Touring Car Championship (NATCC) was announced in July 1995 in the hopes of attracting the same kind of manufacturer support enjoyed across Europe and Asia. According to NATCC President Roger Elliott, with the addition of the United States and Canada, Super Touring races would be held in 20 countries in 1996. "It's the first road racing program under FIA jurisdiction to run in more countries than Formula 1," he said.

The series was open to compact four-door sedans with annual production in excess of 25,000 units. Sheet metal, with the exception of modest front and rear spoilers, remained stock, a key element in linking cars racing in the series to their production counterparts. Competitors could utilize any engine produced by the manufacturer with six cylinders or fewer, and a capacity of less than 2.0 liters. Stock blocks and heads were mandated, along with an 8,500-rpm rev limit. The cars retained catalytic converters and raced on unleaded pump gasoline. Retention of the production car's basic driveline and suspension layout was mandatory, but development of major areas, up to and including the alteration of bore and stroke, was left open. All cars whether front- or rear-wheel drive, utilized a sequential-shift racing gearbox.

CART CEO Andrew Craig spoke at the official launch of the NATCC in Detroit on December 14, 1995. "We've worked with the NATCC to incorporate Super Touring racing with some of our premier road racing and street racing events," he remarked. "A number of IndyCar promoters are very interested in the concept. It provides a different show on race weekends and provides drivers who have stepped out of Indy cars a chance to continue to race in front of familiar fans. Additionally, a number of IndyCar teams have expressed interest in running cars."

PacWest Racing was one of those teams. After spending the 1995 season in a managerial role for the PacWest Indy car team, Dominic Dobson was keen to resume his driving

Chrysler Corporation debuted the Dodge Stratus in 1995 as a modern entry in the compact car class.

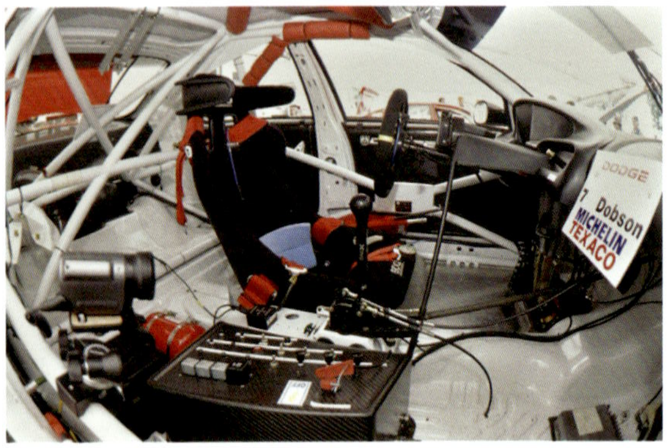

While derived from a production "body in white," the cars that competed in the North American Touring Car Championship were actually highly sophisticated.

career. The NATCC looked like a perfect opportunity. At the Vancouver CART race in September 1995, the team announced that Dobson had started working on setting up a satellite operation that would expand PacWest's footprint in American racing without impacting the organization's Indy car effort.

"I kind of went from owner-driver to owner-manager, back to owner-driver again, in a different series," Dobson explained. "It was a challenging time for me, and frankly I missed driving. To a large extent, my role in the Indy car team was about flying around and being at all the races, but watching somebody else have the fun, so to speak. I guess at mid-summer of that year, the opportunity was presented to me through Pat Wall for the Chrysler Touring Car effort. We started to gather information about the series and found out that Chrysler was building a car—and that Reynard was involved. In fact, Reynard, whose Indy cars we were running, introduced us to Chrysler. We sat down and talked about it and decided to try and make a run for it. Lock, stock, and barrel. Bruce said let's do it under the guise of PacWest Touring Car. We structured a partnership on the Touring Car team between Bruce, Tom Armstrong, and myself. So here I was, kind of back in the owner role of a smaller but separate organization, set up and structured differently. I think that helped Chrysler opt for us over the applications from four or five other serious teams, which included a couple other Indy car teams and two from Trans-Am."

Chrysler Corporation was the first, and ultimately the only, American manufacturer to commit to the NATCC. But it committed in a big way. The company did not compete in NASCAR at the time, so the two-car NATCC effort, using the mid-size Dodge Stratus sedan as the platform, would serve as Chrysler's premier motorsports program. With Dobson as the point man, PacWest was designated as Chrysler's "Development Team" to prepare and manage an ambitious two-car effort.

"The PacWest Touring Car Group's Indy car experience is a fine compliment to the production car engineering expertise we are putting into the Stratus Super Touring Car," commented Lou Patane, executive director of brand marketing for Chrysler. "The international character of this series positions Stratus here and abroad as a dynamic and technologically refined vehicle."

Unlike the competition, which sourced their NATCC-eligible cars from existing touring car programs in Europe and Japan, the Dodge effort started from a clean sheet of paper—or more accurately, a blank computer screen. "This series fit the philosophy of Chrysler to a 'T,'" added Tim Culbertson Chrysler's program manager for the

NATCC Stratus. "Basically, we want to race what we build. What we are doing is very unique, because racing programs are not typically done in-house. But this time we have in-sourced the program to Chrysler Engineering. We've used the same engineers, designers, technicians, and mechanics who work on our other lines of cars. It's also allowing some young engineers to get their hands on the entire car, instead of working their way through one part of the car at a time, which is the usual procedure. The learning experience we're getting from that is outstanding and we're very proud of the final product."

Entries were required to maintain the street car's basic suspension layout, but featured the latest in brake and damping technology.

While Chrysler rightfully took pride in the strong "in-house" element to the NATCC project, including full development of the engine, the company still received plenty of outside help. Of particular importance was the relationship with Reynard, which at the time was not only the world's leading producer of single-seat racing cars, but a key developer of technology for touring car racing. A dedicated computer link allowing for the timely transfer of data was established between Chrysler Engineering in Auburn Hills, Michigan, and Reynard's base in Bicester, England. Chrysler was able to test and utilize its new and proprietary three-dimensional Digital Model Assembly technology and helped Reynard upgrade its computer-aided design (CAD) capabilities.

The formation of PacWest Touring Car Group and the partnership with Chrysler was announced on December 14, 1995, at a press conference in Detroit. The very next day, Dobson hired Steven Costello as team manager for the PacWest Dodge effort. The pair had extensive ties; a former SCCA racer, Costello served as Dobson's race engineer for Spice Engineering in the IMSA Camel Lights series from 1987 to 1989.

A longtime friend and colleague of Dominic Dobson, Team Manager Steven Costello brought a wealth of knowledge to the PacWest Touring Car effort.

"I was actually doing some ski race training at Park City when Dominic called," Costello recounted. "He said, 'Steven, I've got this deal. It's a Touring Car program with Chrysler. Do you want to be the engineer, or do you want to be the team manager?' I said I'd prefer to be the team manager, because I had some ideas about how to do that. We all met at the North American International Auto Show in Detroit in January 1996. That's where the official announcement was made."

Joined by Chrysler Corporation President and Chief Operating Officer Bob Lutz, the first NATCC Dodge Stratus was unveiled onstage at NAIAS on January 4, 1996, less than five months before the May 25th opening round of the championship at Lime Rock Park. In that time, Dobson and Costello were tasked with recruiting a team of mechanics and support personnel, and setting up a race shop at 150 Gasoline Alley in Indianapolis, the facility recently vacated by the PacWest Indy car team.

The team gathers at Memphis Motorsports Park for an early test for the NATCC Dodge Stratus, March 12, 1996: (left to right) Melanie Correll, Pat Wall, Michael Harvey, Eric Dion, "Jake" McLellan, Larry Zelesnik, Josh Browne, Billy Wright, Bill Bergstrom, Steven Costello. Kneeling: Dominic Dobson.

Preparation for the upcoming season of competition generally went smoothly. "I had known Steven since my sports car days, and he did a great job running the organization for us," Dobson said. "He ran that place with a discipline that I sometimes wish we had in the Indy car organization! Of course, it was much smaller and a much easier organization to manage. We had only 12 people, as opposed to 60 or 70. The Indy car team had their new building, so we moved into the old building and that was a nice transition."

Following the official launch at NAIAS, Costello set to work. "After we visited the Chrysler Technical Center, I dropped Dominic for his flight home and continued down to Indianapolis where I shoveled snow so I could walk into an empty building," Costello said. "There was just some office furniture, some dead phones, an old Magnaflux machine, and a few benches that the Indy car team left behind. When we ran our first test at Memphis on March 12th, we had little more than wooden benches to work on. It was a pretty bare bones workshop at the time. We had just gotten the transporter, leased from Brix Racing, and like everything else it was plain white. We had virtually nothing other than hand tools and set-up equipment for the first test. But we eventually managed to purchase enough machine tools that we could do an awful lot of work there. That was a fantastic, proper-size shop for what we were doing."

PacWest took delivery of its first car on March 1 at the Chrysler Technical Center in Auburn Hills, Michigan. The ceremony was attended by more than 2,000 Chrysler employees, including company Chairman and CEO Bob Eaton. By then, the team knew it had been tasked with handling the initial testing of the Stratus, something that was not part of Chrysler's original plan.

"We weren't actually supposed to be doing that first test—it was supposed to be handled by a group of ex-Spice USA people out of Atlanta, headed by Julian Randalls," explained Costello. "They had a deal with Chrysler to do NASCAR truck testing and some Viper testing. The Atlanta group was supposed to do all the initial testing of the Stratus before we took delivery of the cars in May, but we got a call in probably early February from Tim Culbertson, who said, 'Congratulations PacWest, you're doing all the testing!' And it was 27 days of testing, an enormous testing schedule, in addition to trying to complete the second car and finding another driver." Dobson racked up more than 1,600 miles of testing prior to the first race.

Chrysler was keen to put a young American driver into the second car alongside Dobson, but there were few eligible or available candidates. The drive eventually went to David

Donohue, the 30-year-old son of the late Mark Donohue. It was Mark who'd put Penske Racing on the map with a series of road racing championships and the first of Roger Penske's many victories in the Indianapolis 500. Strongly discouraged from pursuing a racing career by his mother (Mark Donohue died in a Formula 1 accident in 1975, when David was eight years old), the younger Donohue nonetheless began a competition career in 1988, and by the mid-1990s was regarded as a talented sports car racer.

Bruce McCaw had worked with Donohue in the hopes of helping the driver take his career into the CART-sanctioned Indy Lights open-wheel series. McCaw purchased one of the second-generation Lola Indy Lights chassis used from 1992 to 1996 with the idea of having Scott Sharp take a step back to Lights after his difficult rookie Indy car campaign in 1994. Sharp and PacWest parted ways, but McCaw and Dobson stayed in contact with Donohue and he was PacWest's first choice for the Touring Car seat.

The decision to retain Donohue to drive the second PacWest Stratus was not finalized until the week before the first race. "That was a long search process," Costello said. "Chrysler desperately wanted an American driver under the age of 30, and David sort of qualified, but he wasn't under 30. We were very pleased, as was everyone, that David was chosen, but he came into the program very late, as did his car."

"David was just such a joy to have around," Dobson added. "He was immediately fast in the car, well spoken, and he got along with everybody. Obviously he had a family name, but I don't think it bought him as much as some other family names because his dad wasn't there. He didn't really know his dad that well; I think he [Mark] spent most of his career gone, but he [David] had spent some time around him."

The series opened at Lime Rock Park on Memorial Day weekend. Dobson claimed pole position for both races, but he stalled at the start of the first contest and was relegated to a third-place finish. Donohue, meanwhile, started from the back of the grid after suffering gearbox problems in practice and qualifying. But by adapting quickly to the unfamiliar car, and driving a clean and steady race, Donohue was able to take the lead from Rod Millen on the 10th lap and maintained it to end of the 25-lap contest to become the first race winner in North American Touring Car Championship history.

"It was such a learning experience, so different to anything else I had driven," Donohue recalled. "I had never driven a sequential gearbox before, I had never raced a front-wheel drive car and I had never driven for a team at that level. I won the first race,

"David was just such a joy to have around. He was immediately fast in the car, well spoken, and he got along with everybody."

Dominic Dobson

Dominic Dobson (right) describes the handling of the Stratus at an early test to Bill Stone and Dave Benbow.

which sounds really admirable. But I was so out of water and not confident that I just made fewer mistakes than everyone else and just motored to victory."

Dobson made up for his Race 1 disappointment by taking a flag-to-flag victory from pole position in Race 2, followed home by Donohue for a PacWest Dodge 1-2. "This is a tribute to the work both Chrysler and Reynard have done to design and build the Stratus," remarked Dobson. "It's also a credit to the PacWest Touring Car team, led by Steven Costello, for the three months of intense testing and development of the car. I'm also very pleased to have a teammate like David Donohue out there to back me up and support the team. He drove two great races this weekend without the benefit of a lot of seat time."

David Donohue gets to grips with a brand new Super Touring Dodge Stratus at Lime Rock.

The next round of the NATCC took place in conjunction with CART's Detroit Grand Prix at Belle Isle. This was an extremely important event for Chrysler, and many of the company's bigwigs turned out to support the Touring Car effort, including Lutz and Patane, along with Chrysler Motorsports Program Manager Bill Tracy and Vice President of Engineering Francois Castaing. Dobson finished fourth in Race 1 and won Race 2. That earned him the $5,000 Dodge Challenge Cup, presented to the NATCC driver who accumulated the most points over the Detroit weekend. "It was important to keep the Dodge Challenge Cup home, not only for PacWest, but for all the Chrysler people who had a hand in the development of this car," Dobson said. "This was a very special win for Dodge and our team."

David Donohue and Dominic Dobson formed an effective pairing for their two years of Touring Car racing.

Subsequent races revealed that while the Stratus generally was able to maintain the same cornering speeds as the competition from Honda and BMW, the car was sorely lacking in straight line speed. Randy Pobst, driving a TC Kline Racing Honda, swept the two races at Portland International Raceway and added a third consecutive win on the streets of Toronto. His teammate Peter Hardman triumphed in the second race. A series of podium finishes kept Dobson in the championship hunt. He cut Pobst's margin to four points following a win in the first race at the Trois Rivieres street course, where the PacWest Dodges traded their white livery for a more distinctive coat of red paint.

After Mid-Ohio, where Honda's Peter Cunningham won both races, Dobson was still just seven points behind Pobst. Dominic qualified on pole position for both races at Vancouver, and scored a thrilling victory in Race 1 after aggressively passing Pobst for the lead. But Dobson again lost his pole position advantage at the start of Race 2 and, at the end of the opening lap, crashed heavily while trying to muscle past Pobst for second place. Pobst recovered to finish fourth, giving him a comfortable championship lead for the final round at Laguna Seca Raceway. A win and a second-place finish at

For 1997, Dobson's car received a bright new livery to highlight sponsorship from PPG Automotive Finishes.

Laguna were more than enough for the BMW driver to claim the title, with insult added to injury for Dobson when his engine blew just three laps into the final round.

Still, the campaign was viewed as a success. Dobson and Donohue finished second and third in the standings; Dobson earned seven poles, and he and Donohue combined for five race wins. "Randy Pobst drove really well and they did a brilliant job of capitalizing whenever we had an issue," assessed Costello. "They basically took a British Touring Car Championship-handoff Honda and he did a beautiful job of both driving and just being in the right place at the right time. Peter Cunningham was also going very well in his Honda, and at that point, I suspect we were somewhere in the area of 25 horsepower down on where we should have been. We started out not even being close to the Hondas on horsepower and it took at least the first year, and well into the second year, until we got to the level of the Hondas and the BMWs."

Dobson was proud of the effort that went into the first year of the Touring Car team and the fact that it earned the first race win for the PacWest organization. But he admits that it may have been difficult for the Indy car team, which was enduring some growing pains in 1996, to watch their "little brother" immediately find success in the NATCC.

"I think the fact that the first PacWest win was Touring Car was bittersweet," related Dobson. "It certainly was nice to have won a race under the PacWest banner, but I think the PacWest organization was hoping to win an Indy car race—which of course it went on to do. But it was almost as if the Touring Car program renewed us. We had immediate success with it. It was a high-tech program; we were involved with Reynard. The cars weren't Indy cars by any means, but it wasn't a big step backwards from a technical standpoint. They were challenging in their own unique way. I thought we had a great series and put on some very good shows."

For 1997, Chrysler planned a series of improvements to the Stratus Touring Car, using the company's new Synthesis of Simulated Technology, one of the first applications of finite element analysis. "In the old days, we designed our cars on the drawing board, but today we design them on a computer," said Culbertson. "I'm taking SST and asking what will happen to our lap times if we do all these things. One of our jobs is to prove that SST can make a difference. If it can do to the production cars what it has done for the racers, the Chrysler hierarchy is going to say that we should keep pushing this stuff."

While outwardly similar, the 1997 Stratus for the renamed North American Super Touring Championship was effectively an all-new car. It featured a new aerodynamic package

PacWest Touring Car co-founders Tom Armstrong and Dominic Dobson chat on the grid.

Dobson calls winning the Dodge Challenge Cup on Chrysler's home turf in Detroit in both 1996 and 1997 a career highlight.

(front splitter and rear wing), the Xtrac sequential-shift gearbox was upgraded, and major improvements were made to the 2.0-liter 4-cylinder engine. "I don't think it shared any components with the '96 car, other than brakes and a few off-the-shelf pieces," commented Josh Browne, a Chrysler engineer who was embedded with the PacWest team in Indianapolis during the course of the Touring Car program. "We even re-optimized the roll cage." Donohue's No. 8 car retained its red and white livery, enhanced by associate sponsorships from Infinity and Silicon Graphics, while Dobson's No. 7 Stratus sported a vivid, new multi-colored paint scheme to represent new title sponsor PPG Automotive Finishes.

Dobson and his wife Kristen welcomed their first child in October 1996, so Donohue handled the testing duties for the new car. "The '96 cars were pretty solid, but not nearly as good as the '97 cars," Donohue remarked. "I think Chrysler really underestimated what was possible with the engines. I think the '96 cars were probably easier to drive. I did all of the testing in '97 and I just got married to the car. It was much more knife-edge in setup, and I was able to gain much more of an understanding about front-wheel drive and learn how to get the most out of the tires, which was so crucial. They were only at their sweetest for one lap and during that testing I was able to get a feel for how to use that to my advantage. I got so used to it that it was easy for me, but I think Dominic struggled with the '97 car, especially early on."

The new car proved to be faster, but it wasn't without its difficulties. The team had a rough opening weekend at Long Beach, where Neil Crompton swept both races in a new Honda entry associated with Steve Horne's Tasman Motorsports Indy car team. Dobson bagged a pair of podiums, but Donohue finished both races in fourth place. With more than a month before the next round of the championship in Savannah, Georgia, PacWest and Chrysler set about trying to solve a perplexing problem.

"The oil tank on the front bulkhead kept getting really damaged somehow and the car wasn't running very well," recalled Donohue. "We couldn't figure out how the oil tank was being damaged until I ended up borrowing some lipstick cameras from Tom Davey that we mounted [on the car, then drove the car] with the hood off. We had this complex under-engine sub-frame that worked as a flat bottom and also housed the roll bar, which was a trick pivoting device with arms going in all directions. It was completely compliant, but when Dominic got out of the throttle, the engine would rock back and slam against the front bulkhead and completely cave in the oil tank. The only way we figured it out was because we filmed it!"

Honda was again dominant at Savannah, as Peter Cunningham outpaced the field to win both races. This time Donohue led the PacWest effort, finishing second and third compared to Dobson's pair of fourths. Suspension geometry modifications helped the 1997 Stratus come good for the all-important Detroit round, with Donohue claiming pole for both races and leading a PacWest 1-2 in the first contest. In the second race, Donohue was punted off track by Crompton, but he recovered to finish fifth. Crompton, meanwhile, was disqualified for reckless driving after finishing second to Dobson. Dobson claimed the Dodge Challenge Cup for the second year in a row. Crompton's disqualification prompted his team owner Horne to skip the next round of the championship at Portland—a development that would significantly impact Crompton's title hopes.

David Donohue and Bruce McCaw catch up in the pits. Although it was a separate entity, McCaw closely followed the Touring Car team.

Donohue took pole for both Portland races, in dry and wet conditions. Race 1 was staged in heavy rain, making things difficult for the drivers. "I remember driving my ass off at Portland in the rain, because I couldn't see anything except out the front," said Donohue. "I had no idea where anyone else was, and I was waiting for someone to either hit me from behind or show up at my door. I had no clue, but then I realized that I could see the leaderboard and, when I went into the Festival Turns, I could see who was in second place. Then when I rounded the next corner, I could see second place going into the chicane, and I realized I had some space. They never told me on the radio! I was just running like a scared puppy."

After winning the first Portland race by more than 13 seconds over Cunningham, Donohue led Race 2 until being sidelined by an electrical problem that left him in seventh place at the flag. "It's great to lead the points and the championship is definitely my goal," Donohue stated post-Portland. "But the tide can turn because this series can get really screwy. Winning at Portland was a real bonus because the incident at Detroit basically turned my car into a banana. My hat's off to the guys, because they had only five days to get it back together, but it ran like a dream."

Donohue and Cunningham competed on equal terms at the next round at Cleveland, with each man winning a race and finishing third in the other. Donohue lost a bit of ground at Toronto, where Cunningham outscored him with a pair of thirds to Donohue's two fourth-place runs in races won by Dobson and Crompton. "It's great to reward everyone at Chrysler and PacWest with a win," Dobson said. "I've had a couple terrible weekends in a row and it was great to turn things around."

At Mid-Ohio, Donohue extended his championship lead to 20 points by winning both races from pole position. "Mid-Ohio was almost easy," he said. "The biggest thing going through my mind was 'Don't make a mistake,' and that felt really good." Although Crompton won the final four races of the season, Donohue still claimed the 1997 North

All smiles for teammates (left to right) Eric Lopez, Donohue, and Jeff Swain after clinching PacWest's first championship.

American Super Touring Championship crown by 22 points over Cunningham, with Crompton (who missed two races) a close third.

"It means a lot to win this championship," Donohue said during the victory celebration after a season in which he collected ten poles and five race wins. "Our entire team made a championship effort and they deserve a championship win. The team outfitted me with the best car in the series this year and we've been fortunate to have tremendous support from Dodge and our corporate sponsors. I'm proud to be part of such a fantastic effort with PacWest and Chrysler. It takes an outstanding effort to build and develop a car from scratch."

The championship finale at Laguna Seca was not without drama for the PacWest team. Donohue was slow off the line from the front row, and he engaged in a fierce battle with Dobson's Dodge for a few laps over third place. "I had to get on the radio to Dominic to suggest that maybe David should have an easier time of it so that David could win the championship," said Costello. "No race car driver wants to hear that!"

Costello also recalled that the atmosphere for the title-deciding weekend was extremely tense. Relations between Chrysler and NASTC management had deteriorated, in part because of how aggressively Chrysler tried to prove some Hondas were gaining an advantage by exceeding the maximum rev limit. As the 1997 season wound down, rumors persisted that Chrysler was contemplating a withdrawal from the series despite the fact that it had a three-year contract with PacWest.

"Everyone was so unnerved that I literally went to the grid for the first race at Laguna Seca with a signed check and a protest form ready to fill in," said Costello. "At the time, there were a lot of internal issues going on within the championship with Roger Elliott and the pressure to do additional years. It got pretty tense at the end. It was more a political fight between Chrysler and the sanctioning body and we, as PacWest, were kind of in the middle of it. The rev limit was very hard to police back then with rudimentary data collecting and there was a lot of thought that some of the cars were running illegal RPM. Chrysler and Dodge took it upon themselves to do some independent testing and that got up some people's noses. There was a lot of tension at the end of the championship, though when David clinched the title, Roger came up and gave me a big hug and said congratulations. I would never have expected that in a million years. But I did see Roger at the 2017 PRI show for the first time since about 1999 and we met like long lost relatives."

A pair of Chrysler corporate guests get the low-down on the Stratus Touring Car program from Bill Tracy and Tim Culbertson (right).

David Donohue (right) and Dominic Dobson celebrate their 1-2 finish in the 1997 Detroit NATCC race. The Detroit event was particularly important to PacWest Touring Car because of the proximity to local Chrysler brass.

"Chrysler had a lot invested in the series and they really wanted to see it succeed, but I think Roger Elliott felt Chrysler was trying to own the series and manipulate things," added Donohue. "I don't know that they were, they just wanted to see it be successful. But they kind of became the white elephant in the room, and people didn't want to get involved in it maybe because of the perception that it was already Chrysler's series. Roger just didn't foster a good relationship with Chrysler. He made it very difficult for them to want to be there, on more of a personal level, let alone a business level."

Dobson added two poles and two race wins but was generally plagued by bad luck during the 1997 season. He did achieve one key goal by defending his Dodge Challenge Cup title at Detroit. "It was really nice to be presented that award both years by Lou Patane who, along with Bill Tracy, was one of ones Chrysler's strongest supporters of the series. There were a couple of years there where the Touring Car team was winning races and the Indy car team was winning races, and certainly 1996 and 1997 were PacWest's glory days."

Unfortunately, Donohue, Dobson, and the PacWest Touring Car team were unable to really enjoy their championship, nor plan for a title defense. About a month after the season ended, Roger Elliott announced that the North American Super Touring Championship would not be staged in 1998. Elliott's proclamation came on the heels of Chrysler's decision to shut down its participation in the American series. Chrysler intended to ship the cars campaigned by PacWest to Europe and South America in an effort to bolster the meager overseas sales of the Stratus.

While the NASTC had produced close, exciting racing, and developed a devoted band of followers, the series rarely featured more than a ten-car field. More importantly, the NASTC failed to attract additional manufacturer-supported programs to go up against the lone Chrysler effort.

"When the series started, Chrysler was promised that Ford and Chevy would be along very soon," remarked Dobson. "That's what Chrysler was interested in—they wanted to beat Ford and Chevrolet. They didn't care so much about beating two-year-old Hondas and Mazdas. They wanted to beat the guys they were competing against in the marketplace. We had a lot of support, but after a couple of years, Chrysler didn't see any other manufacturers coming in and I think at the time they were starting to think about Winston Cup. NASCAR wanted them in Winston Cup very badly and I think NASCAR was gently encouraging them to focus on NASCAR and not Touring Cars with those resources. At the end of the second year, we had won the championship, they didn't see the series going where they wanted, and NASCAR's saying, 'Come join us, we'll look after you.' So, they pulled the plug on it."

"I think had any of the other factory programs said, 'Yeah, we'll be there,' we would have carried on," Costello added. "If we had carried on one more season, the car counts would have been significantly higher, and I think we could have easily jumped onto the tuner car craze that started shortly thereafter. I think we could have been very successful with the championship. The championship itself was remarkable in what it was attempting to do. There were a lot of presentation things going on in our paddock that were really smart, but maybe they were too soon. The overall presentation of the championship was excellent. Certainly ahead of CART at the time. In Chrysler's defense, they were looking around for some support and it didn't happen. They weren't prepared to up the ante on their contribution."

The beautifully-crafted pedal box of a PacWest Dodge Stratus.

Everyone involved with the PacWest effort was stunned, especially when Chrysler informed PacWest that it wanted to honor the final year of the contract by having the team campaign a Dodge in the NASCAR Craftsman Truck Series.

"We were blindsided," Costello said. "It was one of the worst periods of my life. All of a sudden, our championship has gone away and we're boxing up cars and parts that were going to France and Argentina. We thought with Chrysler that we were likely to get a Viper sports car program, which obviously would have been right in our wheelhouse. Our senior people went down to Daytona for a test and we very much thought we were heading toward a Viper program because we still had a year to go on our contract. I vividly remember being in a car with Dominic driving somewhere in Indianapolis, trying to figure out what to make of all this, when we got a call from Bob Waldberger, who was then running the Chrysler NASCAR Truck program. He said, 'Congratulations, PacWest is now a NASCAR Truck team.' That came completely out of the blue."

The news was surprising and deflating for PacWest. After putting together a tight-knit group ideally suited for road racing, the team was being asked to transfer operations to what was literally a foreign form of motorsport. Chrysler did not notify PacWest of its intentions until November, meaning the team scrambled to make the opening race of the 1998 Truck Series at Walt Disney World Speedway in late January. Rich Bickle drove the PacWest truck to a 10th place finish in the team's debut. A two-month gap until Round 2 at Homestead Speedway gave the team time to regroup, but the trip to Homestead resulted in a DNQ, with Dobson running 49th fastest out of 54 entries for a 38-truck grid.

Dobson and the No. 78 Dodge qualified for Round 3 at Phoenix and made the show for the next eight races, including a third-place start at Nazareth Speedway. But Chrysler failed to deliver promised sponsorship and the team encountered financial difficulty. Randy Renfrow brought a small budget and took over driving duties from Dobson,

While on a smaller scale than the Indy car team, the PacWest Touring Car Group also featured hospitality at the track.

qualifying fourth for his first race at California Speedway. But Renfrow's results weren't any better than Dobson's, and Randy Tolsma finished out the final three races of the season. PacWest Super Truck ceased operation at the end of the 1998 campaign.

"That was the most challenging year of my life," remarked Costello. "It took an enormous toll on all of us. Chrysler had some business-to-business relationships that were supposed to pay our sponsorships for the year, with MCI and with VISA. The VISA money never showed up, and though we finally negotiated for MCI to take over the entire truck, that was the summer MCI was taken over by WorldCom and that final payment never materialized. It was an experience where you got to build a quality team and then dismantle it. Sadly, it happens too often. You do everything you can to put together the best possible program you can, with the best people, and the most resources, and treat it as a business. All of a sudden someone makes a decision and it impacts your program and it's over."

Costello paid tribute to the key people in the Touring Car program. "The reason this all worked so well is I filled the team with the best people I knew that I could get," he said. "We had a core group of really strong, experienced endurance car racing people primarily. Michael Harvey had worked the last two years with the Williams Renault team in the BTCC and he was very much on the pulse of what was needed in touring car racing. Melanie Correll, a very experienced racer, was the office manager, and she's the one that continued to point all of us racer guys in the right direction about how to run an effective business.

"An important person to acknowledge is Dave Finch of Racetech, who was actually a consultant to Chrysler during this program. He was also the race engineer for David Donohue for the 1997 season. One of my fabricators from TWR came down for the first year, John "Jake" McLellen, and the second year we had Andy Riggs, who has been involved with Indy car racing forever, as fabricator. Both incredibly talented guys. I got really lucky with the staff. The only problem area, as always, was truck drivers! We had Pete Duffy and John Bright as engineers for the 1996 season, so I really stacked this program with people that I knew and trusted. Ron Mathis came on board at the end of '96 as Dominic's engineer and our design engineer, and he worked very closely with Chrysler and Reynard. He did all of the cockpit and the carbon work inside."

David Donohue's association with PacWest ended after his 1997 championship season. Ironically, Donohue found himself racing a Dodge Viper for the French ORECA team in 1998, taking a class victory in the 24 Hours of Le Mans. Donohue remained with the ORECA for two more years, adding a second-place finish at Le Mans in 2000, before embarking on a successful career in the IMSA Grand-Am Sports Car Championship.

Even though he was no longer part of the PacWest team, Donohue recognized from afar the toll that the 1998 season took on the team, and particularly on Dobson. “Unfortunately, they roped Dominic into that thing,” he said. “He had to over-commit and it darn near ruined him, I think. It was also not the right time to go with Dodge, because they were still learning their way. It was a good program with high expectations, they just hadn’t gotten the bugs worked out yet. You’re not going to go in the first year and run up front like if you have been doing it for 20, 30, 40 years like the other manufacturers had. It was a challenge for sure.”

After the 1997 season, the Dodges were shipped overseas to race in Europe and South America.

Like Costello, Dobson has few fond memories of 1998 and his NASCAR truck experience. “Ninety-eight was truly a disastrous year,” he reflected. “I think Bruce was somewhat reluctant…we were all reluctant to go into it. What we were interested in doing was taking the Viper sports car racing. That was what our group was about. We had English engineers who grew up around sports cars and, all of a sudden, they were asked to go truck racing. Financially it was kind of a disaster and it really sucked a lot of the joy of racing out of me, and it ended my career on a downward note. But we got through it. I think we were a couple of years too early, because Chrysler went on to do very well in NASCAR truck racing. But it wasn’t for me. Our hearts and souls were never into it.”

Pat Wall, who made the introduction between PacWest and Chrysler, believes that PacWest would have had the opportunity to become a leading NASCAR team had it stuck things out.

“As part of my agreement with PacWest, they had a vision of being a preeminent American motorsports company,” Wall related. “My contract covered whatever opportunities I could develop for them, whether it was Indy car, sports car or NASCAR. I guess when they signed it they didn’t think much of NASCAR, but the Dodge opportunity had a back stop in it. It was a three-year deal, and it said if Dodge got out of Touring Cars before the end of the three years, they’d put us into either a sports car program or a NASCAR program. So they put us into the NASCAR Truck program. If we would have stayed there, it would have put us in line to be one of Chrysler’s founding Cup Series teams. That whole Cup program was coming from basically the day we started at Dodge, and the relationship we had with everybody that ran the place would have made it a no-brainer for Bruce to have been there with Ray Evernham when they started that Cup program.”

The PacWest Touring Car team may have ended under sour circumstances, but the 1996 and 1997 seasons remain a career highlight for everyone who was involved with the effort.

When the NASTC folded, the PacWest Touring Car team made an unhappy transition into the NASCAR Truck Series.

"Most people look back at those times as pretty good," said Donohue. "The environment was so much better, with Dominic and Bruce and Tom and Steven. They put together such a great team with Michael Harvey, and all the way down. The chemistry was just really good, and very competent. I had 100% trust in them. I was lucky there."

"That group, and all the associated partners, we all came away from that thinking that was the best program we had ever been involved with," Costello added. "I'd have to say that now, even 20 years later. It continued the Reynard history of winning first time out, which they were very proud of. Bruce was present for the majority of our races and I always got the sense he was enjoying all we were doing, especially when the Indy car team was struggling to get a result. In a lot of ways, it was an amazingly successful program. At one point when you would walk into the entry way at Gasoline Alley, the whole wall was covered in trophies. It seemed if we didn't get the overall win, we probably had one or two cars on the podium at every race. And on the rare times we didn't, it was because there was a very active engine development program going on.

"It was cutting edge, we all got along, and we got it done," he concluded. "There was no in-fighting within the team at all. It's not like we had hundreds of people. It was an amazing amount of work to keep the progression going and the ultimate result was David winning the championship. It was a pretty special time."

A behind-the-scenes look at a promotional photo shoot featuring PacWest's Dodge Ram NASCAR Truck Series entry.

One of the *Driven* Champ Car look-alike cars carries a camera to capture in-car footage from Joe Tanto's perspective.

17

DRIVEN AND OTHER PURSUITS

IN THE LATE 1990s, *Rocky* star and director Sylvester Stallone set out to make a motion picture about Formula 1 racing. When he encountered resistance from F1 impresario Bernie Ecclestone, he turned his attention to the CART FedEx Championship Series. Unlike F1, CART viewed the movie as a business opportunity and pledged full cooperation with Stallone and his producer, Elie Samaha.

"Since I started out with Formula 1, that was almost my only frame of reference about open-wheel racing," Stallone said at a press conference at Homestead Miami Speedway in early 2000 when the production was revealed with the working name *Champs.* "But I said, 'OK, I really haven't investigated the American version.' And the more I got into it, I realized CART was even more of what I was looking for. Here, it's more of a family atmosphere. It's more vital, and the more I got into it, I thought this is one of those disasters that turned in my favor."

Racing-themed movies have been treated with various success over the last 50 years. The stock-car-based *Days of Thunder* (1990) starring Tom Cruise unintentionally featured more comedy than drama, while *Talladega Nights* (2006) made a farce out of NASCAR, and racing in general. The most notable efforts were John Frankenheimer's *Grand Prix* (1966), starring James Garner; *Winning* (1969), featuring Paul Newman and based around the Indianapolis 500 and the USAC Championship Trail; and Steve McQueen's personal tribute to *Le Mans* (1972). More recently, director Ron Howard's *Rush* (2013) documented the fight between Niki Lauda and James Hunt for the 1976 Formula 1 championship, while *Ford vs. Ferrari* (2019) presented a highly dramatized account of the battle for sports car supremacy in the 1960s. The production won a pair of Academy Awards.

Several of the actors who filmed racing-themed movies caught the competition bug. Garner was a frequent visitor to the Indianapolis 500, where he also drove the pace car on several occasions, while McQueen dabbled in professional racing and finished second in the 1970 12 Hours of Sebring. Aside from a successful driving career (see below), Newman attended many races as the co-owner of Newman/Haas Racing, and served as a consultant for Stallone's Indy car movie, eventually renamed *Driven.* Along with CART, Newman thought *Driven* was

PacWest helped convert a fleet of single-seat open-wheel driving school cars into Champ Car look-alikes for the movie *Driven.* This car is rigged to film driver "Jimmy Bly" in action.

Bruce McCaw chats with legendary F1 team owner Frank Williams, who attended the CART race at Chicago in 1999. Burt Reynolds' wheelchair-bound character in *Driven* was inspired by Williams.

the perfect vehicle to promote the FedEx Championship Series at a critical juncture during its fight with the Indy Racing League for control of American open-wheel racing.

"Working with Sylvester and his team is a tremendous opportunity for CART," stated CART marketing director Keith Allo. "The beautiful thing is that not only will the film serve as essentially a two-hour commercial for sponsors that choose to get involved, but they'll get a lasting return. This isn't like a commercial, something that's on for a time and goes away. This will endure in perpetuity—it will never go away. Twenty years from now, this movie will still be popping up in reruns on cable television. It's very powerful."

PacWest Racing, along with corporate partners Motorola and Nextel, played a major role in the production of the movie. In fact, the fictional on-screen team was actually called PacWest, with Burt Reynolds cast in the role of wheelchair-bound team owner Carl Henry, a character modeled more on paraplegic F1 team owner Frank Williams than on Bruce McCaw. Kip Pardue played Stallone's teammate Jimmy Bly, a talented but troubled young racer, while Gina Gershon and Estella Warren were cast in key support roles. Stallone's character was named Joe Tanto, nicknamed "The Hummer" due to his propensity to start humming in his helmet during charged moments on the track. The plot featured several other similarly outlandish activities.

"The first exposure I had to it was at the CART level, long before it was public," recalled McCaw. "At the time, CART was trying to gain some identity and rise above some of the issues that were going on, and push ourselves out in front. If you can get yourselves into the box office in front of mainstream America, it's worth doing. Having seen some great racing movies, I was certainly enthusiastic about the idea if we could do it well—if we could do it professionally and not have a bunch of stuff that was just beyond belief.

"I spent a lot of time with Stallone—we got along pretty well, actually," he added. "We had dinner together I guess three or four times and had some fun. Reynolds only came two or three times. I was never quite sure how to take it, but the first time I met him, he said, 'I guess I'm playing you, aren't I?' I said, 'I'm not sure that's quite right.' I probably could have done without having my character in a wheelchair."

The picture was eventually completed with a budget reported variously between $68 and $94 million, with Motorola and Nextel providing a considerable amount of backing for what would essentially be a two-hour commercial for their brands. PacWest provided technical assistance; former crew chief Butch Winkle set up a shop on the north side of Indianapolis to build and maintain the camera cars and "race cars," which were tube-frame single seaters used by the Andretti Racing Experience, retrofitted with Yamaha motorcycle engines and more accurate bodywork. Racing scenes were filmed during several CART event weekends, including Toronto and Chicago.

The main protagonists of the film were the PacWest cars and drivers—Stallone as Tanto in the Nextel car and Pardue as Jimmy Bly in the Motorola car. The movie helmets were almost identical to those worn by Mauricio Gugelmin and Mark Blundell, with the 'MB' on the top of Blundell's design converted to 'JB' for Bly.

Driven was quickly panned by critics. *Variety* called it "a souped-up, big-canvas actioner with a notably cheesy look to it, that reps the latest manifestation of the [racing movie] genre's apparent built-in limitations." It achieved a score of 14 percent on the Rotten Tomatoes movie rating website, and in 2006, Stallone listed *Driven* among half a dozen films he wishes he had not done.

Although *Driven* opened at No. 1, earning $13 million at the box office in its first week, it grossed less than $33 million domestically, falling well short of its reported budget. The film earned an additional $22 million internationally.

"Obviously the movie turned out to be a huge disappointment," McCaw said. "It certainly didn't do particularly well, and unfortunately, for a couple of reasons, it didn't materialize into all that we had really expected. Paul Newman and I had many discussions about it. He had a lot of concerns about the movie as well and how to keep controls. Unfortunately, much of the input was ignored.

"There were a lot of mistakes made when that rolled out," he noted. "When you're putting up the kind of money that Motorola and Nextel put up, which was serious cash, you have a lot of voice," McCaw continued. "When they wrote the contract, I wrote some letters to them saying these are some very important things you need to maintain control over, or it's going to be an unfortunate thing. We had a lot of similar concerns at CART. As things happen in larger organizations, it ended up being executed by guys who really didn't have the understanding, the dedication, or perhaps even the legal control they should have had. The guy that was handling that became quite enamored with the razzle dazzle of Stallone and the movie set, instead of what we had really gone out to do and why we had done it. I think the fallout of that didn't hit us until the following year."

For the most part, McCaw enjoyed the experience of being so close to the center of the production of a major motion picture, and he believes that PacWest's participation in *Driven* was ultimately good for the team.

"Joe Tanto" (Sylvester Stallone) celebrates a victory in the movie *Driven*.

MORE ABOUT PAUL NEWMAN

Newman, who died from cancer in 2008 at the age of 83, was obviously best-known as one of the most famous actors in the world. He starred in more than 60 movies, including *The Hustler, Cool Hand Luke, Butch Cassidy and the Sundance Kid, The Sting,* and *The Verdict.* Newman garnered 10 Academy Award nominations, including eight for Best Actor. His sole Oscar win came in 1986 (Best Actor) when he reprised his role from *The Hustler* as Fast Eddie Felson alongside Tom Cruise in *The Color of Money.* He was the founder of the popular Newman's Own brand of organic food products, which has donated more than $550 million to charity since 1982.

Newman also cultivated yet another long and successful career in auto racing, as a driver and team owner. He began racing cars in 1972, three years after completing the movie *Winning.* His character, Frank Capua, was a struggling race car driver who turned his career around by winning the Indianapolis 500. The movie's subplot involved a three-way love triangle between Capua, his wife Elora (played by Newman's real-life spouse Joanne Woodward), and rival Luther Erding, portrayed by Robert Wagner.

Newman and Wagner attended the Bob Bondurant racing school to prepare for the movie. While Wagner generally opted to remain on the sidelines, Newman performed many of the at-speed racing scenes himself without the aid of a stunt driver. Several contemporary Indy car drivers made cameo appearances in *Winning,* and during the filming Newman was immersed in a golden era of Indy car racing when stars like Mario Andretti, Bobby Unser and A.J. Foyt were arguably at the peak of their careers. The experience resonated with Newman for the rest of his life.

"I had a great deal of fun filming *Winning* but I never really had a chance to stretch my legs out and find out what I could do in a car," Newman said in 2004. "It actually took me three years of rearranging my schedule before I could find time to get my license and everything. After that, I never made a film between April and September or October. Racing was all I did."

Bob Sharp Racing provided the foundation Newman needed in his formative years as a racer when he claimed four SCCA professional national championships between 1979 and 1986. His greatest accomplishment was a second-place finish in the 24 Hours of Le Mans in 1979, driving a Porsche 935. Newman remained active in endurance racing, making his last professional start at the Rolex 24 at Daytona International Speedway in 2005 at the age of 80.

Newman-Freeman Racing entered cars driven by Elliott Forbes-Robinson, Keke Rosberg, and Danny Sullivan in the "new-era" SCCA Can-Am sports car series from 1977 through 1982. The following year, Newman and his Can-Am archrival Carl Haas formed Newman/Haas Racing, united by the prospect of having Mario Andretti as driver. Newman/Haas became one of the most enduring and successful teams in Indy car racing; Andretti won the 1984 CART championship, and Mario's son Michael added another title in 1991. Newman/Haas compiled 107 Indy car race wins from 1983 to 2008 and won additional championships with Nigel Mansell, Cristiano da Matta, and Sebastien Bourdais.

Newman's love affair with auto racing may have been kindled by filming *Winning* at the Indianapolis Motor Speedway, but in the later years of his life, his relationship with IMS was antagonistic. When the Speedway changed its catering rules in 1995 to allow only IMS-approved suppliers, Newman flaunted authority (and was later fined) by having his team chefs prepare food for the Newman/Haas crew, which he personally delivered into the garage area.

When IMS CEO Tony George split American open-wheel racing in 1996 by forming the Indy Racing League, Newman became a bitter opponent of the IRL and staunch supporter of CART, and later Champ Car. After the 1995 Indy 500, Newman did not again set foot on Indianapolis Motor Speedway grounds until he attended the 2007 Brickyard 400 NASCAR race—to accept money for his charity.

Newman always raced under the name "P.L. Newman" to avoid drawing attention to his status as a Hollywood icon. But despite a reputation for reticence and an understandable desire to maintain a low profile at the racetrack, Newman was willing to do whatever was necessary to help his team or the

CART series in general. He carried no pretense as he interacted with fans or Newman/Haas team guests and he strongly believed in the positive ways that motorsports could be used to promote good causes.

"We bring people to the races and they see the excitement that's going on with the people in the stands," Newman said. "They see highly technical and powerful machines out there moving with alacrity, and they get excited by the package and the presentation that we have here. They can bring their customers and it's a big advantage for them to have a private tent where they can bring 60 or 70 customers or suppliers. They get a jolt out of it and they have a great weekend."

Newman often cited similarities between his racing and acting careers. In 1999, *Champ Car* magazine convinced him to reprise his Capua role from *Winning* for an interview. Andretti donated his 1969 Indy 500 winner's ring for the photo shoot, and not surprisingly, Newman easily slipped back into character 30 years later. The interview ended with "Capua" asked what he would have done differently with his career.

"I think I would have become an actor," he replied. "Acting is a lot like racing. It's the same type of discipline—one and only one person to depend on in your work, on the track or on the stage. Actually, you need a good team around you in both careers."

Newman's enthusiasm for racing and for his team was so great that he attended most CART or Champ Car races until his final year, when his battle with cancer reached the critical stage. Justin Wilson scored an emotional final victory for Newman/Haas in the 2008 Detroit Grand Prix, less than four weeks prior to Newman's death.

"Getting to know Paul was perhaps one of the great highlights of my time in Indy car racing," reflected Bruce McCaw. "He was such a wonderful gentleman. He cared so deeply about racing, for all the right reasons. He kept his ego totally in check, he gave a lot to the sport, and he loved it from the bottom of his heart. His dedication to helping kids was amazing with the Hole in the Wall Gang Camps, along with creating Newman's Own for the sole purpose of helping others."

> "After [getting my racing license] I never made a film between April and September or October. Racing was all I did."
>
> Paul Newman

Nutritionist Jim Leo worked with PacWest chefs Dave Loik and Shane Azevedo to create healthy eating options for team personnel and guests, including a compact salad bar that featured Newman's Own Italian dressing. When McCaw chided Newman about the fat content in the dressing, Newman challenged his chefs to create a healthier alternative. He returned a few weeks later with a small Tupperware that contained a prototype for Newman's Own Light Italian. The low-calorie dressing and a Caesar variation soon went into production. "After that, Paul always thanked me," McCaw recalled. "He said, 'It's the best product we've got!'"

PacWest also particpated in the creation of a commercial for Hollywood cigarettes with scenes filmed around the world.

"It was an interesting time and I viewed it as part of the business we're in," he said. "Maybe it was not a lot different than the Brazilian Hollywood commercial or the other commercials we did over time. Part of what we were doing was trying to get exposure, both for ourselves and ultimately for our sponsors. There was a lot of work involved, but I think it did give PacWest a lot of excitement, focus, and opportunity. There was a lot of activity around us; they were always shooting things in the pits before and after we were on track with the race team. Certainly, it gave us some great opportunities with Motorola and Nextel in doing a lot of movie-related dinners. For a year, there was a lot going on and we had Stallone at a lot of events. It gave us good visibility. We did get income out of it, too. We got hired to do a lot of things that I think were inherently pretty profitable. I think it had a lot of opportunity to help CART and it certainly didn't hurt us."

PacWest created this custom delivery vehicle for its work with Gleaners Food Bank.

CHARITABLE CAUSES

PacWest Racing contributed to numerous charitable events and causes during the team's eight-year run, beginning with a partnership with the United Way in 1995. PacWest ran prominent United Way logos on its cars and hosted major contributors at each of the series' North American venues.

"We got introduced to United Way by Bill Gates' mother, Mary," McCaw said. "Dr. Tommy Frist, who was chairman of the United Way at the time, could see the power of what we could provide with the team. They were very pleased with the results. We did a lot more than just running logos. We not only helped increase name identity in key markets around the US, but also gave them a real opportunity to thank major supporters at some of our race sites."

From 1999 to 2001, PacWest worked with the Muscular Dystrophy Association, hosting guests and raising funds for the charitable organization. In February 2000, Mark Blundell filmed a Public Service Announcement shown during broadcasts of CART races that encouraged fans to tune in to the Jerry Lewis Telethon. Blundell was also one of several celebrities who appeared during the telethon providing information about how to donate.

PacWest was a strong supporter of Championship Auto Racing Auxiliary and CARA Charities. Established in 1981 by Betty Rutherford and several other driver wives, CARA Charities was the driving force behind open-wheel racing's philanthropic efforts which donated some $5 million over the next 30 years to children's health and safety issues.

Wally Dallenbach and his wife, Peppy, enjoy the festivities at Runway Madness.

Mark Blundell shows twins Chris and Marc Schwab his PacWest racing car while filming a Public Service Announcement for the Muscular Dystrophy Association.

In partnership with Bridgestone/Firestone, CARA's "Buckle Up Baby" program alone raised nearly $1 million for needy families and services, and earned the National Highway Traffic Safety Administration's Buckle Up America Champion's Award in 2000. For several years during Federal Express' sponsorship of the CART series, CARA organized an elaborate end-of-year charitable event called Runway Madness in a hangar at Ontario International Airport; the second edition was co-chaired by Bruce and Jolene McCaw.

In 1997, the McCaws kicked off the Portland race week by hosting a charity event at Seattle's Pacific Science Center. Some 250 guests attended a screening of the IMAX documentary *Super Speedway* and a silent auction of donated racing memorabilia raised more than $31,000.

Super Speedway packed a lot of information about Indy car racing into 50 minutes, with Mario Andretti serving as the focus of several storylines. While Andretti reminisced about the first front-engine Indy "roadster" he drove in 1964, his son Michael demonstrated how Newman/Haas Racing developed the latest Lola Indy car. Just two years into "retirement," Mario drove an IMAX camera car in test sessions and occasionally during practice on CART race weekends obtaining some of the most spectacular in-car footage ever recorded. The movie also introduced Martini—Andretti's pet pot-bellied pig—to a wider audience.

"We had an opportunity to raise awareness and make a contribution to an important cause," explained McCaw. "*Super Speedway* was also a great way to introduce CART racing to many of our friends in the Seattle area."

In December 1998 and 1999, "elf" Mauricio Gugelmin drove the PacWest pit stop practice car around Monument Circle in downtown Indianapolis while towing "Santa Claus" in a custom-made sleigh. Santa had a distinctive Australian accent that reminded many observers of John Anderson, who was reported as "mysteriously absent throughout the proceedings." The events annually netted Gleaners Food Bank more than 2,000 pounds of food as well as more than $5,000 in cash donations.

TEAM USA SCHOLARSHIP

Auto racing writer Jeremy Shaw moved to America in the mid 1980s to cover the CART series for *On Track* magazine just as the first wave of international drivers began to descend upon Indy car racing. Shaw soon noticed that the talent transfer was a one-way street; very few American drivers were leaving their home country to race abroad, where the formula car ranks that served as a ladder to Formula 1 were often considered much more competitive, if not cut-throat.

Shaw had covered Formula Ford and Formula 3 for *Autosport* magazine in England and he always made a point of encouraging and spotlighting emerging young drivers. Ironically, his favorites were Brazilians and other South American drivers, who had to adapt to a cold, damp climate in addition to battling cultural differences and a language barrier, all while growing up many miles from home.

In 1990, Shaw rounded up support from several sponsors and created the first Team USA Scholarship, sending rising star Jimmy Vasser to England to compete in the British Formula Ford Festival. Since then, the principal aim of the Scholarship has been to provide young American race car drivers with opportunities to experience international competition at an early stage in their careers. The program also fosters introductions to influential figures within the sport who can provide insight and contacts to assist young drivers in their progress up the racing 'ladder.'

"I just see it as an opportunity for me to give opportunity to deserving youngsters to help forward their careers," said Shaw. "It's an opportunity to get them out of their comfort zone. I'm not interested in doing something here in America, because that's too easy. I want them to be away from their friends and their parents and the people they know, and basically find out whether they really do want to become racing drivers."

Shaw closely follows grassroots single seat racing and taps a network of driver coaches and other motorsports insiders to compile a short list of candidates who are then invited to an Indy car race and embedded with individual teams. Following a meet and greet session, and catered dinner, the candidates' communication skills are assessed by Shaw's panel of experts to determine the finalists to participate in a two-day on-track shootout. Depending on the quality of candidates during any given year, one to three scholarships are awarded.

Bryan Herta was the second recipient of the Team USA Scholarship and he was followed by a who's who of upcoming American racers including future Indy car drivers Memo Gidley (1995), Buddy Rice (1997), A.J. Allmendinger (2001), J.R. Hildebrand (2005), Josef Newgarden (2008), and Spencer Pigot (2010). Tony Renna, who competed for PacWest's Indy Lights team in 1999 and 2000, was a 1996 Team USA Scholarship winner.

"I was at the beginning of my career, and the chance to go race in England was a big opportunity for me," recalled Herta, who won four Indy car races between 1998 and 2005

1991 Team USA Scholarship winner Bryan Herta with program founder Jeremy Shaw.

Mark Blundell wears cake: even drivers were unable to escape the traditional PacWest birthday celebration.

and went on to co-own an Indianapolis 500-winning team. "I tested a Formula 3 car with Alan Docking, and [Formula 1 journalist] Peter Windsor took me around to the Williams factory, and to Cosworth and Lola. I made so many contacts there, because so much of the racing industry is based in England. That's when I first met Adrian Reynard and Rick Gorne, and they actually provided the car for me for the Formula Ford Festival. When I look back at the race, I was proud that we made it to the final, and I think we finished 11th out of about 200 entries. I thought that was a pretty good accomplishment having jumped into an unfamiliar year-old car. But the thing I remember most is making the contacts, and in that respect, it was probably the single most influential moment in my career."

Team members celebrating birthdays quickly learned to never let their guard down.

Since 2009, Shaw has organized an annual dinner on behalf of the Road Racing Drivers Club at the Long Beach Grand Prix. The event rapidly became one of the most prestigious nights on auto racing's social circuit. The RRDC Dinner has honored numerous legends of the sport, including Dan Gurney, Mario Andretti, Parnelli Jones, Jim Hall, Roger Penske, and Emerson Fittipaldi. It also features a silent auction of memorabilia that raises thousands of dollars for the Team USA Scholarship and the Safe Is Fast tutorial program for young drivers.

The common denominator among Team USA Scholarship's individual supporters is a desire to give back to the sport. Over the years, Indy car team owners Rick Galles and Steve Horne made considerable donations to the program; encouraged by Steve Fusek, PacWest Racing was another strong advocate. In addition to financial contributions, for several years the team also hosted the annual meet-and-greet portion of the selection process at the PacWest Summit hospitality area.

"Jeremy put together a really solid program, and a lot of quality drivers have benefitted from his hard work and dedication," observed Bruce McCaw. "Whether a young American driver wants to pursue a career in international racing or compete in a series at home in the United States, the experience the Team USA Scholarship provides is incredibly valuable."

THE LIGHTER SIDE

Racing is serious business, but everyone at PacWest understood the value of humor and keeping the atmosphere light-hearted. No one knew that more than the drivers who, in many ways, functioned like quarterbacks for the teams. They assumed a leadership role that often meant finding ways to boost morale during tough times.

Mauricio Gugelmin was a master of practical jokes. He shared a few of them in a conversation with *Detroit Free Press* writer Steve Crowe in 1998. One of them involved PacWest

PR man Scott Tingwald. Gugelmin presented Tingwald with a briefcase as a parting gift when Tingwald left the team in late 1996 to take up a position with the College Football Hall of Fame in his hometown of South Bend, Indiana. Unbeknownst to Tingwald, Gugelmin had two kilograms of lead sewed into the lining of the briefcase, and the prank remained a secret until Gugelmin sent Tingwald a copy of Crowe's column revealing why that beautiful briefcase was so damned heavy.

But Gugelmin was also on the receiving end of practical jokes. "One day Mo couldn't make it to the shop on the day the guy who was fitting the race suits was there," recounted Brett "Crusher" Murray, who handled PacWest's PR duties in 2000. "He measured Mark Blundell for his suit, and Mark then told the guy that Mo wanted to have the big NASCAR flares, the big Dale Earnhardt flares (bell bottoms), on his suit. So, we arrive at Miami for the first race and the boys are trying their suits on. Mo gets his on, and it's got these big Dale Earnhardt flares about 15 yards wide. He says, 'What the hell is going on here?' The guy says, 'But that's the way you like them!' Blundell and I are in the corner laughing so hard we have tears coming out of our eyes. Quickly we had to find a seamstress and sew cuffs in them, the whole deal."

Rental cars were often the victim of various antics which included impromptu races, bumper tag, and other routines. McCaw recalls one occasion when the conclusion of a spur-of-the-moment car chase from the Laguna Seca circuit to the Monterey Plaza hotel left the reception area of the swank resort swathed in a thick haze of rubber smoke. "You couldn't even see," he marveled. "Ando came in behind me, and his car just kind of came out of this cloud! We took over the bar and had security trying to throw us out. I don't remember this, but Ziggy said I walked over to the manager and said, 'Don't worry, I'll take care of everything—just send me the bill. My name is Roger Penske!'

"Another time when I was testing some vintage cars at Willow Springs, I got out on the skidpad with a Town Car and just started working it to death," McCaw added. "I managed to rip the tread off a couple of the tires—literally, in chunks—and I had to drive from there to the Lancaster Airport. The car shook so badly I had double vision and could hardly see at 40 mph on the freeway."

Anderson was amused by one of his first encounters with McCaw in early 1994. "We were down testing in Big Spring, Texas," he related. "We had rented a car from Walker, done maybe four laps when Bruce arrives in the Lear. He did a quick pass over the top and I thought that was bloody unbelievable. He arrived at the circuit a few minutes later in a Town Car and bugger me, no sooner had he got there that we broke the gearbox. We

Top five things Mark Blundell misses about England:

5. Driving on the right side of the road, which is left.
4. A reasonable speed limit.
3. Fish, and even the chips.
2. Pubs with warm beer.
1. People who actually speak English instead of American (just joking, y'all).

Mauricio (Big Mo) Gugelmin's top five, actually pulled practical jokes:

5. Super Glued team manager's briefcase shut.
4. Saran Wrap over toilet seat.
3. Bouillon cube in shower head.
2. Lead weights in public-relations guy's computer bag — that he's still carrying around a year later!
1. Ex-Lax in chief engineer's chocolates.

PacWest drivers displayed their sense of humor to *Detroit Free Press* writer Steve Crowe.

called up Gerald Davis at Jim Hall's team. They had the bits. It was maybe an hour's drive from Big Spring to Midland, but Bruce says, 'Let's take the Lear…will that work?' It was like an 8-minute flight.

"From there, Bruce was a lot of fun to be around," he added. "He obviously loved his motorcars, and while we were fixing the gearbox, he and Tom Armstrong were out there in a couple of Town Cars beating the bumpers off of each other, having a wonderful time."

"That was probably one of my better buzz jobs," McCaw chuckled. "I got down pretty low—down to about 10 feet or so. There was a fire truck at the end of the straight, and as I pulled up, the firemen jumped out of the truck and dove for cover. They were Vietnam veterans and when they heard this low-flying airplane, thought they were being attacked. When I landed, they were less than thrilled with me."

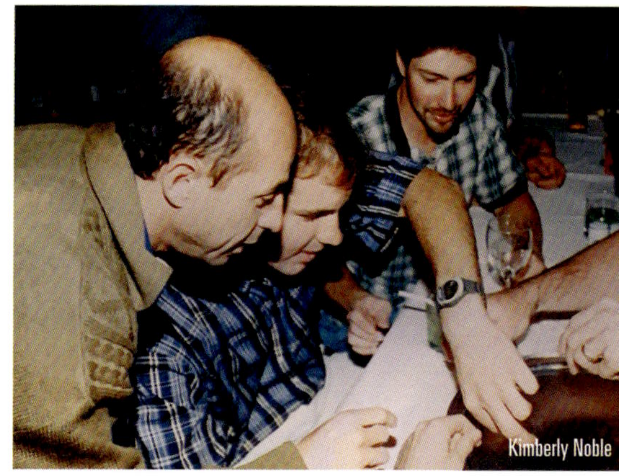

Kimberly Noble

Roberto Moreno's "Hair Races" shocked and surprised all who participated.

Roberto Moreno, who drove eight races for PacWest when Mark Blundell was injured in 1999, had a keen sense of humor. Moreno's 'Hair Races' were legendary. "He got a 3-foot diameter serving tray with a lip and placed it on the dinner table," explained damper engineer Patrick Stufflet. "Then the servers were asked to help fill it with water and Roberto proceeded to explain the rules of the 'Hair Race' we would be having. He went through this awesome buildup, telling us we would be pulling a piece of hair from our own head and racing these hairs across this makeshift pond in the middle of the dinner table.

John Anderson displays the aftermath of a Hair Race.

"We watched intently as Moreno rubbed his hair on his shirt and his arm, like he was trying to build static charge," Stufflet continued. "He made a big production of it, with great showmanship, so some of us copied him. He said, 'Everybody ready?' and after we placed our hairs on one end of the tray filled with water, he did a countdown until we all released them. He immediately started blowing his hair across the 'pond,' and of course we all copied him again. This is where he suckered us all—he backed away and while a handful of us were blowing our hairs intently across this tray full of water to win this race, SMACK! His hand came swiftly across that layer of water and got us all wet. We turned around and he was laughing his tail off. Fun times, great memories, and I guess competitions sometimes get the best of us!"

THE CALEDON EXPERIENCE

From 1995 to 2000, the Molson Indy Vancouver and the CART race at Laguna Seca Raceway in Monterey, California, were scheduled one week apart. With most teams

Nestled in the foothills of the Cascade Mountains, Caledon was a great place to unwind at the end of a long season of racing.

based in Indianapolis or the Midwest, there was no time to return the cars to home base between events, and it often made sense for crew members and others associated with the series to remain on the West Coast. Three days was just the right amount of time to soak in the scenic 1,100-mile coastal drive at a relaxed, yet purposeful, pace.

For the majority of those years, CART's West Coast swing also coincided with the Labor Day holiday, and Bruce and Jolene McCaw hosted several team gatherings at Caledon, a large property near Arlington, Washington, about halfway between Seattle and the Canadian border. In addition to PacWest partners and team members, invited guests included the PPG Pace Car Team and the CART Safety Team, plus other key officials from the corporate and racing divisions.

Coming near the end of a grueling race season, the Caledon trips were a nice reward to the team for their time and hard work. There were plenty of activities to keep everyone busy—an 18-hole golf course, a kart track, and a quarter-scale railroad, among other things. The McCaws added to everyone's enjoyment by featuring live music from HB Radke and the Jet City Swingers, and commissioning private performances from a variety of internationally renowned entertainers, including musician Steve Miller, ventriloquist Ronn Lucas, and magician Steffan Soule. One year, the McCaws engaged Bill Mellberg, a political satirist and impressionist famous for a show called *An Evening with The Presidents,* and Bruce had the team convinced that Bill Clinton would actually be in attendance.

Doubling as the celebration for Mauricio Gugelmin's breakthrough victory at Vancouver, the 1997 version of the Caledon Experience was the undisputed king of PacWest parties. Along with several other team members, Gugelmin and Mark Blundell dyed their hair red and blue to match their car colors, and Lucas brought down the house when he called John Anderson onstage to use as his "dummy." R-rated hilarity ensued.

That was the year that Mark Moore [Gugelmin's longtime chief mechanic on the No. 17 car] had perhaps the most lurid Caledon Experience. "One of my biggest achievements with PacWest was surviving Caledon," Moore said. "We had a little place out away from the main lodge where we were camping, kind of like a yoga retreat. The pathway there was lit by little paper bags with candles in them.

"Late at night a few guys, like Jeff Horton and Ron Endres, thought it was cute to stomp out the little bags," Moore continued. "Somehow, I lost my flashlight, so after a long evening at Caledon, I had to hike back out there. There's a train trestle at Caledon and to make a long story short, I went the wrong direction and fell off the train trestle. I thought

I was going to be there all night, but I managed to find my way out through the lightning storm. I finally made my way back to the house, and there's Bruce out on the balcony, the only one still up."

TEAM-BUILDING ACTIVITIES

In early 1997, Bruce McCaw hosted a PacWest management retreat at the Marriott Key Largo resort in Florida. During the two-day meeting that set the tone for PacWest's most successful season at the Indy car level, the 20 team members present collaborated to create a PacWest Mission Statement encompassing the organization's values:

PacWest Racing Group is a dynamic and profitable organization comprised of a focused team of innovative, quality professionals, dedicated to winning championships, who enjoy working together to be the recognized leader in the racing industry.

Prior to the start of the 1999 season, McCaw engaged motivational speaker Mike Vance, chairman and co-founder of the Creative Thinking Association of America, to conduct a "Think Out of the Box" workshop in Indianapolis that included 93 team members. Vance led a fast-paced discussion that highlighted the following points:

- *Creativity can be learned.*
- *How to develop a corporate culture for continuous innovation and creativity.*
- *Creating team center environments that produce team work activities and become environments of discovery.*
- *How to develop pathfinders who continuously seek out breakthrough solutions.*
- *How to develop a creative living center—a "kitchen for the mind."*

"Mike Vance was a guy who helped the Disney Corporation set up Disney University," noted McCaw. "He was great as an inspirational speaker and team builder. He was an interesting guy, a real character. He would speak very quickly, and supposedly he was the guy who invented the phrase "Think Out of the Box." I met him many years ago and his teachings had a great impact on me both personally and professionally. He helped us develop some new people concepts at Horizon Airlines and had a huge positive effect on our airline. The entire PacWest group was still absorbed by Mike's presentation when it ended, so I think the day was a great success."

Didier André (center) appears to be the innocent victim of a trick by magician Steffan Soule.

A group of 16 team members participated in a skydiving outing wearing PacWest firesuits.

California Speedway was an ideal location for the PacWest/Mercedes-Benz World Party, where the food and entertainment were to a standard even higher than PacWest's norm.

Norbert Haug dropped his inhibitions after a few cocktails at "Stars & Cars."

WORLD PARTY

Mercedes-Benz had a rough time in CART competition in 1998 and 1999, but the company's Formula 1 engines developed into the championship frontrunner in those years in conjunction with the McLaren team. Mika Häkkinen was expected to clinch the 1998 F1 title at the Japanese Grand Prix. Mercedes teamed up with PacWest to throw a viewing party, with the added bonus that guests were encouraged to arrive in Halloween costume. Häkkinen duly clinched the championship and later spoke by satellite video link from Japan to what many people called "the best party of the season." Häkkinen and the World Party both successfully defended their crowns in 1999.

STARS & CARS

Since the resumption of its racing activities in the early 1990s, Mercedes hosted an annual postseason function called "Stars & Cars" to celebrate the firm's motorsports achievements. In the years PacWest was partnered with Mercedes, the event was staged right on the factory grounds in Stuttgart, with thousands of employees in attendance. Bruce McCaw and the PacWest drivers attended from 1997 to 2000, along with a small crew to run a PacWest Indy car and conduct pit stop exhibitions. The team's German hosts knew how to throw a good party. The 1997 festivities ended up in the Hotel Maritim kitchen in the wee hours of the morning, with Mercedes-Benz Motorsports boss Norbert Haug treating Gugelmin, McCaw, Steve Fusek, Mario Illien, Paul Morgan, Greg Moore, and Professor Jurgen Hubbert to an impromptu karaoke show. Following the performance, several additional bottles of red wine, and a few cigars, the assembled group set out to prepare a very large breakfast for themselves and others. A highly inebriated Moore donned waiter's gear and began taking orders from hotel diners when the restaurant opened. "It was quite a sight," laughed McCaw.

DRIVE DAY

For several years starting in 1995, PacWest hosted an annual "Driving Experience" that gave team members, sponsors, and supporters the opportunity to drive one of the team's race cars. Conceived by Dominic Dobson, the partner initiative started small and experienced rapid growth, resulting in a series of venue changes. After debuting at Sebring International Raceway in 1995, Drive Day moved to the Chrysler Proving Grounds in Chelsea, Michigan, the following year, and a special ride-and-drive event was also held at Sebring International Raceway for Hollywood executives and Brazilian media. The event's peak came at the end of the 1997 season, when a total of 133 people had turns behind the wheel of two PacWest Indy cars and a Dodge Stratus Touring Car over the course of three days. The 0.28-mile course ran on runways at Mount Comfort Airport outside of Indianapolis. "Everyone seemed to agree on two things: It was the thrill of a lifetime and it's definitely not as easy as it looks," remarked Darla Elkins, who served as a marketing intern for PacWest in 1997 and later worked full-time for the team.

Because there was no way to detune the Indy cars other than limit revs to 10,500 (the race drivers typically used a 15,000-rpm redline), PacWest equipped them with a remote kill switch so that crew members in the pits could shut the engine off if it looked like a driver was having trouble on the track. In the five-year history of the event, the kill switch was used just one time, for a driver who demonstrated just a little bit too much enthusiasm behind the wheel of a 750-horsepower racing car: John Anderson.

PacWest's longtime racing operations boss had no fears or inhibitions once he was strapped into the cockpit, thrashing the million-dollar machine like it was a cheap rental car. Ando wore out tires and tore up gearboxes, but always emerged from the car with a huge smile on his face.

Paul Haney documented Anderson's antics in *Inside Racing*, the fly-on-the-wall book he developed from spending the 1997 season with PacWest:

They save Ando for last because he's rough on the car. Steve Fusek tells me, "He's okay at the start, but then he gets frustrated." I'm not sure what he's talking about, but that's what happens. The first few laps are slow and careful, then he carries too much speed into the slow corner and goes spinning backwards into the grass, way off into the grass. A few more sane laps, then he drives a 16.17-second lap, very good. Then he just starts spinning donuts raising clouds of white smoke. People either laugh or shake their heads, or both. When Ando gets out of the car his rear tires are showing cord almost all the way across the tread. Mark Blundell is right there asking Ando, "Did you use the bars? What about the weight jacker?"

Watching from the sidelines, Bruce McCaw actually made things more difficult for Anderson. "I took the kill switch from whoever was holding it, and I started flipping it on and off as the car went down the straightaway," he said. "I could watch Ando's head banging back and forth against the headrest and I don't think he had any idea what I was doing. That was really funny."

Many of the team's mechanics, who drove go-karts for recreation, took the idea of setting fast time at Drive Day very seriously. In 1997, Daryl Fox (No. 18 crew chief), Tim Neff

Like everyone else at Drive Day, Ilmor Engineering co-founder Paul Morgan couldn't wipe the smile from his face.

Nobody did Drive Day quite like John Anderson, (aka A. Wanker, according to the driver name placard).

The team had to cut away part of the Reynard chassis to get Chrysler executive Bob Lutz comfortable in the car.

(damper engineer), and Roy Wilkerson (No. 17 mechanic) were separated by 0.04 second with times less than a second off the benchmark established by Mark Blundell.

Those who had less of an attachment to racing were slower, but had just as much fun. Notables over the years who experienced driving a racing car for the first (and possibly only) time in their lives included many local and national media members; a number of high-level Motorola, Souza Cruz, and Chrysler executives, including corporate chairman Bob Eaton and legendary automotive industry figure Robert Lutz.

Lutz proved to be the most challenging amateur driver the team worked with. The 6-foot-3 Lutz complained that he did not fit properly into the 1996 Reynard, which was the last year before CART mandated a wider cockpit with a larger opening. PacWest eventually got Lutz into the car, out of the pits, and up to speed by cutting away (at great expense) a portion of the carbon fiber monocoque.

"We finally got Lutz in the car but he just couldn't move and he was really frustrated," recalled Bruce McCaw. "He had apparently flown to England to drive a Formula 1 car, but he didn't fit, and he had been given some assurance he would fit an Indy car. He was biting my head off, saying, 'I could have gone and flown my fighter jet today (Lutz owns a Czech-built Aero Vodochody L-39 "Albatros").

"I told Ziggy, 'Cut it out—we're not going to race this car again,'" McCaw continued. "Lutz kept saying, 'I can't move,' but I convinced him to try a couple laps and he started getting in the groove. Then we couldn't get him to stop—it was either going to get dark or he was going to run out of fuel. We mounted the pieces of the tub we cut out onto a plaque, with the serial number plate from the chassis, and a picture of him driving the car and gave it to Bob. It turned out to be one of his prized possessions. Every time I see him, he tells me he still has that plaque on his wall. That showed how the drive days proved to be one of the best ways to thank teammates and sponsors alike. It pulled them all together and helped them better appreciate what this was all about."

PACWEST AND PPG INDUSTRIES

When Souza Cruz performed a major re-launch of its Hollywood cigarette brand, with a new logo and pack design, Hollywood unveiled a bold new look for the PacWest Racing car driven by Mauricio Gugelmin. The design underwent several changes in 1998 and 1999, but was characterized by a dayglo-orange base finish with green and blue areas to represent Hollywood's light and menthol offerings, separated by unique zigzags. PacWest

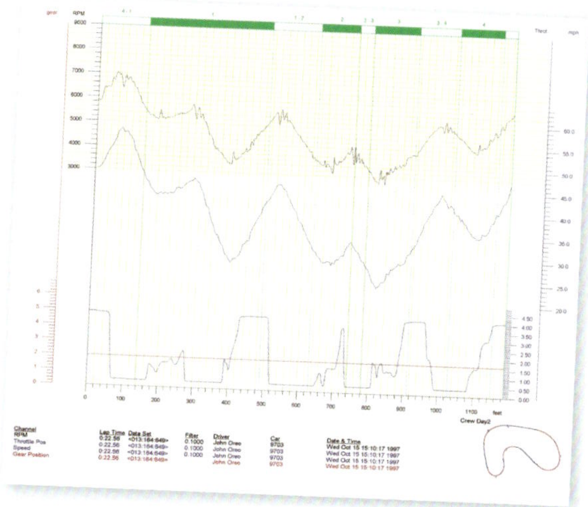

Each Drive Day participant got a computer telemetry printout similar to the data analyzed during race meetings.

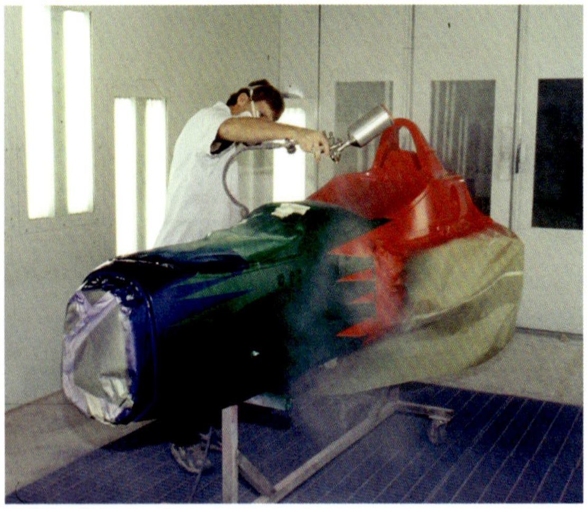

Todd Weed applies PPG paint to a Reynard chassis in PacWest's custom booth.

also incorporated a silver engine cover to visually tie-in its partnership with Mercedes-Benz. The design was a hit with CART fans, who voted to award the No. 17 car the "PPG Best Use of Color and Design" award in 1998 and 1999.

The livery was created by the Brazilian advertising agency DPZ and taken from concept to reality by PacWest painters Randy Smay, Todd Weed, and Carey Hall. They used the state of the art Blowtherm paint booth that was part of the 1997 race shop expansion. It typically took two days to paint a car, with the paint accounting for 16 pounds of weight. "I look at the drawing, then I use my imagination and follow the lines of the car," said Smay. "Everything is done freehand, and it takes experience to get it right."

Hall, who joined the team in mid-1997, stayed with PacWest until the team ceased operation. He died in 2012 from complications of Lou Gehrig's Disease.

PPG Industries served as CART's title sponsor from 1980 to 1997 and maintained strong ties after Federal Express took over in 1998. Aside from the Color and Design Award, the $1 million PPG Cup was presented to the champion of the series. The groundbreaking PPG Pace Car Team, with its all-female driver lineup, played an important promotional role, too.

PPG also began recognizing a series of "Colorful Characters" in the CART series in the mid-1990s, with Bruce McCaw receiving the 1998 honor at his "home" race at Portland International Raceway.

"Bruce McCaw has brought his own personality and a Pacific Northwest sense of style to the competition for the PPG Cup," said Mike Sack, PPG's director of sports marketing. Other notable Colorful Characters included Father Phil DeRea, Tom Carnegie, Rick Mears, Roger Bailey, Leo Mehl, Floyd Ganassi, Wally Dallenbach, Robin Miller, Shav Glick, Mario Andretti, Jim McGee, Al Speyer, Jim Hall, Dan Gurney, Pat Patrick, Dan Luginbuhl, Dr. Steve Olvey, Carl Haas, and Roger Penske.

Much of the success of the PPG/CART alliance was due to the leadership and charisma of legendary marketing executive Jim Chapman. His public relations career dated to 1946 when he joined the Ford Motor Company. One of Chapman's first moves was to hire legendary baseball star Babe Ruth as a Ford spokesman. Chapman struck out on his own in 1951 with Avis Rent-a-Car as his first major client, and his first involvement in auto racing came in 1967 when he landed sponsorship from toilet seat manufacturer Olsonite for Dan Gurney's All American Racers. Chapman pioneered the idea of a trackside hospitality tent, and by the 1990s, PPG hospitality at CART races set a new standard for the industry.

"Jim was one of the most innovative and imaginative PR men ever to grace a pit lane," said Gurney. "However, I think Jim made his greatest contribution to our sport in the early years of CART, when he started to work for PPG Industries. He created a home in the shape of a tent for the Indy Car family. The PPG tent was the centerpiece of any Indy Car paddock. Here, everybody gathered for the family lunch, and it was there that contacts were made, relationships started, networks woven, and friendships cemented."

Chapman retired at the end of 1993, but he stuck around to organize Mario Andretti's 1994 retirement tour known as "Arrivaderci Mario!" Bruce McCaw was one of a handful of people who was asked to lend a hand.

"When Jim Chapman came to me to talk about working on Mario's farewell tour, I was incredibly flattered that he picked me as somebody to help with that," McCaw said. "Of course, he was a remarkable guy and the whole PPG relationship was extremely important. He was a visionary for the whole CART thing, and he was one of the great personalities I got to work with during this time."

BOY SCOUTS MOTORSPORTSMAN OF THE YEAR

Portland International Raceway hosted an Indy car race from 1986 to 2007, and the event was successfully revived in 2018. Starting in 1990, the Cascade Pacific Council of the Boy Scouts of America hosted an annual Motorsports Breakfast honoring a Motorsportsman of the Year. In 1999, the honor went to Bruce McCaw.

"It's a real pleasure to receive this honor," he said. "Over 30 years ago, I drove in my first race at Portland, long before the 'Festival Curves' or even the chicane. Portland International Raceway is special to me and I still love to drive here in vintage events.

"Like the Boy Scout experience, involving kids in racing builds self-esteem, discipline, teamwork, and very strong core values they will take into adulthood," he added. "The Boy Scouts is a superb organization and its members should feel very proud to be a part of it."

Other Motorsportsman of the Year recipients include Mario Andretti, Roger Penske, Tony George and Alex Zanardi. The Motorsports Breakfast raised more than $250,000 in proceeds over the years to benefit the Pacific Cascade council.

The sprawling Indianapolis Motor Speedway facility was studied in-depth by McCaw and his team in preparation for a time when it might come up for sale.

"PROJECT COW PATCH"

As a businessman, Bruce McCaw is always on the lookout for new projects to get involved with, often in conjunction with his hobbies or passions. His lifelong love of cars and driving ultimately spurred him to form PacWest Racing. But he has had other opportunities to maintain an involvement in the sport outside of team ownership, including RaceSport Management's investment in Auto Research Center and other racing-related properties. RaceSport still owns and leases the former PacWest shop at 4001 Methanol Lane in Indianapolis.

McCaw has also used RaceSport as a vehicle for exploring entry into racetrack ownership, beginning with the famed Road America circuit in Wisconsin. "At the time that racetracks were starting to get into public companies, I started looking at it as a potential investment," he remarked. "I invested in both Penske's track company (later sold to International Speedway Corp.) and Speedway Motorsports. I had invested initially in Elkhart Lake; there was a real concern that the shareholders were somewhat split and some of them were possibly interested in seeing the property get developed. There was some stock available, and Augie Pabst asked me if I would buy some. I ended up buying two or three chunks of stock and now I'm probably the largest shareholder in the track. It has been a great investment.

"We made a couple offers on Phoenix International Raceway, and there was a point where I thought Las Vegas Motor Speedway was going to become available, because I thought Bruton Smith was going to have to divest from it," he continued. "I wasn't keen on it but I thought there was an interesting opportunity there and it ended up going for two or three times what we had penciled it in for. I tried to buy Pacific Raceways for years. Road Atlanta was being flogged around at one time and it got pretty cheap, and we made an offer for Sears Point (later known as Infineon Raceway, now Sonoma Raceway) one time, but I just couldn't get comfortable with the partner."

All of those tracks pale in comparison to the most famous track of all, but that didn't stop McCaw and his associates from making a quiet run at investigating the possibility of acquiring the Indianapolis Motor Speedway in the late 1990s.

"There was clearly some dissention in the Hulman family a couple of years into the IRL—it wasn't working very well, it was costing a lot of money, and of course you've got three sisters sitting there (Tony George's siblings Nancy, Kathi, and Josie) who are not getting much out of any of it in terms of cash. It appeared there was a real possibility it would become available because it was owned in a trust, and at some point, the trustees would have to deal with this issue. Mary Fendrich Hulman (Tony Hulman's widow) died at about that time, in the late '90s, and right about the time of her death I thought there might be an opportunity. So I hired an investment banker (Butler, Chapman & Co., Ltd.) in New York and I spent quite a bit of money on a full-blown analysis of the Speedway. I thought maybe it was the opportunity of a lifetime, and I wanted to be ready and understand everything if it suddenly came up for sale. We actually put together a full 'book,' as they call it, on the Speedway."

McCaw's investment bankers from Butler, Chapman & Co. met with IMS officials to discuss the future of the famed race course.

Of course, any secret project needs a code name, and McCaw's exploration into acquiring IMS was no different. "I've never known if this was true or not, but I understand that at least a portion of the Speedway was still taxed as a farm because they kept a couple of cows on the property at least part of the year to legally keep it as an agricultural thing," he said. "So that became 'Project Cow Patch.'"

Armed with as much information as could be determined about a private enterprise such as the Speedway, McCaw's investment bankers eventually met with George and IMS attorney Jack Snyder. "Snyder was blown away with how thorough it was," McCaw related. "He said, 'You know more about this place than we do!'"

McCaw shared some of Butler Chapman's notes from the meeting:

Jack Snyder and Tony George liked Bruce… Tony being aware of Bruce's interest is important and very helpful… Tony wants to build this business… He's at the beginning of his career and is not looking to sell the business… There is a lot of interest in IMS from various people… Bruce is very refreshing and impressive… Most team owners are so wrapped up in racing it's hard to see if they have any other outside interests—that's not the case with Bruce… Of the credible people who have expressed interest over the years, Bruce's interest is very conspicuous… It's the first time we've had a conversation with a CART member… Bruce and Tony have strong similarities, both are serious businessmen who are racing oriented… Tony's primary interests are oval, Bruce's are primarily road races… The IRL is oval and the IRL was created because Tony was fearful CART was threatening the future of oval racing… CART versus IRL and how to figure out a way to present the sport so that both interests are represented and profitable is an interesting question… Tony would like to see an oval in the Pacific Northwest for the IRL and NASCAR, combined with a road racing track—perhaps this is an opportunity with Bruce… What value can Bruce bring besides his money and his familiarity with a family-owned business? … This is an area he wants to think about a great deal more.

The 1952 Le Mans-winning Mercedes-Benz 300SL is one of the premier cars in Bruce McCaw's collection.

McCaw and son Wynn accept a trophy from His Royal Highness Prince Michael of Kent (center) after winning Best in Show at Hampton Court Palace in 2018 with the 1929 Mercedes-Benz S Barker Tourer.

"It was very interesting," McCaw concluded. "It went on for almost a year and a half and nobody knew about it. It was amazing we kept it quiet, but we only talked to Snyder and Tony and nobody else, and they only talked to me and my investment bankers. There were really only four people who were ever in this loop."

IMS was not for sale at the time, but McCaw's bankers put a value on the property of $175 to 225 million in July 1998. The Hulman-George family finally sold the famous track in 2019 to Roger Penske, for an estimated $350 million. "I guess our attempt was just a bit too early," McCaw said.

SENTIMENTAL FAVORITES

Bruce McCaw is a longtime collector of rare vintage automobiles. But some of the cars that hold the most value to him are not multi-million-dollar classics in the traditional sense.

McCaw maintains a pair of 1960 Pontiacs similar to the ones he used to drive around The Highlands when he was a teenager, as well as the 1964 Plymouth Belvedere that served as his transportation at Colorado College. He also still owns the C-Sports Racing Elva-Climax he acquired in 1968 and a reproduction of the Sprite that served as his first racing car. He says it is still one of the most enjoyable cars he takes on track.

Bruce always maintained a special fondness for his first street car, a 1959 Mercedes-Benz 220SE that he purchased for $1,500. When he first acquired the car in late 1962, McCaw soon fitted it with a bank of Lucas "flamethrower" driving lights and began entering in local road rallies. Along with a co-driver, he won the non-equipped class of the 1963 SCCA Rally Northwest, the predecessor to the Olympus Rally.

McCaw was attending the annual concours in Forest Grove, Oregon, in 1990, when he saw a 220SE drive in that he was certain was the same one he had owned. "I found the owner and started telling him about its little idiosyncrasies, like the mounts under the floor mats for the shoulder harnesses and the wiring for the driving lamps—where I'd modified the car for rallying," he recalled. "At first, he didn't believe me, but after we went over the whole car together, he understood that I really had owned this particular Mercedes."

Twenty-three years had passed since McCaw sold the car to a friend, and it took another decade for him to convince the car's most recent owner to sell. "Of all the cars you ever own, only one can be the first," McCaw said. "Your first love is always special, and I grew pretty attached to it. I called the owner every six months, asking to buy the car, and finally, he agreed that if he ever did sell it, I would get the right of first refusal. We finally agreed on a price—$10,000—and once I had a price it was just a matter of motivating him to sell. I sent him a check, including an extra $1,000 if he turned the car over by the end of that year. The guy called me the next day and said, 'Come get the car.'"

McCaw has remained faithful to the Mercedes-Benz brand throughout his driving life. In 1986, he and co-drivers Tom Cufley and Jim Rogers entered the first Mercedes 300E to reach US shores in the "One Lap of America" road rally. For many years, his daily driver was a 1995 E500, the performance version of the W124 sedan engineered and built by Porsche. During the PacWest era, when Mercedes-Benz introduced its first factory-branded AMG model to the American market (the E55 AMG sedan), McCaw and Mauricio Gugelmin were presented with the first two cars to reach the United States.

In spite of some of the challenges they encountered, McCaw continues to have a strong relationship with Daimler-Benz, and he has occasionally been entrusted as the steward of valuable Mercedes racing cars when they are made available for functions in the United States. Through a longterm loan, McCaw is the only private party in possession of one of the eight existing Mercedes 300 SLR; he has permission to demonstrate the car and was delighted to pair with Bernd Maylander in the 60th anniversary celebration of the famous Stirling Moss/Denis Jenkinson triumph in the 1955 Mille Miglia. In return, McCaw frequently loans the factory the 1952 Mercedes Le Mans winner, which he owns.

A 1929 Mercedes-Benz S Barker Tourer owned and restored by McCaw earned the coveted Best in Show honor at the 2017 Pebble Beach Concours d'Elegance. The car was originally owned by Francis Curzon, the 5th Earl of Howe, who won the 1931 24 Hours of Le Mans and was a founding member and president of the British Racing Drivers Club. The car was later owned by Tony Hulman and it sat in the basement of the Indianapolis Motor Speedway Museum for nearly 50 years before McCaw brought it back to life. The same car seized Best in Show at the 2018 Concours of Elegance at Hampton Court Palace, where McCaw and his son Wynn accepted the trophy from His Royal Highness Prince Michael of Kent.

VINTAGE RACING MOTORS

In 1986, Bruce McCaw entered his Elva Mk VII in the South Tacoma Motors Vintage Challenge, a support race for the short-lived Shuck's Tacoma Grand Prix. Run on a 1.5-mile, 10-turn temporary course around the Tacoma Dome, the event ran for two years, headlined by Formula Atlantic single seaters and NASCAR Winston West stock cars.

This Bentley Speed Six Gurney Nutting Sportsman has claimed several prestigious honors, including the Pullman Trophy for Best of Show at the 2013 St. James Concours of Elegance.

Confetti flies as McCaw's 1929 Mercedes takes Best in Show honors at Pebble Beach in 2017.

The floor at Vintage Racing Motors always features an eclectic group of vehicles.

Several PacWest Racing cars are stored at VRM.

McCaw had some trouble getting his Elva's Coventry Climax engine to run cleanly, but a competitor in an adjacent pit stepped in to help. Byron Sanborn worked as a technician at a local BMW dealer, and occasionally drove his neighbor's Shelby Cobra in vintage racing events.

"It was a chance meeting," Sanborn recalled. "I helped Bruce get the Elva running, and the exact same thing happened at the Tacoma Dome the next year. A couple months later, I got a call. I started doing some work for him part-time while I was still working at the dealership. Then that started turning into 35 or 50 hours a week."

McCaw started thinking about creating a business that could consolidate his growing interest in vintage cars and racing, while offering a range of services to car collectors and vintage racers. The key to putting it all together was a third partner—Thor Thorson, a friend of McCaw's dating to his college years in Colorado, who moved to Lake Sammamish, Washington, in the late 1980s. Vintage Racing Motors was formed in 1989.

"Though I was working in the real estate business, I found I was spending more and more time in the car business," said Thorson, who learned the joy of driving by bombing around the high mountains of Colorado in an 850-cc Mini. "Bruce and I decided that it would be a good idea to build a company together. We agreed to form a car dealership/racing operation. The concept was that we would make enough money buying and selling used racing cars, or classic cars, to support our racing habits. It has proven rather successful."

Working from Thorson's garage, their first major project was an Allard J2X in Le Mans specification. VRM set up its permanent base in Redmond, Washington, and for more than 30 years, has restored and maintained an incredible variety of vehicles for a diverse group of customers. VRM also provides transportation services (using an ex-PacWest Racing 53-foot transporter) and on-site race car preparation and hospitality. The company specializes in what Thorson calls "industrial archaeology," or the art of reconstructing mechanical systems when replacement components or even drawings are not available.

"We created a dealership, and it became a means to an end of my hobby," McCaw explained. "By starting VRM, we were able to buy and sell a lot of vintage racing cars and almost by accident created a significant business. We've bought and sold something like 500 cars. We maintain cars of all kinds for customers. You might find anything on the floor from a Morgan trike to a Formula 1 car at any given time. "We've developed a company that has great skills," he added. "We've got great people, many of whom are old racers who got tired of being on the road."

Supported by VRM, McCaw has demonstrated or raced a number of historically significant cars at vintage racing events around the world. Highlights include regular appearances at the Monaco Historic Grand Prix and the Monterey Historic Car Races. McCaw also took part in Mercedes-Benz' 2015 celebration of Stirling Moss's historic victory in the 1955 Mille Miglia, driving the 300SLR he has on permanent loan from Daimler-Benz.

"Driving Graham Hill's BRM at the Monaco historic meeting is an experience I will never forget—racing the car which had won at that very circuit," McCaw said. "My interest in cars parallels my interest in aviation—I enjoy the equipment, but I like the people most of all. Interesting people go racing, and it's fun to be able to race with people who are your heroes, like Stirling Moss, Phil Hill, Dan Gurney, Carroll Shelby, and others."

Bruce McCaw says driving Graham Hill's Monaco Grand Prix winner at the track's vintage race was a highlight of his life.

McCaw poses for a selfie with Derek Hill after McCaw's big win at Pebble Beach in 2017. Hill drove a Formula Atlantic with PacWest support in 1998.

The PacWest reunion inspired many great memories.

18

ONE LAST LOOK BACK

ON MAY 22, 2009, around 200 people associated with PacWest Racing Group gathered in the Grand Ballroom of the Columbia Club in downtown Indianapolis. They were guests of Jolene and Bruce McCaw, who hosted what was informally known as "The PacWest Reunion." The event commemorated the 15th anniversary of the team's two-car entry in the 1994 CART series. Outside, a Reynard show car, with PacWest's 1997 Hollywood and Motorola liveries split down the middle, was parked on Monument Circle, a poignant reminder that the team did not compete in the Indianapolis 500 during its most successful season of operation.

As usual at an event hosted by the McCaws, the food was sumptuous and the drinks flowed freely. Before the end of the night, most of the key players from PacWest's eight-plus years as a full-time racing team came up on stage to share stories. "We've all had some great memories," remarked John Anderson. "It's such a magic occasion to be able to picture everyone as we did back then when we were all associated."

Russell Cameron served as the unofficial emcee as a parade of contributors made their way to the dais. "Bruce helped us all to create an atmosphere of professionalism and camaraderie and friendship that we will carry forever," Cameron said. "It's hard to put it into perspective, but we're all better people because of him. Every time I talk to Mark Moore, or Ziggy, or Ando, or someone on another team, I reflect on the fact that we were doing so many things well. Those days from 1995 to 2001 were magical times. We were really close to the limit with cutting edge cars and drivers and teams that were operating at a very high level of professionalism. I think PacWest helped everyone move on to what they are doing now in their careers. Mark said it was like a Masters program. Bruce pushed the limits and we were trying to be at the top level."

The camaraderie that still existed between the team members was obvious. "We were a very close-knit team," said Ziggy Harcus. "A lot of guys would go out and socialize together, and you don't have a lot of that in the team I'm with now. A lot of funny stories, a lot of good times."

Bruce McCaw brought a split-liveried 1997 Reynard to the PacWest reunion. Clockwise from left: Mauricio Gugelmin, Steve Fusek, Russell Cameron, John Anderson, Ziggy Harcus, Bruce McCaw, Jolene McCaw.

Cameron: *Bruce is the biggest prankster of all. If it's not squirt guns out the windows at Caledon, it's a food fight. One night at Porcao* [the original Brazilian churrascaria in Rio de Janeiro], *we had a really wonderful dinner after the race. Big feed, the drink carts came, and everybody was having a good time. Pretty soon the limes from the caipirinhas started to fly. Bruce wasn't facing my direction, but I had a deadly accurate hit on his left eye. It was kind of twitching and he was in some pain, but he's a tough guy and didn't show it much. I felt for sure it was my last moment at PacWest. But he knew it was a food fight and fair game. Ten or fifteen minutes later, I went over to Bruce to apologize. He stood up and gave me a nice big hug. I thought it was over until I felt the chocolate cake hit the back of my head. The last laugh is with Bruce a lot of times.*

Ziggy Harcus and Flavio de Andrade of Souza Cruz share memories at the reunion.

Alan Mertens: *I have a lot of fond memories, and when I came here tonight, I didn't expect it to generate so much emotion. Bruce was close to tears and several other people have been when they came up here and spoke. It suddenly comes back to you what a good time we had. We went through thick and thin together but basically all of the people in the team were wonderful people. It was a very warm and comfortable place to be.*

Steve Fusek: *Obviously it was a special time with special people. Nowadays I get asked a lot if I miss it, and the answer is that I miss it a lot. But I miss it the way it was. I don't miss it today, and I'm not sure that I'd want to go back today. It's a different time, a different atmosphere. I don't know if you could ever duplicate that era with all those people. I almost feel like a proud parent sometimes, seeing what those guys are doing and what came out of this environment.*

Rick Gorne (Reynard): *I tell you what, PacWest was a very strong team. If you look now at the ex-PacWest personnel in the industry, they are sprinkled everywhere. PacWest was probably the greatest training ground for a bunch of engineers and technicians and race personnel. I've got the greatest respect for Bruce, always have, always will. I think he had a huge impact. A lot of people respected what he had to say. They listened when he spoke. Even when he may not have been overly vocal, when he spoke, it had meaning. I know guys like Chip Ganassi and Roger Penske had great respect for Bruce. PacWest was just seen as a fun team, but a professional fun team. They did things properly with regards to attention to detail and they had a passion for wanting to achieve. That was very evident. It was fun and those were great days. It was a massive growth period for Reynard, but also for Indy car racing. We were on the crest of a wave. We came in at the right time and I'd like to say that we contributed to some of that growth and some of the excitement. The camaraderie between everyone in the paddock was great—the teams, the drivers, the engine manufacturers. For whatever reason, the unity went away.*

Russell Cameron, Tim "Doc" Love and Tony Van Dongen at the reunion.

Colleen Howerton: *I was with PacWest from Day One to the last days. I miss it dearly. Whenever anyone asks if I would go back, I say absolutely. If Bruce said right now 'I want to start a team,' I'd be standing first in line. I learned so much and would never have gotten to where I got without working for Bruce as long as I did.*

Cameron: *It really was a magical time. If you think about the people, and what we were accomplishing, and the results that we were achieving. We were raising the bar consistently as a team, as a group of people, and I think we should be extremely proud of what we did in those times and what we've done since. Time goes on, but what's really great is we're all in this room and we're friends. That's just Bruce and Jolene's personality. They value the friendship of what's created as much as anything. I know tonight is a tribute to the employees of PacWest Racing, but we all know it starts at the top. It trickles down from the top and makes its way to all of us. We become infected with the belief of what can be.*

The last word goes to Bruce McCaw:

One of my attractions to racing was I liked the people," he said. *"Everything I had been involved in in my life were businesses that attracted interesting people. In aviation, I had a chance to meet so many incredible people, from Bill Boeing Jr. and Bill Lear to Kelly Johnson, so many pilots, and I think ten of the twelve guys who walked on the moon. I took Neil Armstrong for a ride on my boat and we flew around the world together. Those are just great people and it's an environment where I enjoyed the people. I found racing was also something that attracted interesting people.*

The racing business clearly taught me that you had to be there. So much is passed up and down the pit lane that if you aren't there, you really miss things. I found that if I missed a day of practice, I never really understood what happened. I could see the times, I could see changes had been made in the cars and listen to all the excuses, but I never really knew. Listening to how people are talking to each other, watching them. You watch how people are interrelating to each other and who is pissed at who and what sort of mood everybody is in. That was something I became increasingly sensitive to. The less time I spent, the less good I thought I could be in terms of a lot of what was going on with the team. I take all those things from a global perspective, and I think I learned a lot and I think I brought a fair amount to the sport that helped the business learn some things from me from other perspectives.

It's funny, the first time Jolene and I went back to the Indianapolis Motor Speedway after PacWest—I guess it was in 2003—we went out on the grid and walked down the pit lane, and we saw so many people that we had worked with," McCaw continued. "It was amazing. I think six out of the top ten drivers had driven for us and every car there had somebody that worked for us. When we walked down the pit lane, there were people in every pit, and they all came out. They were happy to see us and that said a lot. In Gasoline Alley you saw people, from some of the guys that worked in the garages, some of the tire slingers from Firestone and all that. A lot of the people have been around there for years, including some of the Yellow Shirts that I had gotten to know. They were people we cared about.

I think we had an environment at PacWest where people really did care about each other," he concluded. "There were friendships that went way beyond the job. There were times that were not easy when people left, but they had to leave for whatever choices. If people left for better opportunities, I was never bitter about that. I enjoy seeing that we were part of the careers of a lot of people who really have grown. I like to think that at least some of those accomplished their growth with us, that we set a foundation that helped people grow.

I will remain forever grateful to each and every person who was ever part of this team. It has been my great honor to know you and share these times together.

The split livery car sported a specially-designed "PacWest 15 Year Reunion" event logo on the headrest.

ACKNOWLEDGMENTS

JOHN OREOVICZ | SPEEDWAY, INDIANA

I JOINED PACWEST RACING in late 1996 to handle the team's public relations. In one of my first conversations with Bruce McCaw, he advised me to acquire and carry a compact point-and-shoot camera. "You never know what you might see," he said.

Turned out to be prescient advice. These days, we all carry point-and-shoot cameras in our pockets, built into our phones. Thirty years ago, Bruce and his brothers were ahead of that curve, too: once a new-fangled form of communication technology, we now take cell phones for granted. Their forward thinking followed the lead set by their father, J. Elroy McCaw, an aggressive broadcasting pioneer who could be considered the progenitor of modern multimedia conglomerates. It's a remarkable family that I feel privileged to have met.

I worked with PacWest for a little more than two years. I left because I wanted to write stories about the people and places in racing, not pitch them. But those two years were arguably the most important two years of my career. I learned so much about how a racing team operates. I got a priceless insider's look at the sport—the business, to be more accurate—as a whole, and lifelong friendships were sparked. I returned to the media in 1999 much better equipped to understand and analyze what was happening on the track and in the paddock.

I also emerged from PacWest as a better writer, largely thanks to Bruce McCaw himself. For all of the other talents he has displayed in his extraordinary life, Bruce might be the most effective editor I have ever worked with.

"I probably wore all of you PR guys out at one time or another with my drafting and re-writing," he told me. "I remember one time talking to Steve Fusek and telling him, 'If it kills me, I'm going to teach Oreo how to write correctly!'

"Apparently you said something to Steve about it," he added. "I said to Steve, 'Just tell him he'll come to appreciate this one day.'"

I do. Thank you, Bruce. This book was far too long in the making, which is part of the reason it is titled *Time Flies*. I hope it was worth the wait.

I'd also like to express my appreciation to the PacWest team members and others who shared their memories in interviews and candid conversations. It was a pleasure to reflect on the good times, and even the challenges that we faced.

Kudos to Dan Boyd and the other photographers who contributed the brilliant images that illustrate the story. Petyr Beck and the team at Documentary Media pulled it all together and my friend Ryan Long turned it into a beautiful package. I appreciate your talents.

Finally, special thanks to my family—Cheryl and Frank Oreovicz, Mary-Kate Oreovicz, William Flynn, Kathleen Pierce, and Patrick Oreovicz.

Mike Levitt/LAT USA

IN MEMORIAM

REMEMBERING THOSE WHO TOUCHED THE PACWEST TEAM AND HAVE "FLOWN WEST TO THE RACETRACK IN THE SKY"

JOHN ANDERSON	Heart and Soul of PacWest Racing, Vice President of Racing Operations, Spiritual Leader
DEE ANN ANDRETTI	Wife, Mother, Grandmother, Matriarch of the Legendary Andretti Family
JOHN ANDRETTI	Indy Car Driver
TOM ARMSTRONG	PacWest Racing Co-Founder
TONY BETTENHAUSEN	Indy Car Driver, Team Owner
BUDDY BIVENS	PacWest Racing Team Member
DANNY BLUNDELL	Father of Mark Blundell
SCOTT BRAYTON	Indy Car Driver
JOE CLARK	Aviator, Inventor, PacWest Racing's No. 1 Fan
CHARLES "PETE" CONRAD	Naval Aviator, US Astronaut, Third Man to Walk on the Moon, Commander: Gemini 11, Apollo 12 and Skylab 2, Racer
DOUG CONRAD	PacWest Racing Team Member
SANTIAGO "JIM" CUEVAS	Friend and Fan of PacWest Racing
JOHN DELLA PENNA	Indy Car Team Owner
RON FUSEK	PacWest Racing Team Member
MARI HULMAN GEORGE	Chairperson of Hulman & Co./Indianapolis Motor Speedway
CHRIS GRIFFIS	PacWest Racing Team Member
GIULIANO GUGELMIN	Son of Mauricio and Stella Gugelmin
DAN GURNEY	Legendary Driver, Car Constructor, Team Owner, Championship Auto Racing Teams Co-Founder
CARL HAAS	Indy Car Team Owner
CAREY HALL	PacWest Racing Team Member
SAM HANKS	1949 AAA Midget Champion, 1953 AAA National Champion, 1956 USAC Stock Car Champion, Winner of the 1957 Indianapolis 500

PHIL HILL	Three-Time Winner of Le Mans and Sebring, 1961 Formula 1 World Champion, Photographer, Writer, World Class Auto Restorer, Historian
CARL HOGAN	Indy Car Team Owner
MARY FENDRICH HULMAN	Chairperson Emeritus, Hulman & Co./Indianapolis Motor Speedway
JEFF KROSNOFF	Indy Car Driver
BOB LAZIER	Indy Car Driver, Father of Indianapolis 500 Winner Buddy Lazier
WES LEMATTA	PacWest Racing Co-Founder
KEITH MCCAW	Devoted Son, Brother, Husband, Father and Fan, Pilot
MARION OLIVER MCCAW	Devoted Mother, Savvy Businesswoman, Lover of Music and Opera, Racing Fan
GREG MOORE	Indy Car Driver
PAUL MORGAN	Ilmor Engineering Co-Founder
SIR STIRLING MOSS	Legendary Racer, Consummate Gentleman
PAUL NEWMAN	Actor, Philanthropist, Racing Driver, Indy Car Team Owner
GARY NORTH	PacWest Racing Team Member
MORRIS NUNN	Formula 1 and Indy Car Team Owner
TONY RENNA	Indy Car Driver, PacWest Racing Team Member
PAT MATTHEWS RISTER	Mother of Jolene McCaw
GONZALO RODRIGUEZ	Indy Car Driver
BETTY RUTHERFORD	Friend and Fan of Racing, Wife of Johnny Rutherford, CARA Charities Co-Founder
CARROLL SHELBY	Le Mans Winner, Legendary Car Constructor
GREG WATSON	PacWest Racing Team Member
DAN WHELDON	Two-Time Indianapolis 500 Winner, 2005 IRL Champion, PacWest Racing Team Member

TEAM ROSTER

Name	Years
Allbaugh, Gary	1997-2001
Allen, Bill	1993-1994
Anderson, John	1993-2000
André, Didier	1998-1999
Andrus, Michael	1999-2001
Armstrong, Thomas	1993-1996
Atterbury, Neil	1997
Avila, Pete	2000-2001
Azevedo, Carl	1994-1998
Azevedo, Shane	1999-2001
Ball, James	1999-2000
Bauer, Michael	1996-1997
Beaumier, Patrick	1996-2001
Bergstrom, William	1996-2001
Bidding, Brian	1998-2001
Bivens, Buddy	1993
Blinco, Tim	1994
Bloom, Tom	1993-1994
Bloom, Nigel	1993-2001
Blundell, Mark	1996-2000
Bodey, Al	1997-1998
Borland, Matt	1998-1999
Bowe, Theodore	2001
Bowie, Jim	1997-1999
Bowman, Zachary	1997-1998
Bradford, Scott	1999-2001
Brooking, April	1997-1998
Brown, Andy	1993-1998
Brzozowski, David	1999-2000
Burnam, Tim	1996-1997
Byar, Lawrence	1998-1999
Bynum, Steve	1998
Calvert, Frank	1998
Cameron, Russell	1994-2001
Camosy, Mike	1995-1996
Carollo, Jim	1993-1994
Castleman, Andrew	1999-2001
Clark, Steven	2000-2001
Claudio, Mike	1998-1999
Cleary, Matthew	2001
Clutter, Christy	1997
Coffman, Sonya	1999
Confer, Brent	1997
Connell, Daryl	1994
Conrad, Douglas	1994-2001
Correll, Melanie	1996-1998
Costello, Steven	1996-1998
Coxon, Christopher	1999-2001
Creak, John	1996-2000
Crockett, Charlie	1998-1999
Daisher, David	1997-1998
Darragh, Mark	1999-2001
Davis, Wendy	1998
Dawes, Laurin	1999
Derichebourg, Boris	1999
Dimuccio, Mike	1999
Dininger, Bryce	1999
Dininger, John	1998-1999
Dixon, Scott	2000-2001
Dobson, Dominic	1993-1998
Dominguez, Mario	2001
Donohue, David	1996-1998
Douthat, Tim	1994-1998
Durbin, Matthew	2000
Eason, Casey	1994-2000
Edwards, Gerry	1994-1995
Ekeren, Steven	1994-2001
Eldridge, Jeff	1998-1999
Elkins, Darla	1997-2001
Ellingwood, Todd	1999
Ellis, Larry	1998
Endres, Ronald	1994-2001
Erickson, Steven	1999
Fabi, Teo	1996
Faul, Skip	1994-1996
Fellows, Brian	2000-2001
Feltner, Daren	1997
Flint, Mark	1997
Fox, Daryl	1996-2001
Fusek, Mary	1997-2001
Fusek, Ronald	1997-2001
Fusek, Steven	1995-2001
Gerrish, Laurence	1999-2001
Gibson, James	1999-2001
Gibson, Stephanie	2000-2001
Gimbel, Matthew	1999-2001
Glyshaw, Nicholas	1999-2000
Gordon, Jeff	1994-1996
Graffio, Jodi	2001
Gray, Albert	1998-2000
Gray, Brian	2000
Griffin, Joel	1997-2001
Griffis, Chris	1995-2001
Grosshans, Russell	1996-2001
Gugelmin, Mauricio	1995-2001
Guilinger, Charles	1996-2001
Gutierriez, Juan	2001
Hall, Brook	1998-2001
Hall, Carey	1997-2001
Hall, Christopher	1997
Hamilton, Jim	1996-1997
Hamilton, Gavin	1997-2000
Hamilton, Vincent	1996-1998
Harcus, Paul	1994-2001
Harder, Duane	1996-1997
Harvey, Michael	1996-1999
Helman, Robert	1997-1998
Henry, Tom	1997
Herd, Mark	1996-1997
Higgins, Ashleigh	1999-2000
Hollett, Thomas	1999-2001
Holmes, Jennifer	1997-1999
Horton, Gerald	2001
Horton, Jeff	1994-2001
Houk, Tony	1995-2001
Houtin, Pascal	2001
Howard, Joseph	2000-2001
Howerton, Colleen	1993-2001
Hubbert, Mike	1994
Hurford, Rick	1993-1995
Huth, Matt	1993-1996
Irvan, Sean	1997-1998
Isaacs, Nathan	1999-2000
Jackson, Trevor	1996-1999
Jacobs, David	1997-1999
Jasper, Paul	1998
Jaynes, Chris	1995-2001
Jenkins, Daniel	1995-2000
Johnson, Eric	1999-2001
Johnson, Robert	2001
Johnson, Stephen	2001
Jolley, Donald	1997-1998
Joyce, Ken	1994-1996
Julian, Blair	2000-2001
Karras, Julian	1997-2001
Keene, Thomas	1996-1999
Kelley, Bart	1999
Kent, Stephen IV	1997-1999
Kinnaird, Ian	1997-1998
Kivett, Jeff	1999-2001
King, Cooper	1994-1998

Name	Years
Kitasaki, James	1999
Koger, Mike	2001
Koup, Melinda	1999-2001
Kovacik, Dale	2000-2001
Kryder, Bryan	1999-2001
Kuck, Loren	1998-2001
Lacava, Dennis	1994
Lawrence, Brian	1997-1999
Leo, James	1998-2001
Lematta, Wes	1993-1994
Lewis, Andrew	2000-2001
Loik, David	1996-1998
Long, Rick	1994-1996
Lopez, Eric	1997-1998
Love, Timothy	1993-2001
Lowry, Michael	2000-2001
Luckett, Dave	1994
Macedo, Romeo	1998-1999
Mackey, Dave	1999
Mahurin, Rick	1997-2001
Marcus, Bernie	1998-2001
Marks, Pat	1999
Marks, Scott	1999
Martin, Amber	2000-2001
Martin, Joey	2001
Martin, William	2000-2001
Massick, Terry	1996-1997
Mathis, Ron	1996-1998
McCain, Craig	1998-2001
McCann, Bruce	1998
McCauley, Roy	1998-1999
McCaw, Bruce	1993-2001
McCaw, Jolene	1994-2001
McClellen, John	1996
McDonald, Allen	1997-2001
Melson, Steve	1993-1995
Meredith, Richard	1998-2000
Meskis, Rebecca	2000
Metzger, Paul	1997-1998
Milby, David	1999
Minch, Theodore	1999-2001
Mitchell, Scott	2000-2001
Molin, Michelle	1996-1998
Moore, Mark	1993-2001
Moreno, Roberto	1999
Morris, Paul	1998
Mothershead, Garrett	2000-2001
Mullins, Donald	1997-1999
Murray, Brett	1999-2000
Myers, Todd	1998
Natalie, Andy	1997-2000
Neff, Timothy	1995-1998
Nelson, Andrew	1998-2001
Noble, Kimberly	1997-2000
North, Gary	1993
Nott, Benjamin	1999
Oakley, Aron	1999
Oreovicz, John	1996-1998
O'Rourke, Nathan	2001
Oster, Jeff	1996-2000
Patterson, Greg	1998-2000
Paull, Greg	1996-1997
Pena, David	1999-2001
Phillips, Darren	2000-2001
Phillips, William	1994
Pompileo, Chris	1999
Poynter, Justin	1997
Reid, James	1996-1998
Reneau, Ricky	1997-1998
Renna, Tony	1999-2000
Riggs, Andrew	1997-1998
Rinas, Jennifer	1998
Robson, Brian	2000-2001
Rocquelin, Guillaume	2000-2001
Roof, John	1995-1999
Rose, Tom	1998
Sable, Sterling	1999
Salles, Gualter	1999
Schollum, Hugh	2001
Schrier, Brian	1998
Selman, Wayne	1999-2001
Shank, Timothy	1997-2001
Sharp, Scott	1994
Sharpley, David	2000-2001
Sheffler, Chris	2001
Sheldon, Rusty	2000
Simpson, Scott	1996-1998
Slade, Nicholas	1999-2001
Smay, Randy	1995-2001
Smay (Selman), Valerie	1996-2001
Snodgrass, Brad	2000
Snyder, Brett	1999-2000
Sprovtsoff, Mike	1998
Stafford, Jeffrey	1997-1998
Stage, Ed	1994-1995
Start, Thomas	1996-1997
Stepan, Derrick	1998-1999
Stephens, David	1999-2001
Stevens, Rebecca	2001
Storer, JC	2000
Strauss, Eric	2000-2001
Stufflet, Patrick	1997-2001
Sullivan, Danny	1995
Sumner, John	1999-2001
Swain, Jeffrey	1997-1998
Taylor, David	1993-1996
Tingwald, Scott	1995-1996
Todd, Michael	1997-1999
Trevisan, Roberto	1996-1997
Triggs, Clayton	2001
Trotter, Amanda	1999-2001
Trowbridge, William	1999-2001
Trudel, Martin	1996-1997
Ulrich, Mike	1999
Unser, Robby	1997
Vallo, Eric	1999-2001
Van Dongen, Tony	1998
Van Etten, Mark	1997
Vander Well, Victoria	1996-1997
Wall, Pat	1993-1996
Walters, Dennis	2000-2001
Ward, John	2001
Watson, Greg	1997-1998
Weed, Todd	1996-1999
Wethington, Brent	1997
Wheldon, Dan	2001
Whitesides, Richard	2000
Wilkerson, Roy	1993-1998
Williams, Brian	1995-2001
Williams, Don	1993-1994
Williams, Paul	1999-2000
Wilson, Timothy	1999-2001
Winingham, Leann	1995-1997
Winkle, Butch	1996-1998
Wright, William	1996-1998
Woods, Christopher	1996-2001
York, Michael	1998-1999
Zelesnik, Larry	1996-1997

1993 SEASON STATISTICS

RANK	DRIVER	TEAM	PTS	CHASSIS	ENGINE	TIRES	STARTS	RAF	POLES	WINS	BF	LL
1	Nigel Mansell	Newman/Haas Racing	191	Lola	Ford	Goodyear	15	12	6	5	1	603
2	Emerson Fittipaldi	Penske Racing	183	Penske	Chevrolet	Goodyear	16	14	2	3	1	270
3	Paul Tracy	Penske Racing	157	Penske	Chevrolet	Goodyear	16	9	2	5	1	756
4	Bobby Rahal	Rahal-Hogan Racing	133	Rahal-Hogan/Lola	Chevrolet	Goodyear	15	13	0	0	2	58
5	Raul Boesel	Dick Simon Racing	132	Lola	Ford	Goodyear	16	13	1	0	2	102
6	Mario Andretti	Newman/Haas Racing	117	Lola	Ford	Goodyear	16	13	1	1	1	140
7	Al Unser Jr.	Galles Racing	100	Lola	Chevrolet	Goodyear	16	12	0	1	1	55
8	Arie Luyendyk	Chip Ganassi Racing	90	Lola	Ford	Goodyear	16	11	1	0	2	15
9	Scott Goodyear	Walker Racing	86	Lola	Ford	Goodyear	16	10	2	0	2	53
10	Robby Gordon	A.J. Foyt Racing	84	Lola	Ford	Goodyear	16	9	0	0	2	7
35	**Dominic Dobson**	**Burns Racing/ PacWest Racing**	**0**	**Galmer**	**Chevrolet**	**Goodyear**	**3**	**3**	**0**	**0**	**14**	**0**

DATE	CIRCUIT	WINNER	CAR	SPEED	BURNS RACING/PACWEST RACING RESULTS (START/FINISH)
21-Mar	Surfers Paradise	Nigel Mansell	Lola-Ford/Cosworth	97.284	
4-Apr	Phoenix	Mario Andretti	Lola-Ford/Cosworth	123.857	
18-Apr	Long Beach	Paul Tracy	Penske-Chevrolet	93.089	
30-May	Indianapolis	Emerson Fittipaldi	Penske-Chevrolet	157.207	Dobson 27/23
6-Jun	Milwaukee	Nigel Mansell	Lola-Ford/Cosworth	110.97	
13-Jun	Detroit	Danny Sullivan	Lola-Chevrolet	83.116	
27-Jun	Portland	Emerson Fittipaldi	Penske-Chevrolet	96.312	
11-Jul	Cleveland	Paul Tracy	Penske-Chevrolet	127.913	
18-Jul	Toronto	Paul Tracy	Penske-Chevrolet	96.51	
1-Aug	Michigan	Nigel Mansell	Lola-Ford/Cosworth	188.203	
8-Aug	New Hampshire	Nigel Mansell	Lola-Ford/Cosworth	1309.148	
22-Aug	Road America	Paul Tracy	Penske-Chevrolet	118.408	
29-Aug	Vancouver	Al Unser Jr.	Lola-Chevrolet	91.794	Dobson 23/14
12-Sep	Mid-Ohio	Emerson Fittipaldi	Penske-Chevrolet	102.217	Dobson 27/DNS
19-Sep	Nazareth	Nigel Mansell	Lola-Ford/Cosworth	158.685	
3-Oct	Laguna Seca	Paul Tracy	Penske-Chevrolet	106.303	Dobson 29/18

1994 SEASON STATISTICS

RANK	DRIVER	TEAM	PTS	CHASSIS	ENGINE	TIRES	STARTS	RAF	POLES	WINS	BF	LL
1	Al Unser Jr.	Penske Racing	225	Penske	Ilmor	Goodyear	16	12	4	8	1	677
2	Emerson Fittipaldi	Penske Racing	178	Penske	Ilmor	Goodyear	16	11	2	1	1	404
3	Paul Tracy	Penske Racing	152	Penske	Ilmor	Goodyear	16	9	4	3	1	503
4	Michael Andretti	Chip Ganassi Racing	118	Reynard	Ford	Goodyear	16	10	0	2	1	166
5	Robby Gordon	Walker Racing	104	Lola	Ford	Goodyear	12	12	2	0	2	59
6	Jacques Villeneuve	Forsythe-Green Racing	94	Reynard	Ford	Goodyear	16	11	0	1	1	22
7	Raul Boesel	Dick Simon Racing	90	Lola	Ford	Goodyear	16	11	1	0	2	120
8	Nigel Mansell	Newman/Haas Racing	88	Lola	Ford	Goodyear	16	9	3	0	2	103
9	Teo Fabi	Hall Racing	79	Reynard	Ilmor	Goodyear	16	13	0	0	4	0
10	Bobby Rahal	Rahal-Hogan Racing	59	Lola	Honda	Goodyear	16	10	0	0	2	2
18	**Dominic Dobson**	**PacWest Racing**	**30**	**Lola**	**Ford**	**Goodyear**	**16**	**12**	**0**	**0**	**3**	**0**
21	**Scott Sharp**	**PacWest Racing**	**14**	**Lola**	**Ford**	**Goodyear**	**16**	**10**	**0**	**0**	**9**	**0**

DATE	CIRCUIT	WINNER	CAR	SPEED	PACWEST RACING RESULTS (START/FINISH)
20-Mar	Surfers Paradise	Michael Andretti	Reynard-Ford/Cosworth	80.994	Dobson 26/12, Sharp 18/11
10-Apr	Phoenix	Emerson Fittipaldi	Penske-Ilmor	107.437	Dobson 14/24 (Contact), Sharp 13/9
17-Apr	Long Beach	Al Unser Jr.	Penske-Ilmor	99.283	Dobson 17/17, Sharp 21/28 (Engine)
29-May	Indianapolis	Al Unser Jr.	Penske-Mercedes	160.872	Dobson 12/29 (Contact), Sharp 17/16
5-Jun	Milwaukee	Al Unser Jr.	Penske-Ilmor	118.804	Dobson 6/13, Sharp 15/12
12-Jun	Belle Isle	Paul Tracy	Penske-Ilmor	86.245	Dobson 24/25 (Contact), Sharp 26/13
26-Jun	Portland	Al Unser Jr.	Penske-Ilmor	107.777	Dobson 15/17, Sharp 18/18
10-Jul	Cleveland	Al Unser Jr.	Penske-Ilmor	128.026	Dobson 18/25 (Engine), Sharp 20/24 (Suspension)
17-Jul	Toronto	Michael Andretti	Reynard-Ford/Cosworth	96.673	Dobson 16/11, Sharp 20/16 (Header)
31-Jul	Michigan	Scott Goodyear	Lola-Ford/Cosworth	159.8	Dobson 9/3 (First CART Podium), Sharp 18/22 (Driveshaft)
14-Aug	Mid-Ohio	Al Unser Jr.	Penske-Ilmor	110.387	Dobson 20/15, Sharp 18/11
21-Aug	New Hampshire	Al Unser Jr.	Penske-Ilmor	122.635	Dobson 6/6, Sharp 16/24 (Contact)
4-Sep	Vancouver	Al Unser Jr.	Penske-Ilmor	89.166	Dobson 19/17, Sharp 14/12
11-Sep	Road America	Jacques Villeneuve	Reynard-Ford/Cosworth	116.922	Dobson 12/11, Sharp 13/10
18-Sep	Nazareth	Paul Tracy	Penske-Ilmor	131.141	Dobson 16/19, Sharp 17/15
9-Oct	Laguna Seca	Paul Tracy	Penske-Ilmor	92.978	Dobson 14/10, Sharp 20/21 (Engine)

1995 SEASON STATISTICS

RANK	DRIVER	TEAM	PTS	CHASSIS	ENGINE	TIRES	STARTS	RAF	POLES	WINS	BF	LL
1	Jacques Villeneuve	Team Green	172	Reynard	Ford	Goodyear	17	14	6	4	1	280
2	Al Unser Jr.	Penske Racing	161	Penske	Mercedes	Goodyear	16	13	0	4	1	419
3	Bobby Rahal	Rahal-Hogan Racing	128	Lola	Mercedes	Goodyear	17	13	0	0	2	2
4	Michael Andretti	Newman/Haas Racing	123	Lola	Ford	Goodyear	17	9	3	1	1	478
5	Robby Gordon	Walker Racing	121	Reynard	Ford	Goodyear	16	12	2	2	1	69
6	Paul Tracy	Newman/Haas Racing	115	Lola	Ford	Goodyear	17	9	0	2	1	91
7	Scott Pruett	Patrick Racing	112	Lola	Ford	Firestone	17	13	0	1	1	66
8	Jimmy Vasser	Chip Ganassi Racing	92	Reynard	Ford	Goodyear	17	10	0	0	2	20
9	Teo Fabi	Forsythe Racing	83	Reynard	Ford	Goodyear	17	12	1	0	3	103
10	**Mauricio Gugelmin**	**PacWest Racing**	**80**	**Reynard**	**Ford**	**Goodyear**	**17**	**14**	**0**	**0**	**2**	**70**
19	**Danny Sullivan**	**PacWest Racing**	**32**	**Reynard**	**Ford**	**Goodyear**	**13**	**8**	**0**	**0**	**5**	**0**
24	**Juan Fangio II**	**PacWest Racing**	**6**	**Reynard**	**Ford**	**Goodyear**	**4**	**3**	**0**	**0**	**7**	**0**

DATE	CIRCUIT	WINNER	CAR	SPEED	PACWEST RACING RESULTS (START/FINISH)
5-Mar	Miami	Jacques Villeneuve	Reynard-Ford/Cosworth	82.801	Gugelmin 2/2 (First CART Laps Led), Sullivan 6/9
19-Mar	Surfers Paradise	Paul Tracy	Lola-Ford/Cosworth	92.335	Gugelmin 10/4, Sullivan 19/5
2-Apr	Phoenix	Robby Gordon	Reynard-Ford/Cosworth	133.98	Gugelmin 11/13, Sullivan 21/27 (Brakes)
9-Apr	Long Beach	Al Unser Jr.	Penske-Mercedes	91.442	Gugelmin 5/5, Sullivan 17/10
23-Apr	Nazareth	Emerson Fittipaldi	Penske-Mercedes	131.305	Gugelmin 12/17, Sullivan 22/18
28-May	Indianapolis	Jacques Villeneuve	Reynard-Ford/Cosworth	153.616	Gugelmin 6/6 (Led Most Laps), Sullivan 9/18
4-Jun	Milwaukee	Paul Tracy	Lola-Ford/Cosworth	137.304	Gugelmin 10/14, Sullivan 21/17
11-Jun	Belle Isle	Robby Gordon	Reynard-Ford/Cosworth	83.499	Gugelmin 11/15, Sullivan 10/12
25-Jun	Portland	Al Unser Jr.	Penske-Mercedes	103.933	Gugelmin 4/7, Sullivan 18/22 (Fire)
9-Jul	Road America	Jacques Villeneuve	Reynard-Ford/Cosworth	103.901	Gugelmin 18/24 (Contact), Sullivan 19/25 (Contact)
16-Jul	Toronto	Michael Andretti	Lola-Ford/Cosworth	94.787	Gugelmin 14/12, Sullivan 13/18 (Engine)
23-Jul	Cleveland	Jacques Villeneuve	Reynard-Ford/Cosworth	130.113	Gugelmin 12/23 (Fuel Pressure), Sullivan 14/5
30-Jul	Michigan	Scott Pruett	Lola-Ford/Cosworth	159.676	Gugelmin 6/11, Sullivan 9/16 (Contact, Last Indy Car Start)
13-Aug	Mid-Ohio	Al Unser Jr.	Penske-Mercedes	107.11	Gugelmin 4/6, Fangio 14/7 (First Indy Car Start)
20-Aug	New Hampshire	André Ribeiro	Reynard-Honda	134.203	Gugelmin 7/11, Fangio 12/15
3-Sep	Vancouver	Al Unser Jr.	Penske-Mercedes	95.571	Gugelmin 11/20 (Contact), Fangio 24/28 (Contact)
10-Sep	Laguna Seca	Gil de Ferran	Reynard-Mercedes	98.493	Gugelmin 6/3, Fangio 19/13

1996 SEASON STATISTICS

RANK	DRIVER	TEAM	PTS	CHASSIS	ENGINE	TIRES	STARTS	RAF	POLES	WINS	BF	LL
1	Jimmy Vasser	Chip Ganassi Racing	154	Reynard	Honda	Firestone	16	16	4	4	1	162
2	Michael Andretti	Newman/Haas Racing	132	Lola	Ford	Goodyear	16	10	0	5	1	281
3	Alex Zanardi	Chip Ganassi Racing	132	Reynard	Honda	Firestone	16	10	6	3	1	610
4	Al Unser Jr.	Penske Racing	125	Penske	Mercedes	Goodyear	16	13	0	0	2	125
5	Christian Fittipaldi	Newman/Haas Racing	110	Lola	Ford	Goodyear	16	13	0	0	2	80
6	Gil de Ferran	Hall Racing	104	Reynard	Honda	Goodyear	16	11	1	1	1	172
7	Bobby Rahal	Rahal-Hogan Racing	102	Reynard	Mercedes	Goodyear	16	12	0	0	2	1
8	Bryan Herta	Rahal-Hogan Racing	86	Reynard	Mercedes	Goodyear	16	13	0	0	2	41
9	Greg Moore	Forsythe Racing	84	Reynard	Mercedes	Firestone	16	9	0	0	2	73
10	Scott Pruett	Patrick Racing	82	Lola	Ford	Firestone	16	11	1	0	2	12
14	**Mauricio Gugelmin**	**PacWest Racing**	**53**	**Reynard**	**Ford**	**Goodyear**	**16**	**10**	**0**	**0**	**2**	**12**
16	**Mark Blundell**	**PacWest Racing**	**41**	**Reynard**	**Ford**	**Goodyear**	**13**	**9**	**0**	**0**	**5**	**0**
26	**Teo Fabi**	**PacWest Racing**	**0**	**Reynard**	**Ford**	**Goodyear**	**2**	**1**	**0**	**0**	**16**	**0**

DATE	CIRCUIT	WINNER	CAR	SPEED	PACWEST RACING RESULTS (START/FINISH)
3-Mar	Homestead	Jimmy Vasser	Reynard-Honda	109.399	Gugelmin 8/26 (Contact), Blundell 19/15 (First Indy Car Start)
17-Mar	Rio de Janeiro	André Ribeiro	Lola-Honda	117.927	Gugelmin 9/25 (Brakes), Blundell 18/27 (Contact)
31-Mar	Surfers Paradise	Jimmy Vasser	Reynard-Honda	90.218	Gugelmin 11/4
14-Apr	Long Beach	Jimmy Vasser	Reynard-Honda	96.281	Gugelmin 11/15, Fabi 19/18 (Clutch)
28-Apr	Nazareth	Michael Andretti	Lola-Ford/Cosworth	140.953	Gugelmin 16/15, Fabi 19/16
26-May	Michigan	Jimmy Vasser	Reynard-Honda	156.403	Gugelmin 14/2, Blundell 19/5
2-Jun	Milwaukee	Michael Andretti	Lola-Ford/Cosworth	128.282	Gugelmin 9/22 (Suspension), Blundell 12/15
9-Jun	Belle Isle	Michael Andretti	Lola-Ford/Cosworth	75.136	Gugelmin 19/16, Blundell 15/5
23-Jun	Portland	Alex Zanardi	Reynard-Honda	103.837	Gugelmin 10/16, Blundell 21/8
30-Jun	Cleveland	Gil de Ferran	Reynard-Honda	144.932	Gugelmin 9/21 (Engine), Blundell 15/11
14-Jul	Toronto	Adrian Fernandez	Lola-Honda	97.598	Gugelmin 17/12, Blundell 16/11
28-Jul	Michigan	André Ribeiro	Lola-Honda	152.627	Gugelmin 13/3, Blundell 21/6
11-Aug	Mid-Ohio	Alex Zanardi	Reynard-Honda	104.358	Gugelmin 12/26 (Suspension), Blundell 13/10
18-Aug	Road America	Michael Andretti	Lola-Ford/Cosworth	102.947	Gugelmin 5/21 (Engine), Blundell 13/20 (Contact)
1-Sep	Vancouver	Michael Andretti	Lola-Ford/Cosworth	94.374	Gugelmin 9/24, Blundell 17/12
8-Sep	Laguna Seca	Alex Zanardi	Reynard-Honda	102.687	Gugelmin 3/5, Blundell 4/24 (Electrical)

1997 SEASON STATISTICS

RANK	DRIVER	TEAM	PTS	CHASSIS	ENGINE	TIRES	STARTS	RAF	POLES	WINS	BF	LL
1	Alex Zanardi	Chip Ganassi Racing	195	Reynard	Honda	Firestone	16	15	4	5	1	338
2	Gil de Ferran	Walker Racing	162	Reynard	Honda	Goodyear	17	14	2	0	2	165
3	Jimmy Vasser	Chip Ganassi Racing	144	Reynard	Honda	Firestone	17	15	0	1	1	153
4	**Mauricio Gugelmin**	**PacWest Racing**	**132**	**Reynard**	**Mercedes**	**Firestone**	**17**	**14**	**3**	**1**	**1**	**212**
5	Paul Tracy	Penske Racing	121	Penske	Mercedes	Goodyear	16	10	2	3	1	336
6	**Mark Blundell**	**PacWest Racing**	**115**	**Reynard**	**Mercedes**	**Firestone**	**17**	**12**	**0**	**3**	**1**	**138**
7	Greg Moore	Forsythe Racing	111	Reynard	Mercedes	Firestone	17	9	0	2	1	142
8	Michael Andretti	Newman/Haas Racing	108	Swift	Ford	Goodyear	17	9	0	1	1	197
9	Scott Pruett	Patrick Racing	102	Reynard	Ford	Firestone	17	12	2	1	1	66
10	Raul Boesel	Patrick Racing	91	Reynard	Ford	Firestone	17	14	1	0	3	90

DATE	CIRCUIT	WINNER	CAR	SPEED	PACWEST RACING RESULTS (START/FINISH)
2-Mar	Homestead	Michael Andretti	Swift-Ford/Cosworth	135.478	Gugelmin 2/6, Blundell 5/14
6-Apr	Surfers Paradise	Scott Pruett	Reynard-Ford/Cosworth	78.948	Gugelmin 8/17, Blundell 5/8
13-Apr	Long Beach	Alex Zanardi	Reynard-Honda	93.999	Gugelmin 3/2, Blundell 14/13
27-Apr	Nazaerth	Paul Tracy	Penske-Mercedes	118.919	Gugelmin 5/9, Blundell 16/19
11-May	Rio de Janeiro	Paul Tracy	Penske-Mercedes	113.721	Gugelmin 1/22 (Contact/First Career Indy Car Pole/ First PacWest Indy Car Pole), Blundell 20/8
24-May	Gateway	Paul Tracy	Penske-Mercedes	113.984	Gugelmin 3/6, Blundell 20/24 (Ignition)
1-Jun	Milwaukee	Greg Moore	Reynard-Mercedes	119.597	Gugelmin 2/5, Blundell 11/12
8-Jun	Belle Isle	Greg Moore	Reynard-Mercedes	86.047	Gugelmin 8/16 (Out of Fuel), Blundell 10/17 (Out of Fuel)
22-Jun	**Portland**	**Mark Blundell**	**Reynard-Mercedes**	**76.575**	Gugelmin 4/6, Blundell 11/1 (First Career Indy Car Win/ First PacWest Indy Car Win)
13-Jul	Cleveland	Alex Zanardi	Reynard-Honda	111.848	Gugelmin 6/15, Blundell 3/9
20-Jul	**Toronto**	**Mark Blundell**	**Reynard-Mercedes**	**92.779**	Gugelmin 10/6, Blundell 2/1
27-Jul	Michigan	Alex Zanardi	Reynard-Honda	167.044	Gugelmin 2/6, Blundell 11/2
10-Aug	Mid-Ohio	Alex Zanardi	Reynard-Honda	110.456	Gugelmin 6/7, Blundell 13/26
17-Aug	Road America	Alex Zanardi	Reynard-Honda	102.995	Gugelmin 1/2, Blundell 2/16 (Engine)
31-Aug	**Vancouver**	**Mauricio Gugelmin**	**Reynard-Mercedes**	**92.228**	Gugelmin 4/1 (First Career Indy Car Win), Blundell 8/7
7-Sep	Laguna Seca	Jimmy Vasser	Reynard-Honda	109.647	Gugelmin 5/9 (Brakes), Blundell 4/2
28-Sep	**Fontana**	**Mark Blundell**	**Reynard-Mercedes**	**166.575**	Gugelmin 1/4, Blundell 8/1

1998 SEASON STATISTICS

RANK	DRIVER	TEAM	PTS	CHASSIS	ENGINE	TIRES	STARTS	RAF	POLES	WINS	BF	LL
1	Alex Zanardi	Chip Ganassi Racing	285	Reynard	Honda	Firestone	19	18	0	7	1	499
2	Jimmy Vasser	Chip Ganassi Racing	169	Reynard	Honda	Firestone	19	16	1	3	1	296
3	Dario Franchitti	Team Green	160	Reynard	Honda	Firestone	19	11	5	3	1	243
4	Adrian Fernandez	Patrick Racing	154	Reynard	Ford	Firestone	19	15	1	2	1	138
5	Greg Moore	Forsythe Racing	141	Reynard	Mercedes	Firestone	19	12	1	2	1	251
6	Scott Pruett	Patrick Racing	121	Reynard	Ford	Firestone	19	13	1	0	2	2
7	Michael Andretti	Newman/Haas Racing	112	Swift	Ford	Goodyear	19	11	1	1	1	468
8	Bryan Herta	Team Rahal	97	Reynard	Ford	Firestone	19	11	3	1	1	171
9	Tony Kanaan	Tasman Motorsports	92	Reynard	Honda	Firestone	19	13	0	0	3	0
10	Bobby Rahal	Team Rahal	82	Reynard	Ford	Firestone	19	15	0	0	3	2
15	**Mauricio Gugelmin**	**PacWest Racing**	**49**	**Reynard**	**Mercedes**	**Firestone**	**19**	**12**	**0**	**0**	**4**	**69**
17	**Mark Blundell**	**PacWest Racing**	**36**	**Reynard**	**Mercedes**	**Firestone**	**19**	**13**	**0**	**0**	**6**	**1**

DATE	CIRCUIT	WINNER	CAR	SPEED	PACWEST RACING RESULTS (START/FINISH)
15-Mar	Homestead	Michael Andretti	Swift-Ford/Cosworth	144.339	Gugelmin 10/10, Blundell 7/12
28-Mar	Motegi	Adrian Fernandez	Reynard-Ford/Cosworth	159.393	Gugelmin 11/20 (Wheel Bearing), Blundell 7/10
5-Apr	Long Beach	Alex Zanardi	Reynard-Honda	88.946	Gugelmin 22/10, Blundell 23/7
27-Apr	Nazareth	Jimmy Vasser	Reynard-Honda	108.839	Gugelmin 14/17 (Contact), Blundell 21/20 (Contact)
10-May	Rio de Janeiro	Greg Moore	Reynard-Mercedes	132.531	Gugelmin 21/9, Blundell 18/11
23-May	Gateway	Alex Zanardi	Reynard-Honda	125.725	Gugelmin 23/16, Blundell 18/10
31-May	Milwaukee	Jimmy Vasser	Reynard-Honda	131.349	Gugelmin 11/21 (Electrical), Blundell 18/12
7-Jun	Belle Isle	Alex Zanardi	Reynard-Honda	100.052	Gugelmin 22/19, Blundell 21/22 (Contact)
21-Jun	Portland	Alex Zanardi	Reynard-Honda	101.355	Gugelmin 15/7, Blundell 16/22 (Contact)
12-Jul	Cleveland	Alex Zanardi	Reynard-Honda	112.449	Gugelmin 8/20 (Cooling System), Blundell 6/10
19-Jul	Toronto	Alex Zanardi	Reynard-Honda	87.274	Gugelmin 19/12, Blundell 15/26 (Electrical)
26-Jul	Michigan	Greg Moore	Reynard-Mercedes	165.913	Gugelmin 17/13, Blundell 19/17
9-Aug	Mid-Ohio	Adrian Fernandez	Reynard-Ford/Cosworth	98.428	Gugelmin 4/4, Blundell 8/19 (Contact)
16-Aug	Road America	Dario Franchitti	Reynard-Honda	127.145	Gugelmin 21/19 (Brakes), Blundell 15/7
6-Sep	Vancouver	Dario Franchitti	Reynard-Honda	77.081	Gugelmin 13/6, Blundell 18/12
13-Sep	Laguna Seca	Bryan Herta	Reynard-Ford/Cosworth	96.726	Gugelmin 9/27 (Cooling System), Blundell 15/25 (Throttle)
4-Oct	Houston	Dario Franchitti	Reynard-Honda	66.051	Gugelmin 15/18 (Electrical), Blundell 22/14
18-Oct	Surfers Paradise	Alex Zanardi	Reynard-Honda	85.328	Gugelmin 21/12, Blundell 17/11
1-Nov	Fontana	Jimmy Vasser	Reynard-Honda	153.785	Gugelmin 6/5, Blundell 7/6

1999 SEASON STATISTICS

RANK	DRIVER	TEAM	PTS	CHASSIS	ENGINE	TIRES	STARTS	RAF	POLES	WINS	BF	LL
1	Juan Pablo Montoya	Chip Ganassi Racing	212	Reynard	Honda	Firestone	20	15	7	7	1	954
2	Dario Franchitti	Team Green	212	Reynard	Honda	Firestone	20	16	2	3	1	272
3	Paul Tracy	Team Green	161	Reynard	Honda	Firestone	19	14	0	2	1	165
4	Michael Andretti	Newman/Haas Racing	151	Swift	Ford	Firestone	20	16	1	1	1	237
5	Max Papis	Team Rahal	150	Reynard	Ford	Firestone	20	18	1	0	2	329
6	Adrian Fernandez	Patrick Racing	140	Reynard	Ford	Firestone	16	12	1	2	1	167
7	Christian Fittipaldi	Newman/Haas Racing	121	Swift	Ford	Firestone	15	14	1	1	1	46
8	Gil de Ferran	Walker Racing	108	Reynard	Honda	Goodyear	20	13	2	1	1	79
9	Jimmy Vasser	Chip Ganassi Racing	104	Reynard	Honda	Firestone	20	14	1	0	3	56
10	Greg Moore	Forsythe Racing	97	Reynard	Mercedes	Firestone	20	12	1	1	1	102
14	**Roberto Moreno**	**PacWest Racing/ Newman/Haas Racing**	**58**	**Reynard/ Swift**	**Mercedes/ Ford**	**Firestone**	**13**	**11**	**0**	**0**	**2**	**45**
16	**Mauricio Gugelmin**	**PacWest Racing**	**44**	**Reynard**	**Mercedes**	**Firestone**	**20**	**11**	**0**	**0**	**4**	**23**
23	**Mark Blundell**	**PacWest Racing**	**9**	**Reynard**	**Mercedes**	**Firestone**	**12**	**6**	**0**	**0**	**8**	**0**

DATE	CIRCUIT	WINNER	CAR	SPEED	PACWEST RACING RESULTS (START/FINISH)
21-Mar	Homestead	Greg Moore	Reynard-Mercedes	136.671	Gugelmin 10/11, Blundell 13/8
10-Apr	Motegi	Adrian Fernandez	Reynard-Ford/Cosworth	176.195	Gugelmin 2/7, Blundell 16/24 (Mechanical)
18-Apr	Long Beach	Juan Pablo Montoya	Reynard-Honda	87.915	Gugelmin 14/14, Blundell 12/13
2-May	Nazareth	Juan Pablo Montoya	Reynard-Honda	120.225	Gugelmin 15/18, Blundell 5/17
15-May	Rio de Janeiro	Juan Pablo Montoya	Reynard-Honda	125.12	Gugelmin 25/22 (Cooling System), Blundell 23/11
29-May	Gateway	Michael Andretti	Swift-Ford/Cosworth	123.513	Gugelmin 21/18 (Fuel Pressure), Moreno 19/4
6-Jun	Milwaukee	Paul Tracy	Reynard-Honda	128.029	Gugelmin 12/8, Moreno 9/12
20-Jun	Portland	Gil de Ferran	Reynard-Honda	107.457	Gugelmin 16/25 (Turbo), Moreno 11/7
27-Jun	Cleveland	Juan Pablo Montoya	Reynard-Honda	93.931	Gugelmin 9/21 (Contact), Moreno 5/8
11-Jul	Road America	Christian Fittipaldi	Swift-Ford/Cosworth	137.697	Gugelmin 13/12, Moreno 16/19 (Engine)
18-Jul	Toronto	Dario Franchitti	Reynard-Honda	85.897	Gugelmin 16/14, Moreno 17/4
25-Jul	Michigan	Tony Kanaan	Reynard-Honda	186.097	Gugelmin 14/22 (Engine), 13/19 (Handling)
8-Aug	Belle Isle	Dario Franchitti	Reynard-Honda	81.643	Gugelmin 13/24 (Contact), Blundell 15/10
15-Aug	Mid-Ohio	Juan Pablo Montoya	Reynard-Honda	109.606	Gugelmin 17/20 (Engine), Blundell 26/13
22-Aug	Chicago	Juan Pablo Montoya	Reynard-Honda	122.236	Gugelmin 12/19 (Transmission), Blundell 2/21 (Cooling System)
5-Sep	Vancouver	Juan Pablo Montoya	Reynard-Honda	65.279	Gugelmin 10/4, Blundell 5/19 (Contact)
12-Sep	Laguna Seca	Bryan Herta	Reynard-Ford/Cosworth	101.924	Gugelmin 6/11, Blundell 20/12
26-Sep	Houston	Paul Tracy	Reynard-Honda	78.96	Gugelmin 23/6, Blundell 18/24 (Transmission)
17-Oct	Surfers Paradise	Dario Franchitti	Reynard-Honda	91.849	Gugelmin 9/26 (Transmission), Blundell 23/19 (Contact)
31-Oct	Fontana	Adrian Fernandez	Reynard-Ford/Cosworth	171.666	Gugelmin 17/6, Blundell 18/16 (Electrical)

2000 SEASON STATISTICS

RANK	DRIVER	TEAM	PTS	CHASSIS	ENGINE	TIRES	STARTS	RAF	POLES	WINS	BF	LL
1	Gil de Ferran	Penske Racing	168	Reynard	Honda	Firestone	20	15	5	2	1	286
2	Adrian Fernandez	Patrick Racing	158	Reynard	Ford	Firestone	20	17	0	2	1	90
3	Roberto Moreno	Patrick Racing	147	Reynard	Ford	Firestone	20	14	1	1	1	146
4	Kenny Bräck	Team Rahal	135	Reynard	Ford	Firestone	20	14	0	0	2	151
5	Paul Tracy	Team Green	134	Reynard	Honda	Firestone	20	12	1	3	1	132
6	Jimmy Vasser	Chip Ganassi Racing	131	Lola	Toyota	Firestone	20	15	0	1	1	77
7	Helio Castroneves	Penske Racing	129	Reynard	Honda	Firestone	20	12	3	3	1	372
8	Michael Andretti	Newman/Haas Racing	127	Swift	Ford	Firestone	20	12	0	2	1	290
9	Juan Pablo Montoya	Chip Ganassi Racing	126	Lola	Toyota	Firestone	20	8	7	3	1	820
10	Cristiano da Matta	PPI Motorsports	112	Reynard	Toyota	Firestone	20	14	0	1	1	124
17	**Mauricio Gugelmin**	**PacWest Racing**	**39**	**Reynard**	**Mercedes**	**Firestone**	**20**	**9**	**0**	**1**	**2**	**8**
21	**Mark Blundell**	**PacWest Racing**	**18**	**Reynard**	**Mercedes**	**Firestone**	**20**	**9**	**0**	**0**	**7**	**2**

DATE	CIRCUIT	WINNER	CAR	SPEED	PACWEST RACING RESULTS (START/FINISH)
26-Mar	Homestead	Max Papis	Reynard-Ford/Cosworth	164.788	Gugelmin 18/16, Blundell 16/13
16-Apr	Long Beach	Paul Tracy	Reynard-Honda	82.626	Gugelmin 16/10, Blundell 20/8
30-Apr	Rio de Janeiro	Adrian Fernandez	Reynard-Ford/Cosworth	124.256	Gugelmin 21/21 (Engine), Blundell 23/7
14-May	Motegi	Michael Andretti	Lola-Ford/Cosworth	157.154	Gugelmin 7/22 (Header), Blundell 22/19
27-May	Nazareth	Gil de Ferran	Reynard-Honda	101.219	Gugelmin 12/2, Blundell 18/17
5-Jun	Milwaukee	Juan Pablo Montoya	Lola-Toyota	142.684	Gugelmin 23/8, Blundell 17/17
18-Jun	Belle Isle	Helio Castroneves	Reynard-Honda	97.401	Gugelmin 16/17, Blundell 15/11
25-Jun	Portland	Gil de Ferran	Reynard-Honda	109.564	Gugelmin 24/19 (Engine), Blundell 16/20 (Engine)
2-Jul	Cleveland	Roberto Moreno	Reynard-Ford/Cosworth	112.619	Gugelmin 3/10, Blundell 16/12
16-Jul	Toronto	Michael Andretti	Lola-Ford/Cosworth	98.248	Gugelmin 10/15 (Electrical), Blundell 25/15 (Gearbox)
23-Jul	Michigan	Juan Pablo Montoya	Lola-Toyota	177.694	Gugelmin 20/13 (Engine), Blundell 17/19 (Engine)
30-Jul	Chicago	Cristiano da Matta	Reynard-Toyota	114.432	Gugelmin 16/7, Blundell 17/23 (Engine)
13-Aug	Mid-Ohio	Helio Castroneves	Reynard-Honda	106.558	Gugelmin 13/20 (Electrical), Blundell 18/14
20-Aug	Road America	Paul Tracy	Reynard-Honda	136.457	Gugelmin 10/17 (Engine), Blundell 20/11 (Gearbox)
3-Sep	Vancouver	Paul Tracy	Reynard-Honda	85.034	Gugelmin 13/21 (Contact), Blundell 20/25 (Contact)
10-Sep	Laguna Seca	Helio Castroneves	Reynard-Honda	104.949	Gugelmin 7/7, Blundell 21/13
17-Sep	Gateway	Juan Pablo Montoya	Lola-Toyota	155.519	Gugelmin 24/19 (Vibration), Blundell 20/23 (Engine)
1-Oct	Houston	Jimmy Vasser	Lola-Toyota	76.626	Gugelmin 21/23 (Contact), Blundell 20/20 (Clutch)
15-Oct	Surfers Paradise	Adrian Fernandez	Reynard-Ford/Cosworth	81.607	Gugelmin 18/10, Blundell 22/11
30-Oct	Fontana	Christian Fittipaldi	Lola-Ford/Cosworth	139.563	Gugelmin 22/17 (Engine), Blundell 21/15 (Engine/Last Indy Car Start)

2001 SEASON STATISTICS

RANK	DRIVER	TEAM	PTS	CHASSIS	ENGINE	TIRES	STARTS	RAF	POLES	WINS	BF	LL
1	Gil de Ferran	Penske Racing	199	Reynard	Honda	Firestone	20	16	4	2	1	328
2	Kenny Bräck	Team Rahal	163	Lola	Ford	Firestone	20	15	2	4	1	621
3	Michael Andretti	Team Green	147	Reynard	Honda	Firestone	20	14	0	1	1	108
4	Helio Castroneves	Penske Racing	141	Reynard	Honda	Firestone	20	17	3	3	1	411
5	Cristiano da Matta	Newman/Haas Racing	140	Lola	Toyota	Firestone	20	14	0	3	1	104
6	Max Papis	Team Rahal	107	Lola	Ford	Firestone	20	16	1	2	1	222
7	Dario Franchitti	Team Green	105	Reynard	Honda	Firestone	20	13	0	1	1	53
8	**Scott Dixon**	**PacWest Racing**	**98**	**Reynard**	**Toyota**	**Firestone**	**20**	**16**	**0**	**1**	**1**	**74**
9	Tony Kanaan	Mo Nunn Racing	93	Reynard	Honda	Firestone	19	16	1	0	3	179
10	Patrick Carpentier	Forsythe Racing	91	Reynard	Ford	Firestone	20	13	0	1	1	41
24	**Mauricio Gugelmin**	**PacWest Racing**	**17**	**Reynard**	**Toyota**	**Firestone**	**19**	**12**	**1**	**0**	**7**	**6**

DATE	CIRCUIT	WINNER	CAR	SPEED	PACWEST RACING RESULTS (START/FINISH)
11-Mar	Monterrey	Cristiano da Matta	Lola-Toyota	81.548	Gugelmin 17/15, Dixon 14/13 (First Indy Car Start)
8-Apr	Long Beach	Helio Castroneves	Reynard-Honda	86.223	Gugelmin 19/22 (Contact), Dixon 18/19
6-May	**Nazareth**	**Scott Dixon**	**Reynard-Toyota**	**114.84**	Gugelmin (Withdrawn), Dixon 23/1 (First Indy Car Win)
19-May	Motegi	Kenny Bräck	Lola-Ford/Cosworth	178.113	Gugelmin 25/12, Dixon 20/9
3-Jun	Milwaukee	Kenny Bräck	Lola-Ford/Cosworth	122.066	Gugelmin 22/10, Dixon 8/3
17-Jun	Belle Isle	Helio Castroneves	Reynard-Honda	89.008	Gugelmin 12/10, Dixon 18/22 (Driveshaft)
24-Jun	Portland	Max Papis	Lola-Ford/Cosworth	74.606	Gugelmin 11/20 (Contact), Dixon 4/7
1-Jul	Cleveland	Dario Franchitti	Reynard-Honda	118.007	Gugelmin 1/10, Dixon 18/20
15-Jul	Toronto	Michael Andretti	Reynard-Honda	83.375	Gugelmin 19/7, Dixon 10/5
22-Jul	Michigan	Patrick Carpentier	Reynard-Ford/Cosworth	171.498	Gugelmin 10/15, Dixon 12/10
29-Jul	Chicago	Kenny Bräck	Lola-Ford/Cosworth	132.031	Gugelmin 13/22, Dixon 19/4
12-Aug	Mid-Ohio	Helio Castroneves	Reynard-Honda	106.627	Gugelmin 21/14, Dixon 12/12
19-Aug	Road America	Bruno Junqueira	Lola-Toyota	90.721	Gugelmin 15/23, Dixon 3/4
2-Sep	Vancouver	Roberto Moreno	Reynard-Toyota	80.543	Gugelmin 16/15, Dixon 17/13
15-Sep	Eurospeedway	Kenny Bräck	Lola-Ford/Cosworth	155.319	Gugelmin 23/16, Dixon 6/9
22-Sep	Rockingham	Gil de Ferran	Reynard-Honda	153.408	Gugelmin 23/20, Dixon 5/22 (Contact)
7-Oct	Houston	Gil de Ferran	Reynard-Honda	79.521	Gugelmin 9/20 (Gearbox), Dixon 7/18
14-Oct	Laguna Seca	Max Papis	Lola-Ford/Cosworth	84.919	Gugelmin 13/16 (Contact), Dixon 3/4
28-Oct	Surfers Paradise	Cristiano da Matta	Lola-Toyota	97.511	Gugelmin 25/24 (Gearbox), Dixon 8/15
4-Nov	Fontana	Cristiano da Matta	Lola-Toyota	149.073	Gugelmin 15/20 (Engine), Dixon 10/17 (Contact)

GOODYEAR
1 in TIRES
POWERWARE
FIREHAWK
TRD
FREIGHTLINER
BELL
OPEN CLOSED

INDEX

MOTOROLA
NEXTEL